HANDBOOK OF MORAL BEHAVIOR AND DEVELOPMENT

Volume 2: Research

HANDBOOK OF MORAL BEHAVIOR AND DEVELOPMENT

Volume 2: Research

Edited by
WILLIAM M. KURTINES
JACOB L. GEWIRTZ
Florida International University

LAWRENCE ERLBAUM ASSOCIATES, PUBLISHERS

1991   Hillsdale, New Jersey   Hove and London

#2346 3247

Lawrence Erlbaum Associates, Inc., Publishers
365 Broadway
Hillsdale, New Jersey 07642

Library of Congress Cataloging–in–Publication Data
Handbook of moral behavior and development / edited by William M.
Kurtines, Jacob L. Gewirtz.
    p. cm.
    Includes bibliographical references and index.
    Contents: v. 1. Theory — v. 2. Research — v. 3. Application.
    ISBN 0–8058–0206–1 (set). — ISBN 0–8058–0880–9 (v. 1)
—ISBN 0–8058–0881–7 (v. 2). — ISBN 0–8058–0882–5 (v. 3)
    1. Moral development. 2. Ethics. 3. Moral education.
I. Kurtines, William M. II. Gewirtz, Jacob L., 1924–
BF723.M54H35 1991
155.2'5—dc20   91–13908
                                        CIP

Contents

Preface to Handbook

The literature on moral behavior and development, on pro- and anti-social behavior, and on moral and character education has grown enormously in recent years. Work has proliferated and the area continues to attract a broad range of interests and activities. The field has thus emerged as a continuing, separate, substantive area of scholarly and research interest. Yet, despite this substantial interest in the area and the emergence of a substantial body of data, there exists currently no single source of information on developments in the field. The *Handbook of Moral Behavior and Development* is designed to provide researchers and professionals in the area of moral behavior and development with a central source of state-of-the-art information in the field.

The aim of the *Handbook* is to advance work in the area of moral behavior and development by facilitating the dissemination of knowledge and information in theory, research, and application. By bringing together in one place representative writings of prominent scholars, researchers, and professionals in the area, the *Handbook* provides a central source of information about the most important developments that have taken place. Progress in the field will be facilitated by a focal source of information that encompasses a broad range of theoretical, empirical, and practical issues, and that bridges the many gaps in and among theory, research, and application. The central source of information that this *Handbook* constitutes provides a means for the exchange of information and ideas among the diverse theoretical perspectives, research methods, and areas of applied interest that have emerged.

In addition to meeting the need for a central source of information on advances in the field, the *Handbook* also seeks to bridge the gap between theory, research, and application. A critical feature of the *Handbook* is that it includes separate volumes that review developments in theory, research, and application. By bringing together in one place work on diverse topics, the *Handbook* will foster a mutually beneficial exchange not only between alternative approaches and perspectives, but also between "applied" and "pure" research interests. Because the contributors to the volumes in the *Handbook* are active theorists, researchers, and practitioners, it will also serve to define directions that will shape the emerging literature in the field.

The *Handbook* consists of three volumes. Because one of the aims of the *Handbook* is to bridge the gap between theorists, researchers, and practitioners, each volume focuses on a separate topic—Volume 1: Theory, Volume 2: Research, and Volume 3: Application.

EDITORIAL ADVISORY BOARD

The international Editorial Advisory Board for the *Handbook* included distinguished members representing diverse theoretical perspectives and orientations as well as of expertise in various research and applied areas. The topics and issues included in the *Handbook* were selected by the Editors in consultation with members of the Editorial Advisory Board. The goal was to assemble for each volume a range of works representative of current topics and issues by scholars and professionals active in the areas to be represented.

The *Handbook* would not have been possible without the cooperation and assistance of the members of the editorial advisory board whose effort and input helped to make the series possible. We also wish to thank friends and colleagues who provided support and encouragement, the editorial staff of Lawrence Erlbaum Associates, and others whose contribution at various stages were instrumental in its successful completion. In view of recent events we have dedicated the first edition of the *Handbook* to the life and work of the late Lawrence Kohlberg. To this end, the prologue to the first volume is made up of personal observations from his colleagues on his life and work.

William M. Kurtines
Jacob L. Gewirtz

Editorial Advisory Board

Preface to *Volume 2: Research*

Volume 2 of the Handbook of Moral Behavior and Development is comprised of chapters that summarize and interpret the research findings of particular, theory-driven, research programs, review research in areas that have generated substantial empirical findings, describe recent developments in research methodology/techniques, or report research on new and/or emerging issues or topics. The focus of *Volume 2* is on the interpretation/integration of research findings and the consideration of the broader implications of research results and methodology.

Contributors' Biographies

Daniel Bar Tal is professor at the school of education of Pittsburgh and professor at the school of education, Tel Aviv University. He received his Ph.D. in social psychology from the University of Pittsburgh. From the beginning of his career he concentrated on the study of prosocial behavior and specifically on the underlying motivational bases of helping behavior. He has authored *Prosocial Behavior: Theory and Research* (1976) and co-edited *Development and Maintenance of Prosocial Behavior* (1984) and published numerous articles and chapters in this area. Recently, he added to his interest a study of knowledge acquisition and specifically on political beliefs shared by group members. Within this framework he authored *Group Beliefs* (1990) and co-edited *The Social Psychology of Knowledge* (1988), *The Social Psychology of Intergroup Conflict* (1988), and *Stereotyping and Prejudice* (1989).

Yoram Bar Tal is head of the research unit at the nursing department, School of Medicine, Tel-Aviv University. He received his Ph.D. in social psychology from Boston University in 1985. His general area of interest concerns the relationship between cognition and behavior. He published several articles and chapters in this area.

Lyn Mikel Brown is lecturer in education, human development and psychology and research associate at the project for the psychology of women and the development of girls at Harvard University. Her research focuses on female social and personality development and on feminist methodology. Her recent publications include: "Reading for Self and Moral Voice: A Method for Interpreting Narratives With Real-Life Moral Conflict and Choice" (with M. Tappan, C. Gilligan, B. Miller, and D. Argyris) in *Entering the Circle: Hermeneutic Investigation in Psychology.*

Gustavo Carlo is a doctoral student in developmental psychology at Arizona State University. His research interests are in the areas of social and moral development, especially the role of empathy and role taking in moral functioning.

Jeremey Carpendale is a graduate student at Simon Fraser University. His research interests include moral and cognitive development, and the influence of communication and social context on development.

Elizabeth Debold is a doctoral candidate in human development at Harvard University. Her current research involves the social and cognitive development in females and her long range interest is revisioning adult development through the insights of Gilligan and colleagues.

Carol Gilligan is professor of education at Harvard University. She is author of *In a Different Voice: Psychology Theory and Women's Development* and co-editor (with J. V. Ward and J. M. Taylor) of *Mapping the Moral Domain: A Contribution of Women's Thinking to Psychological Theory and Education* and (with N. Lyons and T. Hanmer) of *Making Connections: The Relational World of Adolescent Girls at Emma Willard School.*

John Darley is the Warren Professor of Psychology at Princeton University. He received his doctorate in Social Relations from Harvard University in 1965. His research interests include the determinants of pro-social behavior, and conceptualizations of moral development. With Thomas Shultz, he has recently written a chapter for the *Annual Review of Psychology* on moral development.

Kathy Denton is completing her doctorate at Simon Fraser University. Her research interests include moral development, parent-child relations, and social cognition. Her articles include "From the Scene to the Crime: The Effects of Alcohol and Social Context on Moral Judgment" (with Dennis Krebs) in the *Journal of Personality and Social Psychology,* and "The Evolution of Self Knowledge and Self-Deception" (with Dennis Krebs and Nancy Higgins) in K. McDonald (Ed.) *Sociobiological Perspectives on Human Development.*

Wolfgang Edelstein is director of the Max Planck Institute for Human Development and Education. He received his doctorate in Linguistics, Latin and English Literature from the University of Heidelberg in 1962. His research focus is on cognitive and sociomoral development. He has published books, articles, and chapters in German, English, and Icelandic.

Nancy Eisenberg is professor of psychology in the department of psychology at Arizona State University. She received her doctorate in developmental psychology from the University of California at Berkeley. Her primary interests are in social and moral development, especially the development of empathy, altruism, and prosocial behavior and reasoning. She is author of *The Roots of Caring, Sharing, and Helping* (with Paul Mussen), *Altruistic Emotion, Cognition, and Behavior,* and editor of both *The Development of Prosocial Behavior* and *Empathy and its Development* (with Janet Strayer).

Monika Keller is an assistant professor in development psychology at the University of Heidelberg. She received her doctorate in psychology at the University of Heidelberg in 1974. Since 1981 she has been a senior research scientist at the Max Planck Institute for Human Development and Education. Her research focus is on social cognitive and moral development and socialization. She has published a number of chapters and articles in English.

Melanie Killen is assistant professor of psychology at Wesleyan University. She received her doctorate from the University of California at Berkeley. Her interests are in the development of moral and social judgment and in the influences of early social interactions on social development. She is author of a chapter entitled, "Context, Conflict, and Coordination in Social Development" in L. T. Winegar (Ed.) *Social Interaction and the Development of Children's Understanding.*

George P. Knight is associate professor of psychology at the Arizona State University. He received his doctorate in developmental psychology from the University of California at Riverside. His primary interests are in the areas of cooperation and sociocognitive development, including the role of cognition in moral behavior.

Dennis Krebs is professor of psychology at Simon Fraser University. He received his doctorate from Harvard University, and is a Fellow of the Center for Advanced Study in the Behavioral Sciences. His research interests center around altruism, moral development, and the evolution of social cognition, and self-deception. His books include *Psychology: A First Encounter* (with R. Blackman) and *Sociobiology and Psychology: Ideas, Issues, and Applications* (edited with C. Crawford and Martin Smith).

Darcia Narvaez is currently teaching Spanish in a Minneapolis junior high school, is a research associate at the Center for the Study of Ethical Development, and is pursuing a Ph.D. at the University of Minnesota. In addition to co-authoring several articles on morality, she is undertaking a research project in moral development in the junior high school.

Fritz Oser is professor of education and director of the Pedagogy Institute at the University of Fribourg, Switzerland. His major research interests are sociomoral discussion, religious development, and sociomoral education. He is author and editor of a number of books, including *Moralisches Urteil in Gruppen* as well as *Moral Education: Theory and Application.*

James Rest is professor of educational psychology at the University of Minnesota and research director for the Center for the Study of Ethical Development. His Ph.D. is from the University of Chicago where he began work with Larry Kohlberg, and later followed Kohlberg to Harvard as a post-doctoral fellow. His main line of research has been based on the Defining Issues Test, and he is first author of *Development in Judgment Moral Issues,* 1979 and *Moral Development: Advances in Research and Theory,* 1986.

Cindy L. Shea is a graduate student in developmental psychology at Arizona State University. Her interests are in social development and social psychology, including the development of empathy and the role of emotion in prosocial behavior.

Judith G. Smetana is associate professor of education, psychology, and pediatrics at the University of Rochester. She received her doctorate from the University of California at

Santa Cruz. Her current interests are in moral and social development and in parent-child interactions in early childhood and adolescence. She is the author of *Concepts of Self and Morality: Women's Reasoning About Abortions.*

John Snarey is associate professor of ethics and human development, adjunct associate professor of psychology, and associate director of the Center for Research in Faith and Moral Development. He received his doctorate in human development from Harvard University in 1982. His interests include the development of moral reasoning about the social and natural environments, family studies and human development, and cross-cultural research methods. He is the author of numerous journal publications and he is co-editor of *Conflict and Continuity: A History of Ideas on Social Equality and Human Development* and *Remembrances of Lawrence Kohlberg.* His research has received awards from the National Council for the Social Sciences, the Association for Moral Education, and the American Educational Research Association.

Mark B. Tappan is lecturer in education human development and psychology at Harvard University. He is interested in late adolescent development, female social and person-ality development, and interpretive research methods. His recent publications include "Stories Lived and Stories Told: The Narrative Structure of Late Adolescent Moral Development" in *Human Development.*

Elliot Turiel is professor of education at the University of California at Berkeley. He received his doctorate in psychology from Yale University. His interests are in the development of social judgments, their relations to social actions, and, most recently, ways of conceptualizing cultural categories with regard to social development. He is the author of *The Development of Social Knowledge: Morality and Convention.*

Lawrence J. Walker is associate professor of psychology at the University of British Columbia, Vancouver. He received his doctorate in developmental psychology from the University of Toronto in 1978. Dr. Walker's research interests include factors in the development of moral reasoning, sex and cultural differences, and family interactions.

1 Decision-Making Models of Helping Behavior: Process and Contents

Yoram Bar-Tal
Daniel Bar-Tal

ABSTRACT

This chapter reviews five decision making models of helping behavior. The review concludes that the models include elements that are particular and that cannot be generalized. Based on this observation, the paper proposes a general process model of helping behavior that is based on lay epistemology theory. It is suggested that the motivation for helping behavior derives from discrepancy between the perceived situation and behavioral implications of cognitions that individuals hold, and toward which they have epistemic need for cognitive structure. The helping behavior that is selected to fulfill the motivation has to be consistent with other, more central, cognitions. Finally, the utility of such general model is discussed.

INTRODUCTION

In recent years the study of helping behavior has emerged as one of the central areas in social and developmental psychology (cf. Bar-Tal, 1984a). Within this area, much of the research has focused on the investigation of personal and situational variables (i.e., contents) that influence helping behavior (see reviews by Bar-Tal, 1976; Krebs, 1970; Staub, 1978). This research has identified many situational conditions and personal tendencies that facilitate or inhibit helping behavior. But, it has become apparent that the list of variables can be infinite and that the helping behavior is multidetermined (Bar-Tal, 1984b). Determinants of helping behavior seem to relate in different and complex ways, contingent on

1

specific situations and the specific personal characteristics. Thus, it is not surprising, that in addition to the continuous attempts to isolate specific variables, a number of general elaborative models have been proposed to explain how individuals engage in helping behavior (e.g., Latané & Darley, 1970; Staub, 1978). These models, often referred to as decision making models, propose various phases through which individuals pass while deciding whether to carry out helping behavior. The common denominator of these models is that they were designed to describe a general process which can be applied across individuals and situations, irrespectively of specific limiting variables. In other words, they were proposed as universal models.

We discuss several decision-making models of helping behavior and, while evaluating critically their universality, propose a process model that *explains* helping behavior in general. The basic questions that guide the present review are (a) whether the suggested models are in fact universal or they include specific content elements which can characterize certain people, in certain situations (cf. Bar-Tal & Bar-Tal, 1988), and (b) whether the models properly explain why and how persons move from one phase to another.

REVIEW OF HELPING BEHAVIOR MODELS

Five models of helping behavior process are reviewed. They were selected because they stimulated a considerable amount of empirical research. Thus, this part of the chapter in addition to presenting the models describes a portion of their validating studies.

Latané and Darley's Model

Latané and Darley (1970) proposed a model of decision-making process especially for the cases of emergency situations. Their model consists of five sequential decisions, implying that each decision is contingent on the one in the previous phase. Though the potential helper may cycle back and forth in the five decisions by reconsidering the earlier ones in the later phases of the decision-making process. First, the potential helper has to notice and then decide that something is happening. This decision is important as individuals are usually absorbed with their own thoughts, rushing to meet their own goals. Often, they may not even notice emergency situations happening, especially when other bystanders are around them.

If a person notices that something is happening, the potential helper must decide whether the event is an emergency. Emergency situations are rare and frequently ambiguous. A person may, therefore, have difficulty interpreting what has happened. The interpretation of the nature of the event depends on several variables such as past experience and the reaction of other bystanders.

Third, the person, who notices an event and identifies it as an emergency, has to decide whether it is his or her responsibility to help. Different variables may influence the individual's decision to assume personal responsibility. The relationship with the victim and the presence of other bystanders are only a few examples of variables that influence the third decision. If the person takes responsibility, the fourth decision is how to intervene and what mode of help to use. The two alternatives are indirect and direct help. The indirect help entails reporting the situation to the relevant authority, while direct help involves a personal attempt to cope with the emergency. This decision depends especially on the helper's competency to make a direct intervention. Finally, the person must decide how to implement his or her action. At this point, the helper starts to carry out the intervention.

In their empirical work, Latané and Darley examined especially the first three decisions. Their performed experiments, which simulated emergency situations, focused on the effect of a specific variable on the decisions, namely the presence of other bystanders (e.g. Latané & Darley, 1968; Latané & Rodin, 1969). For example, in one study, Latané and Rodin (1969) simulated an emergency situation that involved a woman who entered an adjoint room, and later sounded a sound of crash and sobbing. Subjects in pairs were less likely to interpret the fall as serious and more likely to decide that it would be inappropriate to intervene than were single subjects. The presence of others inhibited the identification of the emergency, causing pluralistic ignorance. Among the groups, pairs of friends were less inhibited than pairs of strangers. It is possible that people may be less likely to fear embarrassment in front of friends than before strangers, and that friends are less likely to misinterpret each other's inactions than are strangers.

The study by Darley and Latané (1968) concentrated on the third decision in the sequence. In this experiment, subjects were confronted with a case of "epileptic seizure," which could not pass unnoted, either alone, with another person, or with four other persons. The results showed again that the number of bystanders in the situation had a major effect on the likelihood to intervene in the emergency. The more bystanders in emergency situation, the less responsibility the observers felt. Latané and Darley (1970) characterized this situation as diffusion of responsiblity—a common feeling that no one person can be blamed for not having intervened, since the responsibility to help is equally divided among the bystanders.

Piliavin et al. Model

Piliavin, Dovidio, Gaertner, and Clark (1981) proposed a model of emergency intervention that is based on previous models suggested by Pilliavin, Rodin, and Piliavin (1969) and Piliavin and Piliavin (1973). This model describes simultaneous processing and is cyclical and iterative. In their conceptualization, Piliavin et al. (1981) suggested that the decision whether to help or not depends on three intervening variables: arousal, attribution of arousal, and perceived costs and rewards for direct intervention. Specifically, it was suggested that an observation of another's emergency is physiologically arousing to the bystander. In turn, the experienced arousal motivates the person to act. The perceived costs and rewards for direct helping is another variable directly influencing helping behavior. Individuals who face emergency situations, enter into a decision-making process of calculating personal costs and rewards for helping and for not helping. Clearly, helping behavior is facilitated when a person decides that intervention involves low cost for helping and high cost for not helping. Arousal and perceived costs and rewards not only directly affect helping behavior, but also mutually influence each other. For example, a degree of arousal can affect the calculation of costs for not helping and, the high cost for not helping can lead to increased arousal because of the feeling indicating that moral obligation was violated. Attribution of arousal affects only the perceived costs and rewards. That is, the calculated costs and rewards depend on whether arousal is attributed to emergency and on the specific label given to this arousal (for example, disgust or concern). In addition, another intervening variable called "We-ness" was suggested to influence arousal, attribution of arousal, and perceived costs and rewards. "We-ness" is a variable describing the extent of similarity, belongingness, or common fate between the recipient and the potential helper as perceived by the latter.

Finally, three categories of variables were suggested to influence the described intervening variables: situational characteristics, potential helper's traits and states, and victim's characteristics. But, while the first two variables are directly related to all four intervening variables, the variable of victim characteristics influences only the variables "We-ness" and the perceived costs and rewards for direct intervention.

In their book, Piliavin et al. (1981) review studies that provide support for various parts of the model. Some of these are described next.

1. Individuals Experience Arousal While Observing Victims in Emergency Situations.   In one described study, subjects either observed a falling through a television monitor or heard the fall through the wall. The GSR record showed that the emergency's conception increased physiological responses and the audio-visual presentation (T.V. monitor) caused greater responsiveness than the other situation.

2. Arousal Affects Helping Behavior.   Piliavin et al. (1981) reported several studies involving simulated emergency situation of a person's fall in which arousal correlated with helping behavior. Whereas in some studies the arousal was based on self-report of upset and autonomic arousal, in others it was assessed objectively with GSR. In addition, studies showed that ambiguity of the emergency situation and high cost of helping reduced arousal, and subsequently helping behavior.

3. Personal Costs for Helping and not Helping Affect Person's Behavior. Numerous studies investigated the effect of costs for helping and not helping on intervention in emergency situations. The results consistently showed that help that is likely to be costly to the person in such terms as money or time is in general less likely to be offered (Piliavin, Piliavin, & Rodin, 1975; Piliavin, Rodin & Piliavin, 1969). Also, the findings revealed that when subjects do not feel responsibility for helping, the cost for refusing to help is low and, therefore, subjects tend to intervene less. The Piliavin and Piliavin (1972) study demonstrated that the cost of assisting the victim has an effect on helping behavior. In this experiment, a person fell in a subway and in half of the conditions a blood slip appeared in his mouth. The presence of blood decreased the likelihood of helping, since it increased the costs of intervention (blood assumed to cause unpleasantness and inconvenience).

4. Presence of Others (as an Example of Situational Variables) and the Nature of the Bystander-victim Relationship (as an example of Victim's Characteristics) Affect Helping Behavior. Piliavin et al. (1981) suggested that the presence of others and the nature of the bystander–victim relationship seem to affect helping behavior through cost–benefit considerations and arousal. In line with Latané and Darley (1970), they explained the effect of the presence of others with the diffusion of responsibility idea, which implies that individuals in this situation diffuse their responsibility for helping and also the guilt and blame for not helping. A study by Gaertner and Dovidio (1977) examined the relationship between the diffusion of responsibility and arousal. In this experiment, subjects, who were led to believe that they are either alone or with two other bystanders, overheard an emergency situation in which a person was struck by falling chairs. Since the subjects' heart rate was monitored, it was possible to demonstrate not only that subjects who were alone had greater cardiac responsiveness than subjects who believed that they are with additional bystanders, but also that there is a relationship between a latency of intervention and a change in the heart rate. In line with previous findings it was found that subjects who had the opportunity to diffuse responsibility helped the victim less frequently and less quickly than subjects who heard the emergency alone.

Piliavin et al. (1981) review numerous studies which investigated the effect of the bystander–victim relationship on helping behavior. The results in non–emergency situations consistently show that similarity to the victim through a sense of "We-ness" and emotional involvement increases the likelihood of helping. According to Piliavin et al. (1981), these findings are explained by the cost–reward considerations, since helping a similar person involves more reward, and less cost than helping a dissimilar person. Similarly, not helping a similar person involves greater costs than not helping a dissimilar person. In a study by Krebs (1975) that also measured physiological arousal it was found that similarity to a person observed to be experiencing pain is related with greater arousal and to willingness to assist at considerable cost.

Finally, Piliavin et al. (1981) review studies showing that traits such as competence, self-confidence, or commitment to moral standards influence helping behavior through cost–reward calculation. In addition, state factors such as mood affect helping intervention through differential arousal and attention.

Weiner's Model

Weiner (1980) proposed a cognitive model of help giving. According to Weiner, there is a sequence of judgment from attribution as to why a person is in need, to emotions, and to action. Specifically, the model indicates that individuals who observe a person in need exhibit immediately some reflexive reactions (approach or avoidance) and affective reactions such as fear or startle. Subsequently, individuals engage in causal explanation regarding the person in need (what happens with the person—e.g., is he ill or drunk). The outcome of this initial causal analysis separately influences the decision whether to carry out helping behavior and the affective reaction. Furthermore, the potential helper determines the personal responsibility of the person in need for being in this situation by determining the locus of the cause for need to help (internal or external) and its controllability. The outcome of this analysis weakly influences helping behavior and strongly influences affective reaction. Finally, the affective reactions are strongly related to the judgment whether or not to help. Weiner recognized that the described process is affected by various variables not included in the model.

In a series of paper-and-pencil studies, Weiner (1980) investigated the relations of causal attributions and affect to judgments of help giving. In the first experiment he established that the ratings of help were lowest when the cause of the need was perceived as being internally controllable (e.g., lack of effort). The next five experiments found that attributions of the person's need to internal controllable causes maximize negative affect (disgust and distaste) and promote avoidance behavior, whereas attributions to uncontrollable causes increase positive affect (sympathy) and foster helping behavior. In general, the studies demonstrated that the tendency to help is more influenced by the affect than by the causal explanation.

Recently, Weiner, Perry, and Magnusson (1988) replicated the early findings by examining reactions to stigmas. They investigated students' causal attributions, affective reactions, and willingness to help in ten different stigmas' cases (e.g., AIDS, blindness, cancer), which differ in their controllability either by self-understanding (first study) or experimenter's manipulation of each stigma (second study). The results showed that as predicted the attributions were related to affective responses and behavioral tendencies to help.

Schwartz's and Howard's Model

Schwartz and Howard (1981a, 1981b, 1984) proposed a normative decision-making model of helping behavior. The model includes the following five sequential steps, each influenced by situational and personal variables: attention, generation feelings of obligation (motivation), anticipatory evaluation, defense, and behavior. In the first phase of attention, the potential helper becomes aware of the characteristics of the specific situation, which determines whether any decision is needed. Specifically, he or she must notice the person who needs help and must decide that this person is in need. Noticing that someone is in need causes a perceived discrepancy between the expectation that individuals around us should not be in need and the noticed state of need. Individuals are motivated to reduce this discrepancy. Then, the potential helper has to identify the helpful action that might relieve the perceived need. Once potentially helpful actions are recognized, a person considers his or her own ability to execute them.

If, in the first phase, those perceptions necessary for decision making are activated, the potential helper moves to the second phase of considering three implications of the planned actions: (a) physical, material, and psychological implications that follow directly from the action, (b) implications for the actor's internalized moral values, and (c) social implications of other people's reactions. The first consideration involves potential costs that the potential helper might incur. The second involves the implications of the specific considered act in relation to the moral values of the potential helper. This consideration might arouse moral obligation to perform the specific act labeled as personal norm. That is, the potential helper might feel personally responsible for the considered actions in the specific situation. The personal norms consist of self-expectation for behavior and emotions related to this expectation. Finally the potential helper considers the implication of his or her planned action against social norms, that is, the considered question is whether he or she is responsible for action, in accordance with social norms.

In the third phase of anticipatory evaluation, the potential helper calculates the costs and rewards of the helping behavior. If the consideration described in the third phase and the anticipated costs and rewards favor the planned acts, the decision is reached and behavior is executed. But, if moral considerations are unclear and the anticipated costs and benefits are relatively balanced, conflict is experienced. In this situation, the potential helper redefines the situation through methods of defense in the fourth phase.

In the fourth phase, the potential helper, who experiences conflict, weakens his or her feelings of moral obligation through use of a defense. Four types of defenses are suggested by Schwartz and Howard (1984): (a) denial of need from the person in need or reduction in its perceived severity; (b) denial of effective action; (c) denial of personal ability to carry out the necessary help; and (d) denial of personal or social responsibility to conform with moral and normative obligations. The potential helper may use one defense or several of them and if his or her use succeeds, he or she may terminate the decision-making process, or may start the process from the beginning in accordance with new perceptions. The final phase is the behavior that is an outcome of the decision.

Schwartz and his associates performed a number of studies to examine various phases of the decision-making process. Specifically, they concentrated on the investigation of the effects of the personal norms, awareness of the consequences that follow from the action, and feelings of personal responsibility. Also, several studies examined the denial of personal or social responsibility as a variable that affects helping behavior.

In one of his early studies, Schwartz (1968) investigated the relationship between personal norms, awareness of the consequences, responsibility for the behavior, and the helping act. He assessed the description of responsibility for self with a questionnaire (AR) which not only taps person's tendency to accept moral responsibility for his or her action, but also uses a rationale for removing a responsibility from self. With Awareness of Consequences Test (AC) he measured the extent to which a person has an awareness that his potential acts may have consequences for the welfare of others. Finally, the personal norms were inferred on the basis of person's feelings that one ought to help in a specifically described situation. The results showed that the awareness that one's potential acts have consequences for the welfare of others and ascription of responsibility for these acts to self are necessary conditions for the activation of moral norms and their influence upon behavior in the situation.

In another study, Schwartz (1973) measured through mailed questionnaires the personal norm toward donating bone marrow to a stranger and the tendency to ascribe responsibility to the self (AR). Several months later, the female respondents to the questionnaire were asked to join a pool of potential donors from an unrelated source. The results revealed that the volunteering behavior was a function of the tendency to ascribe responsibility toward self (AR) and a personal norm which reflected a moral obligation to donate bone marrow. The multiplicative interaction of AR and personal norm accounted for 23% of the variance in explaining the volunteering act. Schwartz interpreted the findings as evidence for the impact of personal norms through the mechanism of anticipated sanctions.

A study by Schwartz and Ben David (1976) further investigated the effects of responsibility feeling on helping. In this study, subjects who completed the Responsibility Denial (RD) scale, heard a female experimenter scream in panic at the escape of a dangerous rat. In one condition, they were led to believe that they are responsible for the escape, while in other conditions the responsibility was attributed either to the experimenter or to chance. Also, some subjects were told that they had the ability to handle rats. The results showed that those subjects who felt responsible for the situation helped most. Also, helping decreased when the subjects thought they did not have the ability to intervene, especially among those high in the tendency to deny responsibility (RD). Finally, RD was directly related to helping.

The balancing of social and moral implications of the helping act was illustrated by Schwartz and Fleishman (1978) who studied volunteering to aid elderly welfare recipients in need. An appeal to help invoked the social expectation that help should be offered. But, the experimenters varied the legitimacy of the expectation by describing the need as due either to lack of trustworthiness or to arbitrary events beyond control. Women who had indicated feelings of moral obligation either to aid elderly persons or to oppose such aid responded consistently with their premeasured personal norms, regardless of the legitimacy of need. For these women, the moral costs and benefits outweighed the social. On the other hand, women who had reported no personal norms, were significantly more influenced by the legitimacy of the need, volunteering twice as much when the social expectation involved was legitimate rather than illegitimate.

A study by Schwartz and Howard (1980) examined the nature of the responsibility denial, which moderates the relationship of personal norms with helping behavior. Students filled out Responsibility Denial (RD) questionnaires and Personal Norm tests, which measure feelings of moral obligations to perform various altruistic acts (personal norms). Finally, they were asked to volunteer time to read texts to blind children. The results consistently support the defensive strategy explanation: Individuals deny responsibility in order to neutralize the anticipated costs of violating one's own internalized values when facing a moral choice.

Staub's Model

Staub (1978, 1984) proposed a model that integrates personality and situational determinants of behavior. Staub tried to find a limited number of personal characteristics that account for substantial amounts of variance, to define the nature of relevant situational influences and to provide a specification of their joint influence on helping behavior. In principle, the model indicates that both internal stimulation and environment activate personal goals. In turn, some of the personal goals are satisfied by the performance of helping behavior.

Specifically, Staub proposed that personal goals are motivational orientations that imply a preference for certain outcomes and avoidance of other outcomes. Goals are usually associated with a network of cognitions that refer to thoughts, beliefs, or values regarding the desired behavior, other goals, and/or other related subjects. Interpretations based on these cognitive networks give rise to affect, which has motivational properties to reach the goal. In the case of helping behavior, self-gain, prosocial values and norms, and empathy are considered the major classes of motivators of helping behavior. Activation of a goal depends on the nature of the situation, its activating potential, characteristics of the person, and possession of a goal that might be activated in that situation. Upon activation of a goal, a person experiences arousal of tension that continues to exist until the goal has been achieved or some other resolutions regarding the goal have occurred. The intensity of the activated goal is a function of the multiplicative relationship between the importance of the personal goal and the strength of the activation potential of the environment for that goal. Individuals can satisfy their goals in several ways and a varying range of applicability. Several personal characteristics such as self-esteem or ability determine whether individuals will perform the behavior.

Staub recognized the possibility that several goals, some of which may conflict, may be activated at the same time. In this case, the goal with the greater intensity will predominate other conflicting goals. But, when the intensity of two or more goals are similar, a behavior toward any one can be inhibited, or there may be a reevaluation of the situation through a cognitive process. Also, the activation of a conflicting goal can be suppressed by various attentional, perceptual, and cognitive processes.

A number of studies supporting the described model have been described by Staub (1978, 1980, 1984). Several studies found a relationship between personal values or goals and a performance of helping behavior. Finally, in two reported studies, students of Staub found that subjects who differ in their prosocial orientation (goal) react differently in different situations. That is, the behaviors of subjects with high prosocial needs were affected by their desire to satisfy their goal.

In a search for personal goals, Staub (1978) reported a study (Staub, Erhut, & Jaquette cited in Staub, 1978) demonstrating that subjects with advanced level of moral reasoning and with feelings of responsibility for others' welfare helped more when the situation permitted it. Also, subjects with prosocial values helped more than subjects with values that conflicted with the helping act. In general, when later a prosocial orientation was constructed, on the basis of prosocial values, personal responsibility, positive evaluation of human beings, and low manipulativeness, it related to most of the helpful actions, irrespectively of situational variation.

Two dissertations under the supervision of Staub attempted further to test some aspects of this model (Feinberg, 1977; Goodman, 1978). Feinberg (1977) first divided subjects into high and low groups with either prosocial or achievement orientation. Later, all the subjects were exposed individually to a confederate who was either in high or low need. They were instructed to perform a task during which they were observed and their nonverbal responses were coded. The results of the study showed that when in high need the goal was activated, high-prosocial subjects were especially responsive to the distressed person in various ways. They showed a great deal of attention to her, expressed willingness for future interaction with the person, were more willing to help her, and expressed liking for her. Similarly, Goodman (1978) divided his subjects in high and low prosocial groups and exposed them to another person's distress. The results showed that high prosocial subjects looked at the task less, smiled more at the person in distress, expressed more positive verbalizations, and were more helpful than low prosocial subjects.

TOWARD A GENERAL PROCESS MODEL OF HELPING BEHAVIOR

The existence of different process models that describe the same phenomenon raises the possibility that these models not only describe universal phases of decision making, but also refer to specific instances not necessarily generalizable. Indeed, the review reveals certain common features as well as unique elements emphasized by each of the models. The common features center around the questions of how people become aroused; how individuals become motivated to perform the helping behavior; how they decide whether to perform the behavior, and what do individuals, who are initially motivated to help, do when they decide not to engage in the helping behavior after all. The unique elements consist of specific variables and conditions that may or may not serve as antecedents of various phases of the process. For example, while there is an agreement that arousal is an important component in the sequence of deciding on helping behavior, there are differences regarding the specific conditions which cause the arousal. In this vein, Schwartz and Howard (1984) suggested that the discrepancy between the expectation that individuals should not be in need and the noticed state of their need causes the arousal; Staub (1984) indicated that the personal goals activated by the situation cause the arousal; Piliavin et al. and Weiner proposed that the mere observation of a person in need cause arousal. Similarly, each of the models suggested different contents of cognition which may influence the final decision whether to help: Latané and Darley (1970) suggested the potential helper's perception whether he or she is personally responsible to help; Piliavin et al. (1981) suggested among other variables, the mood of the potential helper, the relationship with the potential recipient and self-perception of ability; Weiner (1980) proposed the potential helper's perception of the causes which brought the recipient to the need of help. Schwartz and Howard (1984) suggested that the potential helper examines the implications that follow directly from the action, implications for the actor's internalized moral values, and social implications of other people's reactions.

In principle, then, the models include elements that are particular—they can characterize some individuals, in certain times, in certain situations, but cannot be generalized to all people, in all situations. The unlimited scope of human cognitive repertoire and the endless possibility of what cognition can be accessible and what cognition can be relevant in certain situations leads to the necessity to propose a model free of specific contents.

Staub's model achieves this condition. But, it fails to explain why individuals move from one phase to another in their decision making. Specifically, the model does not explain how the situation activates the goal, how the goal causes arousal, why arousal leads to search of behavior, and how a person generates and selects helping behavior.

Based on this observation, we attempt to outline a general process model that does not include specific contents and explains the sequence of helping behavior. This model may account for the particular contents suggested by the reviewed models. *In principle, it is proposed that the process of helping behavior is based on the relationship between cognitions, arousal, and behavior in a sequential order.* Arousal activates the motivation to behave and, ultimately, the helping behavior may be performed. A state of arousal is evoked by the presence of at least two inconsistent, but relevant cognitions in which the individual believes, while having an interest to resolve this contradiction. It should be noted, however, that an individual, who helps, will not always go through the outlined process. It is also suggested that individuals who hold the schema of ''if situation X, then behavior Y'' (act of helping), may do so as an automatic response.

Recently, Kruglanski has provided an example to a differentiation between particular contents and universal process (e.g., Kruglanski, 1980, 1988, 1989; Kruglanski & Ajzen, 1983), proposing lay epistemology theory about knowledge acquisition. Although Kruglanski's theory deals with a cognitive process, it has important implications for understanding the dynamics of helping behavior. First, because of the proposed distinction between universal process and particular contents. Second, because the lay epistemology theory may provide a common explanatory framework for the understanding of how do cognitions may motivate to perform the helping act and how do individuals decide on the execution of the specific behavior. Since we chose the lay epistemology theory as the general framework for the model, in the next section we outline the base of the theory.

Lay Epistemology Theory

The lay epistemology theory suggests that contents of knowledge consist of various beliefs that a person holds about the world. The process deals with the way individuals acquire knowledge about themselves and the surrounding world. The structure of knowledge consists of conditional propositions in the form of ''if–then''—the proposition, and its implications. The criterion by which individuals assess the validity of their acquired knowledge is the consistency principle. That is, when the individuals desire to validate a certain proposition, they examine the consistency among the proposition and its perceived implications. Perception of an inconsistency between the two entities reduces the certainty in the validity of the proposition.

Another component in Kruglanski's theory is epistemic motivation. Two motivational factors are relevant to the knowledge-seeking process: (a) The degree of epistemic interest that a person may have on a given issue; and (b) the type of epistemic motivational state that the person might have. Three types of epistemic motivational states are proposed to affect the process of knowledge seeking (Kruglanski & Ajzen, 1983).

The need for nonspecific structure is the desire for certainty on some topic as opposed to an ambiguity. This epistemic motivation predisposes individuals to stop testing the validity of their ideas in order to avoid the possibility of loosing their certainty in the validity of the ideas. This motivation is especially apparent in the case where individual has to decide on a course of action under stress in general, and stress of time pressure, in particular. Under these circumstances, any hesitation or rethinking frustrates the individual's need to perform the immediate act.

The fear of invalidity is the desire for valid knowledge or fear of receiving invalid information or making invalid decisions. Under this motivation individuals are predisposed to test as many implications of their hypothesis as possible to insure themselves that they are holding valid knowledge.

The need for specific structure represents the desire to find that certain beliefs the individual holds are correct. With the need for specific structure, individuals tend to seek information that is consistent with their desired content and avoid information that weakens their certainty in the validity of this belief.

Origin of Arousal

Almost regardless of the specific theoretical approach, arousal (specific or nonspecific) has been acknowledged to be an important factor in the process of action activation (e.g., Hull, 1943; Izard, 1978; Lazarus, Coyne, & Folkman, 1982; Locke & Henne, 1986; Weiner, 1974). The different approaches differ, however, in the role they assign to "cold cognitions" in this process. This question is of great importance for the explanation of prosocial behavior, because of the basic assumption regarding the importance of "cold cognitions" such as moral values, norms attitudes, the contents of attributions and perception of the situation in the process of deciding on the prosocial act. In general, it is possible to suggest that *if processed information contradicts content of cognition which individuals hold, and toward which they have epistemic need for specific or non specific structure, then they will experience arousal.*

The idea that arousal appears as a consequence of incongruent cognitions has a long history in psychology (e.g., Festinger, 1957; Harvey, 1963; Heider, 1946; Hunt, 1963; Pepitone, 1966; Rokeach, 1980). In this line, several psychologists suggested that cognitive inconsistency is a causal agent of human action (e.g., Mancuso, 1977; Rokeach, 1980). In the present conception, two major classes of cognition's contents can be singled out as leading to the experience of arousal that may motivate individuals to act. The first class relates to the inconsistency between the mental representation of an end-point of a goal and the perception of the present situation. The second class refers to the perception of events that are incongruent with cognitions (which are not goals) towards which the individuals have need for structure.

Goals as Motivators of Behavior. The word goal implies a preference for certain outcome or end-state (e.g., to see the other happy). Thus, the primary defining characteristics of goals are the desire for valued outcomes and the expectation of satisfaction in reaching them (cf. Staub, 1984). In this vein, Pervin (1983), suggested that an essential property of the goal is that the end point or reference point must be kept in mind. In lay epistemology theory terms, the desire for valued outcome and the expectations of satisfaction imply that individuals have epistemic need for structure toward the outcome. That is, when a goal is evoked in an individual mind, the individual persists in holding the goal and may experience arousal because of the inconsistency between the desired and the perceived state of affairs.

A goal may be triggered as a consequence of internal stimulation (flow of associations) or as a result of perceived cues in a situation. Thus, the specific content of a goal that initiates the helping act is a function of availability and accessibility of various ideas in the cognitive repertoire and availability and saliency of cues in the environment (see Wyer & Srull, 1980). One of the factors contributing to the accessibility of a goal is its centrality (i.e., importance) for the self. Obviously, some goals are more important to self than other goals. A number of psychologists have suggested that goals vary with regard to their centrality to self and are hierarchally arranged along this dimension (Krech, Crutchfield, & Ballachey, 1962; Reykowski, 1982; Staub, 1984). Thus, the more central the goal is, the more accessible it will be in human repertoire (Bar-Tal, 1986). However, it should be pointed out that the repertoire of individuals' goals and their relative importance is dynamic and may likely change over time or circumstances.

Cognitive Inconsistency as a Motivator of Helping Behavior. Several theorists of prosocial behavior recognized the causal relationships between cognitive discrepancy and motivation. Reykowski (1982, 1984) suggested that the motivational effects of arousal that lead to helping behavior are evoked whenever a person is confronted with information that concerns other individuals and contradicts beliefs or attitudes central to self-definition. Other helping behavior theorists proposed more specific contents that when are contradicted, motivate individuals to act. For example, Lerner (1977, 1981) has suggested that individuals have a belief in justice which holds that people should get what they deserve. Whenever information indicates that injustice occurs, individuals display signs of distress which, in turn, motivates them to counter or eliminate this threat. Equity theorists (Walster, Walster, & Berscheid, 1978) suggested that a violation of a belief in equity (e.g., gains are exceeding the inputs in proportion to those of an individual) causes to a distress and willingness to correct the perceived inequity.

It is, however, important to note that inconsistency, as such, need not necessarily cause arousal. Nor can we implicate any specific categories of cognitions such as moral norms, values, or beliefs about just-world as necessarily causing arousal when being contradicted. Similarly, there are *no* cognitions or perceptions of any specific situations that necessary contradict our belief system. Thus, noticing that someone is in need or that there is an emergency situation, does not necessarily cause arousal, even if we believe that individuals around us should not be in need.

It is frustration of the need to be certain in the specific situation which causes arousal (see Kruglanski & Klar, 1987). That is, the stronger the need for specific or nonspecific structure,[1] while the individuals are experiencing the inconsistency, the stronger will be the arousal and, consequently, the motivation to perform the helping act. This argument is supported by empirical findings showing that individuals who were exposed to emotional stress (need for nonspecific structure)[2] reacted more positively to a help request, and the amount of help they gave was larger than subjects who were not exposed to the stress prior to the help request (e.g., Baron, 1978; Baron & Bell, 1976; Yinon & Bizman, 1980).

Activation of a Motivation to Behave

Motivation to behave is activated by arousal. This causal link was suggested by a number of theorists (e.g., Arnold, 1969; Izard, 1965; McClelland, Atkinson, Clark, & Lowell, 1953). Individuals who experience arousal may feel a desire to achieve a certain state or goal. In this vein, motivation is defined as "a cognitive representation of a future goal state that is desired" (Kagan, 1972, p. 54). Similarly, Arnold (1969) defined a motive as a "want that leads to action" (p. 182). A "want" was described as "a goal, or a course of action leading to goals appraisal as desirable. A want will entice or impel to action provided there are no contrary wants, or subsequent appraisals that interdict action" (p. 182). In line with this conception, helping behavior theorists have also suggested that arousal precedes a willingness to perform helping behavior (e.g., Piliavin et al., 1981; Staub, 1978; Weiner, 1980).

The discussion thus far has concentrated on the causal relationships between

---

[1]The need to be certain exists when an individual is either under need for specific or nonspecific structure (cf. Kruglanski & Freund 1983).

[2]For empirical evidence regarding the relationships between stress and need for nonspecific structure see for example, Broadbent (1971), Cowan (1952), Keinan (1987), Sieber (1974), and Smock (1955a, 1955b). See also Bar-Tal (1989) and Janis and Mann (1977) for theoretical discussion about the relationships between stress and need for nonspecific structure.

cognitions, arousal, and motivation. It should be noted, however, that arousal not always is translated into motivation to behave. It is possible that in certain cases arousal can be attributed to other reasons than the one which caused it. This idea was suggested by Schachter and Singer (1962) to explain emotions. It implied that individuals who are aroused by an inconsistency may attribute the arousal to some other causes that become more salient to them (for review of research about the phenomenon of misattribution of arousal, see Reisenzein, 1983). In helping behavior literature, Weiner's (1980) model may be interpreted in this line. That is, when the potential helper blames the person in need for his or her situation, he or she attributes the arousal to anger rather than to the motivation to help.

Moreover, even if the arousal is attributed to the inconsistency, the person may reduce the arousal either by cognitive means (e.g., adding consistent cognitions, changing inconsistent cognitions), or behavioral means (behavior which eliminates the inconsistency). Thus, the person may be motivated to overt or covert action. The important question in the present model concerns which of these two possible ways is chosen. The answer to this question lies in the behavioral implication that a contradicted cognition may have. Behavioral implication, is to a large extent, similar to Kruglanski and Klar's (1985) idea of action schema. According to Kruglanski and Klar, action scheme is a premise; a conditional statement in which its consequence is an intention. In this vein, behavioral implications, as cognitive implications, may be derived on an ad hoc basis, when individuals desire to validate a specific cognition. It is also possible, however, that for certain cognitions individuals develop specific schema of "if–then" nature, which would cause them each time they think about X automatically to be aware of behavioral implication Y. For example, individuals may hold a schema of if "I am good," then "I help when I am asked to." When individuals want to be certain that they are good, they have to help when they are asked to.

A contradiction of a behavioral implication of a cognition causes arousal which activates a motivation to behave. In other words, the present model suggests that *motivations leading to helping behavior are activated in situations where individuals experience inconsistency with behavioral implications of a cognition, while having a motivation to confirm this cognition.*

The Selection and Execution of the Behavior

It is widely accepted that the same behavior might represent different cognitions and that more than one behavior may be consistent with a specific cognition (Bar-Tal, 1982; Reykowski, 1984; Schwartz & Howard, 1981a; Staub, 1978). It is also possible that a behavior that is consistent with one cognition may be relevant, but inconsistent with another cognition. For example, to give money to a friend may be consistent with the positive attitude toward this friend, but inconsistent with the implication of the attitude toward money. Therefore, we suggest that once a person is aroused and he or she attributes the arousal to the contradiction of the behavioral implication with the cognition the person desires to believe in, the person may engage in a process of examining whether the specific behavior does not contradict other relevant salient cognitions or goals. An example of a cognition which its contradiction may prevent the individual from performing the behavior may be the perception of lack of ability to execute the behavior (e.g., Ajzen & Madden, 1986; Bandura, 1977). Some examples of such cognitions, mentioned in the helping behavior literature are perceived cost (physical, material, and psychological) of the helping act (e.g., Bar-Tal, 1976; Piliavin et al., 1981; Schwartz & Howard, 1984), and relationships and past experience with the victim (e.g., Latané & Darley, 1970; Goranson & Berkowitz, 1966).

If the selected behavior does not contradict other cognitions, it is executed. But, if the behavior conflicts with another cognition or its implication, the person may choose among three modes of action: (1) The person may look for another specific behavior which is implied by the cognition and does not contradict other salient cognitions. (2) The person may freeze and not do anything (see Bar-Tal, 1989; Janis & Mann, 1977). (3) The person may choose to perform the specific behavior anyway. It is possible to suggest that the strength and type of epistemic motivation the person has in the moment of the decision toward the cognitions involved in the process, as well as his or her ability to generate alternative specific behaviors, contribute to the final decision of what mode of action the person takes (cf. Bar-Tal, Bar-Tal, Geva, & Yarkin, 1990). If the person has a strong need for non specific structure, he or she will tend to avoid examination of the consistency of the specific behavior with other cognitions or goals (the third mode). Under fear of invalidity[3] the person will tend to produce much more alternative specific behaviors and examine it's consistency with more cognitions (the first mode). The second mode of action may take place when the individual is under strong fear of invalidity, but unable to generate alternative specific behavior which is not contradicting the salient goals (see Janis & Mann's, [1977] description of the hypervigelent type of decision maker) or when the contradicted cognitions (or goals) are more salient and the need for specific structure toward them is stronger than towards the contradicted cognition which initiated the process. In the later case, the person may attempt to further reduce the tension by using cognitive methods such as redefining the situation.

The proposed description of the relations between epistemic motivation and the amount of cognitive processing implies that when the individual has a need

---

[3]Although it was suggested that the arousal involves epistemic motivation of need for structure, it is possible that in the moment of the decision on the specific behavior the person will be motivated by fear of invalidity. Such a situation may occur when the individual thinks that a wrong decision regarding the specific behavior may be very costly for him.

for specific or non specific structure, the process will be shorter and therefore less time consuming. This is especially true in the case of existing schemata, such as a script which the individual applies in the situation.

Automatic Helping Behavior

In some situations, individuals do not go through all the phases of the described process in order to perform helping acts. In situations when individuals repeatedly perform the same helping acts or when the helping acts are defined by learned rules, the behavior may be performed automatically on the basis of learned script. In these cases, cues within a situation or an internal stimulation may elicit a script of helping behavior. For example, a person who contributes every year to the "March of Dimes" campaign may automatically donate, when the campaign is publicized.

The idea that individuals can behave in automatic ways on the basis of stored memory plans has received wide attention in social psychology in the past decade (e.g., Abelson, 1976; Harré, 1977; Langer 1978). Abelson's (1976, 1981) work about script has become especially known because of its attempt to link cognition and social behavior. Scripts are learned courses of action stored in memory and activated more or less automatically whenever the situation is similar to the one experienced in the past. Similarly, Langer and her colleagues (e.g., Langer, 1978; Langer, Blank, & Chanowitz, 1978) named the phenomenon "mindless behavior," and suggested that it occurs when the behavior is performed so many times that the person does not pay attention to the particulars of the situation and/or to the specific behavior he or she is performing. Langer (1978) pointed out that "Much of the interaction that people mundanely enact in the every day world would seem to rely on the script structure of typical activities rather than on the active processing of incoming information" (p. 50). These automatic interactions imply that individuals often utilize simple strategies of behavior which serve cognitive and emotional economy (cf. Jones & Thibaut, 1958).

The phenomenon of mindless behavior, as well as script-base behavior in helping behavior (as well as in social behavior in general), can be interpreted also in the framework of lay epistemology theory (cf. Kruglanski & Klar, 1985). According to the epistemic analysis, in addition to the existence of stored script, mindless behavior would be more likely to occur when individuals are under high need for nonspecific structure, and less likely to occur when they are under high fear of invalidity or when information inconsistent with the schema is made available and salient. Thus, although it is possible that helping behavior will not involve inconsistency between cognitions or a process of selection of specific behavior, it still can be explained by the same principles that govern the decision-making process of helping behavior, suggested earlier.

CONCLUSIONS

The present chapter reviewed various decision-making models of helping behavior and proposed a general process model for explaining helping behavior. The goal was to show that the reviewed models contain also specific contents that characterize certain people in certain time and places, which cannot be applied to all individuals, in all situations and do not explain the basis for the described sequence. Thus, these models differ in particular cognitions, decisions, or considerations which they emphasize. In this respect, they concern particular cases of helping behavior performance rather than the underlying process (cf. Bar-Tal & Bar-Tal, 1988). In contrast, the proposed model describes and explains the general process that underlies the specific decisions of helping behavior. It presents a sequence of stages through which people go in their deciding and performing helping behavior by analyzing the relationships between cognitions, arousal, motivation, and behavior. The proposed process model is described in abstract terms to which specific contents can be inserted. It describes the underlying process of already existing content-oriented models of helping behavior performance. In this sense, it provides an integrative framework to consider various models in common theoretical terms.

Understanding of the process allows the use of specific variables that may characterize certain individuals only. Thus, for example, individuals may have different cognitions with behavioral implications and different information may be collected from different situations, which may contradict the existing cognitions. Furthermore, the originated arousal may activate different motives to behave and different specific behaviors can be selected to satisfy the motives. Finally, people may have different types and strength of epistemic motivation at the moment of the decision about the helping behavior, and thus, to select different course of action.

The model not only describes the sequence of operations involved in the decision about helping behavior, but also explains how and why a person moves from one phase to the next (a progressive process from cognition to arousal; from attribution of the arousal through the cognitive inconsistency to the examination of options, or an "automatic" behavior on the basis of existing scripts or a behavior schemata). Thus, it allows an understanding and even prediction when individuals go through all the phases of the described process in order to perform helping acts and when individuals, in spite of going through all the process, decide finally not to perform the helping act after all.

It is suggested that the proposed process can be utilized in an analysis of specific contents involved in the process of deciding on helping behavior not addressed previously. That is, the underlying process can serve as a basis for a description of a specific type of decision which may be characteristic of certain individuals, at certain time and place. In addition, because the suggested process is general enough, it can explain not just the helping behavior but also the behavioral reaction of the other participants in the situation. Thus, for example, the described process can be used for the analysis of the recipients' or the bystanders's reactions. It can explain not just helping behavior in emergency situations or helping behaviors based on moral values and norms, but helping behavior based more on the need of the helper *to give* rather than on the need of the recipient *to receive*. It can explain the behavior of helping profession individuals who are responding to their role, etc. What might differ in different situations or in different helping acts are the specific variables suggested by the decision making models and the helping behavior research literature (for review see Bar-Tal, 1984b). These variables can be characterized by the contents of cognitions and the epistemic motivations.

It should be emphasized that we do not disregard or underestimate the study of contents. Only on the basis of specific variables it is possible to predict the behavior of individuals. Specific variables must be inserted into the abstract concepts of the process, if one is to study specific individuals. In order to accomplish this, it is essential to identify these specific variables. In fact, only research that uses contents can validate the proposed process. Moreover, an understanding of helping behavior in any specific milieu must be done in relation to contents. But, in our opinion, it is essential that researchers who study a specific milieu will understand the underlying process of the contents they investigate and that they will realize the limitations of content investigations. We believe that the present model provides an important step in this direction.

REFERENCES

Abelson, R. P. (1976). Script processing in attitude formation and decision making. In J. S. Carroll & J. W. Payne (Ed.), *Cognition and social behavior* (pp. 33–45). Hillsdale, NJ: Lawrence Erlbaum Associates.

Abelson, R. P. (1981). Psychological status of the script. *American Psychologist, 36,* 715–729.

Ajzen, I., & Madden, T. J. (1986). Prediction of goal-oriented behavior: Attitudes, intentions, and perceived behavioral control. *Journal of Experimental Social Psychology, 22,* 453–474.

Arnold, M. B. (1969). Human emotion and action. In T. Mischel (Ed.), *Human action.* New York: Academic Press.

Bandura, A. (1977). Self-efficacy: Toward a unified theory of behavioral change. *Psychological Review, 84,* 191–215.

Baron, R. A. (1978). Invasions of personal space and helping: Mediating effects of invador's apparent need. *Journal of Experimental Social Psychology, 14,* 304–312.

Baron, R. A., & Bell, P. A., (1976) Physical distance and helping: Some unexpected benefits of "crowding in" on others. *Journal of Applied Social Psychology, 6,* 95–104.

Bar-Tal, D. (1976). *Prosocial behavior: Theory and research.* New York: Halsted.

Bar-Tal, D. (1982). Sequential development of helping behavior: A cognitive-learning approach. *Developmental Review, 2,* 101–124.

Bar-Tal, D. (1984a). American study of helping behavior—what, why, and where? In E. Staub, D. Bar-Tal, J. Karylowski, & J. Reykoski (Eds.), *Development and maintenance of prosocial behavior: International perspectives* (pp. 5–27). New York: Plenum.

Bar-Tal, D. (1984b). *The limitations of investigating contents: The case of helping behavior.* Paper presented at the meeting of the European Association of Experimental Social Psychology, Tilburg, Holland.

Bar-Tal, D. (1986). The Masada Syndrome: A case of central belief. In N. Milgram (Ed.), *Stress and coping in time of war* (pp. 32–51). New York: Brunner/Mazel.

Bar-Tal, D., & Bar-Tal, Y. (1988). New perspective for social psychology. In D. Bar-Tal & A. W. Kruglanski (Eds.), *Social psychology of knowledge* (pp. 83–108). Cambridge: Cambridge University Press.

Bar-Tal, D., Bar-Tal, Y., Geva, N., & Yarkin, K. (1990). Planning and performing interpersonal interaction: A cognitive-motivational approach. In W. Jones & D. Perlman (Eds.), *Perspective in interpersonal behavior and relationships* (pp. 205–232). London: Jessica Kingsley.

Bar-Tal, Y. (1989, January). *Coping with uncertainty.* Paper presented at the Fourth International Conference on Psychological Stress and Adjustment in Time of War and Peace. Tel-Aviv, Israel.

Broadbent, D. E. (1971). *Decision and stress.* New York: Academic Press.

Cowan, E. L. (1952). The influence of varying degrees of psychological stress on problem solving rigidity. *Journal of Abnormal Social Psychology, 47,* 512–519.

Darley, J. M., & Latané, B. (1968). Bystander intervention in emergencies: Diffusion of responsibility. *Journal of Personality and Social Psychology, 8,* 377–383.

Feinberg, H. K. (1977). *Anatomy of a helping situation. Some personality and situational determinants of helping in a conflict situation involving another's psychological distress.* Unpublished doctoral dissertation. University of Massachusetts, Amherst.

Festinger, L. (1957). *A theory of cognitive dissonance.* Stanford, CA: Stanford University Press.

Gaertner, S. L., & Davidio, J. F. (1977). The subtlety of white racism, arousal, and helping behavior. *Journal of Personality and Social Psychology, 35,* 691–707.

Goodman, S. M. (1978). *The role of personality and situational variables in responding to and helping individual in psychological distress.* Unpublished doctoral dissertation. University of Massachusetts, Amherst.

Goranson, R. E., & Berkowitz, L. (1966). Reciprocity and responsibility reactions to prior help. *Journal of Personality and Social Psychology, 3,* 227–232.

Harré, R. (1977). The ethnogenic approach: Theory and practice. In L. Berkowitz (Ed.), *Advances in experimental social psychology* (Vol. 10). New York: Academic Press.

Harvey, O. J. (1963). Concluding comments on the current status of the incongruity hypothesis. In O. J. Harvey (Ed.), *Motivation and social interaction: Cognitive determinants.* New York: The Ronald Press.

Heider, F. (1946). Attitudes and cognitive organization. *Journal of Psychology, 21,* 107–112.

Hull, C. L. (1943). *Principles of behavior.* New York: Appelton-Century-Crofts.

Hunt, M. J. (1963). Motivation inherent in information processing and action. In O. J. Harvey (Ed.), *Motivation and social interaction: Cognitive determinants.* New York: The Ronald Press.

Izard, C. E. (1965). Affect, awareness, and performance. In S. S. Tomkins & C. E. Izard (Eds.), *Affect, cognition, and personality.* New York: Springer.

Izard, C. E. (1978). Emotion as motivations: An evolutionary-developmental perspective. In R. A. Dienstbier (Ed.), *Nebraska Symposium on Motivation* (Vol. 26, pp. 163–200). University of Nebraska Press.

Janis, I. L., & Mann, L. (1977). *Decisionmaking: A psychological analysis of conflict, choice, and commitment.* New York: Free Press.

Jones, E. E., & Thibaut, J. W. (1958). Interaction goals as bases of inference in interpersonal perception. In R. Tagiuri & L. Petrullo (Eds.), *Person perception and interpersonal behavior* (pp. 151–178). Standard, CA: Stanford University Press.

Kagan, J. (1972). Motivation and development. *Journal of Personality and Social Psychology, 22,* 51–66.

Keinan, G. (1987). Decision making under stress: Scanning of alternatives under controllable and uncontrollable threats, *Journal of Personality and Social Psychology, 52,* 636–644.

Krebs, D. L. (1970). Altruism—an examination of the concept and a review of the literature. *Psychological Bulletin, 73,* 158–202.

Krebs, D. (1975). Empathy and altruism. *Journal of Personality and Social Psychology, 32,* 1134–1146.

Krech, D., Crutchfield, R. S., & Ballachey, E. L. (1982). *Individuals in society.* New York: McGraw-Hill.

Kruglanski, A. W. (1980). Lay epistemologic-process and contents: Another look at attribution theory. *Psychological Review, 87,* 70–87.

Kruglanski, A. W. (1988). Knowledge as social psychological construct. In D. Bar-Tal and A. W. Kruglanski (Eds.), *Social psychology of knowledge* (109–141). Cambridge: Cambridge University Press.

Kruglanski, A. W. (1989). *Lay epistemics and human knowledge: Cognitive and motivational bases.* New York: Plenum.

Kruglanski, A. W., & Ajzen, I. (1983). Bias and error in human judgment. *European Journal of Social Psychology, 13,* 1–44.

Kruglanski, A. W., & Freund, T. (1983). The freezing and unfreezing of lay inferences: effects on impresional primacy, ethnic stereotyping, and numerical anchoring. *Journal of Experimental Social Psychology, 19,* 448–468.

Kruglanski, A. W., & Klar, Y. (1987). A view from a bridge: Synthesizing the consistency and attribution paradigms from a lay epistemic perspective. *European Journal of Social Psychology, 17,* 211–241.

Kruglanski, A. W., & Klar, Y. (1985). Knowing what to do: on the epistemology of actions. In J. Kuhl and J. Beckman (Eds.), *Action control: From Cognition to behavior* (pp. 41–60). New York: Springer.

Langer, E. (1978). Rethinking the role of thought in social interaction. In J. Harvey, W. Ickes, & R. Kidd (Eds.), *New direction in attribution research* (Vol. 2, pp. 35–58). Hillsdale, NJ: Lawrence Erlbaum Associates.

Langer, E., Blank, A., & Chanowitz, B. (1978). The mindlessness of ostensibly thoughtful action: The role of placibic information in interpersonal interaction. *Journal of Personality and Social Psychology, 36,* 635–642.

Latané, B., & Darley, J. M. (1968). Group inhibition of bystander intervention in emergencies. *Journal of Personality and Social Psychology, 10,* 215–221.

Latané, B., & Darley, J. M. (1970). *The unresponsive bystander: Why doesn't he help?* New York: Appleton-Century-Crofts.

Latané, B., & Rodin, J. (1969). A lady in distress: Inhibiting effects of friends and strangers on bystander intervention. *Journal of Experimental Social Psychology, 5,* 189–202.

Lazarus, R. S., Coyne, J. C., & Folkman, S. (1982). Cognition, emotion, and motivation: The doctoring of Humpty-Dumpty. In R. W. Neufeld (Ed.), *Psychological stress and psychopathology* (pp. 218–239). New York: McGraw-Hill.

Locke, E. A., & Henne, D. (1986). Work motivation theories. In C. L. Cooper, & I. Robertson (Eds.), *International review of industrial and organization psychology* (pp. 1–35). New York: Wiley.

Mancuso, J. C. (1977). Current motivational models in the elaboration of personal construct theory. In A. W. Lanfielde (Ed.), *Nebraska Symposium on Motivation 1976* (Vol. 24, pp. 43–97). University of Nebraska Press.

McClelland, D. C., Atkinson, J. W., Clark, R. H., & Lowell, E. L. (1953). *The achievement motive.* New York: Appleton-Century-Crofts.

Pepitone, A. (1966). Problems of consistency models. In S. Feldman (Ed.), *Cognitive consistency: Motivational antecedents and behavioral consequents* (pp. 257–297). New York: Academic Press.

Pervin, L. A. (1983). The statis and flow of behavior: Tward a theory of goals. In M. M. Page (Ed.), *Nebraska Symposium on Motivation 1982* (Vol. 30, pp. 1–54). University of Nebraska Press.

Piliavin, I. M., Piliavin, J. A., & Rodin, S. (1975). Costs, diffusion, and the stigmatized victim. *Journal of Personality and Social Psychology, 32,* 429–438.

Piliavin, I. M., Rodin, J., & Piliavin, J. A. (1969). Good samaritanism An underground phenomenon? *Journal of Personality and Social Psychology, 14,* 289–299.

Piliavin, J. A., Dovidio, J. F., Gaertner, S. L., & Clark, R. D. III (1981). *Emergency intervention.* New York: Academic Press.

Piliavin, J. A., & Piliavin, I. M. (1972). The effect of blood on reactions to a victim. *Journal of Personality and Social Psychology, 23,* 353–351.

Piliavin, J. A., & Piliavin, I. M. (1973). *The good samaritan: Why does he help?* Unpublished module, University of Wisconsin.

Reisenzein, R. (1983). The Shachter theory of emotion: Two decades later. *Psychological Bulletin, 94,* 239–264.

Reykowski, J. Social motivation. (1982). *Annual Review of Psychology, 33,* 123–154.

Reykowski, J. (1984). Spatial organization of a cognitive system and intrinsic prosocial motivation. In E. Staub, D. Bar-Tal, J. Karylowski, & J. Reykowski (Eds.), *Development and maintenance of prosocial behavior: International perspective.* New York: Plenum.

Rokeach, M. (1980). Some unresolved issues in theories of beliefs, attitudes, and values. In M. M. Page (Ed.), *Nebraska symposium on motivation, 1979.* Lincoln: University of Nebraska Press.

Schachter, S., & Singer, J. (1962). Cognitive, social and physiological determinants of emotional state. *Psychological Review, 69,* 379–399.

Schwartz, S. H. (1968). Words, deed, and the perception of consequences and responsibility in action situation. *Journal of Personality and Social Psychology, 10,* 232–242.

Schwartz, S. H. (1973). Normative explanations of helping behavior: A critique, proposal, and empirical test. *Journal of Experimental Social Psychology, 9,* 349–364.

Schwartz, S. H., & Ben David, A. (1976). Responsibility and helping in an emergency: Effect of blame, ability and denial or responsibility. *Sociometry. 39,* 406–415.

Schwartz, S. H., & Fleishman, J. A. (1978). Personal norms and the mediation of legitimacy effects on helping. *Social Psychology Quarterly, 41,* 306–315.

Schwartz, S. H., & Howard, J. A. (1980). Explanations of the moderating effect of responsibility denial on the personal norm-behavior relationship. *Social Psychology Quarterly, 43,* 441–446.

Schwartz, S. H., & Howard, J. (1981a). A normative decision-making model of altruism. In J. P. Rushton & R. Sorrentino (Eds.), *Altruism and helping behavior.* Hillsdale, N.J.: Lawrence Erlbaum Associates.

Schwartz, S. H., & Howard, J. A. (1981b). A self-based motivational model of helping. In V. Derlega & J. Grzelak (Eds.), *Cooperation and helping behavior: Theories and research* (pp. 327–353). New York: Academic Press.

Schwartz, S. H., & Howard, J. A. (1984). Internalized values as motivators of altruism. In E. Staub, D. Bar-Tal, & J. Karylowski (Eds.), *The development and maintenance of prosocial behavior: International perspectives* (pp. 229–255). New York: Plenum.

Sieber, J. E. (1974). Effects of decision importance on ability to generate warranted subjective uncertainty. *Journal of Personality and Social Psychology, 30,* 688–694.

Smock, C. D. (1955a). The influence of psychological stress on the 'intolerance of ambiguity'. *Journal of Abnormal and Social Psychology, 50,* 177–182.

Smock, C. D. (1955b). The influence of stress on the perception of incongruity. *Journal of Abnormal and Social Psychology, 50,* 354–356.

Staub, E. (1978). *Positive social behavior and morality: Social and personal influence: (Vol. 1).* New York: Academic Press.

Staub, E. (1980). Social and prosocial behavior: Personal and situational influences and their interactions. In E. Staub (Ed.), *Personality: Basic aspects and current research*. Englewood Cliffs, NJ: Prentice-Hall.

Staub, E. (1984). Notes toward an interactionist-motivational theory of the determinants and development of (pro)social behavior. In E. Staub, D. Bar-Tal, J. Karylowski, & J. Reykowski (Eds.), *The development and maintenance of prosocial behavior: International perspectives*. (pp. 29–49). New York: Plenum.

Walster, E., Walster, G. W., & Berscheid, E. (1978). *Equity: Theory and research*. Boston, MA: Allyn and Bacon.

Weiner, B. (1974). (Ed.). *Cognitive views of human motivation*. New York: Academic Press.

Weiner, B. (1980). A cognitive (attribution)-emotion-action model of motivated behavior: An analysis of judgments of help-given. *Journal of Personality and Social Psychology, 29,* 186–200.

Weiner, B., Perry, R. P., & Magnusson, J. (1988). An attributional analysis of reactions to stigmas. *Journal of Personality and Social Psychology, 55,* 738–748.

Wyer, R. S., & Srull, T. K. (1980). The processing stimulus information: a conceptual integration. In R. Hastie, T. M. Ostrom, E. B. Ebbessen, R. S. Wyer, D. L. Hamilton, & D. E. Carlston. *Person memory: The cognitive basis of social perception* (pp. 227–300). Hillsdale, NJ: Lawrence Erlbaum Associates.

Yinon, Y., & Bizman, A. (1980). Noise, success, and failure as determinants of helping behavior. *Personality and Social Psychology Bulletin, 6,* 725–730.

2 Reading Narratives of Conflict and Choice for Self and Moral Voices: A Relational Method

Lyn Mikel Brown
Elizabeth Debold
Mark Tappan
Carol Gilligan

ABSTRACT

In this chapter we present a "relational" method for reading and interpreting interview narratives of individuals' lived experiences of conflict and choice. Such a method, focusing as it does on the reading process and the creation of an interpretive account of a narrative, raises questions both about a reader's subjectivity and perspective, and about how a reader can understand the subjectivity and perspective of the person whose narrative he or she reads. The aim of this chapter is to describe this method and to raise and address such issues. We present our theoretical assumptions and a general overview of the method and its interpretive procedures for identifying self and the moral voices of care and justice. We then illustrate this method by presenting an interpretation of an interview text of a 12-year-old girl. Attending to this text allows us to highlight the fundamentally relational character of the act of reading, and thus to consider this method both as a *reader-response* method and as a *feminist* method.

In Margaret Drabble's (1975) short story "The Gifts of War," a nameless woman whose "face had only one expression, and she used it to conceal the two major emotions of her life, resentment and love" goes to town to buy her son, Kevin, "what he wanted" for his birthday: a "Despardo Destruction Machine;" "a grotesque, unjustifiable luxury, a pointless gift" with the "thirty shillings saved, unspoken for" which she really "ought to use . . . to buy him something useful." The luxury is worth it, however, "[b]ecause, amazingly, she had been saved, against all probability: her life which had seemed after that bridal day of white nylon net and roses to sink deeply and almost instantly into a mire of penury and beer and butchery, had been so redeemed for her by her child.'' For this woman, then, this gift was truly an indulgence: an ill-afforded frivolity and a re-payment for the salvation of her son's love. Her act, however, could also be called deeply moral, both in its attempt, in some small way, to rectify the bleakness of her son's life, and in the passionate attention she paid to his small wish.

In the department store, Frances Janet Ashton Hall, who has the right by birth and education to a name and an identity of her own, joins her newfound friend, Michael Swaines, "quite well-brought up," a University student who had a "thing" about "children and violence," in his attempt "to persuade the manager of the Toy department not to sell toy machine guns and toy bombs and toy battleships.'' Frances stops Kevin's mother as she stands with the toy that would "break his heart if he didn't get" and says "in what she thought was a very friendly and reasonable tone, that nobody was trying to stop her buying her little boy a birthday present,'' but "with all the violence in the world today anyway it was silly to add to it by encouraging children to play at killing and exterminating and things like that, and hadn't everyone seen enough bombing . . . so why didn't she buy her boy something constructive like Meccano or a farmyard set?'' Kevin's mother, this woman with the "unnaturally drawn, prematurely aged" face, "started to cry:"

> incredibly, horribly, she started to cry. She dropped the clockwork toy on the floor, and it fell so heavily that she could almost have been said to have thrown it down, and she stood there, staring at it, as the tears rolled down her face. Then she looked at them, and walked off. Nobody followed her: they stood there and let her go. They did not know how to follow her, nor what appeasement to offer for her unknown wound. But Frances knew that in their innocence they had done something dreadful to her, in the light of which those long-since ended air raids and even distant Vietnam itself were an irrelevance, a triviality: but she did not know what it was, she could not know. (p. 347)

Here we have a conflict of moral contexts embedded in a human narrative that, with the complexity of all human reasons and motivations, renders foolish any attempt to define the truly moral stance. Michael and Frances, too, were moved by a moral concern—a wish to make the world a less violent place, so that children like Kevin might have more fertile soil in which to grow. Yet their moral zeal may have destroyed something essential to Kevin's and his mother's world, for she "knew that in their innocence they had done something dreadful to her.'' Frances, in her attempt to show Kevin's mother how to care for Kevin according to *her* standards, took from this woman the only way she knew how to care for her son. For it was only after she had spoken that Frances could see the "immeasurable gap of quality that separated their two lives.''

And why didn't Frances see that gap before?

As students of moral development we are particularly concerned with relationship—born out of seeing, hearing, and recognizing the gap in understanding that difference may create. The method we discuss in this chapter has been developed explicitly to acknowledge the relationship between ourselves and those who share their stories of moral conflict with us. For it is only by bringing ourselves, as researchers, into relationship with the narrator of a moral story that we can possibly understand and maintain the integrity of his or her experience. What would it mean for Frances to know the nameless woman's story?

One could imagine both Frances and Kevin's mother describing their reasons for acting as "care." Individual words and phrases that are used to describe moral thought, feeling, and action—words such as "care" and "justice"—are meaningless in and of themselves to explain the particular "meaning and shape at a particular moment in a socially specific environment" that creates the "living utterance" (Bakhtin, 1981, p. 276). The living language exists in a web of interrelationships that allow the narrator's meaning to become clear only if the context, the narrative, is maintained. Thus, it is only by allowing language to exist in narrative relationship, and by enabling the researcher to acknowledge both the relationships in the narrative itself, and his or her relationship with the narrator, is it possible to begin to interpret and understand another's moral experience. Our way of working, and the method we describe in this chapter, takes these issues seriously as the starting point for psychological research, especially research on moral development.

In this chapter, therefore, we present a "relational" method for reading and interpreting interview narratives of people's experiences of conflict and choice— *A guide to reading narratives of conflict and choice for self and moral voice*— hereafter referred to as the "Reading Guide" (Brown et al., 1988; Brown, Tappan, Gilligan, Miller, & Argyris, 1989; see also Gilligan, Brown, & Rogers, 1990). Such a method, focusing as it does on the reading process and the creation of an interpretive account of a narrative, raises questions both about a reader's subjectivity and perspective, and about how a reader can understand the subjectivity and perspective of the person whose narrative he or she reads. The aim of this chapter, then, is to describe our method and to raise and address such issues. We begin with our theoretical assumptions and move to a general overview of the Reading Guide and its interpretive procedures. We then illustrate this method by presenting an interpretation of an interview text of a 12-year-old girl describing a recent experience of moral conflict and choice in her life. Attending to this case allows us to highlight the fundamentally relational character of the act of reading, and thus to consider the Reading Guide both as a *reader-response* method and as a *feminist* method. Such a focus on the relationship between the reader's and the narrator's perspective directly challenges the strive toward "objectivity"—a disembodied voice and a detached point of view that characterizes traditional empiricist and rationalist approaches to psychological inquiry.

THEORETICAL ASSUMPTIONS

The Reading Guide is premised on a distinction between two voices or orientations heard in moral discourse: a *care* voice and a *justice* voice (Gilligan, 1982, 1986, 1987; see also Gilligan, Brown, & Rogers, 1990; Gilligan & Wiggins, 1987). We hear in these two voices concerns about or visions of ideal human relationship: the care voice articulating concerns about loving and being loved, listening and being listened to, and responding and being responded to; the justice voice reflecting a vision of equality, reciprocity, and fairness between persons. These visions of relationship are experienced as being undercut, in the case of care, by detachment, disconnection, abandonment, inattentiveness, and/or lack of responsiveness; in the case of justice, by oppression, domination, inequality, and/or unfairness of treatment. Insofar as one takes as "blameworthy" detachment, abandonment, inattentiveness, or oppression, domination, unequal treatment, etc., by one person with respect to another with whom she or he is in relationship, one can therefore speak of justice and care not only as *moral* voices, but also as *relational* voices. In other words, actual or potential experiences of vulnerability in relationship are commonly expressed in these moral terms.

From a developmental perspective, we assume that experiences of responsiveness and inequality in relationship are universal human experiences: all children are born into a position of inequality vis-à-vis their parents, and yet no child survives in the absence of some kind of responsive relationships to adults. Since everyone has been vulnerable, therefore, both to abandonment and to oppression, two moral voices and visions—not to turn away from someone in need, and not to treat others unfairly—recur in human experience (see Gilligan, 1987; Gilligan & Wiggins, 1987). Thus, the distinction between the two moral voices of care and justice refers to two dimensions of or two ways of speaking about *all* human relationships, and points to a conception of moral development that considers both changes in the understanding of what constitutes love or care, and changes in the understanding of what justice or fairness means.

Empirical evidence from a number of studies suggests that the voices of care and justice articulate the ways in which individuals both conceive of problems in human relationships and move toward resolutions of interpersonal and intrapsychic conflicts (see Brown, 1989; Gilligan, 1982; Gilligan & Attanucci, 1988; Gilligan, Ward, & Taylor, 1989; Lyons, 1983; Rogers, 1987). Such evidence suggests that while the two voices tend to be *gender-related*—males speak in a justice voice more frequently than females, while females speak in a care voice more frequently than males—they are not *gender-specific*. In addition, individuals do not appear to be limited to a single, monotonic voice when articulating their conflicts and attempts at resolution—that is, both males and females raise and consider issues of both care and justice. Such evidence thus flies in the face of a long-standing tradition in psychology that has tacitly assumed—even against overwhelming evidence to the contrary—that individual "selves" are unitary and monotonic either throughout life or during any particular period of life. We would argue, however, that such a conception of an "individual" is grossly oversimplified. Human beings not only speak in different voices, but they can and frequently do oscillate from one voice to another in their transactions with others (see, for example, Johnston, 1989). Indeed, as Mikhail Bakhtin has argued, human beings are both polyphonic in switching from one voice to another over time and polyphonic in their utterances at any one time (Bakhtin, 1981, 1986; Clark & Holquist, 1984; Emerson & Morson, 1986; also Gilligan, Brown, & Rogers, 1990). Insofar as any notion of human development is dependent on a specific conception of the person, a reconception of human beings as fundamentally polyphonic must therefore lead to a significant change in thinking about what constitutes human social and personality development.

THE READING GUIDE

Construction of the Reading Guide proceeded from evidence that persons know (can recognize, speak in, and respond to) at least two different voices or perspectives in discussing moral conflicts and may indicate a preference for one over the other (see Johnson, 1989). Evidence of the ability of individuals to change voice or switch perspectives suggests that the "narrative self" is, in some sense, both polyphonic and involved in choices about how to speak. In reading texts, therefore, we view persons as "moral agents" with respect to the concerns about relationship they voice and those they keep silent.[1]

The Reading Guide thus highlights both care and justice as moral or relational voices, as well as the sense of tension people often convey in their stories of lived moral experience. In other words, it is a voice-sensitive method that attempts to record the complexity of narratives of conflict and choice, and attempts to capture, in its irreducible polyphony, the personal, relational, and cultural dimensions of psychic life—including language and voice, perspectives and visions, and the relationship between the reader's and the narrator's way of seeing and speaking.

The Reading Guide explicitly acknowledges, therefore, the interpretive nature of the reading process. It is designed to teach a person to read for care and justice in narratives of conflict and choice, highlighting in this process the way in which self is represented in the two voices. That is, it attunes the reader's ear to a

---

[1]We emphasize again, however, that while the moral voices of justice and care are different, they are neither dichotomous nor mutually exclusive (see Rogers, 1987). Rather, they convey different visions of relationship and suggest strengths and vulnerabilities of people in relationships—people's wishes for equality and attachment; their liability to oppression and to abandonment, to violation and to indifference or neglect.

person speaking in an interview text about themselves and talking about a personal moral conflict in terms of concerns about care and/or justice. Thus, this method outlines a particular way of interpreting texts. It does not preclude other readings, but rather clarifies one theoretical frame and highlights what it provides the researcher interested in self, relationships, and morality.

By attending to the reader and the reading process the Reading Guide thus contrasts with coding manuals that are designed to teach coders to match key code words or phrases or target sentences to a predetermined set of categories (see, for example, Colby & Kohlberg, 1987; Gibbs & Widaman, 1982; Loevinger & Wessler, 1970). This shift from a coding method to an explicitly interpretive method—from codifying statements to reading texts—entails several other important distinctions. Methods that rely either on counting considerations (see Lyons, 1982, 1983) or loosely matching justifications or reasons (see Colby & Kohlberg, 1987) may lose much of what seems relevant to understanding the choices people make. The sense of story or narrative account, and therefore the experience of a person telling a story of sometimes unresolvable and therefore tragic conflict, cannot be captured by coding systems that excise certain passages or ideas from the overall narrative. That is, coding systems offer no provision for including the speaker's own reflection on the meaning of the conflict for him or her. The physical reality of an individual speaker who, because of certain circumstances or life experiences, takes certain thoughts or feelings to be of major or minor importance is lost in such systems. Also lost is the engagement and response of the interpreter in his or her life context to such stories. Thus, one of our aims in creating the Reading Guide was to provide a way to acknowledge and explore the relationship between reader and text, and thus to move away from claims to an "objectified" and therefore decontextualized psychology.

In summary, the Reading Guide takes as its starting point the premise that a person, appearing in an interview text as a speaking voice telling a narrative or story, experiences relationships both in terms of attachment and in terms of equality. The care and justice voices are therefore relational voices—that is, they are characterized by the telling of different narratives about relationship. A care voice describes relationships in terms of attachment/detachment, connection or disconnection. *Care narratives,* consequently, focus on the vulnerability of people to isolation and abandonment, and are concerned with the complexities of creating and sustaining human connection. A justice voice describes relationship in terms of inequality/equality, reciprocity, or lack of respect. *Justice narratives* thus focus on the vulnerability of people to oppression, and are centrally concerned with standards or principles of fairness.

Interpretive Procedures

The Reading Guide seeks to provide an approach to interpreting narratives of moral conflict and choice for the relational voices of care and justice; thus it allows a reader to track these two voices and to specify the ways in which a

Table 2.1

Real-Life Conflict and Choice Interview

All people have had the experience of being in a situation where they had to make a decision, but weren't sure what they should do. Would you describe a situation when you faced a moral conflict and you had to make a decision, but weren't sure what you should do?

What was the situation? (Be sure to get a full elaboration of the story).
What was the conflict for you in that situation?
    Why was it a conflict?
In thinking about what to do, what did you consider? Why?
    Anything else you considered?
What did you decide to do?
What happened?
Do you think it was the right thing to do? Why/Why not?
What was at stake for you in this dilemma?
    What was at stake for others?
    In general, what was at stake?
How did you feel about it?
    How did you feel about it for the other(s) involved?
Is there another way to see the problem (other than the way you described it?)
When you think back over the conflict you described, do you think you learned anything from it?
Do you consider the situation you described a moral problem? Why/Why not?
What does morality mean to you? What makes something a moral problem for you?

person orchestrates or chooses between them. The reader first locates a narrative or relational conflict in a larger interview text and then reads this story a total of *four* different times. Each reading considers the narrative from a different standpoint; that is, in each the reader attends to a different aspect of the narrative deemed to be relevant in locating self and relational voices.

We have assumed in developing the Reading Guide that narratives of moral conflict can be read and understood by a careful reader. We have partially assured the coherence of such stories, however, by using a sequence of questions about moral conflict and choice (see Table 2.1) and by training interviewers to ask the narrator additional clarifying or activating questions about his or her construction of the dilemma, resolution of the problem, and evaluation of his or her action. It is important to note, though, that while we have used questions about moral conflict and choice to elicit stories of relational conflict in the majority of our studies, the Reading Guide is designed to enable interpretation of any such stories. That is, it can be used to interpret responses to other interview questions. Since concerns for care and justice emerge from experiences in relationship, any story of conflict in relationship can be read for these two voices.[2]

The first of the four readings is designed simply to establish the story told by

<hr>

[2]The Reading Guide attempts to model a flexible, "open" method of analyzing texts. While justice and care are the two relational voices the Reading Guide currently highlights, it is designed to be modified to reflect the needs of different research questions and interpretive strategies. Thus, readers may use the guide to read for other relational voices. (See, e.g., Zimlicki & Gilligan, 1989).

the narrator. The reader's goal is to understand the story, the context, the drama (the who, what, when, where, and why of the story). The reader, like a literary critic or a psychoanalyst, is also asked to look for recurrent words or images, central metaphors, emotional resonances, contradictions or inconsistencies in style, revisions, absences in the text, as well as shifts in narrative position— the use of first, second, or third person voice. Such close attention to the text helps the reader locate the person telling the story in the narrative told, sets the scene, and establishes the flow of events. In addition, this first reading asks the reader to locate him or herself as a person in the privileged position of interpreting the life events of another and to consider the implications of this act. The reader is asked to reflect on his or her own feelings and thoughts about the story and to consider the issues of commonality and difference with the story's narrator.

The next three readings focus specifically on the ways in which self and the voices of care and justice are represented in the interview-narrative. In the second reading the reader attends to "self": the "I" represented in the story or, in other words, the "I" who appears as an actor in the narrator's story of moral conflict. In the third reading the reader attends to a care voice—the speaker's expressed concerns about attachment, attention, and responsiveness to people. In the fourth reading the reader attends to a justice voice—the speaker's expressed concerns about fair treatment and equal respect.

One can think of the activity of each reading as looking through a different interpretive lens; each lens brings into focus different aspects of the narrative. To switch metaphors, each reading amplifies a different voice. Reading first with one interpretive lens and then another, listening first for one voice and then another, the reader can appreciate the way in which a narrator can see a situation differently, from different perspectives, and can tell a story told from more than one angle, or in different terms. A given statement may therefore have different meanings depending on the lens through which it is seen, and meaning may become apparent with one lens that is hidden from view by another.[3] In this way the Reading Guide highlights a polyphonic view of interview texts:

> Polyphony goes beyond the mere juxtaposition or sequential sounding of contrary voices and ideas. The musical metaphor implies that many voices are heard at the same time, uttering the same word differently. Thus, the same word simultaneously exhibits different values, "pitches," and "rhythms." By repeating this process in the course of a work, the orchestrator—the novelist [or the narrator]—can make the unrepeatable particularity of each utterance resonate. Voices join other voices

---

[3]The reader uses colored pencils to mark passages on the interview text to indicate each reading—colors that represent self (green), care (red), and justice (blue). This visual technique attunes the reader at once to the specific languages or voices of the narrator without losing sight of the larger story or the way these voices are orchestrated to convey the conflict.

to produce the timbre and intonation of a given communication. (Emerson & Morson, 1986, p. 49)

After each of the four readings, the reader is asked to fill in summary Worksheets. The Worksheets provide a place for the reader to document relevant pieces of the text and to make observations and interpretive remarks. The Worksheets are designed to highlight the critical move from the narrator's actual words to a reader's interpretation or summary of them, since they require the reader to substantiate his or her interpretation with quotes from the interview text itself. As such, the Worksheets stand between the Reading Guide (and the reader) and the interview text; they provide a trail of evidence for the reader's interpretations of the narrative.

The final step in the reading process can take several forms. The reader can use the summary Worksheets that focus the reading and capture the details of self, care, and justice to create a descriptive paragraph as a way to summarize the main themes in the narrative or to provide a brief interpretation of the narrator's representation of lived moral or relational experience. The content of such a paragraph will vary depending on the reader's research questions. Such descriptive paragraphs allow the researcher to attend to individual and contextual differences. These paragraphs can be designed to reflect any number of interpretive strategies and foci—such as the ways in which people understand and use these relational voices, the author's narrative style, or the relationship between the interviewer and the interviewee.

The notion of an "interpretive community" (see Fish, 1980, 1989) is especially helpful for the reader considering this form of analysis. That is, a research team must agree on the pertinent research questions within the context of the study (that is, they must first establish themselves as an interpretive community) in order to create descriptive paragraphs that are "reliable"—another word for "meaningful" within their community. Here again we underscore the necessity for openness and flexibility when using the Reading Guide as an interpretive method. Worksheets reflect the interpreter's research questions and the conventions of the interpretive community within which she or he belongs and therefore may vary from project to project.

The reader can also rely on a set of categorical answers to a series of standard summary questions that can then be tabulated to enable a straightforward comparison among narratives collected from a large number of subjects (see Brown, Tappan, Gilligan, Miller, & Argyris, 1989). Categorizing responses to the summary questions is useful when the researcher's questions focus on the simple presence and predominance of justice and care as relational voices or the narrator's choices, in a general sense, about which voice or voices in which to speak (see Gilligan, Ward, and Taylor, 1989). Again, the approach a researcher chooses will depend on his or her research agenda.

A GUIDED READING: THE CASE OF TANYA[4]

To illustrate the Reading Guide, we turn to Tanya, a 12-year-old in one of our studies, a member of the 7th grade. Using this method, what can we learn about Tanya by asking her to tell us about a time when she experienced moral conflict; that is, when she had to make a decision and she was not sure what she should do?[5] One of the things we have learned from our studies is that children, as well as adolescents and adults, will respond to this question, and tell stories in which they appear as the protagonist in a moral drama. We begin with the first reading—asked to speak about an experience of moral conflict, what story does Tanya tell?

The First Reading: Reading for the Story

The first time through the interview text, the reader attempts to understand the narrative; what is the story that is being told?

> When we were at camp [two years ago], I went to camp with my sister and my cousin, and he was really young . . . he was, like, maybe seven, and he got really, really homesick. It was overnight. And he was, like, always crying at night and stuff. And we had this camp guide who was really tough, and I was really afraid of him . . . And he said: "Nobody's allowed to use the phone." And so, my cousin really wanted to call his parents. And it was kind of up to me to go ask the guy if he could. So, either like I got bawled out by this guy and asked, or I didn't do anything about it. And he was my cousin, so I had to help him. So I went and asked the guy if he could use the phone, and he started giving me this lecture about how there shouldn't be homesickness in the camp. And I said, "Sorry, but he's only seven." And he was really young, so he finally got to use the phone. So he used the phone, and then we had a camp meeting, and, um, and the guy starting saying, "Any kid here who gets homesick shouldn't be here." And he didn't say my cousin's name, but like, he was like, almost in tears.[6]

---

[4]This reading of Tanya has been excerpted and adapted from Gilligan, Brown, and Rogers (1990).

[5]The full text of Tanya's interview, and a reader's "Worksheets" and case analysis for self and the relational voices of care and justice are presented in Appendices 1 & 2.

[6]These excerpts represent selections from Tanya's text a reader has deemed relevant, i.e., that best illustrate Tanya's story of conflict and choice. In the self, care, and justice readings, excerpts indicate parts of the text that have been underlined in green (self), red (care), and blue (justice), respectively. These excerpts are transferred from the text to the Worksheets under the appropriate reading, while the reader's interpretation of the excerpts are written alongside. That is, the left-hand column of the Worksheets includes only the narrator's words (although certainly the choice of what to include in this column is, itself, an interpretive step). In this way the reader leaves an interpretive "trail of evidence" that indicates the shift from the narrator's words to the reader's interpretation of those words.

Tanya's story is about her cousin's homesickness, the intransigence of a camp director, and her decision, despite her fear, to help her cousin call his parents. The conflict was, she says succinctly, "me saving myself or saving him." She decided to help her cousin because "nothing bad was going to happen to me"—the camp director might intimidate her and hurt her feelings but he "can't beat me up or anything." She realized that "it was worth, like, letting [her cousin] talk to his parents . . . he was screaming and having nightmares . . . he wasn't being able to have any fun and he paid for it . . . he was like almost sick, you know. That's why I guess they call it homesick." The camp director, she thinks, "was really callous." Looking back Tanya says that it's obvious that her decision was right—at least for her. "It might not be for you or somebody else, but it's helping out my cousin and that camp director, it was a rule, but people are more important than rules." Besides, she notes, the camp director was contradicting himself; they say "We're here to help our kids, to make them have fun." Her cousin, she observes "wasn't having fun, he was just contradicting the whole slogan." Tanya considers the story she has told to be about a moral problem because "I could have gotten out of it easily, and it wasn't my feeling, my cousin's. But he was like really close . . . I wasn't feeling what he was feeling, but I did have a little empathy, but not that much. So either I could have gotten out of it and said, 'I'm not going up to that camp director, you go up yourself,' to my cousin. But he was like very miserable, and I almost felt like he did in a way. So, I did go up, because I felt miserable having him feel miserable."

In addition to understanding the plot or the sequence of events as the narrator tells it, the reader also asks what are the conflicts described and, more generally, what is the landscape of this psychological and social world, as indicated by the relationships mentioned, the use of moral language, repeated words and themes, seeming contradictions, key images and metaphors?

Listening to this narrative of moral conflict, the reader notes that Tanya states the problem on several levels—as a conflict between saving herself and saving her cousin, as a conflict between people and rules, as a conflict between doing nothing and doing something in a situation where she sees the possibility of doing something to help. The relationships involved are Tanya's relationships with her cousin, with herself, with the camp director, and with her friends, as well as the cousin's relationship with his parents. A possible contradiction in the story is between Tanya's sense that the right thing was obvious and she did the right thing, and her sense of moral conflict.

Finally, the reader responds to the story, recording places of connection and disconnection between the narrator's experience as related in the story and the reader's own experiences. The reader asks herself what she knows about the narrator and what this might mean for her interpretation of the story. Through this reflection, we draw attention to the powerful act of one person, the reader, interpreting—"naming"—the experience of another who only speaks within a narrative about a conflict she or he lived with. In Tanya's case, the reader recalls her own experiences of summer camp, of "how powerful the counselors were" and "the rules which seemed arbitrary and unfair." She also wonders "if the fact that [Tanya] is Indian has anything to do with her choice" or "if Tanya's privilege give[s] her confidence in the system." Thus, the reader attends to what she knows about the narrator to raise questions about her interpretation of the story.

The Second Reading: Reading for Self

In the second reading for "self," the reader tunes her ears to Tanya's voice telling her story in the context of the interview and how she wishes to represent herself in the story she tells. Here is Tanya, speaking about herself:

> I went to camp . . . I was really afraid . . . it was kind of up to me . . . either I got bawled out and asked or I didn't do anything about it . . . I had to tell him . . . So I went and asked . . . I considered what was right and wrong . . . I said this guy can intimidate me but he can't beat me up . . . I realized . . . I have to do this . . . I mean . . . I'm sure, I was sure . . . he was my cousin and we've always been kind of close . . . I either helped him out or, like, I helped myself, or I did what was for him, or I couldn't go for myself because I didn't want to be like . . . I was really afraid . . . it was me saving myself or saving him . . . I mean . . . nothing really bad was going to happen to me . . . So I realized . . . so I guess he did kind of realize . . . I mean . . . so I don't . . . I guess it was kind of like a victory . . . I'm sure . . . I don't know what it was . . . It is obvious that it is right for me . . . I felt it . . . I could have gotten out of it easily . . . it wasn't my feeling . . . I wasn't feeling what he was feeling . . . I did have a little empathy, but not so much . . . I could have gotten out of it . . . I could have said I'm not going up to that camp director . . . I almost felt like he did in a way . . . I did go up because I felt miserable having him feel miserable.

In this second reading, Tanya's voice carried the sound of a candid, confident, psychologically astute and shrewd 12-year-old, concerned about her cousin and also about herself, indignant at the camp director's lack of concern, sure of her perceptions and judgments, stubborn, determined, and capable of making intriguing observations: "Either you feel it all the way or you just recognize it" (referring to the difference between her response to her cousin's homesickness and that of her friends). She is also capable of making what would seem, given most descriptions of child development, an astonishing distinction for a 12-year-old: between empathy—feeling another person's feelings—and responding to another person's feeling with feelings of one's own.

In the third and fourth readings, the connection between reader and speaker is forged on the common ground of moral concern about justice and care.

The Third Reading: Reading for Care

Here is Tanya speaking about care:

> He was really young, he was like maybe seven, and he got really, really homesick. It was overnight. And he was always crying at night and stuff. And so my cousin really wanted to call his parents. And he was my cousin, so I had to help him . . . And I said 'Sorry, he's only seven' . . . he was, like, almost in tears . . . the right thing was to go because it was my cousin's good, you know, and he wasn't going to die or anything but, you know, he's afraid to go to camp now, because he's like nine now and he doesn't want to go back . . . This guy can intimidate me, but he can't beat me up or anything . . . I'll realize that that's just the way he is, but I have to do this . . . to help (my cousin) out . . . the conflict was that he was my cousin and we've always been kind of close . . . it was me saving myself or saving him . . . Nothing bad was going to happen to me . . . he felt a lot better . . . my cousin was screaming, has nightmares and it was really bad . . . my cousin lives seven minutes away from us, so I lived with my cousin, but I would never see that [camp director] again . . . [What was at stake was] kind of like the ego, you know, and nothing physically and nothing that anybody else would see. It's just like my feelings being hurt and I hate being yelled at . . . but my cousin, he was like feeling really, really low . . . really bad . . . it's like either you feel it, like all the way, or you just like, recognize it, you know . . . it's helping out my cousin and that camp director, you know, it was a rule, but people are more important than rules . . . He was just a little kid . . . my cousin wasn't having fun . . . He was really close, but I wasn't feeling what he was feeling, but I did have a little empathy . . . he was very miserable and I almost felt like he did in a way, so I did, I did go up because I felt miserable having him feel miserable.

Listening for care draws attention to a contradiction in Tanya's thinking: It was a moral problem, she says, because it wasn't her feelings, it was her cousin's feelings that she was risking her own feelings for in going up to the camp director. And yet, she says, she was miserable because he was miserable. Moral language does not capture Tanya's description of relationship insofar as it implies acting either for another or for oneself. In Tanya's relational orientation, her attentiveness to the feelings of her cousin and her wish to respond to his need are tied in with her own feelings because her cousin's unhappiness affects her. But his feelings are not the same as her feelings, as she states clearly; he is not she. Tanya's care voice draws the reader's attention to her knowledge of human relationships and psychological processes, knowledge which suggests close and careful observations. We notice her fine distinctions first between feeling another person's problem "all the way" as opposed to "just recognizing it"—and, second between empathizing with another versus responding to their feelings with feelings of one's own.

And so, the care voice which runs through Tanya's description of moral conflict speaks of relationships in terms of attachment and detachment—her connection with her cousin, the camp director's "callousness" or apparent lack of concern.

But what about justice?

The Fourth Reading: Reading for Justice

The fourth reading, for justice, highlights Tanya's concerns about fairness and unequal power:

> It was unfair, she implies, that her cousin "wasn't having any fun and he paid for it"—meaning the camp, where the director had said "we're here to help our kids, to make them have fun." She also recognizes the disparity in power between the camp director and her cousin: "The way I saw it by that time was like this guy is a big bully and he can have anything the way he wants it. So I guess it was kind of big, giving in for him [to let my cousin use the phone.] He goes on his reputation, you know, that was a rule and he couldn't break it, but he said, 'yes' but he started giving me this lecture . . . But I did something for him, my cousin, and it's kind of like a victory, kind of like you won over this guy, so be happy.

Put in justice terms, it was unfair for someone not to be happy at camp and not to be able to do anything about it, especially since he had paid to have fun at camp. It also was oppressive for a camp director to place his concern with reputation over the misery of a seven year old and to take advantage of the fact that the seven year old was under his direction while he "could have anything the way he wants it." Tanya also presents a complicated understanding of rules as structures which maintain order in relationships. She sees the camp director's sense of his reputation as "a rule and he couldn't break it," thus, again, making a psychologically astute comment about an internalization of rules and standards. She also alludes to her faith in the protective power of a justice system when she says that the camp director could intimidate her and hurt her feelings but he "can't beat me up or anything."

Summary: Interpretation

Finally, the reader is asked to make a summary interpretation about self and the two relational voices of care and justice: What voices are present in the narrative? What voice, if any, predominates in the overall story of conflict? How are care and justice orchestrated together in the narrative? How does the narrative self speak and make choices within these perspectives? Is one voice given priority? Throughout the story or in certain circumstances?

Twelve-year-old Tanya is cognizant of the claims of both care and justice, the vulnerability of people both to abandonment and to oppression, and the intensity of feelings that lie behind the wish for justice (or at least for fairness) and for love (or at least for care). Taking action that turns out to be effective in securing a response to her cousin's distress, she tells a story which, when told in justice terms, renders her the victor over the callous camp director. But she also knows that the camp director "had another point of view," that he "probably [thought] kids always get homesick and what difference does it make, he's not going to die." In the end Tanya relies on a system of justice that will hold the camp director accountable and thus she feels will prevent him from beating her up—which would leave evidence, something that someone else could see. To protect herself and her cousin from psychological violence—where what was at stake was "the ego, you know and nothing physically and nothing that anybody else would see, like my feelings being hurt," Tanya draws on an ethic of care to support her capacity to respond, and guided by this ethic she finds an inclusive solution to the dilemma—people are more important than rules, she says, and in the end, her cousin felt better, she no longer felt miserable, and the camp director, albeit at her cousin's expense, salvaged his reputation by giving a lecture.

Reading first with one interpretive lens and then another, listening first for one voice and then another, we hear and convey the way in which a situation can be seen differently from different perspectives and a story told from more than one angle, or in different terms by Tanya and also by ourselves. In the Reading Guide, our procedures for attending to moral or relational voices reflect our recognition that the same words in an interview text can be used as evidence for justice and as evidence for care, depending on the lens through which one is reading. A case in point is Tanya's statements, "He was my cousin, so I had to help him" or "Sorry, he's only seven." Reading for care, one could understand these statements to reflect her attentiveness and her response to her cousin's distress. One also could cite them as evidence of the necessity for response which she feels and of her belief in her ability to do something to help her cousin. Tanya's care narrative is premised on her ability to talk to the director and her belief that he will listen to her—a belief in her efficacy as a person who is able and willing to care for another, which may be why she remembers and tells this story.

Yet reading for justice, a reader may see in these same statements evidence for Tanya's felt sense of obligation or duty contingent upon occupying the role of cousin (a good cousin takes care of her cousin) or upon being an older child. The fact that Tanya is Indian suggests the possibility that she may be bound by a cultural norm of family responsibility and obligation.

Thus Tanya's interview text reveals how care and justice themes may be interwoven throughout the narrative or how both care and justice may resonate in a single statement. It also reveals how value judgments can be made, both by Tanya and by the reader, about different renditions of justice and care. So that, for example, one can see "bad justice" in the rigid or blind adherence to moral principles or rules and "good justice" in the attentiveness to differential power and the potential for oppression which it creates. Similarly one can see "bad care" in the strategies of exclusion which often are valorized in the name of care—the sacrifice of self or of other—just as one can see "good care" in the search for inclusive solutions that are responsive to everyone involved.

REFLECTIONS ON TANYA: THE READING GUIDE AS A RELATIONAL METHOD

Central to the Reading Guide is the issue of perspective and the relationship between the reader and text; hence we have come to see the Reading Guide fundamentally as a "relational method." Its relational character is illustrated in the case of Tanya by distinguishing the first two readings—reading for the story, and reading for self—from the second two readings—reading for care and justice.

In the first reading the reader is asked explicitly to attend to the text of lived experience in light of her own knowledge and experience—that is, to be an active listener, to acknowledge the interaction or relationship between her own subjectivity as a woman reader and the text before her. As a function of this relationship, the reader considers seriously what similarities with the narrator might create openings and channels for connection and what differences might inhibit understanding or a free-flowing communication. In the case of Tanya, who is Indian, upper-middle class, attending a private all-girls' day-school in the Midwest, and on the brink of adolescence, one must ask, according to this method, from what perspective is her narrative interpreted?

Indeed, the reader, in response to Tanya's story, acknowledges her own memories of being Tanya's age and being at camp, at the mercy of powerful counselors. This shared experience of fear of an authority's power to harm provides a channel of connection that allows for understanding. Yet, she wonders how Tanya's ethnic background may have affected her actions, noting, in particular, that Tanya's felt responsibility for her cousin may be grounded in cultural conventions she is not privy to. She notes both that there are differences between herself as a reader and this 12-year-old narrator—differences in age and ethnic background—but that there are additional channels of connection in the common ground of socioeconomic status, educational privilege, and gender.

In the second reading for self, the reader attempts to attune her ear to the voice of the person speaking; that is, to open her eyes and ears to the words of another, taking in her story. Specifically, this exercise of directing the reader's attention to the way Tanya speaks about herself is designed to highlight or amplify the terms in which she, as the narrator of a particular story, sees and presents herself. In this way, the reader comes into relationship with Tanya, by paying attention to her way of seeing and speaking. Put simply, the reader listens to Tanya's voice and attends to her vision, and thus makes some space between Tanya's way of speaking and seeing and her own.

In the process of reading for self, then, the reader becomes engaged with or involved with Tanya as the teller of her own story, and as the reader attends to the way in which Tanya speaks about herself, she is likely to experience herself coming into a relationship, so that she begins to know Tanya on her own terms and to respond to what she is saying emotionally as well as intellectually. As Tanya's words about herself enter the reader's psyche, a process of connection begins between Tanya's feelings and thoughts and the feelings and thoughts of the reader in response to hers, so that Tanya affects the reader, who begins to learn from her—about Tanya, about herself, and about the world they share in common, here specifically the world of relationships and its geography of moral concern.

Once the reader allows the voice of another to enter her psyche, she can no longer claim a detached, "objective" position. She is affected by Tanya whose words may lead her to think about a variety of things and to feel sad, or happy, or jealous, or angry, or bored, or frustrated, or comforted or hopeful. But by allowing Tanya's words to enter her psyche, the reader gains the sense of an entry, an opening, a way into Tanya's story in Tanya's terms. Thus relationship or connection, rather than blurring perspective or diminishing judgment, signifies an opening of self to other creating a channel for information, an avenue to knowledge.

We would liken these first two readings, then, to what literary critics call "subjectivist criticism" (see Suleiman, 1980). That is, as readings, they are designed to highlight the actual reading experience of an individual person to a specific text, to represent the relationship between a reader's life history and context and that of the narrator's as represented in the interview text. In this way, like Slatoff's (1970) teacher-critic, the reader:

> would be sharply aware of what took place during [her] act of reading and might well describe changes in [her] experience in successive readings or differences in [her] experiences while reading and reflecting upon the work. . . . Such a critic would try to be aware of [her] biases and open about them, and [she] might well wonder aloud at times about the effect [of a particular reading] on [her] literary experience. . . . The main thing is that [she] would sound like *somebody*, and if not a particular somebody, at least a recognizably human creature. (p. 171)

After reading for the story and for self, the reader shifts focus to read for the relational voices of care and justice. That is, the reader moves from a "reader-response" approach that highlights the relationship between a particular reader and a particular text (see Suleiman & Crossman, 1980; Tompkins, 1980), to a focus on reading as itself a relational activity among a group or community of readers; that is, to reading as a communal, context-specific act. Unlike self, care and justice are voices that have specific characteristics, properties, or recogniz-able features as defined by a community of readers within which these terms have meaning. Therefore, these latter two readings require the reader to construct an interpretation using what Jonathan Culler (1982) calls "reading conventions" or what Stanley Fish (1980) calls "reading strategies." In other words, in order for a reader to "recognize" or hear aspects of care and justice as relational voices, s/he must first be taught certain conventions or strategies; s/he must be admitted to the "interpretive community" (Fish, 1980, 1989) within which care and justice as relational voices are publicly understood and intelligible and rele-vant. One of the purposes of the Reading Guide (like any other method) is thus to admit others to such an interpretive community by making such conventions of interpretation clear. By creating a public method the boundaries of such a com-munity become negotiable—they may shift, they may widen—since with new members come different research questions, contexts, findings.

Thus, both the first two readings and the latter two readings in this method are based on the "reader's response" to the text, but they are distinguished by the nature of the response the reader is called upon to make. In the first readings, s/he is asked to consider biases, potential blind spots to understanding as well as places in which s/he identifies and connects with the narrator's story through shared experience. In the second readings, s/he is required to know and to use particular, agreed-upon conventions of reading; that is, to know what s/he is reading for and why it is relevant within the community of which s/he is a member.

Yet one might ask, then, why do the first two readings at all? It is our belief that the power of the Reading Guide as a method *depends* on the reader acknowl-edging this shift in relationship—from the experience of connection to the nar-rator (in the form of a text) to the experience of membership within an in-terpretive community. By first tuning the reader's ear to the voice of the speaking self—the "I" in the interview text—and then by amplifying moral voice and vision, the Reading Guide draws attention to a danger which inheres in psycho-logical research: namely, the danger of striving for safety, clarity, or justification at the expense of voice or vision, and thus of oversimplifying or reducing the experience of conflict in the search for agreement or justification. In other words, the reader who listens for the voice of the person speaking, who searches for the places of connection, and who struggles with the issue of difference as a prereq-uisite to learning something from the narrator, stands in a different relationship to the narrator and to the text than the reader who seeks only to confirm the existence of predefined categories, or who seeks only to affirm agreement in interpretation based on particular interpretive conventions. The power of this method resides in the fact that both of these readers are the same person—the person who finds him or herself involved with, and therefore accountable to, a complex life story; a story s/he has, at some level, participated in.

Moreover, it is the naming of this relational shift that leads us to claim the

Reading Guide as an explicitly *feminist* method. That is, a participating reader who acknowledges his/her social and cultural embeddedness does so within the male-based constraints of this culture at this time. Patrocinio Schweickart (1986b) claims, in fact, that reader-response methods have generally overlooked "the issues of race, class, and sex, and give no hint of the conflicts, sufferings, and passions that attend these realities." "To put the matter plainly," she says, "reader-response criticism needs feminist criticism:"

> The pervasiveness of androcentricity drives feminist theory beyond the individualistic models . . . of most reader-response critics. The feminist reader agrees with Stanley Fish (1980) that the production of the meaning of a text is mediated by the interpretive community in which the activity of reading is situated: the meaning of a text depends on the interpretive strategy one applies to it, and the choice of strategy is regulated (explicitly or implicitly) by the canons of acceptability that govern the interpretive community. However, unlike Fish, the feminist reader is also aware that the ruling interpretive communities are androcentric, and that this androcentricity is deeply etched in the strategies and modes of thought that have been introjected by all readers, women as well as men. (p. 50)

We argue, therefore, that the first two readings shift the focus of attention inherent in most "individualistic" reader-response methods from "the drive to get it right" or the need to determine who controls the meaning of the text—the narrator or the reader—to the experience of relationship between reader and text (see Schweickart, 1986a). Inherent in this method, then, is the recognition that in complex ways a reader at some level must deal both with the issue of difference and with the issue of identification with the narrator—and thus with issues of gender, race, and class. And, as we have said earlier, this participation in the life of another person represented by the text changes the reader's relationship to the care and justice readings that follow. Having been in this relationship, any attempt to belie that experience either by giving authority for the meaning of the text to the narrator alone, or by claiming it for oneself, requires giving up a certain degree of knowledge, a certain reality, and, we would add, a certain accountability, derived from this experience of relationship.

CONCLUSION

In this chapter we have described a method for reading interview-narratives of lived experience of moral conflict and choice. We have provided an elaborate example of the interpretation of a story of conflict told by a 12-year-old girl. In addition, we have used this example to explore how the Reading Guide is fundamentally a relational method and thus contributes to a view of psychological inquiry itself as an inherently relational enterprise, as opposed to an "objec-

tive'' or decontextualized activity. Seen in this light, a consideration of gender—
both the gender of the reader and of the narrator—is important to the interpretive
process, to the degree that gender, like race and class, is an example of a
difference that makes a difference in this culture at this time.

The view that psychology can be nothing more or less than a relational, and
thus an interpretive, enterprise necessarily heightens attention to context, to
cultural and relational histories. However, we do not think such a view means we
are without foundation, with no firm ground on which to stand to claim our
interpretations as "meaningful." It seems to us, following Fish (1989), that
relationships, rather than being purely subjective and therefore completely inde-
terminate, by virtue of shared history and cultural convention provide a place to
stand, but that this place is not the same for everyone at all times. In other words,
we cannot at any time stand outside our relational ties, but ought to be made
responsible, accountable to them—to what we can and cannot know. The interpretation of texts is such a relational activity to which we ought to be
accountable.

This brings us around again, full circle, to Frances Janet Ashton Hall. Why
didn't Frances see the gap before? What did she miss and why? Frances, named,
identified in her own right, saw for a brief moment in the face of the nameless
women—herself identified through the one important relationship in her life—
something of the meanings and passions of her life that she, Frances, could not
fully know or appreciate outside of this encounter. In this act of recognition, at
the level of human compassion, Frances, herself, has the power to name their
commonalities and respect their differences.

What we seek to do as readers, as researchers, as psychologists, is to come
into relationship with those we study and so to be aware of our power to define
the right, the good, the best, the ideal; to become accountable to the power of
naming, and thus, unlike Frances, not to violate, unwittingly, "the dividing
spaces," "the immeasurable gap of quality" that separates two lives.

ACKNOWLEDGMENTS

Preparation of this chapter was supported by grants from the Lilly Endowment,
the George Gund Foundation, and the Cleveland Foundation.

REFERENCES

Bakhtin, M. (1981). *The dialogic imagination.* Austin, TX: University of Texas Press.
Bakhtin, M. (1986). *Speech genres and other essays.* Austin, TX: University of Texas Press.
Brown, L. (1989). *Narratives of relationship: The development of a care voice in girls ages 7 to 16.*
    Unpublished doctoral dissertation, Harvard University.
Brown, L., Argyris, D., Attanucci, J., Bardige, B., Gilligan, C., Johnston, K., Miller, B., Osborne,

D., Tappan, M., Ward, J., Wiggins, G., & Wilcox, D. (1988). *A guide to reading narratives of moral conflict and choice for self and moral voice* (Monograph No. 1). Cambridge, Harvard Graduate School of Education, Center for the Study of Gender, Education, and Human Development.

Brown, L., Tappan, M., Gilligan, C., Miller, B., & Argyris, D. (1989). Reading for self and moral voice: A method for interpreting narratives of real-life moral conflict and choice. In M. Packer & R. Addison (Eds.), *Entering the circle: Hermeneutic investigation in psychology.* Albany: SUNY Press.

Clark, K., & Holquist, M. (1984). *Mikhail Bakhtin.* Cambridge, MA: Harvard University Press.

Colby, A., & Kohlberg, L. (1987). *The measurement of moral judgment.* New York: Cambridge University Press.

Culler, J. (1982). Reading as a woman. In J. Culler (Ed.), *On deconstruction: Theory and criticism after structuralism.* Ithaca, NY: Cornell University Press.

Drabble, M. (1975). The gifts of war. In S. Cahill (Ed.), *Women and fiction.* New York: New American Library.

Emerson, C., & Morson, G. (1986). Penultimate words. In C. Koelb & V. Lokke (Eds.), *The current in criticism.* West Lafayette, IN: Purdue University Press.

Fish, S. (1980). *Is there a text in this class?* Cambridge, MA: Harvard University Press.

Fish, S. (1989). *Doing what comes naturally.* Durham, NC: Duke University Press.

Gibbs, J., & Widaman, K. (1982). *Social intelligence: Measuring the development of sociomoral reflection.* Englewood Cliffs, NJ: Prentice-Hall.

Gilligan, C. (1982). *In a different voice.* Cambridge, MA: Harvard University Press.

Gilligan, C. (1986). Exit-voice dilemmas in adolescent development. In A. Foxley, M. McPherson, & G. O'Donnell (Eds.), *Development, democracy, and the art of trespassing: Essays in honor of Albert O. Hirschman.* Notre Dame, IN: University of Notre Dame Press.

Gilligan, C. (1987). Remapping the moral domain: New images of self in relationship. In T. Heller, M. Sosna, & D. Wellber (Eds.), *Reconstructing individualism: Autonomy, individuality, and the self in Western thought.* Stanford, CA: Stanford University Press.

Gilligan, C. (1989). Teaching Shakespeare's sister: Notes from the underground of female adolescence. In C. Gilligan, N. Lyons, & T. Hanmer (Eds.), *Making connections: The relational worlds of adolescent girls at Emma Willard School.* Troy, NY: Emma Willard School.

Gilligan, C., & Attanucci, J. (1988). Two moral orientations: Gender differences and similarities. *Merrill-Palmer Quarterly. 34*(3), 223–237.

Gilligan, C., Brown, L., & Rogers, A. (1990). Psyche embedded: A place for body, relationships, and culture in personality theory. In A. Rabin (Ed.), *Studying persons and lives.* New York: Springer.

Gilligan, C., Ward, J., & Taylor, J. (Eds.). (1989). *Mapping the moral domain.* Cambridge, MA: Harvard University Press.

Gilligan, C., & Wiggins, G. (1987). The origins of morality in early childhood relationships. In J. Kagan & S. Lamb (Eds.), *The emergence of morality in early childhood.* Chicago: University of Chicago Press.

Johnston, D. (1989). Adolescents' solutions to dilemmas in fables: Two moral orientations—two problem solving strategies. In C. Gilligan, J. Ward, & J. Taylor (Eds.), *Mapping the moral domain.* Cambridge, MA: Harvard University Press.

Loevinger, J., & Wessler, R. (1970). *Measuring ego development I. Construction and use of a sentence completion test.* San Francisco: Jossey-Bass.

Lyons, N. (1982). *Conceptions of self and morality and modes of moral choice: Identifying justice and care in judgments of actual moral dilemmas.* Unpublished doctoral dissertation, Harvard University.

Lyons, N. (1983). Two perspectives: On self, relationship, and morality. *Harvard Educational Review. 49*, 125–145.

Rogers, A. (1987). *Gender differences in moral thinking: A validity study of two moral orientations*. Unpublished doctoral dissertation, Washington University.

Schweickart, P. (1986a). Engendering critical discourse. In C. Koelb & V. Lokke (Eds.), *The current in criticism*. West Lafayette, IN: Purdue University Press.

Schweickart, P. (1986b). Reading ourselves: Toward a feminist theory of reading. In E. Flynn & P. Schweickart (Eds.), *Gender and reading: Essays on readers, texts, and contexts*. Baltimore, MD: The Johns Hopkins University Press.

Slatoff, W. (1970). *With respect to readers: Dimensions of literary response*. Ithaca, NY: Cornell University Press.

Suleiman, S. (1980). Introduction: Varieties of audience-oriented criticism. In S. Suleiman & I. Crossman (Eds.), *The reader in the text*. New Jersey: Princeton University Press.

Suleiman, S., & Crossman, I. (Eds.). (1980). *The reader in the text*. New Jersey: Princeton University Press.

Tompkins, J. (1980). *Reader-response criticism*. Baltimore, MD: The Johns Hopkins University Press.

Zimlicki, B., & Gilligan, C. (1989). *Two languages of love*. Unpublished manuscript, Harvard University.

APPENDIX 1

Tanya's Interview Text*

I: Can you tell me a situation where you faced a moral conflict, you had to make a decision, but you weren't sure what was the right thing to do?

R: I guess that's kind of one, the one I just told you.

I: With your friend?

R: Who's getting out of line, yah. But also when we were at camp, I WENT TO CAMP with my sister and my cousin, and he was really young, he was like maybe seven, and he got really, really homesick. It was overnight. And he was like, always crying at night and stuff. And we had this camp guide who was really tough and I WAS REALLY AFRAID of him, it was like two years ago and I WAS REALLY AFRAID OF HIM. **And he said, "nobody is allowed to use the phone,"** and so my cousin really wanted to call his parents, (Yah) and it was kind of up to me to go ask the guy if he could. So, EITHER LIKE I GOT BAWLED OUT BY THIS GUY AND ASKED, OR I DIDN'T DO ANYTHING ABOUT IT, **and he was my cousin, so I HAD TO HELP HIM,** SO I WENT AND ASKED the guy if he could use the phone and **he started giving me this lecture about how other shouldn't be homesickness in the camp. AND I SAID, "SORRY, BUT HE'S ONLY SEVEN."** (Yah!) And he was really young and so he finally got to use the phone, so he used the phone. And then we had a camp meeting, and um, and the guy started saying **"any kid here who gets homesick shouldn't be here,"** and he didn't say my cousin's name, but like, he was like, almost in tears.

I: Oh, and your cousin was there when he said that? Oh, that wasn't very nice.

R: Yah. It was really mean.

I: When you were in this situation, you knew the camp counselor had this policy that you couldn't call, but you also knew that you wanted to help your cousin out. What kinds of things did you consider in thinking about what to do?

R: Well, mostly that, first of all, what was right and wrong. (Um, hum) **And the right thing was to go because it was my cousin's good, you know.** (Um, hum) And he wasn't going to die or anything, but, you know, he's afraid to go to camp now, because he's like nine now (Yah) and he doesn't want to go back, (Hmm) and SO I, **LIKE I SAID, "THIS GUY CAN INTIMIDATE ME, BUT HE CAN'T BEAT ME UP OR ANYTHING."** (Yah) I'LL REALIZE THAT THAT'S JUST THE WAY HE IS, **BUT I HAVE TO DO THIS,** so. I mean, he might be . . . he might say no, but it can't hurt asking.

I: Ah, ha. So, can you think of what was the conflict for you when you were trying to decide between, um, between the two options?

47

R: Just to either KEEP ON MY COUSIN for the week, you know, JUST HELP HIM, OUT, (Um, hum) or have him, like the thing he wanted to do was go home, (Yah) but I'M SURE, I WAS SURE he wouldn't be able to do that, so if he just talked to his mom, he did feel better, (Okay) but the conflict was that HE WAS MY COUSIN AND WE'VE ALWAYS BEEN KIND OF CLOSE, AND I EITHER HELPED HIM OUT OR, LIKE I HELPED MYSELF OR I DID WHAT WAS FOR HIM, OR I COULDN'T GO FOR MYSELF, BECAUSE I DIDN'T WANT TO BE LIKE, I WAS REALLY AFRAID of that guy, and IT WAS ME SAVING MYSELF OF SAVING HIM. So I MEAN, **NOTHING BAD WAS GOING TO HAPPEN TO ME. SO I REALIZED** that it was **worth letting him talk to his parents.**

I: Do you think this was the right thing to do?

R: Yah.

I: Why?

R: Why? Because he felt a lot better and even though the guy was, was like giving us a lecture and getting really mean, he was, he was like, he let us use the phone, so I GUESS HE DID KIND OF REALIZE cause, my cousin was screaming, has nightmares, and it was really bad, he was with his friends, so he let him use the phone, but still, I MEAN I would never see the guy again, you know, if I didn't go back to the camp, but I LIVED, like my cousin lives seven minutes away from us, SO I LIVED WITH MY COUSIN BUT I WOULD NEVER SEE THAT GUY AGAIN.

I: I see, okay. So that factored into it, that you were going to see your cousin over and over and over.

R: Yah, so . . .

I: Okay. What was at stake for you in the dilemma?

R: Kind of like the ego, you know, and nothing physically and nothing that anybody else would see, IT'S JUST LIKE MY FEELINGS BEING HURT AND I HATE BEING YELLED AT, SO . . .

I: Ah, okay. All right, um, and then what was at stake for the other people involved?

R: The camp director, nothing, but my cousin, just kind a like, to be able to feel better, you know, (Um, hum) he was like feeling really, really low. **He wasn't being able to have any fun and he paid for it, so he had to do something** and he was just like really bad. He was like almost sick, you know. That's why I guess they call it homesick, but.

I: Right. Well now, why do you think there was nothing at stake for the camp director?

R: Because, I'm sure there was, BUT THE WAY I SAW IT by that time was like **this guy is a big bully and he can have anything the way he wants it.** SO I DON'T, I GUESS **it was kind of big giving in for him,** you know. (Ah, huh) And I GUESS that kind of showed he was thinking, I KNOW he was now, SO I WAS REALLY SURPRISED, letting him use the phone, but he goes, **see his like reputation, you know, that was a rule and he couldn't break it,** but he said yes, <u>but</u> he started giving us this lecture.

I: All right, okay. So how did you feel about it?

R: How did I feel? (Um, hum) I FELT GOOD, BUT I FELT REALLY BAD when the camp director went out and said that in the meeting, (Yah) I WAS JUST LIKE, but **I DID SOMETHING for him, my cousin,** and IT'S KIND OF LIKE A VICTORY, YOU KNOW, IT'S LIKE YOU WON OVER THIS GUY SO BE HAPPY.

I: Oh, okay. Even if he did act like a creep the next day or whatever?

R: Yah.

I: Do you think there is another way to see the problem, from anybody else's perspective?

R: Yah, I'M SURE, I DON'T NOW WHAT IT WAS, but the camp director had another point of view. **He was probably, like, "kids always get homesick and what difference does it make, he's not going to die,"** you know, <u>but he</u> <u>wasn't that kid,</u> (Yah) and so he had a totally different point of view from my cousin and I. (Um, hm) And then like my friends probably, they knew about it, and they were like, "I understand but it's not, why does he cry all the time," you know. (Yah) <u>It's like, either you feel it, like all the way or you just, like,</u> <u>recognize it, you know?</u>

I: Sure, sure. It sounds like the camp director wasn't doing either of those two.

R: I know, he was really callous.

I: Yah. Okay, so when you think back over the conflict that you just described, do you think you learned anything from it?

R: It's obvious that I was right.

I: It's obvious that you were right?

R: Yah. The decision was right, you know.

I: Now, why is it obvious?

R: <u>It's obvious because,</u> no it isn't, BUT IT IS FOR ME. It might not be for you or somebody else, but <u>it's helping out my cousin and that camp director,</u> you know, **it was a rule,** but <u>people are more important than rules,</u> you know. So he was just a little kid, you know, and they were trying out things, and the camp director, **they were saying, "we're here to help our kids, to make them have fun," but my cousin wasn't having fun, he was just contradicting the whole slogan,** (Yah) you know, (Right . . .) so it wasn't for that, and it was just like, I guess if you did ask somebody they would say, "that is right," but then you say the answer, and "I don't know . . . the reason, you know."

I: But you felt it was right?

R: Yah, I FELT IT WAS RIGHT.

I: Do you consider this situation you described a moral problem?

R: What's that?

I: I don't want to define it, because then you have my definition. But, um, oh, okay, let me try this one: what does morality mean to you? When you hear that word, what does that mean?

R: Morality? Probably it has to do with the person . . . Oh! We did this in English the other day.

I: (laughs) So I hear.

R: Morality, it's like the difference between right and wrong, you know, and it's when the person like chooses the right thing, it's like, in the long run, or, um, even in that little experience or that little incident, but, um, it's just like what's deep down what you think is going to be right, and what's going to help you out or help the other person out, and then the conflict is what is a decision, but it's like not going to do anything, it's just gonna maybe make things, life, easier.

I: Okay, well, then I would like to ask you, what is a moral problem for you? What do you think makes a moral problem?

R: Maybe when, you know, it has something to do with people or your friends, or just even a dog or something, and it's going to be easier, I mean, it's like if you're lazy, it's easier to take the wrong one, so it's like a decision.

I: Okay. Do you think the situation, the story with your cousin and the camp director, would that be considered a moral problem for you?

R: Yeah, because I COULD HAVE GOTTEN OUT OF IT EASILY, you know, and IT WASN'T MY FEELING, my cousin's, but he was like really close, but I WASN'T FEELING WHAT HE WAS FEELING, but I DID HAVE A LITTLE EMPATHY, BUT NOT THAT MUCH. So, either I COULD HAVE GOTTEN OUT OF IT AND SAID "I'm not going up to that camp director, you go up yourself," to my cousin, but he was like very miserable and I ALMOST

FELT <u>LIKE HE DID IN A WAY, SO I DID GO UP BECAUSE I</u> FELT
<u>MISERABLE HAVING HIM FEEL MISERABLE.</u>

I: Right. I bet.

*KEY:

SELF=CAPITAL LETTERS
Justice=**Bold Face**
Care=<u>Underlining</u>

APPENDIX 2
WORKSHEETS FOR TANYA'S INTERVIEW TEXT

I. First Reading—Understanding the Story

A. *Please Make Notes Here on the First Reading*—e.g., relationships, general moral language, repeated words and themes, contradictions, and key images and metaphors.

Relationships—Her family relationships, between herself and her cousin, are very important to her. She mentions that she was in camp with her sister, too, who wasn't mentioned. Were they not close? She does say that she was close to her cousin. Also, she seems to understand that even though her relationship with the camp director means that he was "in charge" he still has a responsibility to her and the other campers.

Repeated themes—she says 3 times "I was really afraid" of counselor. (p. 47)

Contradictions—she notes a contradiction in the camp directors' belief that "we're here to help our kids, to make them have fun," when her cousin was obviously "contradicting the whole slogan."
—She says, "either you feel it, like all the way or you just, like, recognize it, you know?" And "he was like really close, but I wasn't feeling what he was feeling." This seems contradictory but I think actually it's a very complex idea of empathy.
—Possible contradiction in her narrative—her sense that the right thing to do was obvious for her, and her experience of this as a moral conflict. "I felt good but I felt really bad." (p. 49)

Moral language—[Note that they discussed morality "in English the other day."] Morality is "what's deep down what you think is going to be right, and what's going to help you out or help the other person out. . . ." She considers the story to be a story about morality because "I could have gotten out of it easily . . . it wasn't my feeling, my cousins, but he was like really close . . . so either I could have gotten out of it easily . . . but he was very miserable and I almost felt like he did in a way, so I did go up because I felt miserable having him feel miserable." (p. 51)
—Most of what she says is phrased in terms of helping others (see above definition). She's astute enough to have a complicated idea of the psychology of rules: there are the camp rules (not allowed to phone home) and the internalized "rules" of the camp director's perception of his own reputation.

B. *Reader Response—Where do you stand in relationship to this story?* e.g., where did you feel most connected to the interview? Where did you feel disengaged? What do you know about the narrator? How is s/he like you? Different from you? What might this mean for your interpretation?

52

I was very moved and impressed by this story. I've been to summer camp and I remember how powerful the counselors were—they could make you completely miserable if they wanted to. I also remember the rules which seemed arbitrary and unfair: You have to eat two spoonfuls of everything; you have to dive down to the touch the snake-filled bottom of the lake to be allowed to swim at all. I can remember how frightening it could be. So, I feel I can understand her fear and sense of intimidation. I also understand how having someone you care about be hurt can impel you to action. But, I'm not sure if I would have been so brave as to take this camp director on in such an unfamiliar context as camp. She really seems to trust that he couldn't hurt her physically. Also, she sees the hurt to herself as being "ego." She seems very strong to me! That's not a little thing to have at stake, at risk. I wonder if her close relationship with her cousin, and perhaps sister and friends, gave her the confidence to speak up? I also wonder if the fact that she is Indian has anything to do with her choice. And what does the fact that I am a white woman have to do with ways we might differ that I'm not aware of. Does that allow her to risk this—a slightly different sense of authority and obligation (of authority and familial ties)? Does her privilege give her confidence in the system that would keep the camp counselor from being violent or seriously harmful? Then, too, I remember being very outspoken and outraged about injustices and hypocrisy in 7th grade—it wasn't until a little later that I learned that our systems and authorities don't always obey the rules that they ask us to follow. I wonder if she will learn that, too.

C. *Briefly Note All Conflicts* in the section of the interview entitled "Moral Conflict and Choice" (please cite page numbers where found).

—(p. 47) "I guess that's kind of one, the one I just told you." [May want to refer to previous section to pick up this conflict with her friend "getting out of line." She does not elaborate here.]

—(pp. 47–51) " . . . I went to camp with my sister and my cousin, and he was really young . . . and he got really homesick . . . And we had this camp guide who was really tough and I was really afraid of him . . . And he said, "nobody is allowed to use the phone" . . . my cousin really wanted to call his parents . . . and it was kind of up to me to ask the guy if he could. So either like I got bawled out by this guy and asked, or I didn't do anything about it . . . but the conflict was that he was my cousin and we've always been kind of close, and I either helped him out or like I helped myself . . . it was me saving myself or saving him . . .

Summary Interpretation—Conflict(s)

Her conflict here seems to be pretty clearly defined as helping her cousin and risking getting in trouble or getting "out of it easily" by telling her cousin to fend for himself. This seems to be what makes this a moral problem for her, that it's a decision where "it's easier to take the wrong one" but doing so would be against "what's deep down what you think is going to be right." Embedded in here is a very interesting discussion of empathy which raises questions about moral action: if you can feel how miserable another feels, does this imply action if you know you could help? (But she says "it's like not gonna do anything."??) I find it interesting that as she talks this through, the "rightness" of her choice becomes clear to her. I don't think she is denying her feelings of conflict in the situation, but she is saying that now, with hindsight and having made a choice, it's clear that's what she should have done. My sense is that this was a real learning experience for her.

II. SECOND READING—SELF

A. Self and the Narrative of Action—What actions does self take in the conflict?

1. Choosing self—Does the narrator see or describe a choice? What is the choice? How is the choice made?	Summary/Interpretation
(p. 47) "I was really afraid. . . . it was kind of up to me. . . . either I got bawled out and asked or I didn't do anything about it. . . . I had to tell him. . . . So I went and asked. . . ."	The choice seems to be between risking getting yelled at (which hurts her feelings and she hates) or helping her cousin. She sees herself as the only one who could practically do anything. She also felt she 'had' to take action. (A moral imperative?)
2. What is self describing him/herself as saying and/or doing	
(p. 47) I had to tell him. . . . so I went and asked. . . .	A sense of imperative.
I said, 'this guy can intimidate me but he can't beat me up.'	She believes and can trust that the camp director's power/authority does not extend to physical violence.
(p. 51) I did go up because I felt miserable having him feel miserable.	Ability to empathize with her cousin's distress seems to motivate action/commit her to response.
3. What is self thinking or considering or feeling?	

(p. 47) I was really afraid. . . . it was kind of up to me . . . either I got bawled out and asked or I didn't do anything about it.

She was frightened for herself and felt she was the only one who could do something.

I considered what was right and wrong . . .

(pp. 47–48) He was my cousin and we've always been kind of close . . . I either helped him out or, like I helped myself. . . . it was me saving myself or saving him . . .

The closeness between herself and her cousin is a reason for her conflict. She also phrases this in terms of "saving" herself or him. This isn't borne out by how she later describes it. (Feeling miserable because he felt miserable.)

(p. 48) " . . . nothing bad was going to happen to me . . . ["Kind of like the ego . . . and nothing physically and nothing anybody else would see"]

Re: to the fact that counselor "can't beat me up." She knows that while her "ego" would be hurt, she wasn't risking physical violence.

(p. 49) I guess it was kind of like a victory.

Note she doesn't dwell on this, or gloat.

(p. 50) . . . it wasn't my feeling . . . I wasn't feeling what he was feeling . . . I did have a little empathy . . . I almost felt like my cousin did in a way . . . I did go up because I felt miserable having him feel miserable.

She seems to be distinguishing her cousin's feelings from her own, while trying to explain her feelings of empathy for him . . . and her felt need to respond to his misery. She distinguishes her feelings from relational fusion or an idealized sympathy or empathy in which she *is* he.

B. Self in Relationship

What is organizing frame for the relationship(s) described in the conflict?

Summary/Interpretation

(p. 47) With her cousin—it was kind of up to me to go ask the guy if he could (use the phone) . . . he was my cousin, so I had to help him . . . he was really young . . . it was my cousin's good . . . we've al-

She describes her feelings of attachment to her cousin, and her felt need to respond seems connected to these descriptions. Yet she also observes his vulnerability and distress, connected to his young age, and may

ways been kind of close . . . (p. 48) my cousin lives seven minutes away from us . . . (p. 51) I almost felt like he did in a way . . .

feel responsible for him, both because she is older and witnesses this (and therefore has more power than he does to act) and because she is a relative, and may feel it is her role or her duty to act on his behalf (Not clear whether she was given special responsibility for her cousin by her/his family? Could this relate to her being Indian?)

With the camp counselor—(p. 47) I was really afraid of him . . . so either I got bawled out by this guy and asked . . . he started giving me this lecture . . . I said sorry, but he's only seven . . . this guy can intimidate me, but he can't beat me up or anything . . . (p. 47) I would never see that guy again . . . this guy is a big bully and he can have anything the way wants it . . . it was big giving in for him . . . (p. 49) was like a victory . . . like you won over this guy so be happy.

Her fear of him, his relative position and power, point to a relationship of inequality that is understood within a structure where his power has limits. This makes her experience of victory over him sensible. And makes her act of speaking up (I said, "sorry but he's only seven") seem quite brave. Her awareness of his limits seems to allow her to speak up in reaction to her cousin's distress.

With herself—(p. 47) so, like I said, this guy can intimidate me, but he can't beat me up or anything . . . (p. 48) it was me saving myself or saving him . . . kind of like the ego . . . nothing that anybody else would see . . . my feelings being hurt and I hate being yelled out . . . (p. 49) it's like you won over this guy so happy.

she seems to be letting us in on a series of internal dialogues . . . her way of sorting through the issues in this conflict that represent different parts of herself—fear, potential embarrassment, damage to her ego, final sense of victory. This dialogue sets up the conflict in a way that represents her in relation to herself, and includes concern for herself (selves?) as central in the choices she makes. She finally concludes that her action was right, and right for her. Thus, based on her decision, her choice allows her to stay with herself and what was right: "what's deep down what you think is going to be right."

C. What is at Stake for Self

(p. 48) I was really afraid of him . . . it was me saving myself or saving him . . . kind of like the ego . . . nothing physically and nothing that anybody else would see, it's just like my feelings being hurt and I hate being yelled at. . . .

While she seems, in stating that it was only her ego that could be hurt, to be almost trivializing the fear that she felt, what's at stake seems to be her feelings about or relationship to herself as that is played out in the drama of her response to her cousin. Her sense that she was the only one who could help him, that her close relationship meant she felt for him, and her realization of the limits of the camp director's power, leave her with a struggle between acting from what "deep down" she knew was right or being "lazy." What does it mean, though, that she claims that what is moral is "*just* like what is deep down" but "it's like not going to do anything, it's just gonna maybe make things, life, easier?"

Summary Interpretation—Reading for Self

I hear in her struggle a claiming of her integrity. She seem to be genuinely frightened of this powerful bully, the camp director. Yet, her feelings for her cousin and her sense that she had to do something, both out of her feeling miserable because he did and her sense of responsibility—being the only one in the position to act—led her to confront him. She explains her sense of security that he could not physically harm her. When the director capitulates, and even though he takes a jab at the cousin in the lecture, she realizes that it was a kind of victory. Interestingly, she doesn't exult in this. The conflict, it seems, wasn't about wining over him: it was about her helping her cousin and being true to herself.

I find myself admiring her in her choice. She has considered the complexity of this situation from a number of perspectives. She is responsive—listening not only to her cousin but to her own needs and responding. In so doing, she stays "true" to herself. Yet, I wonder if what I alluded to at the end of my reader-response will play out over time—that she, too, will learn that systems of authority are unresponsive, untrustworthy, because she sees moral action as "not going to do anything." Will she then disconnect?

III. THIRD READING—CARE

A. Is the Care Orientation Articulated?   Yes

—How would you characterize care?	Summary/Interpretation
(p. 47) . . . he was really young . . . he got really home-sick . . . he was almost in tears . . .	Attention to cousin's distress.
. . . he was my cousin, so I had to help him . . . the right thing was to go because he was my cousin . . . he was my cousin and we've always been kind of close . . . (p. 48) cous-in lives 7 minutes away from us, so I would live with my cousin, but I would never see that guy again . . . he (cousin) was like really close . . .	Description of close relationship with cousin, which will be maintained be-yond this situation.
(p. 48) . . . so I realized it was worth letting him talk to his par-ents . . . what's going to help you help the other person out (re: def. of morality, p. 50) . . . he was like very miserable and I almost felt like he did in a way, so I . . . did go up because I was miserable having him feel miserable.	Response to need of the cousin based on relationship with him and the im-pact of that relationship on her (interdependence).
(p. 47) . . . I said sorry, but he's only 7. (p. 50) . . . people are more important than rules . . . but my cousin wasn't having fun, he was just contradicting the whole slogan.	Consideration of cousin and particu-lar circumstances, over the rule as a whole.
Understanding of counselor's view— (p. 47) I'll realize that's the way he is, but I have to do this . . . (p. 49) I guess it was kind of big giving in for him . . . Awareness of impact of her own view on situation—(p. 47) This guy can intimidate me . . . I was afraid . . . my feelings being	Attention to and understanding of perspective of others as concerns rel-evant to outcome of conflict; includ-ing attention to her own as one of many possible views.

hurt . . . Awareness of cousin's view
(p. 47) . . . he was really homesick.

B. If Care is Not (Clearly) Articulated?

(p. 48) . . . it was me saving myself
saving him . . .

How does care of self fit in here?
Her assurance that she cannot be
physically hurt or that ''nothing bad
was going to happen to me,'' seems
at odds with this dichotomy . . . here
she makes it sound as though choosing her cousin is self-sacrificial?

C. Does Self Align with Care? How Do You Know?

Appears so—Awareness of her own needs and the extent to which she could be
harmed (what's at stake was the ego) mitigates the few phrases in which she
sounds self-sacrificial. Deciding her fears and hurt feelings were not as important
as her cousin's distress, she responds to her cousin. She focuses on their closeness, and distinguishes between feeling what he was feeling and feeling empathy. She believes that people in general, and her cousin in this situation in
particular, are more important than rules, at least those that are enforced without
exception or attention to particularities of the situation.

IV.   FOURTH READING—JUSTICE

A. Is the Justice Orientation Articulated?   Yes

—How would you characterize
justice?

Summary/Interpretation

(p. 49) . . . re: counselor: his reputation (was at stake) . . . that was a
rule and he couldn't break it . . . (p.
49) He was probably, like kids always get homesick and what difference does it make . . .

Reference to an understanding of
rules (but rejects their enforcement
without attention to the particular
case).

(p. 50) . . . people are more important than rules . . . camp directors
say we're here to help our kids, to
make them have fun, but my cousin

Understanding the spirit of the law
vs. the letter of the law . . . counselor was not paying attention to the
exception in cousin's case.

wasn't having fun, he was just contradicting the whole slogan.

(p. 48) . . . He wasn't being able to have any fun and he paid for it, so he had to do something . . .	Not to let the cousin call would be unfair, since cousin was not getting what he was due for his money, what the camp promised.

B.   If Justice is Not (Clearly) Articulated in this Conflict?

−What would constitute justice in
this conflict?

(p. 47) . . . this guy can intimidate me, but he can't beat me up or anything . . .	she seems aware that the system (or convention) will protect her from physical abuse . . .
(p. 49) . . . but I did something for him, my cousin, and it's kind of like a victory . . . you won over this guy so be happy . . .	Framing the outcome as a victory makes most sense in the context of a struggle between what she perceived as unfair about the counselor's actions, and her (and her cousin's) less powerful position with respect to him.
(p. 47) . . . and he was my cousin, so I had to help him . . .	Not clear if she experienced a sense of duty to care for him, or was given responsibility for him?

C.   Does Self Align with Justice? How do you know?

No . . . though she does allude to protection from a system that would limit the
actions of the counselor, she seems most attentive to her own fears and her
cousin's distress, and pits this against a definition of justice that is blind to
particular circumstances; that is blind to the spirit of the law.

V.   INTERPRETIVE SUMMARY—SELF IN RELATION TO JUSTICE AND CARE

She is cognizant of the claims of both care and justice, the vulnerability of people
both to abandonment and to oppression. Taking action that turns out to be
effective in securing a response from the camp counselor to ameliorate her

cousin's distress, she tells a story, which when told in justice terms, renders her the victor over the callous camp director. But she also knows that the camp director "had another point of view," that he probably thought "kids always get homesick and what difference does it make, he's not going to die." In the end she relies on a system of justice which will hold the camp director accountable and thus she feels, will prevent him from beating her up. To protect herself and her cousin from psychological violence, however, she calls on, and *aligns* with, an ethic of care to support her capacity to care, and guided by this ethic she finds an inclusive solution to the dilemma—"people are more important than rules," she says, and in the end, her cousin felt better, she no longer felt miserable, and the camp director, albeit at her cousin's expense, salvaged his reputation by giving a lecture.

Both care and justice are present; at times certain phrases can be understood from either perspective, depending on the lens—e.g., "He was my cousin and so I had to help him," can refer to their closeness or to the fact that she was responsible due to her role as older relative, perhaps related to particular cultural conventions (there is less evidence for this latter interpretation in the text). Also, "I said, sorry he's only seven," can refer to her empathy for her cousin's distress at being homesick at such a young age, or her anger at the counselor's advantage in power and oppressive treatment.

She rejects a form of justice that places importance of reputation or rules for the sake of rules (i.e., that do not consider exceptions) over persons in need . . . She focuses *predominantly* on care concerns—the relationship with her cousin, her own fears and needs, and her cousin's distress.

3 Empathy-Related Responding and Cognition: A "Chicken and the Egg" Dilemma

Nancy Eisenberg
Cindy L. Shea
Gustavo Carlo
George P. Knight

ABSTRACT

The concepts of empathy, sympathy, and role taking frequently are embedded in theories and models of moral development. However, these various terms frequently have not been adequately differentiated; for example, empathic reactions generally have not been differentiated from sympathetic and personal distress responses. Moreover, the interrelations of empathy, sympathy, personal distress, and related cognitive processes (such as role taking and accessing relevant cognitions from memory) have not been adequately explored, conceptually or empirically. Consequently, in this chapter we consider definitions of the aforementioned terms, review empirical research on relations among the constructs of interest, and hypothesize about possible links among vicariously induced emotional reactions and cognitive processing. The cognitive processes considered are conditioning/direct association, labeling, elaborated networking, and role taking; the various vicarious emotional processes are empathy, sympathy, and personal distress. Alternative tentative causal models are presented and discussed. In particular, the possible sequencing of these various processes is addressed. Issues concerning the elicitation and maintenance of vicariously induced emotional responses and related cognitive processes are viewed of importance to an understanding of pro- and antisocial behavior.

Empathy and related vicarious response such as sympathy often have been viewed as playing an important role in social and moral development (e.g., Allport, 1937; Blum, 1980; Hoffman, 1984; Staub, 1984). However, there has been considerable debate regarding the definition and nature of empathy and how empathy relates to other cognitive and vicarious affective processes.

In this chapter, we discuss the aforementioned issues. In brief, we try to differentiate among various responses that frequently have been labeled as empathy, speculate about the roles of cognition and affect in empathy and related responses, and consider the interrelations among relevant modes of cognitive processing and vicarious affective responses. In the process of discussing these topics, selected issues related to the development of empathy are examined. Although we refer to data when possible, in much of this chapter we deal with issues for which there are few directly relevant data. Thus, the goal of this chapter is to stimulate thinking about several important issues in the study of empathy, rather than to attempt to resolve these difficult issues.

The issues examined in this chapter are of direct relevance to an understanding of morality. In general, indexes of empathy and related responses (such as sympathy) have been shown to relate positively to prosocial behaviors (Eisenberg & Miller, 1987) and negatively to aggressive, antisocial behaviors (Miller & Eisenberg, 1988). However, some other types of vicariously induced emotional responses (i.e., personal distress) seem to be sometimes negatively and sometimes positively related to prosocial behavior (Batson, 1987); thus, it is important to consider factors that may differentially affect the likelihood of people experiencing sympathy and/or personal distress. Cognitive processes such as role taking also have been conceptually linked to higher-level moral judgment (e.g., Kohlberg, 1976) and altruism (e.g., Batson, 1987; Hoffman, 1984), and there seems to be empirical support for these assumptions (see Selman, 1980; Underwood & Moore, 1982). Clearly, then, a better understanding of the links between vicarious emotional responding and related cognitive processes is essential for an understanding of both moral development and the enactment of moral behaviors.

For readers who desire further discussion of the links between vicarious emotional responding or role taking and moral behavior or reasoning, relevant information and references are provided in numerous books and papers, including Batson (1987), Eisenberg (1986), Hoffman (1984, 1987), Krebs and Russell (1981), Staub (1978, 1984), and Underwood and Moore (1982).

DEFINITIONAL ISSUES

Over the years, empathy has been defined in many different ways (Eisenberg & Strayer, 1987; Wispe, 1986, 1987). As there is no way to ascertain which definition is correct, it is perhaps most useful to base our definitions on current usage of terms and to differentiate carefully among the various processes which have been called empathy.

In much of the recent social psychological and developmental literature (Batson, 1987; Feshback, 1978; Hoffman, 1984), empathy has been defined as having an affective basis (sometimes in combination with a cognitive basis;

Davis, 1983b; Feshbach, 1978). Our definition of *empathy* is consistent with this view. Specifically, we define empathy as *an emotional response that stems from another's emotional state or condition and is congruent with the other's emotional state or condition.* Further, empathy is defined as *involving at least a minimal differentiation between self and other* while empathizing. In other words, the empathizer is assumed to realize that another's experience is not one and the same as one's own. Whereas some theorists believe that empathy need not involve any self—other differentiation (Hoffman, 1982a), we believe that vicarious emotional responding which does not involve any differentiation is more primitive than empathy and may be a precursor thereof. Our definition of empathy is quite similar to Staub's (1987) definition of affective empathy, particularly parallel affective empathy (empathy in which one matches or parallels the other's affective state).

In line with our definition of empathy, several subtle distinctions related to the term should be noted. First, at times individuals may experience or "catch" another's emotion without realizing that it comes from another (pure emotional contagion) or without making the distinction between one's own or the other's emotional state (e.g., in the case of reflexive crying; see Hoffman, 1982a; Thompson, 1987). Such responses are especially likely in infants and, as noted previously, may be precursors (developmentally or in a time sequence) of empathy. Second, it is important to note that empathy based on perceiving another's emotional cues and empathy based on interpreting the other's situation may require different cognitive capabilities (Hoffman, 1984). Finally, people and animals (Plutchik, 1987) sometimes may experience the same emotion as another not because they are empathizing but because the other's emotional state has significance for the self. In other words, the observer may not enter into the other's experience; rather, the other's experience may generate the same experience in the self (Staub, 1987). An example of this is when another's emotional behavior serves as a signal of danger to the observer. We do not consider this type of responding to be empathic.

Many theorists have not differentiated between the concepts of *sympathy* and *empathy* (e.g., Batson, 1987; Feshbach, 1978), or have considered sympathy to be a developmentally mature type of empathy (Hoffman, 1984). We define sympathy as distinct from empathy, although it may often stem from empathy. Specifically, *sympathy* is defined as *a vicarious emotional reaction based on the apprehension of another's emotional state or situation, which involves feelings of sorrow or concern for the other.* Thus, the sympathizer does not necessarily feel the same emotion as the other person (or does not simply experience the emotion likely to stem from the other's situation); rather, he or she feels the other-directed emotion of concern for another. This concern is seen as involving the other-oriented desire for the needy other to feel better and the desire for the other's negative state to be alleviated (note that sympathy usually occurs in regard to negative states or emotions). Thus, although sympathy is viewed as a vicariously induced emotional response, it also is viewed as involving more cognition than does empathy (e.g., cognitions about the other's state). Our definition of sympathy is consistent with Batson's (1987) definition of empathy, Wispe's (1986) definition of sympathy, and Staub's (1987) definition of reactive affective empathy and participatory empathy.[1]

Another type of emotional reaction that frequently has not been differentiated from empathy or sympathy is personal distress (Batson, 1987). When people perceive cues (emotional or situational) indicative of another's negative state, observers may experience *personal distress, an aversive, vicariously induced emotional reaction such as anxiety or worry which is coupled with self-oriented, egoistic concern.* Batson (1987) has suggested that experiencing personal distress leads to the motive of alleviating one's own, not the other's distress. For example, people experiencing personal distress appear to assist a needy other primarily when doing so is the easiest way to alleviate their own aversive arousal. Self-oriented personal distress, then, differs in its focus and motivational component from empathy (which is neither self- or other-oriented) and sympathy (which is other-oriented and involves feelings of concern) and usually should involve more cognitive elements than should empathy (e.g., the person would be expected to be thinking about their own aversive feelings and how they can best be alleviated).

In our definitions of empathy, sympathy, and personal distress, emotion is central. However, empathy often has been defined in solely cognitive terms, as involving person perception skills (Dymond, 1949) or, more frequently, role taking (Deutsch & Madle, 1975; Mead, 1934). Although cognition is no doubt involved in most if not all instances of empathy and sympathy (depending on one's definition of empathy; Feshbach, 1978; Hoffman, 1984), it is important to differentiate between processes called empathy that involve emotion and those that do not. In recent years, some people (e.g., Shantz, 1975; Underwood & Moore, 1982) have made this distinction by labeling the cognitive processes involved in understanding another's cognitions or emotional state (or the ability to do so) as *role taking* or *perspective taking.* Specifically, three types of perspective taking have been identified (Shantz, 1975): visual or spatial perspective taking (the ability to understand what another perceives, usually visually), affective role taking (the ability to understand what another feels), and cognitive or communicative role taking (the ability to comprehend what another is thinking or understands).

Although we do not consider it further in this chapter, *projection* is one other mode of response that sometimes has been confused with empathy. Projection is

---

[1]It differs dramatically, however, from Goldstein and Michaels' (1985) view that "the sympathizer, in contrast [to the empathizer], is more preoccupied with is or her own feelings in response to the other and thus is less able to respond to, for, or with the other in a manner sensitive to the other person's actual ongoing emotional world and context" (p. 8).

"the act of ascribing to someone or something else one's own attitudes, thoughts, etc." (*Random House College Dictionary*, 1980, p. 1058). Thus, projection differs from our definition of empathy in two ways: (1) It is a process that frequently is solely cognitive, and (2) The direction of the process is from the self to other rather than vice versa (see Feshbach, 1978). Nonetheless, it frequently is difficult to determine whether an individual is empathizing or projecting (Strayer, 1987).

Delineation of Cognitive Processes in Vicarious Emotional Responding

There are numerous cognitive processes that are likely to be involved in empathy and sympathy. At this time, we briefly discuss and try to differentiate among some of these various processes (i.e., conditioning and direct association, simple categorization/labeling, retrieval of elaborated cognitive networks, and role taking). Doing so will be helpful when we turn to the issue of the antecedents and consequences of empathy, sympathy, and personal distress.

Feshbach (1978) has argued that two cognitive abilities are critical to empathy: (1) the ability to discriminate the emotional states of others (an elementary form of social comprehension), and (2) the ability to assume the perspective and role of the other. Similarly, Hoffman (1982a, 1984) has suggested that some rudimentary forms of empathy involve the discrimination between self and other as sources of emotion and that higher-level forms of empathy involve the ability to role take and/or use information from language-mediated associations. In fact, he sees cognition as a necessary component for more developmentally advanced modes of empathy. For example, empathy for another's general plight (Hoffman's most sophisticated form of empathy) involves the ability to use others' expressive cues, relevant situational information, and knowledge of the other's life condition to imagine the other's feelings and condition beyond the immediate situation.

Feshbach's and Hoffman's views reflect the common assumption that the abilities to label others' emotional states and to understand how others feel and think contribute to empathy, especially developmentally sophisticated forms of empathy. However, investigators frequently have lumped most or all the cognitive skills discussed by Hoffman or Feshbach under the label of perspective taking (or role taking). Contrary to this assumption, we maintain that there are probably important differences in the nature of the various types of cognitive capabilities that contribute to empathizing or sympathizing. Specifically, we delineate four different modes of cognitive responding: conditioning/direct association, labeling, retrieving elaborated cognitive networks, and role taking.

As the label role taking has most often been used by researchers investigating the role of cognitive responding in empathy, we first define what we mean by role taking. According to Higgins (1981), role taking requires going beyond the stimulus information given in a situation by using inferential abilities, controlling one's own viewpoint when making judgments about others (rather than using projection or making an egocentric judgment), and relating two or more elements (e.g., viewpoints). Thus, consistent with Higgins's view, we define *role taking* as *making an inference about a target's viewpoint or situation and basing the inference on these rather than on one's own perspective.* With this definition in mind, we now describe three other modes of cognitive processing that may contribute to empathy, sympathy, or personal distress, but which do not meet the criteria for role taking.

At the most rudimentary level, empathy may be evoked by *conditioning and direct association* (Hoffman, 1984). For example, the sight of another's blood may elicit fear or distress in a viewing child because the child's own blood has been linked with the child's own distress in the past (see Aronfreed, 1968, 1970). We are assuming that some elementary level of cognition is needed in most cases to make such a connection. However, the relevant cognitive processing is very simple, automatic, and does not involve an intentional memory search. If the viewer is unaware that the blood reflects the other's condition rather than one's own or is reacting only to the sight of blood, we would not consider the child's affective response to be truly empathic. If, however, the child has the simple cognitive ability to differentiate between self and other, is not simply alarmed by the blood, and has some recognition of the other's emotional state or condition, the affectively responsive viewer may be seen as empathizing (depending on the match between the viewer's affective response and that of the other).

As was noted previously, Feshbach (1978) has argued that the ability to disciminate other's emotional states is an important precursor of empathy in some situations. However, all that is required to interpret cues in some situations is a basic knowledge of the meanings associated with perceptual cues; the ability and/or desire to interpret the situation using the other person's viewpoint is not necessarily involved. We call this type of cognitive processing *labeling* (although others such as Borke, 1971, have called this type of processing role taking.) For example, an observer may know that a downturned mouth indicates sadness, and thus would label someone with a frown as feeling sad, regardless of the other cues in the situation. Likewise, an observer may know that children at a birthday party are normally happy, and therefore may label someone in that situation as being happy, regardless of the person's facial cues. As for conditioning and direct association, this mode of cognitive responding is presumed to be fairly automatic, involving relatively little, if any, intentional processing or inference on the observer's part. Thus, labeling (along with conditioning/direct association) is considered to be a lower level than is role taking.

Karniol has suggested that the inference that another is in need often does not depend on role taking; rather, this inference is based on retrieval processes that are initiated by situational stimuli. She writes:

Specifically, we contend that the observation of social stimuli such as another person's behavior in a given setting initiates cognitive processes in which the observer attempts to match the observed event with some prestored chunk of stereotyped knowledge. . . . Once the appropriate knowledge store or theoretical structure is accessed, the observer is in possession of adjunct information that has either been prestored or inferentially derived, and that is relevant to the situation. This adjunct knowledge may include information about the motivation of actors, the internal psychological processes they would experience as a consequence of either achieving or failing to achieve the goal that motivated their behavior, and knowledge about how goal attainment can be facilitated or circumvented. (1982, p. 256)

Thus, upon the observation of particular cues, complex *elaborated cognitive networks* of relevant information can be accessed, including social scripts in which extensive information about other situations and people in general can be embedded (Schank & Abelson, 1977).[2] These networks develop as a consequence of direct or vicarious experiences, and the cues that elicit stored information can be perceptual (e.g., visual) or coded semantically (e.g., words in a letter). For example, the awareness that another is bleeding may be used as a cue to indicate an injury, which may then stimulate the retrieval of information related to various types of injuries, how the injured other must feel, and what one does when confronted with an injured other.

In brief, Karniol has argued that we often need not role take to understand that another is in need. Similarly, one can argue that people frequently can understand how another feels or what another is thinking without role taking. It is likely that young children have less and simpler information stored in memory and fewer social scripts, with the result that their inferences based on retrieval processes may be less accurate and elaborated than those of adults. However, it is clear that even 3-year-olds have social scripts related to common experiences such as going to a restaurant (Nelson, 1981), and it is likely that even the very young have simple cognitive networks in which the sequencing of everyday events, their consequences, relevant social roles, and related emotional responses are embedded.

An important issue is when do people role take rather than simply rely on their elaborated cognitive networks? Consistent with Higgins's (1981) thinking, we assume that role taking is most likely when the judge's own viewpoint, characteristics, or feelings are different from those of the target person. In addition, role taking is probably more likely when the judge or viewer is in a situation which is unfamiliar, one for which he or she does not have elaborated cognitive informa-

---

[2]A *cognitive script* is defined as "a coherent sequence of events expected by the individual, involving him either as a participant or an an observer" (Abelson, 1976, p. 33).

tion stored in memory. For example, when individuals are in an unfamiliar culture dealing with people with different belief systems, they are likely to try to use what information they have about the other people's beliefs and traditions and the culture to determine the other's viewpoint. In such a context, information and social scripts derived from experience in one's own culture are less reliable than when one is dealing with people from a similar background; thus, it is advantageous to try to role take. Another factor that would be expected to affect to what degree people role take is the level of their motivation to act in a manner pleasing to another; if a judge is highly motivated to please, he or she may be more likely to take the extra effort needed to try to discern the other's perspective.

In summary, we have reviewed several types of cognitive processes that may play major roles in empathic, sympathetic, or personal distress responding, each of which can be used to provide information about another. At the simplest level, people can merely associate cues emanating from others with their own experiences (direct association, conditioning; Hoffman, 1982a, 1984). For example, the sight of another crying may involuntarily elicit feelings of sadness in the viewer, due to the pairing of others' tears with the viewer's own sadness in the past. Individuals can also use situational information to make judgments about others and their situations based on either simple categorization and labeling processes (e.g., blood means that the other person is hurt) or the accessing of complex chunks of information stored in memory (e.g., blood is used as a cue to indicate an injury, which then stimulates thinking about the various types of injuries that might have occurred, how the injured other must feel, and what one should do in various cases). Finally, in some contexts people undoubtedly role take actively in an attempt to understand another's feelings or situation. In doing so, the role taker no doubt must access existing information (including social scripts) stored in his or her memory; however, role taking ultimately involves the use of information about the other and his/her situation to try to make new inferences about the specific situation at hand. We now consider the role of these various processes in vicarious emotional responding.

ROLE OF SOCIOCOGNITIVE PROCESSES: THE EMPIRICAL DATA

It is a common assumption that empathy and sympathy often are a consequence of role taking (e.g., Batson, 1987; Feshbach, 1978; Hoffman, 1982a). However, this assumption has seldom been investigated empirically. Additionally, many researchers who have addressed this issue have actually utilized indexes that assess the ability to label another's emotion or use simple retrieval processes rather than the ability to role take. For example, with some instruments assumed to assess role taking, children have been asked simply to label how another feels based on overt situational or facial cues (e.g., Borke, 1971; see Chandler & Greenspan, 1972) or have been asked to select different and appropriate gifts for person of different ages or sex (a task which probably involves social categorization skills and stored information about what various categories of people like; see Higgins, Feldman, & Ruble, 1980). For the aforementioned reasons, the existing empirical research is not very informative with regard to the task of delineating the precise nature of the interrelations among various cognitive processes and vicarious emotional responding. Nonetheless, we briefly review this body of literature because it is relevant to our discussion.

In the limited empirical literature, there is some empirical support, albeit not entirely consistent, for the assumption that cognitive skills are associated with empathy and sympathy. In a study with 6- and 7-year-olds, Feshbach and Roe (1968) found that children's skill in identifying story characters' emotions from situational cues was positively related to their verbal report of experiencing the same emotion as the story protagonist. Eisenberg–Berg and Lennon (1980) found that a similar index of the ability to label another's emotional state was significantly, positively related to a nonverbal index of 4- to 5-year-olds' empathy (i.e., the children indicated what emotion they experienced after hearing the vignettes by pointing to pictures of various facial expressions) but was not significantly related to the children's verbal report of empathy.

In another study, Iannotti (1977, 1978) obtained evidence suggesting that the type of cues boys use when determining another's state is related to the cues that affect their empathic responding. Iannotti assessed role taking with two tasks involving inferential abilities and the maintenance of the difference between various perspectives (Selman & Byrne's, 1974, task, and Flavell, Botkin, Fry, & Wright, and Jarvis's, 1968, nickel/dime task). He also assessed the ability to label another's state from pictures; in some pictures situational and facial cues concerning the other were consistent (e.g., the child was happy at the birthday party). Empathy was assessed by asking the boys how they felt when they viewed the incongruent and congruent pictures.

For both age groups (6- and 9-year-olds), children who frequently used facial cues to identify how the person in the picture felt reported feeling an emotion consistent with the same facial cues. Similarly, the use of situational cues to identify the other's state generally was paired with report of feeling the emotion indicated by the situational cues. When situational and facial cues were consistent, measures of labeling and empathy were significantly positively related for 6-year-olds, whereas 9-year-olds who reported feeling the emotion indicated by both types of cues scored high on the use of situational cues to label the other's affect in the incongruent picture tasks. In addition, a composite score of the two role-taking tasks was negatively related to 6-year-olds' report of feeling the emotion depicted by the facial cues in the incongruent situations. This same composite score was unrelated to 9-year-olds' or the 6-year-olds' empathy when tested 1 year later; however, it was positively related to the 9-year-olds' use of situational cues when empathizing with characters in incongruent situations. Empathy based on situational cues increased with age over the year among the 6-year-olds and empathy based on facial cues in incongruent contexts was negatively correlated with age. Thus, it is likely that empathy based on situational cues is more developmentally mature than is empathy (or labeling) based on facial cues that conflict with situational cues. If one makes this assumption, Iannotti generally found that mature levels of the ability to infer others' emotions was positively related to the children's own empathizing and that the way in which children determine another's emotional state affects what emotional state children empathize with.

Similarly, Iannotti and Pierrehumbert (1985) found that 2-year olds' cognitive role-taking abilities were positively related to their use of situational rather than facial cues to label another's emotion and to empathize at age 5. Thus, Iannotti obtained additional support for the view that cognitive skills are related to developmentally advanced modes of empathic responding.

In a more recent study, Iannotti (1985) administered to preschoolers two role-taking tasks, one most likely involving the retrieval of social information (i.e., the selection of gifts for various people), and his picture measure of empathy and labeling of others' emotions. Iannotti's index of empathy was unrelated to the two role-taking tasks or to the gift selection task. Thus, the results of this study are not consistent with those in his other studies. In addition, it should be noted that the picture/story mode of assessing empathy used in all of Iannotti's studies as well as in Feshbach and Roe's (1968) work has been criticized for a variety of reasons, including the likelihood of salient demand characteristics and the possibility that the stories are not really emotionally evocative (Eisenberg & Lennon, 1983; Hoffman, 1982b). Moreover, contrary to theory (e.g., Feshbach, 1978; Hoffman, 1984), such indexes of empathy generally have not been significantly related to prosocial behavior (Eisenberg & Miller, 1987) or related to aggressive behavior (Miller & Eisenberg, 1988). Therefore, it is questionable whether picture-story indexes of empathy are valid measures.

In studies involving other types of indexes of empathy, positive relations between empathy or sympathy and role-taking measures generally have been obtained. For example, Strayer and Roberts (1984) obtained a significant, positive relation between an index of role taking and 6- and 8-year-olds' report on Bryant's (1982) questionnaire index of empathy (which probably assesses some combination of empathy, sympathy, personal distress, and role taking). Similarly, in studies with adults, self-report of dispositional role taking (i.e., the trait of tending to role take) has been positively related to self-report of dispositional sympathy (e.g., Batson, Bolen, Cross, & Neuringer–Benefiel, 1986; Davis, 1983b; Eisenberg, Miller, Schaller, Fabes, Fultz, Shell, & Shea, 1989).

In another study in which role taking was induced, Chovil (1985; reported in Strayer, 1987) asked children to either imagine themselves in a character's role

(role taking), imagine what it would be like if the events depicted were happening to them (believed to be projection), or simply listen and watch videotaped stimuli. She found that the two former conditions were related positively to report of experiencing the same affect as the story characters and to Bryant's (1982) questionnaire index of empathy (which contains items that could reflect role taking, empathy, sympathy, personal distress, and other related capabilities). Thus, Chovil's findings suggest that imaginal processes such as role taking facilitate empathic responding. Similarly, a number of researchers have found that instructing adults (Davis, 1983a; Shelton & Rogers, 1981; Toi & Batson, 1982) or children (Howard & Barnett, 1981) to imagine how a needy other feels increases their reports of feeling sympathy or empathy for the needy other. These findings are also consistent with those of Larsen, Diener, and Cropanzano (1987). They found that people who scored high on a self-report index of characteristic emotional intensity reported trying to understand how another felt ("I can feel the grief the mother must feel in that situation") or personalized another's situation (imagined themselves in the other's situation) when confronted with slides depicting people in positive or negative situations.

The aforementioned studies in which individuals were asked to role take in laboratory contexts suggest that role taking or other cognitive processes used to determine another's condition facilitate sympathetic and empathic emotional responding in a given context. However, the causal relation between the trait or enduring tendency to respond empathically or sympathetically and the characteristic tendency to use role taking and other cognitive procedures to enhance one's understanding of another's situation is unclear.[3] Many people seem to assume that people who typically role take should, as a consequence, be relatively likely to empathize or sympathize with others. However, it is also possible that people who are prone to respond empathically or sympathetically, that is people who typically respond emotionally to others' states (Larsen & Diener, 1985, 1987), are more likely than other people to engage cognitive processes that increase emotional arousal. Larsen (Larsen et al., 1987) has suggested that this is because people high in characteristic emotional intensity are typically under-

---

[3]There is some evidence that there really are dispositions to be sympathetic or personally distress, and to role take. For example, Davis (1980) obtained test–retest reliability on his sympathy, personal distress, and role-taking questionnaires scales for adults over a period of 60–75 days. Reliabilities ranged from .61 to .81 (for seven item scales). Similarly, test–retest reliabilities for Bryant's (1982) scale ranged from .74 to .83 for children in first, fourth, and seventh grades. Although we realize that test–retest reliabilities are not an ideal test of individual stability on a given trait, the fact that adequate test–retest coefficients were obtained is consistent with such a conclusion. Unfortunately, in many studies in which multiple measures of a concept were used, it is very likely that the different indexes actually assessed different constructs (e.g., role taking vs. labeling of emotions or sympathy vs. affective matching). However, in one study in which similar but not identical measures of empathy/sympathy were administered a week apart, Lennon, Eisenberg, and Carroll (1986) obtained significant correlations between the indexes of facial intensity ($r = .50$) and latency response ($r = .38$) over time.

aroused physiologically and consequently seek stimulation. In support of this view, Larsen and Diener (1987) found that populations known to have low baseline arousal levels and consequently a high need for stimulation (e.g., extroverts) are higher on their characteristic intensity of affective response (also see Davis, Hull, Young, & Warren, 1987).

In summary, the data regarding the interrelations of sociocognitive skills and indexes of empathy or sympathy are limited. Moreover, in much of the relevant research, the indexes of empathy are of questionable validity (especially the picture-story indexes) and few inferences can be drawn regarding causal links (due to the correlational nature of much of the data). Nonetheless, the data from laboratory studies in which people are induced to role take generally are consistent with the view that role taking enhances sympathizing. One could argue that verbal instructions to role take are likely to create a demand for subjects to report that they sympathized; the fact that the instructions to role take increased helping as well as report of sympathy in some studies (e.g., Shelton & Rogers, 1981; Toi & Batson, 1982; see Eisenberg & Miller, 1987) suggests that the positive relation obtained between role taking and report of sympathizing may not be entirely artifactual (especially because the indexes of helping involved some potential cost and therefore were less likely to be affected by demand characteristics). Thus, at this point in time, there seems to be some empirical support for theoretical assertions linking role taking or other cognitive processes involved in assessing another's state and sympathy or empathy (especially the former). However, the nature of any existing interrelations certainly is not clear.

CONCEPTUAL SPECULATIONS

Interrelations of Empathy, Sympathy, and Personal Distress

Prior to examining the interrelations of the various aforementioned cognitive and vicarious, emotional processes, it is useful to consider the relations solely among empathy, sympathy, and personal distress. Once this is done, we consider the possible causal relations among cognitive processing and these three modes of emotional responding.

In our view, sympathy and personal distress often stem from empathizing. This may not be the case for the very young child who experiences another's emotion and has some awareness that the other's and one's own emotions are not one and the same, but does not process his or her own responding any further (due to cognitive immaturity). Such children may remain affectively aroused without considering what to do about this arousal. In contrast, for persons 1–2 years or older, we hypothesize that empathic responding usually leads individuals to focus on the other's need or state (which results in sympathizing), on one's own aversive state (which results in personal distress), or on both. They would be expected to do so in an attempt to understand and/or deal with the emotion. One exception to this generalization may be if the empathic arousal is very mild and transitory, or if the empathizer's attention is drawn elsewhere prior to his or her focusing much attention on the vicariously induced affect. In brief, we are arguing that, unless attention is diverted and/or empathy is not processed further, empathy usually is followed by some sort of cognitive processing that results in the empathizer experiencing sympathy, personal distress, or both (see Fig. 3.1a).

For the young child who often is still partly confused about the boundaries of one's own and the other's distress (Hoffman, 1982a; Radke–Yarrow & Zahn–Waxler, 1984; Zahn–Waxler & Radke–Yarrow, 1982), empathizing most likely leads to a self focus and a predominance of personal distress. Moreover, for children (or adults) with only a limited ability to understand why the other feels as he or she does, a predominance of personal distress may be expected. In addition, if one's empathic arousal involves a negative emotion and is very intense, the empathizer may experience "empathic overarousal" (Hoffman, 1982a), which may be so aversive that it leads primarily to personal distress (Fig. 3.1b).

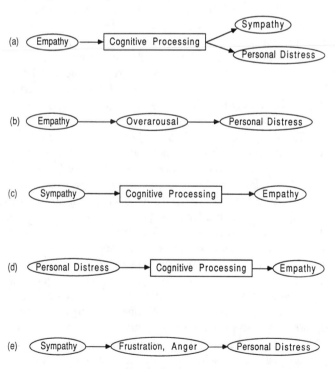

FIG. 3.1.   Interrelations of empathy, sympathy, and personal distress.

In other situations, for example, when people do not feel overwhelmed by the vicarious affect and for individuals who have the ability to amplify internally (via cognitive processes) the other's emotional state or condition, empathizing may lead to a predominance of sympathetic responding (see p. 67 for more discussion of relevant cognitive processes). This should be especially likely for people who have internalized other-oriented values (see Eisenberg, 1986; Staub, 1978, 1984) or are positively disposed toward other people (Staub, 1984). This is because such people should be predisposed emotionally to orient to others' needs, to role take, and to retrieve social scripts that include an other-oriented response and helping. Because the use of other-oriented moral reasoning (Eisenberg, 1986; Eisenberg et al., 1987), and role taking (Hoffman, 1982a; Shantz, 1975, 1983) increase with age, we would expect the likelihood of sympathetic responding to increase with age, at least in the early years and middle childhood (also see Hoffman, 1976, 1982a).

According to observational evidence, this is the case. For example, children less than a year of age frequently respond to others' distresses with general agitation whereas in the second year of life, children begin to try to assist or comfort those in distress (e.g., Dunn & Kendrick, 1982; Zahn–Waxler & Radke–Yarrow, 1982). By 2, children exhibit even more behaviors consistent with sympathizing: "Children bring objects to the person who is suffering, make suggestions about what to do, verbalize sympathy, bring someone else to help, aggressively protect the victim, and attempt to evoke a change in affect in the distressed person (Radke–Yarrow, Zahn–Waxler, & Chapman, 1983, p. 481). Moreover, there is some evidence from self-report data and facial indexes of sympathy (i.e., facial sadness/concern rather than facial anxiety/distress) that sympathy is increasing during the late preschool years. Facial indexes of sympathy/empathic sadness were found to correlate positively with age in the preschool years for girls (Eisenberg, McCreath, & Ahn, 1988), whereas self-report indexes of sympathy seem to increase from the preschool- to schoolyears (Eisenberg, Fabes, Bustamante, Mathy, Miller, & Lindholm, 1988; see Lennon & Eisenberg, 1987).

What we have been arguing is that sympathy and personal distress frequently stem from empathizing, with the likelihood of empathy leading to sympathy increasing during the early years of life. We are not, however, asserting that personal distress and sympathy always stem from empathy. It is our view that they sometimes may result from cognitive processing (see the next section). Moreover, we are not assuming that empathy can never be a consequence of sympathizing or personal distress, although we view such causal sequences as much less likely than the reverse. As a consequence of being concerned with another (sympathizing), people may try to gather more information about the other (e.g., may role take and retrieve relevant information from memory), which might then result in empathizing (Fig. 3.1c). In such a case, sympathy indirectly leads to empathy. However, given that personal distress involves a focus on one's own aversive state and possibly avoiding the aversive stimulus (Batson, 1987), it seems rather unlikely that the experience of personal distress would enhance the likelihood of subsequent empathizing. Nonetheless, it is possible that in the process of trying to reduce or validate the origin of one's personal distress, the individual occasionally will cognitively analyze the situation of the needy other in more detail, which could then lead to empathizing (based on the new information processed; Fig. 3.1d).

In addition, although people may experience sympathy and personal distress simultaneously (Batson, 1987), it seems rather unlikely that one would engender the other. If an individual is focused on his or her own aversive state and is motivated to alleviate this state, he or she is unlikely to be oriented to the person who was the aversive stimulus. Similarly, if an individual is focused on the other and is feeling concern for the other, he or she should be relatively unlikely to shift to a self-focus as a consequence. One exception might be if a person sympathizes greatly with another in a context in which he or she can do nothing to assist; in such a situation, sympathizing may result in frustration or anger, which may then be experienced as aversive (see Fig. 3.1e).

To summarize, we have suggested that empathy is a common causal antecedent of sympathy and personal distress, and that other causal relations among sympathy, personal distress, and empathy, although less likely, may occur. When other causal relations do occur, it is likely that they are due to intervening cognitive or emotional responses quite distinct from the antecedent mode of vicarious emotional responding.

Cognition as a Cause of Vicarious Emotional Responding

Now that we have considered the various ways in which vicarious emotional responses may be causally interrelated, it is appropriate to explore the ways in which the previously discussed cognitive processes (p. 67) may lead to the experiencing of vicariously induced emotions. In this discussion, it is assumed that once one vicarious reaction is induced (e.g., empathy), it may lead to further emotional responding in the ways delineated in the prior discussion.

A first assumption in regard to the role of cognition in engendering vicarious emotional responding is that very simple forms of cognition (i.e., conditioning/direct association and labeling/categorization) do not in isolation lead to sympathy (see Fig. 3.2a). This is because sympathy by definition involves more sophisticated cognitions regarding the other and his or her condition or emotional state. Rather, a conditioned reaction to cues related to the other's state or direct associations with such cues are most likely to engender either empathy or personal distress (e.g., cues embedded in the other's facial expression may elicit similar emotional responding in the observer due to prior pairing of such cues with one's own distress; see Aronfreed, 1970, and Fig. 3.2a). Of course, the empathy

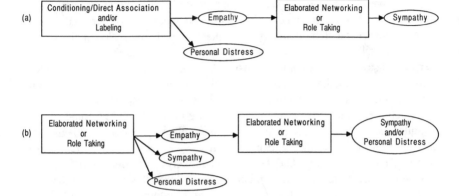

FIG. 3.2.   Cognition as a cause of vicarious emotional responding.

evoked by conditioning or direct association could, with additional cognitive processing, result in sympathetic responding. Similarly, labeling would be expected to most often result in empathy or personal distress; only if the labeling/categorization results in role taking and/or the retrieval of more complex information stored in memory would we expect such processes to indirectly cause sympathy (Fig. 3.2a).

In contrast, the retrieval of elaborated cognitive networks or role taking could logically result in personal distress, sympathy, empathy, or any combination thereof (Fig. 3.2b). If empathy is elicited, it would be expected to occur prior to sympathy or personal distress (while the individual is involved in further cognitive activity) or to occur simultaneously with sympathy or personal distress. Sympathy and personal distress are likely outcomes of higher-level cognitive processing because such processing is likely to involve an analysis of the source of the vicarious feeling and, consequently, should lead to a focus on the self or other (or both). In such a situation, empathy, sympathy, and personal distress may all initially co-occur without causal relations among them, although the experiencer's empathy is likely to then result (causally) in additional cognitive elaboration or role taking, and possibly sympathy or personal distress (Fig. 3.2b).

Whether elaborated cognitions and role taking result in personal distress, empathy, sympathy, or no vicarious emotional response is likely to be a function of characteristics of both the person and the situation. Different persons will have very different cognitive networks stored in their memories, depending on their prior experiences and perhaps on person characteristics (e.g., the individual's ability to deal with emotional arousal and to cope in general). For example, some people will associate cues concerning another's need with cognitions related to how needy others feel, how one alleviates the other's needs, and other-oriented values. Others, in the same situation, may retrieve cognitive networks in which they have stored information regarding the negative consequences of getting involved with others' problems, social scripts related to avoiding contact with needy others, negative attributions about the poor, and egoistic values (Karniol, 1985). The former set of cognitions would be expected to lead to feelings of sympathy, whereas the latter would be expected to result in the experience of personal distress.

Situational factors that affect whether cognitive elaboration and role taking result in empathy, personal distress, or sympathy probably are many and varied. For example, the aversive properties of the cues emanating from the other (e.g., the degree of blood and gore involved) should affect the probability that viewers will experience personal distress, empathy, or sympathy. The more aversive the cues, the more likely are viewers to respond to cues indicative of the other's state with personal distress (due to factors such as overarousal or negative associations). Similarly, degree of liking of the other and the valence of the relationship with the other (e.g., cooperative or competitive; Lanzetta, personal communication, July, 1987; Miller, 1987) would be expected to moderate individuals' vicarious reactions. If the stimulus other is liked or is in a positive relation with the another, the likelihood of experiencing sympathy would be expected to increase. Situational cues that provide information concerning the origins of the other's need or distress (e.g., whether the other's need is due to factors within the other's control) also appear to affect whether observers experience sympathy or negative emotions such as disgust and distain (Meyer & Mulherin, 1980; Reisenzein, 1986; Weiner, 1980; see Eisenberg, 1986; Weiner, 1986 for reviews), even for children (Barnett & McMinimy, 1988). Other situational variables that are likely to influence vicarious reactions include salience of the other's need (Pearl, 1985; see Piliavin, Dovidio, Gaertner, & Clark, 1981), similarity of the needy other to the self (Batson, 1987; Feshbach, 1978; Krebs, 1975), similarity of the situation to one which the viewer him or herself has experienced (Barnett, 1984), the cost of assisting (see Piliavin et al., 1981), and one's own ability to deal with the other's distress (Barnett, Thompson, & Pfeifer, 1986). People seem to be more likely to sympathize if (a) The other's need is clear (albeit not overwhelming), (b) The other's need is not due to factors in the needy other's control, (c) The other is perceived as similar to the self, (d) The potential sympathizer has had a similar experience as the other (although this could lead to personal distress if the prior experience was very bad), and (e) One has the competence to deal with the other's problem.

Although many situational cues will have rather uniform effects across observers, the impact of the processing of situational cues on consequent vicarious emotional responding will vary somewhat as a function of the subjective meaning of the cues to actors. For example, the same aversive cues that might result in personal distress for most people who view a drunk person lying in the gutter may elicit cognitions and social scripts related to the victim's neediness for others who have dealt with such situations more frequently and/or have developed sympathetic attitudes toward alcoholics. Obviously, the subjective meaning of a given situation will vary as a function of the individual's prior experience and learning. Thus, both personal and situational factors must be determinants of mode of vicarious emotional responding in a given situation, as well as whether or not an individual even responds affectively.

Vicarious Emotion as a Cause of Cognitive Responding

In the previous section, we discussed the ways in which cognition might elicit vicarious emotions and touched upon causal sequences in which these resulting vicarious emotions may lead to further cognitive processing and subsequent emotional responses. Here we elaborate on the ways in which cognitions could be a consequence of vicarious emotional responding.

Because empathy involves some degree of self–other differentiation and at least the partial recognition of the source of one's vicarious responding, empathy (as thus defined) cannot occur without some prior cognitive processing. However, in most instances, one would expect additional cognitive processing subsequent to the onset of the empathic affect. This additional cognition could be relatively primitive (conditioning, direct association, or simple categorization) or more sophisticated (retrieval of elaborated cognitive networks and/or role taking; see Fig. 3.3). In some instances, the experience of empathizing with a negative affect may elicit further anxiety due to a simple association between experiencing the given emotion and negative consequences. For example, a boy who has been ridiculed by his parents for exhibiting fear may experience anxiety as a consequence of empathically induced fear due to cognitions that link fear with ridicule (see Buck, 1984). In such an instance, personal distress would be a likely

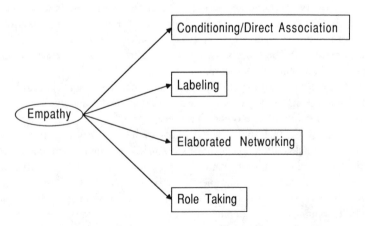

FIG. 3.3. Vicarious emotion as a cause of cognitive responding.

consequence of the simple cognitions that were evoked by the child's empathic fear (assuming that additional simple cognitive processes were used to identify the anxiety as an aversive feeling).

In many situations, however, empathizing is likely to result in higher-level cognitive processing because the empathic reaction will stimulate efforts to understand the origins of the vicarious affect and/or the situation which elicited the response. Especially if the empathic affect is strong enough to capture the empathizer's attention, he or she is will probably retrieve relevant information from memory, including entire networks of associated cognitions. Moreover, the empathizer may use any information stored in memory relevant to the other to try to make inferences about the other's state or situation (i.e., role take). Given that one's relevant cognitive network would be expected to become more elaborated with experience and that role-taking skills increase with age (Shantz, 1983), it is reasonable to assume that older and more experienced persons will be more likely than younger and less experienced persons to engage in higher-level cognitive processing as a function of empathizing.

As was discussed previously, we assume that sympathy cannot occur without the involvement of higher-order cognitive processing. Thus, it is only when empathy instigates the retrieval of relevant information from memory (e.g., concerning the needy other or values related to social behavior) or role taking that sympathy can be expected to be a result of empathizing.

Now we have come full circle; we have discussed causal sequences in which vicarious emotion elicits cognitive processing and vice versa. Clearly, there are many possible patterns of relations, although it can be argued that some sequences are logically impossible or are unlikely to occur. Those that we see as most likely are diagrammed in Fig. 3.4; entry points into a sequence are multiple and are indicated in this figure.

Traits and Relations Among Cognitive and Affective Responding

Thus far, we have discussed the relations among vicarious emotions and cognitive processes in a given situation. Therefore, we have been discussing *state* emotional and cognitive responses, not characteristic ways of responding emotionally or cognitively. However, in some of the research reviewed previously, researchers have examined the relations between vicarious affective responding and cognition using dispositional indexes of one or both constructs. Indeed, it is a common assumption in the literature that people who characteristically role take are those who are high in trait or state empathy and sympathy (e.g., Batson, 1987; Davis et al., 1987; Eisenberg, 1986; Krebs & Russell, 1981).

As reviewed previously, there is some evidence for these assumptions; significant relations frequently have been found between role taking (often operationalized in ways that could reflect labeling or retrieval of elaborated cognitive

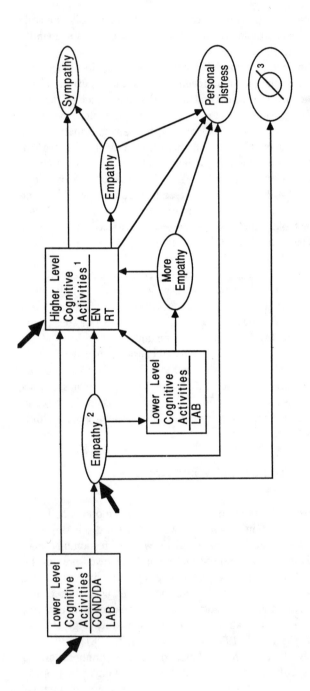

Possible entry points into the causal chain.

1. Any individual or combination of listed cognitive activities may be performed and there causal links between those listed within a box.
2. Empathy always requires at least some very simple cognitive activities (simpler than those listed as lower level) that are not represented in this model.
3. Emotional reaction is terminated if attention is diverted, the affect is fleeting, or the empathy is not processed further.

LEGEND

COND/DA = Conditioning or Direct Association
LAB = Labeling
EN = Elaborated Networking
RT = Role Taking

FIG. 3.4. A model of the various causal relations among vicarious emotion responding and cognition.

82

networks) and empathy/sympathy when one or both were operationalized as a trait (see p. 73). However, as has been noted frequently, role taking, as well as the retrieval of networks of information, are cognitive processes that can be used for a variety of purposes, egoistic or altruistic. For example, role taking can be used to understand others so that one can better manipulate people and achieve egoistic goals. Indeed, people who are especially adept at figuring out and managing other people may excel in role-taking capabilities. Thus, one would not expect a strong, consistent relation between the trait (or state) of role taking and the trait (or state) of sympathetic or empathic responding.

The variability in the link between cognition and vicarious emotional reactions has important implications for the causal models we have presented. This variability suggests that the paths in our models are at best probabilistic because there are individual differences not only in the availability of cognitive strategies that may lead to various vicarious emotional responses, but also in the specific function for which the cognitive strategies may be used. Although the psychological constructs that are the source of these individual differences are at present unclear, it seems reasonable to speculate that constructs such as social motives, social values, or social orientations are likely candidates. For example, social orientations that are other-oriented are likely to lead to different cognition-emotion links than do social orientations that are self-oriented (Staub, 1984), and there is limited evidence of consistent individual differences in the social orientations of adults and children (e.g., Bem & Lord, 1979; Karylowski, 1982; Knight, 1981; Kuhlman & Marshello, 1975; Liebrand, 1984). Moreover, there seem to be individual differences in the tendency to augment or avoid vicarious emotional responding by means of processes such as empathy, role taking, and elaborating and personalizing others' situations and reactions (e.g., Larsen et al., 1987), differences that may be present from an early age (Radke–Yarrow & Zahn–Waxler, 1984). People who seek affective intensity appear to engage cognitive processes (such as role taking) that enhance the likelihood of responding emotionally (Larsen et al., 1987). Thus, some people are more likely than others to even engage in the processes presented in our models (rather than simply ignoring, minimizing, distorting, or misinterpreting cues related to others' states). Clearly the ways in which individual difference variables affect the interrelations of vicarious affective responding and cognitive processing is a topic which merits further attention.

CONCLUSIONS

In summary, although cognitive processes and/or emotional responses (especially empathy) are critical concepts in many theories and models of moral development (e.g., Batson, 1987; Eisenberg, 1986; Feshbach, 1978; Hoffman, 1984), there has been debate concerning the definitions of various emotional responses and the relations of these responses to cognitive processes. We have attempted to address some of the definitional issues apparent in this research and to speculate on the interrelations among relevant cognitive processes and emotional responses. We believe that the causal relations between these cognitive processes and emotional responses clearly are not simple or unidirectional. In addition, it is likely that the causal links among cognitive processes, vicarious emotional responses, and moral behaviors also are not simple or unidirectional. For example, we can easily envision circumstances in which empathy, sympathy, or personal distress could lead to behavior that outwardly appears to be moral (although some apparently moral behavior is not motivated by moral concerns). Similarly, we can envision circumstances in which moral behaviors result from some particular cognitive processes (such as retrieval of a cognitive network) and then lead to a subsequent cognitive processing and emotional responding. Ultimately, a better understanding of moral behavior and moral development will likely require greater understanding of the links between cognitive processes and vicarious emotional responding, as well as the links between these and moral behavior.

REFERENCES

Abelson, R. P. (1976). Script processing in attitude formation and decision making. In J. S. Carroll & J. W. Payne (Eds.), *Cognition and social behavior* (pp. 33–45). Hillsdale, NJ: Lawrence Erlbaum Associates.

Allport, G. W. (1937). *Personality: A psychological interpretation.* New York: Holt.

Aronfreed, J. (1968). *Conduct and conscience: The socialization of internalized control over behavior.* New York: Academic Press.

Aronfreed, J. (1970). The socialization of altruistic and sympathetic behavior: Some theoretical and experimental analyses. In J. Macaulay & L. Berkowitz (Eds.), *Altruism and helping behavior* (pp. 103–126), New York: Academic Press.

Barnett, M. A. (1984). Similarity of experience and empathy in preschoolers. *Journal of Genetic Psychology, 145,* 241–250.

Barnett, M. A., & McMinimy, V. (1988). Influence of the reason for the other's affect on preschoolers' empathic response. *Journal of Genetic Psychology, 149,* 153–162.

Barnett, M. A., Thompson, M. A., & Pfeifer, J. R. (1986). Perceived competence to help and the arousal of empathy. *Journal of Social Psychology, 125,* 679–680.

Batson, C. D. (1987). Prosocial motivation: Is it ever truly altruistic? In L. Berkowitz (Ed.), *Advances in experimental social psychology* (pp. 65–122). New York: Academic Press.

Batson, C. D., Bolen, M. H., Cross, J. A., & Neuringer–Benefiel, H. E. (1986). Where is the altruism in the altruistic personality? *Journal of Personality and Social Psychology, 50,* 212–220.

Bem, D. J., & Lord, C. A. (1979). Template matching: A proposal for probing the ecological validity of experimental settings in social psychology. *Journal of Personality and Social Psychology, 37,* 833–846.

Blum, L. A. (1980). *Friendship, altruism and morality.* London: Routledge & Kegan Paul.

Borke, H. (1971). Interpersonal perception of young children: Egocentrism or empathy. *Developmental Psychology, 5,* 262–269.

Bryant, B. (1982). An index of empathy for children and adolescents. *Child Development, 53*, 413–425.

Buck, R. (1984). *The communication of emotion.* New York: Guilford Press.

Chandler, M. J., & Greenspan, S. (1972). Ersatz egocentrism: A reply to H. Borke. *Developmental Psychology, 7*, 104–106.

Davis, M. (1980). A multidimensional approach to individual differences in empathy. *JSAS Catalog of Selected Documents in Psychology, 10*, 85.

Davis, M. H. (1983a). The effects of dispositional empathy on emotional reactions and helping: A multidimensional approach. *Journal of Personality, 51*, 167–184.

Davis, M. H. (1983b). Measuring individual differences in empathy: Evidence for a multidimensional approach. *Journal of Personality and Social Psychology, 44*, 113–126.

Davis, M. H., Hull, J. G., Young, R. D., & Warren, G. (1987). Emotional reactions to dramatic film stimuli: The influence of cognitive and emotional empathy. *Journal of Personality and Social Psychology, 52*, 126–133.

Deutsch, F., & Madle, R. A. (1975). Empathy: Historic and current conceptualizations, and a cognitive theoretical perspective. *Human Development, 18*, 267–287.

Dunn, J., & Kendrick, C. (1982). *Siblings: Love, envy, and understanding.* Cambridge, MA: Harvard University Press.

Dymond, R. F. (1949). A scale for the measurement of empathetic ability. *Journal of Consulting Psychology, 13*, 27–33.

Eisenberg, N. (1986). *Altruistic emotion, cognition and behavior.* Hillsdale, NJ: Lawrence Erlbaum Associates.

Eisenberg, N., Fabes, R. A., Bustamante, D., Mathy, R. M., Miller, P. A., & Lindholm, E. (1988). Differentiation of vicariously induced emotional reactions in children. *Developmental Psychology, 24*, 237–246.

Eisenberg–Berg, N., & Lennon, R. (1980). Altruism and the assessment of empathy in the preschool years. *Child Development, 51*, 552–557.

Eisenberg, N., & Lennon, R. (1983). Sex differences in empathy and related capacities. *Psychological Bulletin, 94*, 100–131.

Eisenberg, N., McCreath, H., & Ahn, R. (1988). Vicarious emotional responsiveness and prosocial behavior: Their interrelations in young children. *Personality and Social Psychology Bulletin, 14*, 298–311.

Eisenberg, N., & Miller, P. (1987). The relation of empathy to prosocial and related behaviors. *Psychological Bulletin, 101*, 91–119.

Eisenberg, N., Miller, P. A., Schaller, M., Fabes, R. A., Fultz, J., Shell, R., & Shea, C. (1989). The role of sympathy and altruistic personality traits in helping: A re-examination. *Journal of Personality, 57*, 41–67.

Eisenberg, N., Shell, R., Pasternack, J., Lennon, R., Beller, R., & Mathy, R. M. (1987). Prosocial development in middle childhood: A longitudinal study. *Developmental Psychology, 23*, 712–718.

Eisenberg, N., & Strayer, J. (1987). Critical issues in the study of empathy. In N. Eisenberg & J. Strayer (Eds.), *Empathy and its development* (pp. 3–13). Cambridge, England: Cambridge University Press.

Eisenberg–Berg, N., & Hand, M. (1979). The relationship of preschoolers' reasoning about prosocial moral conflicts to prosocial behavior. *Child Development, 50*, 356–363.

Feshbach, N. D. (1978). Studies of empathic behavior in children. In B. A. Maher (Ed.), *Progress in experimental personality research* (Vol. 8, pp. 1–47). New York: Academic Press.

Feshbach, N. D., & Roe, K. (1968). Empathy in six- and seven-year-olds. *Child Development, 39*, 133–145.

Flavell, J. H., Botkin, P., Fry, C., Wright, J., & Jarvis, P. (1968). *The development of role-taking and communication skills in children.* New York: Wiley.

Goldstein, A. P., & Michaels, G. Y. (1985). *Empathy: Development, training, and consequences.* Hillsdale, NJ: Lawrence Erlbaum Associates.

Higgins, E. T. (1981). Role taking and social judgement: Alternative perspectives and processes. In J. H. Flavell & L. Ross (Eds.), *Social cognitive development* (pp. 119–153). Cambridge, England: University of Cambridge Press.

Higgins, E. T., Feldman, N. S., & Ruble, D. N. (1980). Accuracy and differentiation in social prediction: A developmental analysis. *Journal of Personality, 48*, 520–540.

Hoffman, M. L. (1982a). Development of prosocial motivation: Empathy and guilt. In N. Eisenberg (Ed.), *The development of prosocial behavior* (pp. 218–231). New York: Academic Press.

Hoffman, M. L. (1982b). The measurement of empathy. In C. E. Izard (Ed.), *Measuring emotions in infants and children* (pp. 279–296). Cambridge, England: Cambridge University Press.

Hoffman, M. L. (1984). Interaction of affect and cognition on empathy. In C. E. Izard, J. Kagan, & R. B. Zajonc (Eds.), *Emotions, cognition, and behavior* (pp. 103–131). Cambridge, England: Cambridge University Press.

Hoffman, M. L. (1987). The contribution of empathy to justice and moral judgement. In N. Eisenberg & J. Strayer (Eds.), *Empathy and its development* (pp. 47–80). Cambridge, England: Cambridge University Press.

Howard, J. A., & Barnett, M. A. (1981). Arousal of empathy and subsequent generosity in young children. *Journal of Genetic Psychology, 138*, 307–308.

Iannotti, R. J. (1977). *Empathy and the relationship to role taking and altruism: A longitudinal investigation.* Unpublished manuscript, Marietta College, OH.

Iannotti, R. J. (1978). Effect of role-taking experiences on role taking, empathy, altruism, and aggression. *Developmental Psychology, 14*, 119–124.

Iannotti, R. J. (1985). Naturalistic and structured assessments of prosocial behavior in preschool children: The influence of empathy and perspective taking. *Developmental Psychology, 21*, 46–55.

Iannotti, R. J., & Pierrehumbert, B. (1985, April). *The development of empathy in early childhood.* Paper presented at the biennal meeting of the Society for Research in Child Development, Toronto.

Karniol, R. (1982). Settings, scripts, and self-schemata: A cognitive analysis of the development of prosocial behavior. In N. Eisenberg (Ed.), *The development of prosocial behavior* (pp. 251–278). New York: Academic Press.

Karniol, R. (1985). Children's causal scripts and derogation of the poor: An attributional analysis. *Journal of Personality and Social Psychology, 48*, 791–798.

Karylowski, J. (1982). Two types of altruistic behavior: Doing good to feel good or to make the other feel good. In V. J. Derlega & J. Grzelak (Eds.), *Cooperation and helping behavior: Theories and research* (pp. 397–413). New York: Academic Press.

Knight, G. P. (1981). Behavioral and sociometric methods of identifying cooperators, competitors, and individualists: Support for the validity of the social orientation construct. *Developmental Psychology, 17*, 430–433.

Kohlberg, L. (1976). Moral stage and moralization: The cognitive-developmental approach. In T. Lickona (Ed.), *Moral development and behavior: Theory, research, and social issues* (pp. 84–107). New York: Holt, Rinehart, & Winston.

Krebs, D. (1975). Empathy and altruism. *Journal of Personality and Social Psychology, 32*, 1134–1141.

Krebs, D., & Russell, C. (1981). Role-taking and altruism. In J. P. Rushton & R. M. Sorrentino (Eds.), *Altruism and helping behavior: Social, personality, and developmental perspectives* (pp. 137–165). Hillsdale, NJ: Lawrence Erlbaum Associates.

Kuhlman, D. M., & Marshello, A. (1975). Individual differences in game motivation as moderators of pre-programmed strategy effects in prisoner's dilemma. *Journal of Personality and Social Psychology, 32*, 922–931.

Larsen, R. J., & Diener, E. (1985). A multitrait-multi method examination of affect structure: Hedonic level and emotional intensity. *Personality and Individual Differences, 6*, 631–636.

Larsen, R. J., & Diener, E. (1987). Affect intensity as an individual difference characteristic: A review. *Journal of Research in Personality, 21,* 1–39.

Larsen, R. J., Diener, E., & Cropanzano, R. S. (1987). Cognitive operations associated with individual differences in affect intensity. *Journal of Personality and Social Psychology, 53,* 767–774.

Lennon, R., & Eisenberg, N. (1987). Gender and age differences in empathy and sympathy. In N. Eisenberg & J. Strayer (Eds.), *Empathy and its development* (pp. 195–217). Cambridge, England: Cambridge University Press.

Lennon, R., Eisenberg, N., & Carroll, J. (1986). The relation between empathy and prosocial behavior in the preschool years. *Journal of Applied Developmental Psychology, 17,* 219–224.

Liebrand, W. B. G. (1984). The effect of social motives, communication and group size on behavior in a N-person, multi-stage, mixed-motive game. *European Journal of Social Psychology, 14,* 239–264.

Mead, G. H. (1934). *Mind, self, & society.* Chicago: University of Chicago Press.

Meyer, J. P., & Mulherin, A. (1980). From attribution to helping: An analysis of the mediating effects of affect and expectancy. *Journal of Personality and Social Psychology, 39,* 201–210.

Miller, R. S. (1987). Empathic embarrassment: Situational and personal determinants of reactions to the embarrassment of another. *Journal of Personality and Social Psychology, 53,* 1061–1069.

Miller, P. A., & Eisenberg, N. (1988). The relation of empathy to aggression and psychopathology: A meta-analysis. *Psychological Bulletin, 103,* 324–344.

Nelson, K. (1981). Social cognition in a script framework. In J. H. Flavell & L. Ross (Eds.), *Social cognitive development: Frontiers and possible futures* (pp. 97–118). Cambridge, England: Cambridge University Press.

Pearl, R. (1985). Children's understanding of others' need for help: Effects of problem explicitness and type. *Child Development, 56,* 735–745.

Piliavin, J. A., Dovidio, J. F., Gaertner, S. L., & Clark, R. D., III. (1981). Responsive bystanders: The process of intervention. In V. J. Derlega & J. Grzelak (Eds.), *Cooperation and helping behavior: Theories and Research* (pp. 279–304). New York: Academic Press.

Plutchik, R. (1987). Evolutionary bases of empathy. In N. Eisenberg & J. Strayer (Eds.), *Empathy and its development* (pp. 38–46). Cambridge, England: Cambridge University Press.

Radke–Yarrow, M., & Zahn–Waxler, C. (1984). Roots, motives, and patterns in children's prosocial behavior. In E. Staub, D. Bar-Tal, J. Karylowski, & J. Reykowski (Eds.), *Development and maintenance of prosocial behavior: International perspectives on positive behavior* (pp. 81–99). New York: Plenum Press.

Radke–Yarrow, M., Zahn–Waxler, C., & Chapman, M. (1983). Children's prosocial dispositions and behaviors. In P. H. Mussen (Ed.), *Handbook of child psychology. Vol. 4: Socialization, personality, and social development* (pp. 469–545). New York: Wiley.

Reisenzein, R. (1986). A structural equation analysis of Weiner's attribution-affect model of helping behavior. *Journal of Personality and Social Psychology, 50,* 1123–1133.

Schank, R. C., & Abelson, R. P. (1977). *Scripts, plans, goals, and understanding.* Hillsdale, NJ: Lawrence Erlbaum Associates.

Selman, R. L. (1980). *The growth of interpersonal understanding: Developmental and clinical analyses.* New York: Academic Press.

Selman, R. L., & Byrne, D. F. (1974). A structural-developmental analysis of levels of role taking in middle childhood. *Child Development, 45,* 803–806.

Shantz, C. U. (1975). The development of social cognition. In E. M. Hetherington (Ed.), *Review of child development research* (Vol. 5, pp. 257–323). Chicago: University of Chicago Press.

Shantz, C. U. (1983). Social cognition. In P. H. Mussen (Ed.), *Handbook of child psychology. Vol. 3: Cognitive development* (pp. 495–595). New York: Wiley.

Shelton, M. L., & Rogers, R. W. (1981). Fear-arousing and empathy-arousing appeals to help: The pathos of persuasion. *Journal of Applied Social Psychology, 11,* 366–378.

Staub, E. (1978). *Positive social behavior and morality. Vol. 1: Social and personal influences.* New York: Academic Press.

Staub, E. (1984). Steps toward a comprehensive theory of moral conduct: Goal orientation, social behavior, kindness and cruelty. In J. Gewirtz & W. Kurtines (Eds.), *Morality, moral development, and moral behavior: Basic issues in theory and research* (pp. 241–260). New York: Wiley.

Staub, E. (1987). Commentary on Part I. In N. Eisenberg & J. Strayer (Eds.), *Empathy and its development* (pp. 103–115). Cambridge, England: Cambridge University Press.

Strayer, J. (1987). Affective and cognitive perspectives in empathy. In N. Eisenberg & J. Strayer (Eds.), *Empathy and its development* (pp. 218–244). Cambridge, England: Cambridge University Press.

Strayer, J., & Roberts, W. L. (1984). *Children's empathy, role-taking, and related factors.* Unpublished manuscript, Simon Fraser University, Burnaby, British Columbia.

Thompson, R. A. (1987). Empathy and emotional understanding: The early development of empathy. In N. Eisenberg & J. Strayer (Eds.), *Empathy and its development* (pp. 119–145). Cambridge, England: Cambridge University Press.

Toi, M., & Batson, C. D. (1982). More evidence that empathy is a source of altruistic motivation. *Journal of Personality and Social Psychology, 43,* 281–292.

Underwood, B., & Moore, B. (1982). Perspective-taking and altruism. *Psychological Bulletin, 91,* 143–173.

Weiner, B. (1980). A cognitive (attribution)-emotion-action model of motivated behavior: An analysis of judgements of help giving. *Journal of Personality and Social Psychology, 39,* 186–200.

Weiner, B. (1986). *An attributional theory of motivation and emotion.* New York: Springer–Verlag.

Wispe, L. (1986). The distinction between sympathy and empathy: To call forth a concept, a word is needed. *Journal of Personality and Social Psychology, 50,* 314–321.

Wispe, L. (1987). History of the concept of empathy. In N. Eisenberg & J. Strayer (Eds.), *Empathy and its development* (pp. 17–37). Cambridge, England: Cambridge University Press.

Zahn–Waxler, C., & Radke–Yarrow, M. (1982). The development of altruism: Alternative research strategies. In N. Eisenberg (Ed.), *The development of prosocial behavior* (pp. 109–137). New York: Academic Press.

The Development of Socio-Moral Meaning Making: Domains, Categories, and Perspective-Taking

Monika Keller
Wolfgang Edelstein

ABSTRACT

This chapter presents an integrative approach to social cognitive and moral development by showing how descriptive (social) and prescriptive (moral) reasoning are interconnected in socio-moral meaning making. It is argued that socio-moral meaning making is based on processes of perspective differentiation and coordination through which persons come to understand descriptive and prescriptive aspects of social reality. In order to clarify structure and content aspects of socio-moral reasoning, first, conflicting theoretical positions about perspective-taking and domains of reasoning are discussed. Second, a reinterpretation of structure and content aspects of socio-moral meaning making in an action-theoretical framework is proposed. Third, this approach is exemplified with reference to longitudinal data about the development of socio-moral meaning making in a morally relevant conflict in a close friendship.

INTRODUCTION

This chapter deals with the development of socio-moral meaning making in intimate relationships such as friendship. We argue that growing interpersonal and moral awareness is based on processes of perspective differentiation and coordination through which persons come to understand descriptive aspects (what is the case) and prescriptive aspects (what ought to be the case) of social relations. Thus we pursue an integrative approach to social cognitive and moral development by showing how descriptive and prescriptive aspects of social reasoning are interconnected in the developing understanding of relationships and moral rules.

Three basic assumptions characterize this approach:

1. We understand the unfolding of socio-moral meaning as the construction in and through development of a naive theory of social action. In the course of development, the categories of the naive theory of social action are differentiated and coordinated into more encompassing systems of meaning.

2. A central part of socio-moral meaning making is the development of a conception of self as an intentional and responsible agent.

3. The different forms of organization of the categories of the naive theory of social action and moral agency can be described and explained in terms of processes of perspective differentiation and coordination.

In the following, we *first,* discuss conflicting theoretical positions about the concept of perspective-taking in social and moral development. *Second,* we develop our own approach to socio-moral meaning making and, *third,* empirical data are presented about the development of notions of obligation and responsibility in friendship.

PERSPECTIVE-TAKING AND DOMAINS OF SOCIAL AND MORAL REASONING

The cognitive-structural tradition reaches back to the work of Piaget (1970, 1983) and Mead (1934). The focus of concern in this tradition is on formal competence to differentiate and coordinate perspectives of self and other. But because structural theories neglect content, significant aspects of interaction, the intrapsychic world of self and others (e.g., feelings, intentions, expectations) and the types of relationships and social rules that serve to coordinate the transactions of self and other have virtually been ignored by these theories. Only recently have domains and categories of social reasoning been specified. Two contradictory positions have been formulated with regard to the meaning of perspective-taking and the meaning of content domains in social cognition: On the one hand Selman (1980) and Kohlberg (1976, 1984) distinguished the two broad domains of descriptive social understanding and prescriptive moral judgment. The concept of perspective-taking represents the logical core of these two domains. On the other hand Turiel (1983a, 1983b) has argued that different domains of social reasoning represent distinct conceptual systems with distinct organizational features. The concept of perspective-taking is defined as a cognitive skill which is not amenable to description in structural terms. These contrasting positions are discussed.

The Position of Kohlberg and Selman

According to Kohlberg (1984; Colby & Kohlberg, 1987) and Selman (1980) the domain of *descriptive* social reasoning encompasses reflections on the psychological states of the self, on other persons, and on relationships between persons. The *prescriptive* domain encompasses deontic judgments of what is right and obligatory in terms of moral standards that regulate relationships between persons. Both Selman and Kohlberg argue that the two realms form distinct conceptual systems but that they develop in parallel sequences. To account for content, both realms are subdivided into subdomains and categories. Thus, Selman distinguishes the understanding of persons from the understanding of relationships. Within the subdomain of "persons" specific categories of understanding are differentiated, such as understanding the subjective world of others in terms of thoughts, feelings, and motives. Within the subdomain of "relations" the concept of friendship is defined by categories such as closeness, trust, and conflict resolution. In the domain of prescriptive reasoning content is represented through the different types of moral rules or norms (issues) such as property, promise-keeping, or authority and the moral values (elements) supporting the validity of these norms.

Within each domain reasoning is taken to be homogeneous, and both authors present empirical evidence to the effect that stages form structured wholes (Colby, Kohlberg, Gibbs, & Lieberman, 1983; Selman, 1980). Thus, content aspects in social and moral reasoning seem to be of little developmental importance. According to Kohlberg and Selman the consistency found in the two domains is due to the structure of perspective-taking, which is seen as the organizational or logical core common to both descriptive and prescriptive reasoning. Selman (1980) defined five levels of social perspective-taking which form a hierarchically ordered sequence in which each lower level is integrated into a more differentiated and more complex level above it. The sequence starts with level 0 where the child confuses the perspectives of self and other. At level 1 perspectives of self and other can be differentiated and the individual realizes that thoughts and feelings of self and others can be distinct. At level 2 perspectives of self and other are coordinated in the sense that self knows that other can consider self's subjective viewpoints and that self can reflect on his or her own subjectivity. At level 3 self and other can mutually and simultaneously reflect on each other's subjective points of view. At level 4 a general societal viewpoint is constructed that transcends individual perspectives. This formal sequence of perspective fusion, differentiation, and various forms of coordination of perspectives is reconstructed within the different content domains and categories of social reasoning.

In his recent research, Selman (Selman, Beardslee, Schultz, Krupa, & Podorefsky, 1986) has used the concept of perspective-taking as a heuristic tool for the analysis of understanding strategies of interaction both at the conceptual and at the behavioral level. It is noteworthy that when the focus is on interpersonal strategies (which in fact represent a content category within the subdomain of understanding relationships, namely the issue of conflict resolution) different types of relations are treated as content categories. Thus, friendship and authority relationships represent different contexts for the analysis of interpersonal negotiations (Adalbjarnardóttir & Selman, 1989). We shall return to this question below (see p. 00)

In Kohlberg's work two contrary positions can be distinguished with regard to the concept and the meaning of perspective taking in moral judgment. In his earlier statements, Kohlberg (1976) distinguished a descriptive social perspective and a prescriptive socio-moral perspective: "From our point of view, however, there is a more general structural construct which underlies both role-taking and moral judgment. This is the concept of socio-moral perspective, which refers to the point of view the individual takes in defining both social facts and socio-moral values or oughts" (p. 33). Thus a socio-moral perspective is taken to underlie both descriptive social reasoning and prescriptive moral judgment.

In his later work Kohlberg appears to adopt a different position: "Let us again say that we believe the perspective-taking underlying the moral stages is intrinsically moral in nature rather than a logical or social-cognitive structure applied to the moral domain. In this interpretation we agree with Turiel (1979) and Damon (1983) in their contention that there are many types of perspective-taking, each of which develops separately, although not necessarily independently, as a result of experience in a particular domain. In this view spatial, social, and moral perspective-taking are fundamentally different processes rather than applications of a single general structure to different content areas" (Colby & Kohlberg, 1987, p. 16). Although the basic distinction between a descriptive social and a prescriptive moral perspective is maintained here, it is no longer claimed that the latter represents a more general structure underlying both social and moral reasoning and defining both social facts and moral values. The assumed general structure has been transformed into partial structures of perspective-taking, among which moral or *prescriptive* perspective-taking represents but one.

This socio-moral perspective defines the types of relationship between the self and society's moral rules and expectations (Kohlberg, 1976; Colby & Kohlberg, 1987). At the preconventional level—the first two stages of moral judgment— the perspective is that of "isolated individuals," a perspective where social expectations are something external to the self. Stage 1 perspective represents the naive generalization of the concrete individual's point of view. Different interests of others are neither recognized nor considered. At stage 2 an awareness of different points of view emerges and the solution of moral conflicts is deter-

mined by pragmatic exchanges. "At stage two, in serving my interests, I anticipate the other guy's reaction, negative or positive, and he anticipates mine.
(And, the present authors would add: I know that he anticipates mine.) Unless we
make a deal, each will put his own point of view first. If we make a deal each of
us will do something for the other" (Colby & Kohlberg, 1987, p. 23). At the
conventional level—stages 3 and 4 of moral judgment—the person takes the
shared viewpoint of the participants in a relationship or a group. The stage 3
perspective is that of a member of relationships where shared feelings and expectations take primacy over individual interests. At stage 4 the member-of-society
perspective serves to assess individual relationships in view of their function in
the social system that defines rules and roles. The postconventional level—
stages 5 and 6 of moral judgment—is characterized as the perspective of any
rational moral human being. This implies the distinction between moral and legal
points of view: "That is, the moral perspective is a prior-to-society view of basic
human rights and welfare, and social systems are seen as derivative from this
prior, ethical perspective." The socio-moral perspective forms the structural
core of the level specific moral judgments as assessed through the different
content-issues (Colby et al., 1987).

Turiel's Position

Turiel (1983a, 1983b) has established a comprehensive frame of reference for the
study of social and moral reasoning. He proposed three broad domains that in his
view correspond to well-defined domains of social reality that are also the object
space of specific social science disciplines (psychology, sociology/an-
thropology, and moral philosophy): These three domains are defined as follows:

1. The psychological domain encompasses knowledge or concepts of persons, including self and others, with regard to psychological attributes such as
feelings, motives, intentions as well as stable or enduring personality characteristics.

2. The social domain contains knowledge about how people interact or relate
to each other, more specifically about social rules and conventions, social roles,
relations and institutions.

3. The moral domain refers to knowledge about what is right in terms of
concepts of justice (or other moral principles).

This domain classification is not incompatible with that of Selman and
Kohlberg as far as the demarcation of content domains and categories is concerned. Yet, Turiel differs from Kohlberg and Selman in the amount of specificity he ascribes to such content domains in terms of underlying organization and
structure. The knowledge systems, even within domains, do not necessarily form

structured wholes. Rather they are taken to represent partial structures, each with their own organizational principles and developmental logic. It is the task of the researcher to define meaningful domains, delineate the boundaries between them, and reconstruct their developmental logic.

Furthermore, in Turiel's view, the concept of perspective-taking has no explanatory function for the structural organization of such content domains. In contradistinction to the definition of *domains of knowledge* as objects of structural analysis, perspective-taking is defined as a *method* of gaining information about the social world. Some examples follow: Knowledge about behaviors and psychological states (thoughts and feelings); knowledge of social groups, and of rules, laws and regulations of social systems. Through the use of the method of perspective-taking the individual attempts to reproduce what is given in the external environment. The method therefore does not constitute an organized system and does not undergo structural change. Rather, with increasing age there may be *quantitative* changes in methods, such as increments in their accuracy and scope (Turiel, 1983a, p. 70). Thus, in contradistinction to the cognitive-structural position that Selman and Kohlberg adopt, perspective differentiation and coordination is not the central cognitive process in the construction of meaning within knowledge systems. Rather it is interpreted as an ''information processing skill'' in the service of acquisition or reproduction of information about different aspects of the social world.

RECONSTRUCTING PERSPECTIVE-TAKING: STRUCTURE AND CONTENT ASPECTS OF SOCIO-MORAL MEANING MAKING

The distinction of structure and content aspects in social and moral reasoning is a necessary and relevant task. Yet at present sufficient clarification of this question has not been achieved. There are problems with regard to both structure and content aspects. In what follows our concern is first with the system for classifying content and then with the structural aspect.

While the differentiation of descriptive and prescriptive social cognition and the within-domain differentiation of persons, relations, and rules represent necessary conceptual distinctions, the reconstruction of their meaning—whether in general or in the context of defining and solving specific problems—necessarily draws on more than one category. Therefore, understanding within one domain must be seen, in principle, as mediated by the others. We exemplify this with reference to the concept of friendship, which is central for the empirical data presented in this chapter. Reconstructing the meaning of a relationship such as friendship necessarily implies understanding of the intrapsychic dimensions of persons, such as their feelings, intentions, or expectations towards each other. On the other hand, understanding friendship involves not only descriptive, but also prescriptive knowledge according to which actions, feelings, intentions, expectations, or persons performing such actions or characterized by such intra-psychic processes are judged as responsible or irresponsible in the light of normative standards of how one ought to act as a good friend. Thus, friendship cannot be exclusively subsumed under the domain of descriptive social reasoning or knowledge. Rather, it depends on the person and the situation or context whether in reconstructing the meaning of friendship descriptive or prescriptive aspects become salient.

Furthermore, in making descriptive or prescriptive judgments, persons may draw on the same conceptual categories, e.g., feelings, intentions, expectations or relations. Thus, in our opinion, there is no reason to distinguish between social, and socio-moral perspective-taking, as Kohlberg (p. 00) proposes. Rather, perspective-taking operates in either descriptive or prescriptive contexts. It is an empirical question to determine which categories persons use in reconstructing the meaning of actions, relations, and rules in different contexts (e.g., descriptive or prescriptive) at different points in development.

Socio-moral Meaning Making as the Development of Naive Concepts of Action

In an earlier work we proposed that the distinction between components and categories of socio-moral meaning making should be derived from the concept of action (Keller & Reuss, 1984). This approach was predicated on the assumption that socio-moral meaning making develops in contexts of human action (Damon, 1989; Eckensberger, 1984). Thus, the study of socio-moral meaning making calls for a phenomenological and hermeneutic approach where the focus is on the person's construction and interpretation of situations.

The categories of socio-moral meaning making concerning a specific action context comprise both typical (general) and situation-specific knowledge about actions, persons, and relationships, as well as rules governing interactions and relationships. They refer to both social facts (what is the case) and moral facts (what ought to be the case in view of normative standards). *Descriptive* social knowledge refers to social facts or explanatory categories, such as "reasons for action" in terms of a person's intentions. Descriptive social knowledge encompasses subjective preferences, hopes, interests, expectations, or feelings as well as knowledge about consequences of actions for others, self and the relationship between self and other; finally knowledge about strategies that serve to achieve certain goals. *Prescriptive* knowledge refers to actions that are allowed, prohibited, responsible, or irresponsible in view of normative standards, such as moral or conventional standards. This type of knowledge refers to shared or intersubjectively valid norms or values according to which the members of a group, or people in general, ought to orient their behavior. These norms provide persons not only with "reasons for action" in the sense of descriptive social cognition, but with "good" or "prima facie" and morally justified reasons (Ross, 1963) and with evaluative standards according to which actions or persons are judged in cases of complying with or violating norms. From the validity claims of these norms individuals derive the knowledge that certain intentions and the means used to pursue them are responsible or irresponsible. Violations of normative standards give rise to external or internal (self-evaluative) sanctions (e.g., anticipation of punishment or guilt) and call for acts of compensation, such as justifications or excuses (Döbert & Nunner-Winkler, 1978; Keller, 1984a; Sykes & Matza, 1957). On the other hand, acting in accordance with normative standards may give rise to external or internal evaluations (e.g., anticipation of praise or pride).

The naive concepts or theories of action represent typified knowledge available to persons for the interpretation of situations (Schutz, 1967). It may be more or less differentiated and more or less comprehensive and more or less general or situation-specific. It is accessible to consciousness in principle (Toulmin, 1974), but it may, in general, function as background or "tacit knowledge" (Cicourel, 1978; Edelstein & Keller, 1982; Glick, 1978) from which the specific interpretation of a situation and the process of negotiation of conflicting claims is derived more or less implicitly.

The components of the naive theories of action represent the content on which the processes of perspective-taking operate. The relevant components of the naive theories of action can be summarized as follows (see also Keller & Reuss, 1984): They comprise typical (general) or situation-specific knowledge about *actions, persons,* and *situations.* This includes the representation of *persons,* self, and others, in terms of their intentionality: motives, feelings, expectations, and subjective preferences; the representation of *relationships* and the *regularities* and *rules* governing actions and relationships; the representation of *consequences* of actions for persons (including the self) as well as for the relationship between persons; *normative standards* that call for or prohibit actions; *evaluative standards* that permit to judge actions and persons (in terms of short-term psychological attributes or long-term dispositions); and *regulatory strategies* serving to maintain relationships or reestablish a moral balance in the case of the violation of normative standards.

Socio-moral Development as the Development of a Conception of Agency and Responsibility

Socio-moral development implies growing awareness of the self as an intentional and responsible agent. To function in social reality the self must be aware of the concerns of others since only such awareness will enable the self to maintain relationships. The individual thus has to take into account the standards of rightness that define certain actions or intentions as acceptable or inacceptable in the light of one's responsibilities toward others. The development of a conception of a responsible self encompasses both cognitive and affective processes. Cognitively, any person in order to be able to engage in relationships with other persons must be aware of normative standards, of the consequences that violations of such standards have for those concerned, and of actions that serve to compensate violations of the legitimate concerns of others. As a person's naive concepts of action develop, he or she comes to experience him- or herself as an intentional and responsible agent. He or she begins to anticipate the evaluation of actions by others and to experience the necessity to justify, excuse, or compensate violations of another person's legitimate concerns. In order to achieve this task adequately, persons must not only be able to understand concerns of others. They must also feel responsible for the consequences of their actions for others. This implies empathy with others' feelings and concerns (Eisenberg, 1982; Hoffman, 1975, 1984) as well as the development of a self-evaluative system. The self-evaluative system leads to feelings of shame or guilt when the concerns of others have been violated or when others have been treated unfairly or irresponsibly (Keller, 1984b; Melden, 1977). Such feelings are basic to the motivation to morally compensate for the effects of unfair or irresponsible actions, e.g., by providing justifications or excuses. The self-evaluative system includes the development of the 'moral ideal' (Blasi, 1984; Damon, 1984) that functions as a standard according to which moral choices are made. Positive moral feelings are derived from action in congruence with such standards. Thus, empathic feelings as well as the cognitions and feelings derived from the self-evaluative system serve to regulate moral judgment and action.

The Role of Perspective-taking in the Development of Naive Concepts of Action and of Responsibility

The development of the categories of naive concepts of action and the development of responsibility derive from complex operations of perspective differentiation and coordination. Through these operations individuals construct the meaning of the social world and of the self as part of this social world. The self comes to understand how his or her actions influence others and others' view on the self. It is through the self-reflective structure of the perspective-taking process that intersubjectivity is established.

We thus agree with the position adopted by Selman and Kohlberg that processes of perspective differentiation and coordination constitute the core structure of social and moral reasoning. However, we do not agree with Kohlberg's distinction of a social-descriptive and a socio-moral prescriptive perspective. We propose that perspective-taking is the fundamental organizational structure through which naive concepts and categories of action are differentiated and coordinated in both descriptive and prescriptive knowledge and reasoning.

We approach the concept of perspective-taking in the framework of theories of social action (Berger & Luckmann, 1966; Blumer, 1969; Habermas, 1984;

Lidz & Meyer Lidz, 1976; Mead, 1934) starting from the assumption that perspective-taking is a fundamental process in human interaction and communication, grounded in interaction as interaction is grounded in perspective-taking. In the symbolic-interactionist tradition where the concept originates (Blumer, 1969; Mead, 1934), perspective-taking was defined as a process of interpretation that serves to establish interaction and mutual consent. This requires that the interacting subjects be reflexively oriented towards the *meaning* of each other's actions (Lidz & Meyer Lidz, 1976). Thus, negotiating the meaning of a situation and achieving mutual consent implies cognitive processes of structuring and restructuring the different aspects of the situation. It is in this process that perspective-taking and the reflexive orientation towards the self that is made possible by perspective-taking play a major role.

In an action-theoretical framework the concept of reciprocal expectations takes on both descriptive and prescriptive meaning. By taking the perspective of the other, persons are able to coordinate their expectations and understand them as mutual, and thus develop a notion of the expectability both of behaviors and of expectations about behavior (Parsons, 1964). The concept of expectation has explanatory (predictive) meaning in the framework of descriptive social cognition when shared meaning about actions is established. In the normative framework of ethics, however, the concept of expectability implies mutually accepted and binding patterns of action (Habermas, 1984). The members of a social group are justified in expecting certain types of behaviors in certain situations. This legitimacy is derived from the intersubjectively shared norms that regulate behavior in certain situations. In this normative framework, understanding action means to be able to reconstruct it with regard to reciprocal expectability and to differentiate between subjective preferences and moral preferability (Keller & Reuss, 1984; Lenk, 1979). Understanding social processes and social regularities such as moral or conventional norms, social roles, and institutions means the ability to reconstruct such generalized patterns of action or invariances of interaction that derive from the validity of norms.

In order to be fully justifiable and morally acceptable, action must be oriented toward the reciprocity of complementary perspectives (Berger & Luckmann, 1966). Therefore, when assessing the validity and generalizability of a norm (Habermas, 1984) and establishing a moral point of view (Hare, 1952; Rawls, 1972) the role switch between those performing an action and those concerned by the effects of an action and the generalized (reflective) perspective of the independent observer are critically important.

We therefore argue against the redefinition of perspective-taking as an information-processing skill as Turiel (1983a, 1983b) proposed. Rather, perspective-taking is taken to represent the formal structure of coordination of the perspectives of self and other as they relate to the different categories of people's naive theories of action. The differentiation and coordination of the categories of action and the self-reflexive structure of this process are basic to those processes of development and socialization in which children come to reconstruct the meaning of social interaction in terms of both what *is* the case and what *ought* to be the case in terms of morally responsible action. In order to achieve the task of establishing consent and mutually acceptable lines of action in situations of conflicting claims and expectations, a person has to take into account the intersubjective aspects of the situation that represent the generalizable features, as well as the subjective aspects that represent the viewpoints of the persons involved in the situation. In its fully developed form, this complex process of regulation and interaction calls for the existence and operation of complex socio-moral knowledge structures and a concept of self as a morally responsible agent. The ability to differentiate and coordinate the perspectives of self and other thus is a necessary condition both in the development of socio-moral meaning making and in the actual process of solving situations of conflicting claims.

CONTEXT AND DEVELOPMENT

The naive concepts of action and the conception of a moral self must be reconstructed within specific action contexts. It is an empirical question which specific content categories of the naive theories of action are differentiated within given action contexts, how the categories are coordinated in the interpretation and solution of action problems, and which conception of agency or responsibility is achieved at different points in development. Action context refers to both the *content* categories of the naive theories of action (such as different types of rules or norms or different types of relationship) and the type of *situation* in which the categories are assessed (such as reasoning about a dilemma or interacting in a situation of social conflict). The literature concerned with social cognitive and moral development (Damon, 1984, 1989; Eisenberg, 1982; Rest, 1983; Shantz, 1983; Turiel, 1983) presents evidence that the specific action context is important in the person's socio-moral meaning making. Otherwise, there would be no explanation of the obvious décalages in the use of categories and processes. Examples of such déalages between contexts and/or contents of socio-moral functioning have been found in the development of empathic understanding (Eisenberg, 1982; Hoffman, 1983, 1984) and in the understanding of moral rules by young children (Dunn, 1987; Turiel, 1983a, 1983b). Thus, children at an early age show empathic concerns in their interactions (Hoffman, 1975, 1983, 1984) and an awareness of moral rules (Dunn, 1987). In rather simply structured situations where the validity of a moral rule is at stake (Turiel, 1983b), preschoolers take an internally oriented moral point of view by showing empathic concern for the feelings of others, and judge moral norms such as physical integrity as universally valid compared to conventional norms, such as dressing conventions. In Kohlberg's dilemmas of conflicting moral duties even adolescents appear externally oriented, i.e., motivated by sanctions, punishment and authority, or concern for self's interests (see Keller, Eckensberger, & von Rosen, 1989, for a critique).

Given these findings, it is plausible to expect that the moral stage scores achieved by 10- or 12-year-olds in Kohlberg's study (stage 1 or stage 2 at best, Colby et al., 1983) should be viewed as specific to the task in which conflicting moral obligations have to be weighed against each other. Conversely, it does not appear plausible that these stage scores indicate the general level of children's moral competence as tapped by their interpersonal and moral understanding. In other words, it is not plausible that children scoring at the preconventional level of moral judgment should be generally unable to recognize different interests in a moral conflict, or that children should be generally unable to consider actions in terms of the psychological interests of others, and that they should not possess a conception of obligation. As expected, the literature reports evidence that children and adolescents not only possess rich understanding of the psychological world in terms of motives, feelings, and intentions (Flavell & Ross, 1981; Shantz, 1983), but also of moral rules (Damon, 1989; Kagan & Lamb 1987; Turiel, 1983a, 1983b).

The relevant parameters for the appraisal of context are, of course, largely conjectural at this point. However, types of relationship such as reasoning about authority or peer relationships (Damon, 1989; Youniss, 1980), or types of moral rules such as moral duties (Colby et al., 1983) or moral responsibilities (Eisenberg, 1982; Gilligan, 1982) are promising candidates. Further, it is necessary to take into account the *type* of situation where moral agents interact.

The Development of Socio-moral Meaning Making in Friendship: Results of a Longitudinal Study

Next, we present empirical data that exemplify the development of a naive theory of action and of moral responsibility in the context of reasoning about an action problem in close friendship (Keller, 1984b).

Method and Sample

Socio-moral understanding was assessed in a longitudinal study of 121 subjects at the ages 7, 9, 12, and 15 years (57 female, 64 male). Subjects were interviewed about an everyday action dilemma occurring between friends. The dilemma was based on Selman's (1980) friendship dilemma. The protagonist (actor) promised to meet his or her best friend on their special meeting day. Later, the protagonist receives a more attractive invitation from a third child (movie or pop concert depending on age) who has only recently moved into the neighborhood. This invitation happens to be at the same time the protagonist had promised to meet the best friend. Various psychological details are mentioned that complicate matters further, for example that the best friend has problems he or she wants to talk about and that he or she does not like the new child.

Since the interpretation and the solution of the dilemma involve clashes of interest as well as conflicts between norms, an adequate reconstruction of meaning entails both descriptive and prescriptive aspects. During the interview the categories of the naive theory of action and of a moral self become increasingly salient. The interview is structured according to the phases of an action sequence.

First, in the phase of orientation, the subject has to define the action problem in a preliminary way. *Second,* the subject has to make a (hypothetical) choice for the protagonist and to give reasons for the choice as well as for the alternative option. Reasons can refer to preferences or preferability and thus give rise to the consideration of problematic or illegitimate aspects of a choice in terms of self's responsibility. *Third,* these considerations are reflected in anticipation and (moral) evaluation of consequences of choices for those concerned (protagonist, best friend, new child). *Fourth,* the subject explores regulative strategies that are available to avoid or compensate unintended and undesirable consequences for self and others. *Fifth,* the action choice is evaluated in terms of moral rightness. Intensive awareness of the problematic aspects of the conflict may result in a revision of the action choice and thus in a renewed sequence of evaluating preferences and consequences in the light of (moral) preferability. Depending on the ability to differentiate and coordinate the categories of the naive theory of action, the coordination of different phases of action can take place successively (for example, when consequences are regulated after facts have been established) or simultaneously (for example, when consequences are anticipated and taken into account in making an action choice).

Scoring

Developmental levels were determined for the arguments given in each category. Levels vary from the lowest level 0 to the highest level 3 with transitional levels (e.g., 0/1, 1/2, 2/3). Exact percentage agreement for sublevels varied between 75% and 100% for the categories. Average agreement across categories within age groups was 86%, 86%, 85%, and 89% for the 7, 9, 12, and 15-year-olds.

Qualitative Results
Levels of Socio-moral Meaning Making[1]

In the following the developmental levels of socio-moral meaning-making and moral agency are described. Table 4.1 summarizes this information (see Table 4.1).

---

[1]See Keller & Reuss (Human Development, 1984).

TABLE 4.1.
Developmental Levels of Socio-Moral Meaning Making: Differentiation and Coordination of Action Categories

Level	Conception of Perspectives	Conception of Actions and of (Moral) Agency
0	no differentiation between subjective perspectives	isolated actions no conception of action conflicts no sense of agency
1	differentiation of subjective perspectives from the viewpoint of given needs, interests, expectations beginning coordination in terms of action sequences (action in reaction to action)	construction of an elementary action conflict agency as: ---awareness of conflicting options ---anticipation of (intended and unintended) consequences of choices (cognitive expectations)
2	beginning differentiation of subjective perspectives in light of intersubjective perspectives coordination of perspectives from the viewpoint of what is legitimate in terms of shared standards (beginning of a relationship perspective)	conflict of action as conflict of relationship actions/interactions evaluated in terms of obligations and responsibilities as concrete behavioral requirements agency as knowledge about obligations (normative expectations)
3	full intersubjectivity integration of a generalized perspective (norms) with a particular perspective (persons, situations) (generalization and individuation) ideal role-switch	Actions and interactions are evaluated in light of general and personalized obligations and responsibilities actions oriented towards establishment and maintenance of trust agency as personal commitment to norms (moral responsibility) consense orientation

Level 0.   At level 0 no differentiation between the subjective perspectives of self and other has emerged. The situation is not yet interpreted in terms of conflicting claims, i.e., in terms of self's needs and interests versus other's (friend's) needs, interests, or expectations. Self's mostly hedonistic perspective is attributed to other as well (friend wants to go to the movie). Therefore, no differentiation is possible between preferences and preferability (in the sense of what would be right to do). The preferential behavior is not yet oriented towards the representation of alternative options, goals, or action strategies. Action decisions are primarily oriented towards objects (movie, toys) while disregarding intersubjective invariances and established action patterns in the context of an ongoing relationship (friendship). Persons are representatives of certain gratifying objects, and perceived in their instrumental function (offers made to the actor). Relations are not organized over time nor are they tied to specific persons, or specified by definite characteristics (such as old friendship, situation of new child). Actor may achieve a first differentiation of subjective perspectives with regard to the anticipation of various consequences of decisions for ego and alter: satisfaction of needs leads to positive feelings, dissatisfaction to negative ones. Thus, even when negative consequences of self's action decision for other are anticipated (friend will feel bad if actor goes to movie), such understanding does not have a regulatory or modifying function for self's preferences concerning decisions, goals, and means. Consequences are interpreted in terms of "effects" for which the actor is not yet held responsible. Actions are not perceived as objects of justification so that no necessity is felt to devise strategies of compensation for negative consequences for other. Strategic and communicative forms of action are not yet differentiated even in the most elementary form.

Level 1.   At this level a beginning differentiation between subjective-particular and intersubjectively *right* perspective emerges (actor should go to the friend). At this level subjective perspectives of self and other are differentiated in terms of specific needs, interests, and expectations and can be perceived as conflicting (actor wants to go to the movie, friend wants actor to come). Expectations achieve quasi-normative status resulting, first, from ego's declaration of intent (actor said he or she would come). Second, they result from the relationship between self and other (actor and friend), a relationship interpreted in terms of the intersubjective invariance of action orientations. These are based on the given regularities of established patterns of action (they always meet and play together). Third, expectations may refer to the nonnormative circumstances and the corresponding needs and feelings of the new child (new in town, alone). Therefore, a first differentiation between preference and preferability becomes possible. Preference relations are based on naive hedonistic criteria (which option provides more or less fun) and/or the quasi-obligatory aspects of the situation (actor does not want to leave out one or the other child). They take into account consequences of a decision for self and other. Consequences relate back to the self in terms of consequences and consequences of consequences (if actor does not go to friend, friend will never play with actor and then . . .). The actor is construed as a person who knows about other's expectations towards him- or herself, and about negative evaluations that result from the violation of such expectations. Regularities in the context of friendship can be seen as precursors of rules and, therefore, or moral claims. Their quasi-obligatory nature is evidenced by the fact that action orientations violating expectations that result from such regularities are subject to criticism and in need of justification (friend will ask actor where he or she has been). Justifications as well as strategies of regulation make use of simple material compensations (actor will invite friend at another time) as well as of imperfect discourse strategies (actor hides action from friend). This strategy serves the function of avoiding negative consequences for the self.

Level 2.   At this level a clear distinction between subjective-particular perspectives and intersubjectively *right* orientations of action is achieved. At the same time, both dimensions are differentiated and elaborated. Action is no longer oriented merely toward given regularities but also toward rules, i.e., toward normative expectations that self and other mutually accept as legitimate (actor has given a promise). Yet, these rules are still represented as isolated and abstract moral requirements. The differentiation between the descriptive and the prescriptive levels of social-cognitive reasoning—between *is* and *ought*—is presupposed by the ability to coordinate perspectives under a moral point of view— in a critical, self-reflective manner (actor knows that friend will think he or she is deceiving him). The distinction between given preference and preferability in a moral sense makes possible an interpretation of the situation as a conflict between desire and duty (wants to go to a movie but has promised). Understanding the inner world of others gains a moral dimension, but the conflict is not yet understood as an inner conflict of a moral self as is the case at the next level.

Preference behavior is now based, first, on formal rules, i.e., on "institutional facts"—such as having given a promise—and on the normative expectations based on these facts. It is based second on interpersonal rules, i.e., on the regularities of established action patterns that have achieved quasi-normative significance. Thus, the friendship relationship as such is taken to contain obligations that specify rules about how one should act towards a friend. Normative expectations are interpreted in abstract and general terms whose claims to validity are raised independently of the (concrete) persons, the circumstances, and the specifying context that potentially may restrict the validity claim of a norm (e.g., "a promise must be kept"). This type of interpretation presupposes a social-cognitive generalization in a dual form: temporal and social-interpersonal, implying that the rule is valid always and for everyone.

Relations are seen as more exclusive and intimate (being best friends). At the same time, when the situation is evaluated in view of appropriate action, particular conditions of the relationship are taken into account (friends have their special day, friend does not like new child). Formal rules and the consequences of their violation are interpreted on the background of such a specifying interpretation of the situation. Consequences can also be constructed with regard to their long-term effects for the ongoing relationship (they will stop being friends). In the case of violation of obligations actor is aware that other (friend) morally evaluates his or her actions and ascribes certain personality attributes to him or her (e.g., being somebody who will deceive or betray others).

Level 3.   At this level the components of intersubjective rightness are further differentiated (preferability). Single rules and regularities are integrated into systems of norms of reciprocity basic to intimate relationships like friendship. The perspectives of self and other are tied to a role-bound understanding of how one generally acts and should act towards a friend. The norm of reciprocity and its derivatives such as dependability, reliability, and trustworthiness constitute the superordinate viewpoint that guides action in the context of an ongoing relationship. At the same time the moral point of view is elaborated. This leads to the view of an actor as bound by a strict obligation to conduct action under these norms (if she is a good friend she must go to her friend as promised, good friends must be able to trust each other). Obligations to the friend become part of an actor's self-evaluative system. Violating friendship norms would lead to a negative self-evaluation (he would feel guilty if he let his best friend down, he would feel that he was a traitor, that he is not a trustworthy friend). A strict orientation towards these general norms also implies taking into account the particular circumstances of the friend's situation as well as that of the new child. Friend's situation-specific needs and problems become dominant factors that codetermine the structuring of action.

There is now a clear distinction between strategic and communicative action. This implies that illegitimate and legitimate strategies of regulation have become differentiated. A justification of an action that violates reciprocity norms is generally avoided. In the case of problematic actions that are subject to criticism, dialogue is used to attempt regulation: Actors engage in negotiation and communication in order to achieve consensual interpretation and mutual validation in the decision-making process and to define mutually accepted reasons for action. In case of violation of reciprocity norms, self attempts to elicit other's assent by appealing to excuses and justifications of self's motives, circumstances, and constraints (either the appeal of the offer made to the actor, or the situation of the new child). Thus, self tries to restore the moral balance in order to ascertain the long-term existence of the relationship.

Hypothetical role-taking or exchange serves the function of considering possible actions and reactions from the viewpoint of others (asking friend to take self's perspective or the perspective of the new child). This is the basis for the regulatory principle of universalization that leads to the potential exchange of the roles of actor, those concerned by an action, and those adjudicating, evaluating, as observers, the moral quality of an action.

Quantitative Results

The results of the empirical analyses of the longitudinal data reveal progression in the development of the categories of general socio-moral understanding. Figure 4.1 presents the data for the 7- to 15-year age span. (N = 92 subjects, 49 male and 43 female) for whom a complete data set is available.

Developmental change proceeds in a regular fashion with progression rates of about one half of one stage on the average between two measurement occasions. Regression between adjacent measurement occasions varied between 2% and 10% for the various categories of socio-moral reasoning, mean regressions contribute about 4%. These numbers are within the conventional boundaries of the reliability of measurement. No sex effects were found in the developmental patterns. In sum, the longitudinal patterns show that the transformation of the categories of socio-moral meaning making is a regular, sequential and cumulative developmental process.

In general the results document that the various content categories over time develop in a systematic and interconnected way. Yet, even in this relative homogeneous situation, context effects obtain as well. As Fig. 4.2 evidences it holds

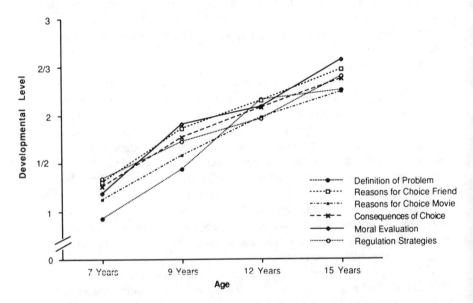

FIG. 4.1. Development of categories in reasoning about friendship-dilemma.

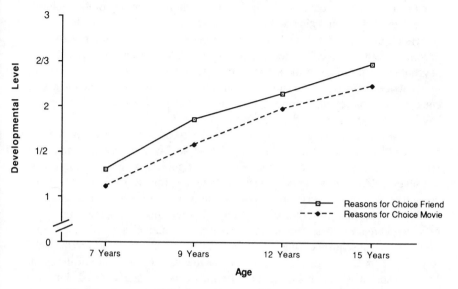

FIG. 4.2.   Context effects in reasoning about friendship-dilemma.

for all measurement occasions that reasoning about the motives for the action choice to go to the friend is developmentally advanced compared to reasoning about the motives for the action choice to go to the movie.

Further, the data show a highly significant association between level of socio-moral reasoning (represented by the summary score of the categories) and action choice (see Table 4.2). While the majority of subjects at level 1/2 and below choose to go to the movie with the new child, a majority of subjects at level 2 and most subjects at level 2/3 or 3 decide to go to the friend.

Discussion

The analyses show that the development of socio-moral meaning making in friendship is part of the more encompassing development of the ability to understand persons, relations and actions. Understanding what it morally means to

TABLE 4.2.
Level of Socio-Moral Reasoning and Action Choice

	≤ Level 1/2	Level 2	≤ Level 2/3	total
Movie	89	50	9	148
Friend	47	85	85	216
Total	135	135	94	364

| Chi-square | 74.100 | $p \leq 0.001$ |

stand in a relationship develops in conjunction with the unfolding of the subject's naive theory of social action and responsibility. At the lowest level, the subject centers on one perspective and perceives other persons merely in terms of their hedonistic value for self's interests. At this level, action has not yet acquired psychological meaning in the sense of reconstructing and differentiating intentional action sequences. The subject is neither aware of reasons for action nor of consequences of action. It follows that a moral perspective that implies agency has not yet been established at this level.

At level 1 basic categories of the naive theory of action are established as evidenced by the representation of the psychological world of persons and their relations to each other. A conception of what is right is beginning to emerge. At this level children do not refer spontaneously to the promise given, neither in the context of descriptive reasoning about the motives or consequences of choices, nor in the context of prescriptive reasoning. Children appear to possess a concept of *quasi-obligations* based on the regularities of interactions and on the anticipation of the consequences that self's actions have for others or for the self. Regulatory strategies begin to appear when subjects become aware of the problematic aspects of the situation where friend's concerns are violated, but they remain deficient in terms of standards of discourse. In the context of prescriptive reasoning physical sanctions are not mentioned as moral reasons. Rather, sanctions play a role when consequences of violating a rule are anticipated. Yet, already at level 1, consequences are also interpreted psychologically (friend's anger). In contrast to Kohlberg (1976, 1984) and in agreement with Turiel (1983a, 1983b) our data also provide indications that, already at level 1, the validity of a moral rule such as promise-keeping is not supported by external sanctions like physical punishment. Punishment is not a cause of (reason for) abiding by the rule, but a mere consequence of violating the rule (see also Keller, Eckensberger, & von Rosen, 1989).

At level 2 the construction of the conflict encompasses psychological details of persons' relationship with each other (regularities of interaction) as well as formal moral rules. Thus, preferences (what is the case) and preferability (what is right) can be clearly differentiated. In various segments of the naive theory of action there is evidence of increasing coordination of perspectives. Compared to the preceding level, the inner world of the other is interpreted at a deeper level of psychological understanding. In case of violation of the concerns of others, increased psychological understanding provides a sense that regulatory strategies are indeed necessary. A genuine concern with the relationship in terms of obligations and commitment to a friend emerges at this level. Grounded in the awareness of shared experience in an ongoing relationship, obligations and commitments are interpreted as rather specific behavioral requirements such as having to keep one's promises to the friend, or maintaining established routines of interaction. The reasons given for choices and moral evaluation may indicate genuine moral concern anchored in the nature of the relationship, as well as empathic concern and reciprocal sharing of feelings. The concrete reciprocity and instrumental exchange types of reasons invoked by Kohlberg as reasons for keeping a promise are absent from our data. Instead, at level 2 we find reasoning which, adopting a Kohlbergian perspective, one might tend to evaluate as stage 3 reasoning because of a concern for the good of the other and of the relationship (Keller et al., 1989).

At level 3 the child has mastered the double prerequisites of responsible action: (a) to understand that others have subjective and particular perspectives grounded in their specific circumstances and life conditions and, (b) simultaneously to take into account the intersubjective standards of rightness. Individuals are aware of basic norms of reciprocity and have established a moral self. Being a "good friend," in the sense of being loyal, trustworthy, and dependable is the superordinate viewpoint from which the categories of the naive theory of action are interpreted. Actions are evaluated in the light of what is fair and responsible towards a friend. Adolescents at this level tend to take a moral or prescriptive view when they think spontaneously about reasons for action and focus on the question how a good friend ought to act.

At level 3 criteria of moral precedence are established that determine why it is "more right" to join the friend than to accept the new child's invitation in spite of the acknowledged moral responsibility that actor has also incurred toward the new child. Interestingly, moral obligations and responsibilities toward the third child are also more salient at this level which is characterized by a conception of intimacy and exclusiveness, tainted by feelings of jealousy toward the new child. This interpretation of level 3 is in basic agreement with Kohlberg's stage 3 of moral development. What is interesting and novel compared to what we know from Kohlberg's data is that moral obligations and duties based on the relationship come to be seen as negotiable under standards of discourse (Keller & Reuss, 1985, 1988). But in spite of the possibility of negotiation, action choices at this level are based on obligations and responsibilities towards the friend. The results show a systematic relationship between level of socio-moral reasoning and the hypothetical action choice in the conflict situation. Subjects at lower levels of reasoning frequently show a split between what they judge to be the right action choice (going to the friend) and what they actually choose (going to the movie). It is only at level 2/3 or 3 that the hypothetical action choice is consistently based on what is judged to be right. At this level a moral self is established that simultaneously defines the nature of the social relationships in which the subject engages: Commitments and obligations will then be experienced as binding to the person. It follows that action choice and moral judgment are consistent in situations where obligations are experienced as personally meaningful and binding.

To summarize, let us relate these findings to the three theoretical premises discussed in the beginning. The description of the developmental levels has highlighted the process of differentiation and coordination of the categories of the naive theory of social action and responsibility. Each level entails more encompassing coordinations that build on previous achievements and thus generate new and more comprehensive forms of descriptive and prescriptive meaning making. The analysis has produced rather general results, and more detailed analyses of the coordination processes are both desirable and possible (Eckensberger, 1984). However, even the present analysis grants insight into fundamental social-cognititive prerequisites of the interpretation of social relations.

In the description of the levels we focus on general features or "ideal types." Empirically, the subjects fit these ideal type descriptions to a greater or lesser extent by scoring at full or transitional levels. Individuals usually function at more than one level and thus are mostly encountered in the process of reconstructing current forms of meaning making and constructing new ones. Turning again to the question of distinct social knowledge systems we discussed earlier, our data show that reasoning about an action conflict draws on selected aspects from all three domains distinguished earlier (persons, relations, and social structures). Therefore it appears reasonable to explain socio-moral meaning making as a process of differentiation and coordination of the categories of action.

In general the results presented here document that the various content categories of socio-moral reasoning as assessed with the interview about the action-dilemma over time develop in a systematic and interconnected way. Yet, context effects of socio-moral reasoning were observed as well. Thus, in the dilemma presented the action choice to go to the friend - which is also perceived as the morally legitimate one - pulls for a higher level of socio-moral understanding. This result can also be interpreted in such a way that even among the oldest age group the level of reasoning or justification for an action choice which is not perceived as fully morally legitimate is not at the same developmental level than reasoning about the morally legitimate alternative.

Context effects in socio-moral development become even stronger when reasoning is compared across domains or tasks (Keller, 1990). Thus, we could show that reasoning about the promise-keeping (e.g., why in general must a promise be kept) is developmentally advanced compared to reasoning about friendship (e.g. what makes friendship really close). This décalage again is observed across all age groups from age 7 to age 15 years. The same décalage holds true in the comparison of general reasoning about friendship and the situation-specific application of reasons referring to friendship in the action dilemma described above. In this case the reconstruction of friendship in the specific action context is developmentally advanced at all measurement occasions. We can conclude from these results that context is an important factor in the development of socio-moral meaning making. It is a task for future research to develop a theory of socio-moral understanding that takes into account and specifies contexts of development in order to reconstruct the dynamics of the developmental process.

We conclude with some hypotheses about the developmental dynamics of socio-moral development. We assume that the developmental transformations depend on, and result from, the experience of standing in relationships. The levels show how shared experience becomes represented at the symbolic level. This is true both for cognition and affect: Standing in a relationship implies ongoing negotiation of intentions, goals, and expectations, as well as sharing experiences and feelings. It is through these processes that the child becomes aware of the other's inner world of subjective experience, gradually learns to anticipate the other person's reaction schemata, and finally comes to construct generalized expectations about behavior in relationships. Simultaneously, interactions extending over time in the context of shared experience constitute affective bonds which make other's reactions emotionally meaningful to the self. The anticipation of psychological reactions of emotionally significant others gives interpersonal meaning to moral rules that, in the early stage of interpersonal-moral meaning making, are perceived as merely abstract commands.

Another question that has not been adequately addressed concerns the issue of universal vs. person-specific aspects of socio-moral meaning making. Our emphasis has been on universal aspects of the organization of meaning making systems. Clearly, there are individual differences both in terms of intraindividual change (Edelstein, Keller, & Schröder, 1990) and the (sub)culturally normative valence of particular aspects of the system of action. Moreover, specific ("idiosyncratic") performance conditions located in the psychological makeup of particular persons and/or their socialization experiences may generate valences, interaction modalities and rules of interpretation (such as defensive operations) specific to these person. The interface between universal and person-specific aspects of development, a question mostly unresearched to date may prove a fruitful field for the cooperation of developmental, personality and social psychologists.

REFERENCES

Adalbjarnardóttir, S., & Selman, R. L. (1989). How children propose to deal with the criticism of their teachers and classmates: Developmental and stylistic variations. *Child Development, 60,* 539–550.

Berger, P. L., & Luckmann, T. (1966). *The social construction of reality.* Garden City, NY: Doubleday.

Blasi, A. (1984). Moral identity: Its role in moral functioning. In W. Kurtines & J. Gewirtz (Eds.), *Morality, moral behavior, and moral development* (pp. 128–139). New York: Wiley.

Blumer, H. (1969). *Symbolic interactionism.* London: Prentice-Hall.

Cicourel, A. V. (1978). Interpretation and summerization: Issues in the child's acquisition of social structure. In J. Glick & K. A. Clarke-Stewart (Eds.), *The development of social understanding* (pp. 251–281). New York: Gardner Press.

Colby, A., & Kohlberg, L. (1987). *The measurement of moral judgment. Vol. 1. Theoretical foundations and research validation.* New York: Cambridge University Press.

Colby, A., Kohlberg, L., Gibbs, J., & Lieberman, M. (1983). A longitudinal study of moral judgment. *Monographs of the Society for Research in Child Development, 48*(1–2, Serial No. 200).

Colby, A., Kohlberg, L., Speicher, B., Hewer, A., Candee, D., Gibbs, J., & Power, C. (1987). *The measurement of moral judgment. Vol. 2. Standard issue scoring manual.* New York: Cambridge University Press.

Damon, W. (1983). *Social development from childhood through adolescence.* New York: Norton.

Damon, W. (1984). Self-understanding and moral development from childhood to adolescence. In W. Kurtines & J. Gewirtz (Eds.), *Morality, moral behavior, and moral development* (pp. 109–127). New York: Wiley.

Damon, W. (1989). *The moral child.* Cambridge, MA: Harvard University Press.

Döbert, R., & Nunner-Winkler, G. (1978). Performanzbestimmende Aspekte des moralischen Bewußtseins. In G. Portele (Ed.), *Sozialisation und Moral* (pp. 101–121). Weinheim: Beltz.

Dunn, J. (1987). The beginnings of moral understanding: Development in the second year. In J. Kagan & S. Lamb (Eds.), *The emergence of morality in young children* (pp. 91–112). Chicago: The University of Chicago Press.

Eckensberger, L. (1984). *On structure and content in moral development.* Unpublished manuscript, Universität des Saarlandes, FRG.

Edelstein, W., & Keller, M. (1982). Perspektivität und Interpretation: Zur Entwicklung sozialen Verstehens. In W. Edelstein & M. Keller (Eds.), *Perspektivität und Interpretation* (pp. 9–43). Frankfurt am Main: Suhrkamp.

Edelstein, W., Keller, M., & Schröder, E. (1990). Child development and social structure: Individual differences in development. In P. B. Baltes, D. L. Featherman, & R. M. Lerner (Eds.), *Life-span development and behavior (Vol. 10).* Hillsdale, NJ: Lawrence Erlbaum Associates.

Eisenberg, N. (1982). The development of reasoning regarding prosocial behavior. In N. Eisenberg (Ed.), *The development of prosocial behavior* (pp. 219–249). New York: Academic Press.

Flavell, J. H., & Ross, L. (Eds.). (1981). *Social cognitive development.* New York: Cambridge University Press.

Gilligan, C. (1982). *In a different voice.* Cambridge: Harvard University Press.

Glick, J. (1978). Cognition and social cognition: An introduction. In J. Glick & K. A. Clarke-Stewart (Eds.), *The development of social understanding* (pp. 7–10). New York: Gardener Press.

Habermas, J. (1984). *Vorstudien und Ergänzungen zur Theorie des kommunikativen Handelns.* Frankfurt am Main: Suhrkamp.

Hare, R. M. (1952). *The language of morals.* Oxford: Oxford University Press.

Hoffman, M. (1975). Developmental synthesis of affect and cognition and its implications for altruistic motivation. *Developmental Psychology, 11,* 607–622.

Hoffman, M. (1983). Affective and cognitive processes in moral internalization. In E. T. Higgins, D. Ruble, & W. Hartup (Eds.), *Social cognition and social behavior* (pp. 236–274). New York: Cambridge University Press.

Hoffman, M. (1984). Empathy, its limitations, and its role in a comprehensive moral theory. In W. Kurtines & J. Gewirtz (Eds.), *Morality, moral behavior, and moral development* (pp. 283–302). New York: Wiley.

Kagan, J., & Lamb, S. (1987). *The emergence of morality in young children.* Chicago: The University of Chicago Press.

Keller, M. (1984a). Rechtfertigungen. Zur Entwicklung praktischer Erklärungen. In W. Edelstein & J. Habermas (Eds.), *Soziale Interaktion und soziales Verstehen* (pp. 253–299). Frankfurt am Main: Suhrkamp.

Keller, M. (1984b). Resolving conflicts in friendship: The development of moral understanding in everyday life. In W. Kurtines & J. Gewirtz (Eds.), *Morality, moral behavior, and moral development* (pp. 140–158). New York: Wiley.

Keller, M. (1990, June). *Intra- and interindividual differences in social cognitive development:*

Results of a longitudinal study in 7 to 15 year old children. Paper presented as part of the invited symposium "Structure & Context in Individual Development: Impact of Longitudinal Research on Piagetian Theory" at the Twentieth Anniversary Symposium of the Jean Piaget Society, Philadelphia.

Keller, M., Eckensberger, L., & von Rosen, K. (1989). A critical note on the conception of preconventional morality: The case of stage 2 in Kohlberg's theory. *International Journal of Behavioral Development, 12,* 57–69.

Keller, M., & Reuss, S. (1984). An action-theoretical reconstruction of the development of social cognitive competence. *Human Development, 27,* 211–220.

Keller, M., & Reuss, S. (1985). The process of moral decision-making: Normative and empirical conditions of participation in moral discourse. In M. W. Berkowitz & F. Oser (Eds.), *Moral education: Theory and application* (pp. 109–123). New York: Erlbaum.

Keller, M., & Reuss, S. (1988, July). *Development of negotiation strategies in an interpersonal-moral conflict situation.* Paper presented at the First International Conference on Human Development and Counseling Psychology, Porto, Portugal.

Kohlberg, L. (1976). Moral stages and moralization: The cognitive developmental approach. In T. Lickona (Ed.), *Moral development and behavior* (pp. 31–53). New York: Holt, Rinehart & Winston.

Kohlberg, L. (1984). *Essays on moral development. Vol. 2. The psychology of moral development.* San Francisco: Harper and Row.

Lenk (1979). Handlungserklärung und Handlungsrechtfertigung unter Rückgriff auf Werte. In H. Lenk (Ed.), *Handlungstheorien interdisziplinär (Vol. 2).* München: Fink.

Lidz, C. W., & Meyer Lidz, V. (1976). Piaget's psychology of intelligence and the theory of action. In J. J. Loubser, R. C. Baum, A. Effrat, & V. Meyer Lidz (Eds.), *Explorations in general theory in social science, Vol. 1* (pp. 195–239). New York: Free Press.

Mead, G. H. (1934). *Mind, self and society.* Chicago: University of Chicago Press.

Melden, A. S. (1977). *Rights and persons.* Berkeley: University of California Press.

Parsons, T. (1964). *Social structure and personality.* London: Collier-Macmillan.

Piaget, J. (1970). *Structuralism.* New York: Basic Books.

Piaget, J. (1983). Piaget's theory. In P. H. Mussen (Series Ed.) & W. Kessen (Vol. Ed.), *Handbook of child psychology: Vol. 1. History, theory, and methods* (pp. 103–128). New York: Wiley.

Rawls, R. (1971). *A theory of justice.* Cambridge, MA: Harvard University Press.

Rest, J. R. (1983). Morality. In P. H. Mussen (Series Ed.) & J. H. Flavell & E. Markman (Vol. Eds.), *Handbook of child psychology: Vol. 3. Cognitive development* (pp. 556–629). New York: Wiley.

Ross, D. (1963). *Foundations of ethics.* Oxford: Clarendon Press.

Schutz, A. (1967). *The phenomenology of the social world.* Evanstown, Ill.: Northwestern University Press.

Selman, R. L. (1980). *The growth of interpersonal understanding.* New York: Academic Press.

Selman, R. L., Beardslee, W., Schultz, L., Krupa, M., & D. Podorefsky, C. (1986). Assessing adolescent interpersonal negotiation strategies: Toward an integration of structural and functional methods. *Developmental Psychology, 22,* 450–459.

Shantz, C. U. (1983). Social cognition. In P. H. Mussen (Series Ed.) & J. H. Flavell & E. Markman (Vol. Eds.), *Handbook of child psychology: Vol. 3. Cognitive development* (pp. 495–555). New York: Wiley.

Sykes, G. M., & Matza, D. (1957). Techniques of neutralization: A theory of delinquency. *American Sociological Review, 22,* 664–670.

Toulmin, S. E. (1974). Rules and their relevance for understanding human behavior. In T. Mischel (Ed.), *Understanding other persons* (pp. 185–215). Oxford: Blackwell.

Turiel, E. (1979). *Social-cognitive development: Domains and categories.* Paper presented at the 9th Annual Symposium of the Jean Piaget Society, Philadelphia.

Turiel, E. (1983a). Domains and categories in social cognitive development. In W. Overton (Ed.), *The relationship between social and cognitive development* (pp. 53–90). Hillsdale, NJ: Lawrence Erlbaum Associates.

Turiel (1983b). *The development of social knowledge. Morality and convention.* Cambridge: Cambridge University Press.

Youniss, J. (1980). *Parents and peers in social development.* Chicago: Chicago University Press.

5 Social and Moral Development in Early Childhood

Melanie Killen

ABSTRACT

The focus of this chapter is on social-cognitive development in early childhood and on some of the studies which have examined social judgment and moral behavior in the preschool period. It is asserted that in order to understand early social development it is necessary to be explicit about the criteria used for determining social and moral categories of behavior. In addition, a sensitivity to the context needs to be incorporated into both research methodologies and theoretical interpretations of early behavior and development. It is argued that research which has taken these issues into account has provided a more differentiated model of early social and moral development than has been previously postulated.

INTRODUCTION

The focus of this chapter is on social-cognitive development in early childhood and on the existing evidence for social judgment and moral behavior in the preschool period. This chapter makes two central points: (1) that in order to understand early social and moral development it is necessary to be explicit about the criteria for analyzing "social" and "moral" categories of behavior, and (2) that it is essential to conduct detailed analyses of the social context. It is argued that the movement towards the use of explicit criteria and a sensitivity to the context has led to a characterization of early development as differentiated, rather than global, and as reflecting a moral, rather than premoral orientation.

This new characterization differs from the traditional one espoused by the predominant theoretical models in the field which initiated much of the work on social and moral development.

In this chapter, the theoretical foundations of research on early social and moral development are described followed by an examination of selected research in social and moral development. In addition, current research on preschoolers' social interactions and social judgments is discussed. The aim of this research has been to analyze how children resolve conflicts in the preschool setting. This has been done by investigating the role of context variables on social exchanges and by determining the social and moral components of conflict episodes.

THEORETICAL FRAMEWORK: SOCIAL-COGNITIVE DOMAINS

In the original ground-breaking work on moral development by Piaget (1932) and Kohlberg (1969), morality was defined in terms of philosophical theories of justice and fairness. Children in early to middle childhood were characterized as premoral since they did not base their evaluation of moral violations on principles of justice, but on the commands of authority (referred to as "heteronomy" in Piaget's theory) or an avoidance of punishment (referred to as "Stage 1: The punishment and obedience orientation" in Kohlberg's theory). Subsequently, studies were designed to assess moral reasoning with issues relevant to the child's world (Damon, 1977, 1983; Eisenberg & Hand, 1979) and with questions directed at the criteria that elementary school-aged children use to evaluate actions as right or wrong (Davidson, Turiel, & Black, 1983; Nucci & Nucci, 1982; Weston & Turiel, 1980). These studies showed that children *in middle childhood* were capable of moral reasoning, that is, of evaluating acts on the basis of justice, welfare, and rights.

A model of social reasoning, referred to as a social-cognitive domain approach, was proposed in order to examine how children evaluate social and moral components of everyday events (Turiel, 1983). In this model, moral transgressions are defined as acts which violate rules about respecting others' welfare, fair distribution, and rights. Social-conventional transgressions are defined as acts that violate rules about social order, customs, rituals, and institutional norms. Work in cognitive development that has utilized "domain" approaches (Feldman, 1980; Keil, 1985; Siegler, 1989) has shown that children's knowledge differs by the type of issue or concept under investigation. Similarly, work from the social-cognitive domain model has shown that children's judgments about issues of harm and justice differ from those revolving around conventions and pragmatics.

For example, research has shown that when posed with direct questions about what makes moral transgressions wrong children use reasons other than authority and punishment to evaluate acts (Turiel, 1983). When posed with the question "Would it be all right to hit someone if the teacher said it was all right? Why/why not?" or "Would it be all right to hit someone if you didn't get in trouble for it? Why/why not?," children in middle childhood state that acts of harm are wrong even in the context of teacher approval and in the absence of punishment (Davidson et al., 1983). Children evaluate acts of harm as wrong on the basis of the negative intrinsic consequences that occur from inflicting harm on others ("he or she will get hurt and cry"). This differs from their evaluation of social-conventional transgressions, which are judged as wrong on the basis of the commands of authority and social consensus. Other criteria used to examine children's judgments have included generalizability (whether an act is wrong in other countries or social environments), rule alterability (whether the rule about the act can be changed), and group consensus (whether an act is all right if everyone agrees with it).

More recently, research has been conducted on preschoolers' moral reasoning and has shown that young children also make some of the same distinctions between moral and social-conventional transgressions as shown in middle childhood (Dunn, 1988; Nucci & Turiel, 1978; Nunner-Winkler & Sodian, 1988; Smetana, 1985). If early conceptual development is more differentiated than previously characterized, then early social experience may also be more differentiated. This expectation is based on the theory that social knowledge stems from social action. And in fact, research in diverse settings has shown that young children's interactions are highly differentiated; adult-child interactions differ from child–child exchanges in the home (Dunn, 1988; Smetana, 1989) and in preschool and daycare settings (Much & Shweder, 1978; Nucci & Turiel, 1978; Sanderson & Siegal, 1988).

Interestingly, much of the research on early social experience stems from the social development, rather than the moral development, literature. Unfortunately, these two areas have not influenced each other. A close examination of research in these two areas shows that each provides information relevant to the other. For example, some of the theoretical distinctions between social and moral categories in the moral developmental literature can be applied to the research on social development, particularly with respect to criteria that delineate social, cooperative, or prosocial behavior. Conversely, findings in the social developmental literature provide hypotheses for developing theories of the acquisition of social concepts.

RESEARCH ON MORAL DEVELOPMENT IN THE PRESCHOOL PERIOD

In order to examine preschool moral judgment, Smetana (1981) investigated preschoolers' judgments about the seriousness, rule contingency, rule relativism, and amount of deserved punishment for moral and social-conventional transgressions. In her study, social-conventional transgressions were defined as acts that violate rules about social order, social customs, and social regulations. Moral transgressions were defined as ones that violate principles of fairness, welfare, and rights. Her results showed that children evaluated moral transgressions as more serious than conventional ones and more deserving of punishment. In addition, moral transgressions were less likely to be evaluated as contingent on the rule and relative to the context than conventional transgressions.

Other studies have shown differentiated aspects of preschoolers' social and moral reasoning using hypothetical stories and events. Eisenberg-Berg, Haake, Hand, and Sadalla (1979) examined children's differential responses to toy ownership with respect to sharing toys in the preschool setting. When children were told that a toy belonged to the class, as opposed to an individual child, older children were more likely to share than younger children were likely to share. Eisenberg and Hand (1979) also showed that sharing behaviors were significantly related to moral reasoning whereas helping behaviors were only related to general sociability. This indicates that there is a distinction between children's sharing and helping behavior; sharing behavior is tied to moral reasoning whereas helping behavior is not. Other research has shown that children evaluate affiliative, aggressive, and prosocial possession episodes differently (Ramsey, 1987).

Evidence that preschoolers systematically evaluate a range of moral and social-conventional transgressions in qualitatively different ways supports a model of early development that characterized conceptual development as differentiated rather than global and undifferentiated (as asserted by Piaget and Kohlberg). What remains unknown is the extent to which preschoolers are capable of applying their judgments to a variety of situations since studies have typically used only one or two scenarios. In addition, the process of acquisition of social concepts has not been systematically examined.

Recent research by Dunn (1988) has examined experiential sources for social and moral judgments by studying interactional sequences in the home. Her findings show that toddlers, at 18 months, display greater emotional reactions to moral transgressions in the home than to social-conventional ones; interestingly, toddlers at 24 and 36 months do not make this distinction. Dunn hypothesizes that the emotional quality of particular relationships may influence the child's development of moral understanding. In her research, she analyzes transgressions that are discussed in social interaction in the home as initiated by the child, the sibling, or the mother. The categories Dunn examines include: possession, politeness, destruction/dirt, place/order, sharing, and hurting others. Thus, these categories vary by the domain of the transgression (as in Smetana's study); some pertain to moral issues, such as possession and sharing, and others to social-conventional ones, such as politeness and order. Dunn finds that there are differences in who initiates discussions around these transgressions: mothers initiate discussions about destruction, dirt, place, and order more than any of the other categories analyzed, whereas children initiate discussions about possessions and sharing most often. As Dunn states, the data show that it is not just the mother or the peer that contribute to the child's moral understanding. Yet, there are differences in the types of topics that are particularly salient to mothers and peers. Other studies have shown that toddlers respond to moral and social-conventional transgressions differently in daycare settings as well (Siegal & Storey, 1985; Smetana, 1984) and that emotions themselves may be a source for differentiating types of transgressions (Nunner-Winkler & Sodian, 1988).

Several general findings can be gleaned from this research. First, not all rule violations are treated alike; evaluations vary depending on the specific social and moral aspects of the transgression. This leads to the hypothesis that aspects of social interactions, other than rule violations, take on different forms depending on the social and moral features. And, in fact, research described shortly on preschoolers' conflicts shows that conflicts and conflict resolutions differ depending on social and moral aspects of interaction episodes.

Second, children as young as 4-years-of-age recognize the difference between moral rules and rules designed to achieve nonmoral social goals, such as social order. This is important as it provides evidence for rejecting a moral/selfish dichotomy as a predominant characterization of early childhood. Rather than analyzing behavior as moral *or* selfish, analyses should encompass nonmoral social categories, such as those which pertain to social groups, rituals, norms, and social organization. Third, the findings indicate that preschoolers have the capacity to critically evaluate decisions by authorities; young children do not condone certain moral violations supported by authority figures. This suggests that the adult–child relationship is more complex than characterized in some theories; rather than viewing the adult–child relation as unilateral (in which adults transmit values to children who passively adopt them), the relationship should be viewed as bilateral or mutual. An implication is that adults may be only one of a multitude of sources from which the child constructs social and moral judgments.

The acquisition process is still largely unknown. In order to address the issue of how children acquire social and moral concepts, an examination of the different sources of experience is necessary. This information will provide a systematic basis from which to make hypotheses about the relationship between a child's social relations (and experience) and social knowledge. As an example, recent research has challenged some of the basic claims that Piaget made about connections between adult–child and child–child relations about moral judgment (Youniss, 1980). Piaget characterized adult–child relations as ones of constraint and child–child relations as cooperative. The importance of these characterizations were that they formed part of the basis for Piaget's theory about the acquisition of moral concepts; as children form cooperative relations with peers they also reason in moral terms (that is, in terms of principles of fairness). The limitation of Piaget's explanation of acquisition may lie with the unilateral characterization of adult–child relations.

Interestingly, most of the social-cognitive research conducted on the acquisition of moral judgment has focused on peer relations in middle childhood (Bearison, in press; Damon, 1983). Less work has analyzed peer relations in early childhood or adult–child relations with respect to moral judgment. For the most part, research in moral development has looked at whether children exhibit moral behavior in their interactions with others and the extent to which their conceptual development encompasses an understanding of moral rules. How preschoolers construct morality from interaction with peers has also been examined but not in comparison to their interactions with adults or the role that different types of relationships take in the development of moral knowledge.

Patterns of social interaction between peers and between adults and children in the preschool setting have been examined in some detail in the social development literature; the difference is that these studies have not been designed to assess the relation between interactive patterns and the development of social and moral knowledge. Analyzing adult–child relations in the context of the development of moral knowledge should include ways in which adults, teachers, and parents discuss, respond to, and conceptualize social and moral events involving preschoolers, and how their interactions with young children structure the types of social exchanges that children experience (which may ultimately contribute to the acquisition of moral concepts). Thus, research which shows adult–child relations to be other than characterized by constraint, or child–child as other than cooperative, provides a basis from which to construct alternative hypotheses about the acquisition of moral knowledge (from the cognitive-developmental model).

RESEARCH ON SOCIAL DEVELOPMENT IN THE PRESCHOOL PERIOD

The three major variables considered in most research are: (1) the behavior observed; (2) the interactants; and (3) the setting. Each of these variables is discussed in turn.

Behavioral Categories

The behavioral categories used to examine social developmental patterns have included cooperation, competition, aggressiveness, and communication. An examination of the categories used in the social developmental literature reveals several general patterns. First, much of the behavioral data encompass acts, such as sharing, that are similar to those looked at by the moral development researchers. Yet the interpretation of the data is grounded in a social, rather than a moral, framework. Part of this different interpretation is deliberate; researchers studying social behavior choose to stay away from "moral" terminology since it is couched in different philosophical traditions and is not unanimously agreed upon. Part of the different view is happenstance; research that comes out of different traditions often taps into similar phenomena and different terminology prevents much cross-referencing in the literature.

Second, dichotomies are prevalent. Implicit in these dichotomies are assumptions about social behavior as positive *or* negative. Studies have investigated whether preschoolers' social behaviors are: cooperative or competitive, cooperative or aggressive, cooperative or agonistic, cooperative or simple, dominant or subordinate, prosocial or aggressive, deviant or nondeviant, object controlled or socially controlled, and possessive or behavioral, to name a few (Addison, 1986; Camras, 1984; Dodge, Asher & Parkhurst, 1989; Eisenberg, 1982; Howes & Farver, 1987; LaFrenière & Charlesworth, 1987; Laursen & Hartup, 1989; Shantz & Hobart, 1989; Stingle & Cook, 1986).

An advantage of using dichotomies to categorize social behavior is that it provides a context for the goal of the behavior studied. That is, without a dichotomy, there is a problem as to how to describe the social meaning of the interaction. For example, cooperative behavior in and of itself, can be positive *or* negative (e.g., cooperating to help someone who is in need or cooperating with a group to gang up on another child). However, cooperative behavior *in contrast* to aggressive behavior is assumed to be prosocial. A limitation of this approach is that the definition of the terms are ambiguous in the absence of the dichotomy, particularly with respect to the social purpose of the interaction. If the research question is to find out to what end a child is cooperative or aggressive, these terms should be defined with reference to a category of behavior that includes the social meaning of the interaction.

As an example, Abramovitch, Corter, Pepler, and Stanhope (1986) observed a number of agonistic and prosocial behaviors in the preschool setting and analyzed children's responses to such initiations. Agonistic behaviors included command with a reason, commands regarding possessions, competitive statements (of superiority), bribing, and teasing. Play-related behaviors included play initiation, initiation of rough-and-tumble play, clowning, establishing roles, and turn-taking. While both of these categories are well delineated, the subcategories entail acts that could have either positive, negative, or neutral intentions towards others. For example, "command with a reason" (under agonistic behaviors) could be an act of assertion, without a negative intention towards treatment of others, whereas "teasing" could be a negative act towards others. Likewise, play-related behaviors, such as "clowning," could be neutral and "turn-taking" could be positive, with respect to treatment of others.

When agonistic behaviors, as a whole, are contrasted to play-related ones, the comparison gives a positive connotation towards the play-related category. Yet, the subcategories within the "play-related" categories reflect acts with a mixture of intentions, and the positive or negative aspects of these categories have not been specified. Thus, although this analysis on the surface seems straightforward, there is more complexity in the meaning of the interaction than is stated, and this needs to be clarified.

In fact, most studies that examine cooperative or prosocial behavior do not specify what makes prosocial behavior positive, or what makes antisocial behavior negative. That is, social behaviors are positive with respect to what? Is the relevant criterion school norms, parental values, societal codes, and/or universal principles? Little differentiation is made within these global categories (e.g., prosocial and cooperative behavior) and when they are made, analyses usually require that the categories be collapsed for general comparisons to other variables. A limitation of this method of analysis is that general categories are often used to characterize diverse phenomena. For example, in some cases prosocial behavior is equated with morality (such as sharing toys) and in other cases it is synonymous with friendship (such as smiling to others). A violation of a moral code, however, has different social implications from the violation of expectations about etiquette.

From a moral developmental viewpoint, the use of social categories, without including the moral/nonmoral status of the interaction, is ambiguous; one can be cooperative, be good at reading social cues, communicate well, and be quite popular, all for negative purposes (e.g., communicating with another to deceive). It is proposed here that analyses of social skills must include an analysis of the social meaning of the interaction. This point was also recently emphasized by Dodge, Asher, and Parkhurst (1989) who critiqued definitions of social competence based on the "achievement of one's goals." In their argument, they stated that because some goals may be socially deviant, the definition of social competence as the achievement of one's goals is not necessarily social. Their solution to the ambiguity of the definition was to stress a process analysis, in which children's goal selection strategies are analyzed from an information-processing perspective. From a moral developmental view, it is essential to include social and moral categories in analyses of social behavior; this would include determining whether social acts pertain to the violation of norms about how people ought to treat one another (e.g., preserving fairness, protecting others' welfare) or to other social norms, such as conventions and personal decisions that do not affect the treatment of others.

Categories Pertaining to Interactant and Setting Variables

The two other predominant variables that have been investigated in social developmental research include the type of interactant, and the setting—variables that are often inextricably linked, especially in naturalistic studies. For example, analyses of adult–child and child–child interactions usually refer to parent–child and sibling–sibling in the home, respectively, (although some studies include nonsibling peers in home observations) and to teacher–child and peer–peer in the preschool setting, respectively.

In fact, most of the research on preschool children's social behavior has been conducted during one kind of activity: school-time free play under adult supervision. Issues like popularity (Masters & Furman, 1981; Putallaz & Gottman, 1981), frequency of contact, and preschoolers' conflicts (Bakeman & Brownlee, 1982; Shantz, 1987) have been examined in the context of school-time free play. These studies have provided valuable information about children's social behavior in the school environment. For example, in peer groups, children develop methods of play and rituals that are not always structured by adults (Corsaro, 1985). Yet, little is known about how preschoolers respond to social transgressions in diverse settings; those vary depending on the interactive partner (e.g., a teacher or a child).

Recently, researchers have argued that studies which examine children's interactions, and do not differentiate whether the interactants are friends or nonfriends, familiar or unfamiliar, confound the results by obscuring the source of influence and/or the process of the acquisition of social knowledge (see Berndt, 1987). For example, studies have shown ways in which children differentially interact with friends and nonfriends (Doyle, Connolly, & Rivest, 1980; Drewry & Clark, 1985; Masters & Furman, 1981; Werebe & Baudonniere, 1988), mixed-age and same-age groups (Brody, Graziano, & Musser, 1983), close vs. distant associates (Hinde, Easton, Meller, & Tamplin, 1983) and younger vs. older playmates (Howes & Farver, 1987).

Preschool social behavior is typically observed in the preschool environment although recent studies have been conducted in the home (Dunn, 1988). One of the important differences between the home environment and that of the preschool is that the preschool environment involves new sets of relationships and social expectations. Thus, in the new setting, children are confronted for the first time with large peer groups involving new friendships and mixed-age social groups. Although there is a fair amount of documentation regarding young children's social interaction patterns, little is known about the role that these contextual variables play in children's developing social knowledge. Most of the research in the social developmental literature on contextual constraints has been designed to show differences regarding different types of peer exchanges without direct comparisons between adult and child interaction patterns or the role of setting effects on behavior.

An exception to this trend is the Vygotskyan-inspired research that looks specifically at the role of context on social development, particularly differences between adult–child and child–child exchanges (Rogoff & Lave, 1985; Wertsch, 1985). Although these studies provide detailed analyses of the role of context on social interaction, the end-goal for analyses is cognitive, rather than social-cognitive. That is, adult–child and child–child interactions are examined for the purposes of determining their differential influence on children's successful completion of cognitive tasks (e.g., memory, computer skills, or information-processing) rather than social and moral reasoning. A few studies which have compared the nature of moral discussions between adult–child and child–child dyads (or groups) and their impact on children's moral reasoning have shown differential effects (Damon & Killen, 1982; Kruger & Tomasello, 1986). In addition, research in development has begun to examine the influence of different social contexts on children's communication and use of social strategies (Selman, Schorin, Stone, & Phelps, 1983). So far, these studies have not been conducted with preschoolers; the results suggest, however, that this type of analysis could contribute to our understanding of the acquisition process of social knowledge.

RESEARCH ON SOCIAL CONFLICTS IN THE PRESCHOOL SETTING

The studies from the moral developmental and social developmental literature suggest that research needs to examine both the patterns of interactions that exist in preschoolers' social experience and their social and moral judgments about such exchanges. In order to analyze these aspects of early experience, a set of studies was conducted to determine whether preschoolers and adults differ in the way they respond to, resolve, and conceptualize social conflicts and their resolutions (Killen, 1989; Killen & Turiel, in press; Rende & Killen, 1989; Slomkowski & Killen, 1989). Social conflicts were the focus of this research for several reasons. First, conflicts are a measure of the potential problems that children experience in the social environment of the preschool setting. A small number of important studies have been conducted on acts that initiate conflicts, the outcome of conflicts, and resolutions (Dawe, 1934; Garvey & Shantz, 1988; Hay, 1984; Hartup, 1983). These studies have shown that not all conflicts are aggressive (Sackin & Thelen, 1984; Shantz, 1987), and that the most frequent event that creates conflicts in early development is the possession and use of objects (Bronson, 1981; Mueller, 1989; Shantz & Shantz, 1985).

In addition, a large area of research in middle childhood has focused on children's verbal conflicts. This work has shown that conflictful situations provide an important focus for social communication and moral development (Berkowitz, 1985; Blatt & Kohlberg, 1975; Camras, 1984; Eisenberg & Garvey, 1981; Killen, 1990). Yet, little is known about how preschool children resolve conflicts and how features of the social setting bear on this process (see Shantz, 1987, for an extensive review).

Second, conflicts serve as a broader category of behavior for analyses of social interaction than rule transgressions which have usually been the focus of research in social and moral development (Nucci & Turiel, 1978; Smetana, 1984). Rule transgressions, by definition, are violations of rules, which are imposed by adults. Conflicts, however, are defined as instances in which one child protests, resists, or retaliates against the actions of another (see Hay, 1984). Thus, they are events generated by children; that is, the determination of a

conflict episode derives from the child's spontaneous response to another's behavior rather than from the observation of a violation of an adult-imposed rule.
Third, conflict has been theorized to play an important role in development
(Colby & Kohlberg, 1987; Damon, 1983; Piaget, 1932). Yet, little empirical
work has been conducted on the structure of conflict in interpersonal exchanges
(see Shantz, 1987). As mentioned earlier, recent work from different perspectives has called attention to the influence of contextual variables on social interaction processes (Bearison, in press; Brownell, 1989; Higgins, Ruble, &
Hartup, 1983; Rogoff & Lave, 1985; Serafica, 1982). For the most part, contextual influences on preschoolers' social conflicts have not been systematically
examined (Hartup, 1983). How children resolve conflicts in peer situations, and
how this contrasts with preschool free play (when adults are continually present)
will shed light on the different social roles played by peers and adults in early
social development.

The guiding theoretical framework for this research is the social-cognitive
domain approach described above (Nucci, 1984; Smetana, 1989; Turiel, 1983).
The implication of this work for research on children's social conflicts is that the
structure of conflicts may differ depending on the type of social and moral issue
involved. For example, a conflict over sharing toys may take a different form
from one over how to sit at juice time; the former has potential moral features to
it, whereas the latter has potential social-conventional ones. In order to assess the
domain features of a conflict, a set of criteria were applied to the verbal and
nonverbal responses of the participants in a given exchange. Because past research has shown that adults and children differ in their responses to moral and
social-conventional transgressions (Nucci & Turiel, 1978; Smetana, 1989),
adults and children most likely differ in their responses to conflicts revolving
around moral and nonmoral social issues (see also Youniss, 1980). Thus, the
social-cognitive domain perspective provides a theoretical framework for classifying types of conflicts and conflict resolutions.

Further, the domain approach provides another way to examine contextual
features of conflictful interactions. The social context is determined, in part, by
the social-cognitive meaning of the event for the participants (see Turiel,
Smetana, & Killen, this volume). This meaning can be analyzed by assessing
how children, parents, and teachers evaluate a range of conflicts from a social-
cognitive viewpoint and whether preferences for resolutions vary on the basis of
moral, social-conventional, psychological, or pragmatic features of acts.

In the research that follows, children were observed in two social settings,
school-time free play and semistructured peer group sessions. The major context
variables included the setting, the role of adults, and the nature of child–child
relationships, including friendship alliances and familiarity with one another
over the course of a 6-month observational period. These variables were examined in relation to children's conflicts and methods of resolving conflicts. Preliminary research (Killen & Turiel, in press) produced measures for reliably classi-

fying social and moral components of conflicts (e.g., sources, outcomes, and resolutions) and social and moral judgments about conflict resolutions in the preschool context. Analyses focused on how preschoolers resolve social and moral conflicts, how resolutions differ by the type of conflict, and how variables, such as friendship, gender make-up of groups, and interactional states influences the type of conflicts that arise and their resolutions.

In addition to collecting behavioral data, preschoolers, teachers, and parents were interviewed about resolutions to conflicts. These data were collected in order to determine whether preschoolers, teachers, and parents make social-cognitive domain distinctions when evaluating social conflict resolutions. In addition, these data were compared with behavioral observations in order to compare how preschoolers' conceptualizations about conflict resolutions are similar and different to their parents' and teachers' conceptualizations.

In the first study, (Killen & Turiel, in press), an event-sampling method was used to observe conflicts in free-play settings in three preschools and in both free-play settings and peer group sessions at one preschool (ages of children ranged from 3- to 4½ years-of-age). In this study, results showed that in free-play settings, sources of conflicts differed by school; the percentage of teacher intervention in conflicts, however, was not different. While one school had a greater percentage of conflicts that stemmed from violations of social-conventional rules than the other schools, teachers intervened at an average of 53% of the time in conflicts. Further, analyses showed that teachers intervened in social order conflicts most often (66%), followed by physical harm conflicts (60%) and conflicts over sharing resources (48%). Teachers rarely intervened in conflicts stemming from psychological harm (27%). Thus, teachers differed in their intervention strategies depending on the social or moral characteristic of the conflict.

Comparisons of the conflicts in free-play settings and peer group sessions at one preschool showed that the source of conflicts varied across the settings within the school. Conflicts that stemmed from sharing resources occurred 76% in the peer groups and only 33% in the free-play sessions. One of the important findings for the setting was that child-generated resolutions to conflicts were shown at a higher rate during peer group sessions (36%) than during free play (19%).

In a subsequent study (Killen, in preparation), children were observed for four sessions in order to determine whether the findings of the first study were due to the predominance of certain highly active children contributing to the overall findings more than the other children. Using this method, each child was observed four times in the free-play setting and participated in four peer group sessions. This ensured that each child in the study was observed the same number of times, thus preventing the possibility a minority of children would contribute to the bulk of the data conducted. This method also provided a check on whether the degree of teacher intervention recorded in free play with the event sampling method was due to the fact that teachers may have intervened more often with conflicts in which highly active children were involved rather than more passive ones. As shown in Table 5.1, the majority of conflicts in the peer group sessions were again over the distribution of toys and were more diverse in the free-play setting (see Table 5.1).

As shown in Table 5.2, analyses of conflict resolutions revealed that child-generated resolutions to conflicts occurred more often in peer group sessions than during free play at each of three preschools. Out of 177 conflicts observed in peer groups, 69% involved compromising and bargaining, 24% involved reconciliation by the instigator, and 7% involved appeal to adults (with 0% adult intervention). Out of 193 conflicts observed in free play, 60% involved reconciliation by the instigator, 23% involved intervention by an adult, 9% involved compromising and bargaining, and 7% involved appeal to adults. Reconciliation by the instigator referred to instances in which the instigator immediately adhered to the protests of the respondent, whereas compromising and bargaining referred to extended discussions between the participants about the conflict. Thus, there were more active discussions about conflicts in the peer group setting than during free play. Teacher intervention was recorded less often, however, when observing children a set number of times than when using the event-sampling method.

Further, conflict resolutions varied by the source of the conflict in the two settings. Compromising and bargaining occurred quite often (74%) in the peer group sessions for conflicts about how to distribute the toys. In the free-play sessions, most of the resolutions involving reconciliations by the instigators occurred in response to conflicts about social order (70%) and, to a lesser extent, in response to conflicts about distributing resources (53%). This indicates that conflicts about the distribution of toys may be an important context in which children develop reciprocal methods of interaction, unlike conflicts about social order which do not promote the same degree of interaction.

Since there was a high percentage of reconciliation by the instigator during the free-play setting, analyses were conducted to assess whether these interactions were reflective of child–child or adult–child exchanges at each school. It was found that there were school differences regarding the relationship between the type of resolution to a conflict, its source, and whether teachers were active participants or not. For example, child-generated resolutions occurred when teachers were not active participants in a conflict episode more often than when they were participants. At some schools, however, children reconciled their conflicts more often than negotiated them, and did so when teachers were immediately present. This pattern of results indicates that the role of the teacher is complex, and that in some schools, teachers allow children to generate their own resolutions more often than in other schools. In general, children engaged in more discussion and dialogue over their own conflicts in situations in which adults did not intervene, and in which there was sustained interaction.

Qualitative analyses revealed that the way young preschoolers (3- to 4-years-

TABLE 5.1.
Percentage of Source of Conflict by Setting for Three Preschools

Source of Conflict

Setting	Physical Harm	Psychological Harm	Distribution of Resources	Rights	Social Order	Pragmatics	Friendship Expectations	Total
Peer-Group	3 (19)	4 (21)	72 (449)	13 (80)	8 (51)	0	0 (0)	(620)
Free-Play	7 (22)	6 (18)	29 (85)	18 (52)	35 (104)	4 (12)	1 (1)	(294)
Total	(41)	(39)	(534)	(132)	(155)	(12)	(1)	(914)

Notes. Frequencies in parentheses.

TABLE 5.2.
Percentage of Types of Resolutions to Conflicts for Two Settings

	Type of Resolution				
Setting	Compromising and Bargaining	Retribution and Appeal to Adults	Reconciliation by Instigator	Intervention by Adult	Total
Peer-Group	69 (122)	7 (13)	24 (42)	(0)	(177)
Free-Play	9 (19)	7 (15)	60 (114)	23 (45)	(193)
Total	(141)	(28)	(156)	(45)	(370)

Notes. Frequencies in parentheses (conflicts which were not resolved were excluded from this table).

of-age) discuss conflicts is quite different from old preschoolers (4- to 5-years-of-age). To illustrate this difference, consider the following two excerpts from actual transcripts of the peer group sessions (in which adults were absent):

> The toys (Fisher-Price people, trucks, cars, and blocks) are in a pile on the table. Three three-year olds, M, J, & D, enter the room and look at the toys. M takes a Fisher-Price person and all three sit down.
> M: You got a sister? (holding up a female Fisher-Price person) (to J)
> J: No.
> M: I do (shows her the doll again). Cause I . . .
> J: I've got this, this, this . . . (J is pulling toys from the pile toward her. D sits and watches. M starts to pull toys toward herself. D is left with a few toys to play with.)
> M: You got too many blocks and I just got two.
> J: Hey, M, here (gives her one).
> M: I need another block.
> J: Not this one (holds one in her hand).
> M: I need another block. J could you give me one block?
> J: I don't need any. I got lots of blocks. I forgot.
> M: Then give me one. (M gets up from the table and grabs the block out of J's hand. J does not resist. D watches without saying anything.)
> J: Now look. We have three and three.
> M: Yeah. Hey, you have four silly . . let's count ours.
> J: Count yours. One, two, three, four.
> M: You have four. So give one to, give some to D and give some to me. Give some to D because she has none, because you have four. (J looks over at D's few toys. J goes back to playing.)
> J: Let's just play, M.
> M: Okay.
> J: She (referring to D) doesn't get any.
> M: No, she's a silly girl.

J: She gets only two cars and a square. We don't let her have any of ours. (D watches passively.)

M: No. Now let's start to make something. (Plays with her own toys.) See how I'm making mine real different. So I want to, want to make mine like this. (M and J begin to play a naming game with their toys while D watches.)

In this example, two of the participants are more actively engaged than the third group member and appear to exclude her from the play; they appear to resolve their own conflicts about sharing the toys. An overture to share with the third child is rejected and the topic is dropped. Contrast this exchange with a group session with three 4-year olds:

L, M, and R enter the room and sit down to play with the toys at the table.

L: I need the work things . . . I want the work things. (L grabs a few of the toys). (To M) You can have the train. Can I have the work things? (Grabs a toy truck) Can I have this piece?

R: No. (R pulls back the truck and looks upset.)

M: I'll give you one of the trains. (To R) I'll give you one of the trains if you give that to L. Okay?

R: No.

L: I want all of the work things.

M: (To R) Then I won't give you the train.

R: I don't want the train. Hey, M, you want to trade cars?

M: No . . . I don't want another car.

L: (To M) Can I have this train?

M: Okay, (Looking at the pile of toys that each one has) you guys have more.

R: I have the cookie monster too. (M looks a little upset, but she is distracted by R.) Look, this moves (playing with one of the trucks).

L: Well, this is the Oscar thing.

R: Look, this moves.

M: Hey, look, watch this. (M grabs the truck from L and shows him how it works. L watches and is not bothered that M has taken his toy. M gives it back to L.)

L: How do you work it?

(There is some discussion about the trucks and how they work.)

M: I don't want this truck anymore.

R: I know (she takes a toy from L's pile).

L: (To M) You can have this one (hands her a toy).

R: Now, I only have two.

L: And I only got one.

M: Me too.

R: I know . . .

M: Let's share this one (holds up an unclaimed toy).

R: No (putting M's hand down). Since you (referring to M) have two, you (L) can have this (gives L a toy).

(All three seem content and continue to play.)

In this session, the children solicit views from one another about how to play with the toys. In addition, there is third-party intervention (in which one child makes a deal to resolve a conflict between the other two children); moreover, the level of group coordination is much higher in this session than in the group session with the younger preschoolers.

Other variables that were examined in the peer group sessions, in relation to conflict resolutions, included the types of relationships (friends or not), familiarity (history of interaction), pattern of interactive states (solitary, dyadic, or triadic), and gender make-up of the groups (there were same-sex and mixed-sex groups). Preliminary analyses revealed that friends resolve conflicts more often than nonfriends (Slomkowski & Killen, 1989), and that mixed-gender groups had fewer conflicts than same-gender groups (Killen, in preparation). Analyses conducted on the social interactional states (i.e., solitary, dyadic, or triadic) that preceded conflicts showed that when solitary or dyadic states occurred before conflicts, protests by victims were often ignored, whereas when triadic states preceded conflicts, the protests were often responded to in a positive way (with the outcome of an active resolution by the participants in the group). This supports the notion that increased levels of coordinated play and interaction are related to methods of conflict resolutions. The relationship between coordinated play and history of interaction (and friendship) needs further investigation.

In addition to observing children's social interaction patterns, interviews were conducted with preschoolers, parents, and teachers about conflict resolutions (Killen & LaFleur, in preparation). Conflicts that reflect moral and social-convention issues and that occurred frequently in the preschool setting (e.g., hitting, not sharing, knocking over someone else's toys, standing rather than sitting at the snack table, changing a game rule, and playing with the lego blocks in the sandbox) were selected and described to subjects (six conflicts in the adult interview and four conflicts in the child interview).

After the description of each conflict, a range of resolutions (six for the adult interview and four for the child interview) were presented (depicted as drawings for the preschoolers) and the interviewer asked the subject to choose the best resolution to the conflict. The resolutions (like the conflicts) varied along moral and social-conventional lines. For example, "morally oriented" conflict resolutions involved the teacher explaining the moral consequences that occurred in a conflict (e.g., "the teacher explains to Eric that he should share with others so that everyone gets a chance to use the toys") and social-conventionally oriented resolutions involved the teacher explaining the social-conventional consequences that occurred in a conflict (e.g., "the teacher tells Eric that it looks messy for him to have all of the toys on his side of the sandbox, so he should share with Joe"). Both types of resolutions were presented for each type of conflict and variations along extrinsic and intrinsic dimensions were incorporated into the design (as described by Hoffman, 1977). Extrinsic resolutions emphasized rules and punishment (e.g., "the teacher tells Eric that he is breaking a rule in the preschool, and that therefore, he must share the toys with Joe") while intrinsic resolutions emphasize explanations. Further, parents and teachers were asked to give preferences for "ideal" resolutions and for "practical" resolutions, and all subjects were asked about resolutions which included letting children work it out on their own.

Preliminary results from interviews with mothers and fathers showed that the majority of parents preferred intrinsic moral explanations for moral conflicts (80%) and intrinsic social-conventional explanations for social-conventional conflicts (65%) when asked about ideal conditions. A minority of parents (11%) chose resolutions which called for the teacher to let the children work out conflicts on their own, and almost no parents (2%) chose punishment as the ideal resolution.

When asked about practical resolutions, parents still preferred domain-consistent resolutions but their preferences for resolutions based on punishment increased (32% for moral conflicts and 27% for social-conventional ones) and their preferences for letting children work it out on their own decreased dramatically (6% for moral conflicts and 8% for social-conventional ones). Thus, overall, parents were domain consistent in their choice for resolutions to conflicts. Parental preferences for resolutions based on punishment or letting children work it out, however, changed depending on whether the condition was "ideal" or "practical." These findings indicate that parents believe that teachers should emphasize the underlying rationales when intervening in children's conflicts. However, parents do not yet believe that letting children work out conflicts on their own is practical in the preschool setting. Whether this judgment derives from a view that children are not capable of working out conflict or from a view that the preschool environment does not make teacher nonintervention feasible remains to be investigated.

These results are interesting in light of Nucci's (1984) findings that children in elementary school prefer teachers who use domain-consistent teaching strategies over ones who are often inconsistent. Perhaps effective parental strategies are also ones that are domain-consistent, which would support Nucci's conclusions. Other studies which have examined parental evaluations of preschoolers' social interactions indicate that parental perceptions are related to children's social competence (Dix, Ruble, Grusec, & Nixon, 1986; Ladd & Golter, 1988).

Analyses of interviews with teachers and preschoolers are currently in progress. The results analyzed so far show that children were also domain consistent in their preference for teacher resolutions. The majority of children, 66% and 57%, preferred moral resolutions for moral conflicts (not sharing and hitting, respectively); 65% and 62% of the children preferred social-conventional resolutions for social-conventional conflicts (playing with toys in the wrong area, and violating a juice-time convention, respectively).

Thus, children's choice of resolution was consistent with the type of conflict. Children's reasons for their decision were even more domain differentiated than their choices in that moral reasons were given for moral conflicts and social-conventional reasons for social-conventional conflicts. Very little pragmatic reasoning was shown for this choice.

When asked about a choice between punishment or letting children work out conflicts on their own, one-third of the children preferred resolutions in which children would be allowed to work it out on their own. Thus, while more children preferred punishment to nonintervention, one-third of them chose the latter. Interestingly, some children gave moral reasons for choosing punishment. As an example, some children said that an instigator of a hitting conflict should be sent to "time-out" so no one would be getting hurt. This reason has a moral basis to it since the subject is discussing the alleviation of pain. This differs from traditional characterizations of children's reasoning about punishment in which they are oriented towards retribution and authority. Here some of the children were discussing a way to end the infliction of harm to another. One of the aims of this research is to directly compare children's, parents', and teachers' evaluations of conflict resolutions with one another and to analyze the relationship between individuals judgments about resolutions with what actually occurs (as measured by observational data in the preschool setting).

Thus, in this research, criteria were used to classify social conflicts that occur in the preschool setting and to analyze individuals' social judgments about how such conflicts should be resolved. Children and adults responded to, and treated social exchanges (in this case, conflicts) differently depending on whether they pertained to moral or social-conventional issues. The results showed that conflicts about the distribution of toys were more interactive than those pertaining to social order; this suggests that children are more involved in these issues, and that they serve a different role in children's construction of social and moral judgments than exchanges that revolve around matters of social order.

These findings reveal that the use of criteria for classifying social behavior is instrumental in revealing patterns of interaction which in turn allows for a more detailed understanding about processes of development. Moreover, the results present a differentiated view of the context. Rather than characterizing the context in terms of a broad template of experience (e.g., permissive, restrictive), these results suggest that it is important to define context in terms of the patterns of interactions, especially since it was shown that exchanges differ depending on the social and moral issues at stake.

CONCLUSIONS

To summarize, the focus of this chapter was on social-cognitive development in early childhood and on studies which show evidence for social judgment and moral behavior in the preschool period. Studies which used explicit criteria for "social" and "moral" categories and which conducted detailed analyses of the context, provided evidence for a differentiated, rather than a global model of development, and for a moral, rather than a premoral orientation in early development. Differentiation was shown in children's evaluations of rule transgressions and sharing norms. Children's conflicts with adults and peers also showed diversity; adult–child conflicts concerned sharing issues just as child–child conflicts pertained to social order. Moral orientations were evident in preschoolers' reasoning about rule transgressions; how children acquire such judgments requires further investigation. This calls for more research on the influence of contextual variables on children's social interactions. This can be accomplished by conducting detailed observations of social interactions as well as obtaining information about how individuals (children, parents, and teachers) interpret such social exchanges from a social and moral viewpoint. Investigating how individuals interpret and evaluate their social experience provides information about the meaning of the exchanges to the interactants as well as about the nature of the relationship between social experience and judgment. For a comprehensive theory about the acquisition of social knowledge, it is necessary to understand how children and adults engage in, and conceptualize their social exchanges.

ACKNOWLEDGMENTS

This research was supported by a Spencer Foundation Grant, a Wesleyan University Project Grant, and a Ford Foundation Faculty-Student Summer Award (granted to the author and Lara Anderson). The author would like to thank Judith G. Smetana for her thorough comments on the manuscript, and Rosemarie LaFleur, Richard Rende, and Cheryl Slomkowski for their collaboration on the design of the preschool research project. I gratefully acknowledge the research assistance of Lara Anderson, Sue Breton, Heather Ferguson, Karen Handler, and Cassie Kisiel. In addition, I extend my gratitude to the teachers, parents, and children at the Neighborhood Preschool, the Durham Cooperative Preschool, and Young Horizons Day Care in the Middletown, Connecticut, area, for their cooperation and participation in the research reported in this paper.

REFERENCES

Abramovitch, R., Corter, C., Pepler, D. J., & Stanhope, L. (1986). Sibling and peer interaction: A final follow-up and comparison. *Child Development, 57,* 217–229.

Addison, W. (1986). Agonistic behavior in preschool children: A comparison of same-sex versus opposite sex interactions. *Bulletin of the Psychonomic Society, 24,* 44–46.

Bakeman, R., & Brownlee, J. R. (1982). Social rules governing object conflicts in toddlers and preschoolers. In K. H. Rubin & H. S. Ross (Eds.), *Peer relationships and social skills in childhood* (pp. 99–111). New York: Springer-Verlag.

Bearison, D. J. (in press). Interactional contexts of cognitive development: Piagetian approaches to sociogenesis. In L. Tolchinsky (Ed.), *Culture, cognition, and schooling.* Norwood, NJ: Ablex.

Berkowitz, M. W. (1985). The role of discussion in moral education. In M. W. Berkowitz & F. Oser (Eds.), *Moral education: Theory and application.* Hillsdale, NJ: Lawrence Erlbaum Associates.

Berndt, T. (1987). The distinctive features of conversations between friends: Theories, research, and implications for sociomoral development. In W. M. Kurtines & J. L. Gewirtz (Eds.), *Moral development through social interaction.* New York: Wiley.

Blatt, M., & Kohlberg, L. (1975). The effects of classroom moral discussion upon children's level of moral judgment. *Journal of Moral Education, 4,* 129–161.

Brody, G. H., Graziano, W. G., & Musser, L. M. (1983). Familiarity and children's behavior in same-age and mixed-age peer groups. *Developmental Psychology, 19,* 568–576.

Bronson, W. C. (1981). *Toddler's behaviors with agemates: Issues of interaction, cognition and affect.* Norwood, NJ: Ablex.

Brownell, C. A. (1989). Socially shared cognition: The role of social context in the construction of knowledge. In L. T. Winegar (Ed.), *Social interaction and the development of children's understanding* (pp. 173–205). Norwood, NJ: Ablex.

Camras, L. A. (1984). Children's verbal and nonverbal communication in a conflict situation. *Ethology and Sociobiology, 5,* 257–268.

Colby, A., & Kohlberg, L. (1987). *The measurement of moral judgment.* New York: Cambridge University Press.

Corsaro, W. A. (1985). *Friendship and peer culture in the early years.* Norwood, NJ: Ablex.

Damon, W. (1977). *The social world of the child.* San Francisco: Jossey-Bass.

Damon, W. (1983). The nature of social-cognitive change in the developing child. In W. Overton (Ed.), *The relationship between social and cognitive development.* Hillsdale, NJ: Lawrence Erlbaum Associates.

Damon, W., & Killen, M. (1982). .Peer interaction and the process of change in children's moral reasoning. *Merrill-Palmer Quarterly, 28,* 347–367.

Davidson, P., Turiel, E., & Black, A. (1983). The effect of stimulus familiarity on the use of criteria and justifications in children's social reasoning. *British Journal of Developmental Psychology, 1,* 49–65.

Dawe, H. C. (1934). An analysis of two hundred quarrels of preschool children. *Child Development, 5,* 139–157.

Dix, T., Ruble, D. N., Grusec, J. E., & Nixon, S. (1986). Social cognition in parents: Inferential and affective reactions to children at three age levels. *Child Development, 57,* 879–894.

Dodge, K. A., Asher, S. R., & Parkhurst, J. (1989). Social life as a goal-coordination task. *Research on Motivation in Education, 3,* 107–135.

Doyle, A. B., Connolly, J., & Rivest, L. P. (1980). The effect of playmate familiarity in the social interactions of young children. *Child Development, 51,* 217–223.

Drewry, D. L., & Clark, M. L. (1985). Factors important in the formation of preschoolers' friendships. *The Journal of Genetic Psychology, 146,* 37–44.

Dunn, J. (1988). *The beginnings of social understanding.* Cambridge, MA: Harvard University Press.

Eisenberg, A. R., & Garvey, C. (1981). Children's use of verbal strategies in resolving conflicts. *Discourse Processes, 4,* 149–170.

Eisenberg, N. (1982). (Ed.) *The development of prosocial behavior.* N.Y.: Academic Press.

Eisenberg, N., & Hand, M. (1979). The relationship of preschooler's reasoning about prosocial moral conflicts to prosocial behavior. *Child Development, 50,* 356–363.

Eisenberg-Berg, N., Haake, R., Hand, M., & Sadalla, E. (1979). Effects of instructions concerning ownership of a toy on preschoolers' sharing and defensive behaviors. *Developmental Psychology, 15,* 460–461.

Feldman, D. H. (1980). *Beyond universals in cognitive development.* Norwood, NJ: Ablex.

Garvey, C. J., & Shantz, C. U. (1988, March). *Varieties of children's conflicts.* Paper presented at the Conference on Human Development, Charleston, SC.

Hartup, W. W. (1983). Peer relations. In E. M. Hetherington (Ed.), P. H. Mussen (Series Ed.), *Handbook of child psychology: Vol. 4. Socialization, personality, and social development,* 4th ed. (pp. 103–196). New York Wiley.

Hay, D. F. (1984). Social conflict in early childhood. In G. Whitehurst (Ed.), *Annals of child development* (Vol. *1,* pp. 1–44). Greenwich, CT: JAI.

Higgins, E. T., Ruble, D. N., & Hartup, W. W. (1983). (Eds.). *Social cognition and social development.* Cambridge, England: Cambridge University Press.

Hinde, R. A., Easton, D. F., Meller, R. E., & Tamplin, A. (1983). Nature and determinants of preschoolers' differential behavior to adults and peers. *British Journal of Developmental Psychology, 1,* 3–19.

Hoffman, M. L. (1977). Moral internalization. In L. Berkowitz (Ed.), *Advances in experimental social psychology* (Vol. 10). New York: Academic Press.

Howes, C., & Farver, J. A. (1987). Social pretend play in 2-year-olds: Effects of age of partner. *Early Childhood Research Quarterly, 2,* 305–314.

Keil, F. (1985). On the structure dependent nature of stages of cognitive development. In I. Levin (Ed.), *Stage and structure: Reopening the debate* (pp. 144–163). Norwood, NJ: Ablex.

Killen, M. (1990). Children's evaluations of morality in the context of peer, teacher-child, and familial relations. *Journal of Genetic Psychology, 151,* 395–410.

Killen, M. (1989). Context, conflict, and coordination in social development. In L. T. Winegar (Ed.), *Social interaction and the development of children's understanding* (pp. 119–146). Norwood, NJ: Ablex.

Killen, M. (in preparation). *Social conflicts in preschool peer groups.* Manuscript.

Killen, M., & LaFleur, R. (in preparation). *Parents' and preschoolers' judgments about social conflict resolutions.* Manuscript.

Killen, M., & Turiel, E. (in press). Conflict resolutions in preschoolers' social interactions. *Early Education and Development.*

Kohlberg, L. (1969). Stage and sequence: The cognitive-developmental approach to socialization. In D. A. Goslin (Ed.), *Handbook of socialization theory and research.* Chicago: Rand McNally.

Kruger, A. C., & Tomasello, M. (1986). Transactive discussions with peer and adults. *Developmental Psychology, 22,* 681–685.

Ladd, G. W., & Golter, B. S. (1988). Parents' management of preschoolers' peer relations: Is it related to children's social competence? *Developmental Psychology, 24,* 109–117.

LaFrenière, P. & Charlesworth, W. K. (1987). Effects of friendship and dominance status on preschooler's resource utilization in a cooperative/competitive situation. *International Journal of Behavioral Development, 10,* 345–358.

Laursen, B., & Hartup, W. W. (1989). The dynamics of preschool children's conflicts. *Merrill-Palmer Quarterly, 35,* 281–297.

Masters, J. C., & Furman, W. (1981). Popularity, individual friendship selection, and specific peer interactions among children. *Developmental Psychology, 17,* 344–350.

Much, N., & Shweder, R. (1978). Speaking of rules: The analysis of culture in the breach. In W. Damon (Ed.), *New directions for child development: Vol. 2. Moral development.* San Francisco: Jossey-Bass.

Mueller, E. (1989). Toddler's peer relations: Shared meaning and semantics. In W. Damon (Ed.), *Child development today and tomorrow* (pp. 312–331). San Francisco: Jossey-Bass.

Nucci, L. P. (1984). Evaluating teachers as social agents: Students' ratings of domain appropriate and domain inappropriate teacher responses to transgressions. *American Educational Research Journal, 21,* 367–378.

Nucci, L. P., & Nucci, M. (1982). Children's social interactions in the context of moral and conventional transgressions. *Child Development, 53,* 403–412.

Nucci, L. P., & Turiel, E. (1978). Social interactions and the development of social concepts in preschool children. *Child Development, 49,* 400–407.

Nunner-Winkler, G., & Sodian, B. (1988). Children's understanding of moral emotions. *Child Development, 59,* 1323–1328.

Piaget, J. (1932). *The moral judgment of the child.* London: Routledge & Kegan Paul.

Putallaz, M., & Gottman, J. M. (1981). An interactional model of children's entry into peer groups. *Child Development, 52,* 986–994.

Ramsey, P. G. (1987). Possession episodes in young children's social interactions. *Journal of Genetic Psychology, 148,* 315–325.

Rende, R., & Killen, M. (1989). *Social interactional antecedents of object conflict in young children.* Manuscript.

Rogoff, B., & Lave, J. (1985). (Eds.). *Everyday cognition: Its development in social context.* Cambridge, MA: Harvard University Press.

Sackin, S., & Thelen, E. (1984). An ethological study of peaceful associative outcomes to conflict in preschool children. *Child Development, 55,* 1098–1102.

Sanderson, J. A., & Siegal, M. (1988). Conceptions of moral and social rules in rejected and nonrejected preschoolers. *Journal of Clinical Child Psychology, 17,* 66–72.

Selman, R. L., Schorin, M., Stone, C., & Phelps, E. (1983). A naturalistic study of children's social understanding. *Developmental Psychology, 19,* 82–102.

Serafica, F. C. (Ed.). (1982). *Social-cognitive development in context.* New York: Guilford Press.

Shantz, C. U. (1987). Conflict between children. *Child Development, 58,* 283–305.

Shantz, C. U. & Hobart, C. J. (1989). Social conflict and development: Peers and siblings. In T. J. Berndt & G. W. Ladd (Eds.) *Peer relationships in child development* (71–94). New York: Wiley.

Shantz, C. U., & Shantz, D. W. (1985). Conflict between children: Social-cognitive and sociometric correlates. In M. W. Berkowitz (Ed.), *Peer conflict and psychological growth: New directions for child development* (pp. 3–21). San Francisco: Jossey-Bass.

Siegal, M., & Storey, R. M. (1985). Day care and children's conceptions of moral and social rules. *Child Development, 56,* 1001–1008.

Siegler, R. S. (1989). How domain-general and domain-specific knowledge interact to produce strategy choices. *Merrill-Palmer Quarterly, 35,* 1–26.

Slomkowski, C., & Killen, M. (1989). *Children's concepts of friendship in relation to conflict resolution and peer exchanges.* Manuscript.

Smetana, J. G. (1981). Preschool children's conceptions of moral and social rules. *Child Development, 52,* 1333–1336.

Smetana, J. G. (1984). Toddler's social interactions regarding moral and conventional transgressions. *Child Development, 55,* 1767–1776.

Smetana, J. G. (1985). Preschool children's conceptions of transgressions: The effects of varying moral and conventional domain-related attributes. *Developmental Psychology, 21,* 18–29.

Smetana, J. G. (1989). Toddlers' social interactions in the context of moral and conventional transgressions in the home context. *Developmental Psychology, 25,* 499–508.

Stingle, S., & Cook, H. (1986). Age and sex differences in the cooperative and noncooperative behavior of pairs of American children. *Journal of Psychology, 119,* 335–345.

Tisak, M. (1986). Children's conceptions for parental authority. *Child Development, 57,* 166–176.

Turiel, E. (1983). *The development of social knowledge: Morality and convention.* Cambridge, England: Cambridge University Press.

Werebe, M. J. G., & Baudonniere, P. M. (1988). Friendship among preschool children. *International Journal of Behavioral Development, 11,* 291–304.

Wertsch, J. (1985). *Culture, communication, and cognition: Vygotskyan perspectives.* New York: Cambridge University Press.

Weston, D., & Turiel, E. (1980). Act-rule relations: Children's concepts of social rules. *Developmental Psychology, 16,* 417–424.

Youniss, J. (1980). *Parents and peers in social development.* Chicago: University of Chicago Press.

6
Structural and Situational Influences on Moral Judgment: The Interaction Between Stage and Dilemma

Dennis L. Krebs
Sandra C. A. Vermeulen
Jeremy I. Carpendale
Kathy Denton

ABSTRACT

Kohlberg advances a rational model of moral judgment based on the assumption that people "construct moral meaning" in terms of their "current developmental stage," and, therefore, that moral judgment is highly homogeneous, organized in structures of the whole. In this chapter we review past research on the structural consistency of moral judgment, and describe our own research on the issue—reviewing studies on moral judgment about AIDS, impaired driving, prosocial behavior, business transactions, prostitution, and actual moral dilemmas experienced by people in their everyday lives. The evidence indicates that moral judgment is sometimes homogeneous and sometimes heterogeneous. We argue that a more interactional model than Kohlberg's constructivistic model is needed to explain the observed pattern of relationships. People possess a set of stage-structures that include their "current stage" and all stages they have acquired in the past. Situations and dilemmas exert varying pulls for and resistances against the activation of these stage-structures. The structures that individuals invoke depend on the distribution of stages they possess, the strength of pull and resistance of the dilemmas they face, and contexts in which they make moral decisions. Kohlberg's dilemmas tend to evoke the highest stages people have acquired; his test assesses moral competence. Although people often fail to perform at their level of competence on less philosophical dilemmas, those who score high on Kohlberg's test are significantly less prone than those who score lower to invoke Stage 2 judgments about other issues.

No psychologist has contributed more to the study of moral development than the late Lawrence Kohlberg. According to Kohlberg, individuals interpret moral issues in terms of cognitive structures—"general organizing principles or patterns of thought" (Colby & Kohlberg, 1987, p. 2)—that define their current stage of moral development. Kohlberg believes that moral judgment is highly consistent, organized in "structures of the whole" such that "under conditions that support expression of the individual's most mature thinking, his or her reasoning will form a coherent system best described by one of Kohlberg's five stages or a mixture of at most two adjacent stages" (Colby, Kohlberg, Gibbs, & Lieberman, 1983, p. 123). The emphasis in Kohlberg's model is within the person: people "construct moral meaning" across varying content in terms of the structures that define their current stage of moral development. If you determine an individual's stage by giving him or her Kohlberg's test, you will be able to predict how the person will interpret or construct all the moral issues he or she may face. Kohlberg's model is hopeful because it construes humans as rational thinkers motivated to determine what is right. Although Kohlberg acknowledges that high levels of moral judgment do not guarantee high levels of moral behavior, he believes they are prerequisites.

How valid is Kohlberg's model of moral judgment? Recent research on cognition suggests that human inference is not as rational as Piaget or Kohlberg assume (see Wason & Johnson-Laird, 1972). Research on social cognition has revealed that social judgments are plagued by a variety of self-serving biases (see Nisbett & Ross, 1980; Snyder, Higgins, & Stucky, 1983). And, as pointed out by Brown and Herrnstein (1975), a spate of studies on social influence paint a much less hopeful picture of human nature than that intrinsic to Kohlberg's model. Such studies demonstrate that people at relatively high stages of moral development are easily induced to behave aggressively (Krebs & Miller, 1985), to inflict power (Zimbardo, Haney, Banks, & Jaffe, 1973), to obey the commands of destructive authorities (Milgram, 1963), and to ignore victims in emergencies (Latané & Darley, 1970). What happens to their capacity to make high-level moral judgments in situations such as these?

The guiding purposes of the program of research we have been pursuing for the past several years are (a) to examine the nature of moral judgment in everyday life (in particular, to determine whether it is structured in terms of Kohlbergian stages), (b) to determine the extent to which moral judgment stems from rational deductive reasoning, and is susceptible to corrupting biases, (c) to explore the structural consistency of moral judgment across a variety of moral issues, and, ultimately, (d) to explain the link between moral judgment and moral behavior. Our focus in this chapter is on structural consistency and the constructivistic model of moral judgment it implies. Do people base all their moral judgments on their current developmental stage, as Kohlberg's model suggests, or do they tend to invoke lower-stage structures in certain situations, as a more interactional model would suggest?

EVIDENCE ON HOMOGENEITY: KOHLBERG'S LONGITUDINAL STUDY

The primary evidence adduced by Kohlberg in support of the structural consistency of moral judgment stems from the pattern of judgments given to his test by the subjects in his 20-year longitudinal study. As scored and counted by Colby, Kohlberg, and their colleagues (1987), the mean percentage of judgments at each subject's modal stage was approximately 70%, with virtually all judgments at adjacent stages (p. 90): only "9% [of the subjects] . . . show a third stage of reasoning greater than 10%" (p. 91). Colby and Kohlberg acknowledge only two clear cases where "the lack of consistency is a real phenomenon" (p. 91).

In cognitive-developmental theories such as that of Kohlberg, two inconsistent cases constitute a threat to the assumption that the processes mediating structural wholeness are invariant and universal. If two subjects show stage heterogeneity, other people might as well. More problematically, other investigators who have reviewed Colby and Kohlberg's longitudinal data have found more stage inconsistency than Colby and Kohlberg claim. According to Fischer (1983):

> Different dilemmas produced different modal stage assignments for many subjects and alternate forms of the interview produced different stages as well . . . The moral judgment study, then, does not allow the conclusion that moral development demonstrates a strong form of the structured-whole hypothesis. With substantial variations in task and context, moral behavior seems instead to fit what is becoming the standard empirically based portrait of cognitive and social-cognitive development. Considerable variability in stage within an individual is the norm (Flavell, 1971; Martarano, 1977; Piaget, 1972; Rest, 1979) (pp. 99–100).

EVIDENCE ON HOMOGENEITY: KOHLBERG DILEMMAS VS. OTHER DILEMMAS

Even if moral judgments to the dilemmas on Kohlberg's test were structurally homogeneous, as Kohlberg claims, this would not, of course, establish that people structure their moral judgments to other dilemmas and issues in terms of the stages they display on Kohlberg's test. Gilligan (1982), Eisenberg (1982), and others have argued that in their concern with justice, Kohlberg's dilemmas neglect the prosocial or "care" side of morality. Baumrind (1978) and Damon (1977) criticize Kohlberg's dilemmas for failing to reflect the types of moral conflicts people experience in their everyday lives. Haan (1978) chastises Kohlberg for overlooking the interpersonal side of morality. And, from our frame of reference perhaps most importantly, Kohlberg's dilemmas evoke hypothetical judgments about imaginary characters, as opposed to actual judgments with real consequences to the self.

At least ten studies have examined the consistency between stage use on Kohlberg's tests and on other types of moral dilemma. Three studies support Kohlberg's homogeneity claim; seven do not. The three studies in which moral judgment was consistent involved dilemmas about public policy (Lockwood, 1975), Israeli soldiers' justifications for refusing to fight in the Lebanon war (Linn, 1987a) and actual moral conflicts (Walker, de Vries, & Trevethan, 1987). Five studies found that subjects scored significantly lower on the non-Kohlberg dilemmas than on Kohlberg's dilemmas. The non-Kohlberg dilemmas in these studies involved moral issues relating to sexual relationships (Gilligan, Kohlberg, Lerner, & Belenky, 1971), problems in prison (Kohlberg, Scharf, & Hickey, 1972), relations in high school (Higgins, Power, & Kohlberg, 1984), daycare (Linn, 1984), and an actual strike staged by 50 Israeli physicians (Linn, 1987b).

Finally, two studies found that subjects made higher stage judgments on non-Kohlberg dilemmas involving the Free Speech Movement in the 60s in Berkeley (Haan, 1975) and personal decisions about abortion (Gilligan & Belenky, 1980).

Several of the foregoing studies relied on earlier versions of Kohlberg's scoring system—versions plagued with reliability problems, subjective scoring, and failure to distinguish content from structure (Colby & Kohlberg, 1987). For example, Candee and Kohlberg (1987) rescored the Kohlberg dilemmas in Haan's (1975) study using Kohlberg's revised scoring system, and found substantial differences between the original and revised stage assignments. Only six of the studies—Gilligan & Belenky, 1980; Higgins et al., 1984; Linn, 1984, 1987a, 1987b; and Walker et al., 1987—employed Colby and Kohlberg's revised Standard Issue Scoring System.

The conclusion that seems to follow from past research on the structural consistency of moral judgment is that individuals sometimes base their moral judgments on the same stages they display on Kohlberg's test, but they more often base their judgments on other structures. In his latest work, Kohlberg acknowledges that moral judgment is sometimes inconsistent. Let us consider how he deals with this issue.

Kohlberg's Explanation For Stage Heterogeneity

Because all stage theories posit a transitional period in which individuals change from one stage to another, no stage theory expects perfect homogeneity (see Flavell, 1982). People don't change from one stage to another overnight. It is on this basis that Kohlberg sets his criteria for homogeneity as adjacent stages rather than same stage.

In recent formulations of his theory with Colby and other colleagues, Kohlberg acknowledges another source of heterogeneity—"performance factors'': In "situations with a significant downward press" such as the "low-level 'moral atmosphere' of a traditional prison" (Colby & Kohlberg, 1987, p. 8), individuals may base their moral judgments on stages lower than the ones they obtain on Kohlberg's test. Indeed, Colby and Kohlberg (1987) state that the "stage properties" of Kohlberg's theory, including the assumption of structured wholeness, "characterize competence though not necessarily performance in moral judgment" (p. 8). Of course, all measures of competence are based on tests of performance, but Colby and Kohlberg argue they minimize the gap between competence and performance on Kohlberg's test "by using hypothetical dilemmas, by using probing questions that attempt to elicit the upper limits of the subject's thinking, and by . . . scoring rules according to which only the most mature expressed version of a particular moral idea is scored" (p. 7).

Because our goal is to explain moral judgment in everyday life, our focus is on performance, not competence. We take as a starting point Kohlberg's acknowledgment that people do not always perform at their level of competence—indeed, we suspect people *usually* fail to perform at their level of competence, and we seek to uncover the "performance factors" that mediate low-level moral reasoning. We turn now to our own research on this issue.

OUR RESEARCH ON THE HOMOGENEITY OF MORAL JUDGMENT

Our research on homogeneity follows a general format. Subjects respond to a set of dilemmas from Kohlberg's test before or (usually) after they respond to another dilemma or dilemmas—either (a) a standard Kohlberg dilemma that has been modified in some way, (b) a dilemma created by us based on issues experienced by people in real-life, or (c) a dilemma actually experienced by subjects in their everyday lives. The set of non-Kohlberg dilemmas we have examined is outlined in Table 6.1.

We score the Kohlberg dilemmas in accordance with the 17-step procedure outlined by Colby and Kohlberg (1987). We break down the prescriptive judgments (should statements) made by our subjects into discrete interview judgments, and match them with criterion judgments in the Colby and Kohlberg (1987) scoring manual. Through this matching procedure, we assign stage scores to all scoreable interview judgments, which are then weighted and summed to produce Global Stage Scores (GSS) and Weighted Average Scores (WAS). We obtain GSS on a 9-point scale (Stage 1 followed by Stage 1/2 and Stage 2, etc.). WAS (also called moral maturity scores) range from 100 (corresponding to stage 1) to 500 (corresponding to Stage 5).

Scoring non-Kohlberg moral judgments is more difficult, because the content of such judgments usually differs from the content of the criterion judgments in Kohlberg's scoring manual. It is, however, possible to match the stage structure

TABLE 6.1.
Overview of Studies

Study	Gender	Mean Age	N	Kohlberg WAS	Non-Kohlberg WAS	r*	p value**	Kohlberg GSS	Non-Kohlberg GSS	Interrater Reliability % Agreement***
1. Modified Kohlberg: Self	M & F	24	40	329	333	.53	n.s.	3/4	3/4	90(90)
2. Modified Kohlberg: AIDS	M	27	40	335	329	.43	n.s.	3/4	3/4	90(90)
3. AIDS	M	27	40	335	331	.35	n.s.	3/4	3/4	85(94)
4. Impaired Driving	M & F	27	60	325	247	.51	p<.001	3/4	2/3	90(80)
5 Prosocial	M & F	27	60	325	284	.32	p<.001	3/4	2/3	90(80)
6. Business Sale	M	28	40	344	249	.18	p<.001	3/4	2/3	80(93)
7. Free Trade	M	28	40	344	301	.32	p<.001	3/4	3	80(80)
8. Prostitution	F	16	60	245(Pro)	232	.17	n.s.	2/3	2/3	85(75)
				236(JD)	225	.41	n.s.	2/3	2/3	85(75)
				269(Cont)	261	.33	n.s.	2/3	2/3	85(75)
9. Real-Life	M & F	25	50	335	298	.21	p<.001	3/4	3	80(80)
10. Interpersonal Conflict	M & F	25	52	325	299	.28	p<.001	3/4	3	91(83)
11. Family Conflict	M & F	43(Mo)	63	340	327	.43	n.s.	3/4	3	87(87)
		44(Fa)		347	313	.29	p<.005	3/4	3	87(87)
		14(Dau)		278	251	.46	p<.005	3	2/3	87(87)

* correlations between the Kohlberg WAS and the Non-Kohlberg WAS

** p value for the differences between the mean Kohlberg and Non-Kohlberg WAS

***Interrater reliability on the WAS is calculated separately for the Kohlberg and Non-Kohlberg. The interrater percent agreement for the Non-Kohlberg is bracketed.

of interview judgments with the underlying stage structure of criterion judgments, even though the content differs. We were able to match enough non-Kohlberg judgments with criterion judgments in the Colby and Kohlberg manual in all of our studies to obtain reliable GSS and WAS. Examples of non-Kohlberg interview judgments from each of our studies matched with corresponding criterion judgments from Colby and Kohlberg's scoring manual are outlined in Table 6.2.

All dilemmas are scored blind to subjects' scores on other dilemmas. Twenty-five percent of each sample of dilemmas are selected at random for interrater reliability. Our criterion for interrater reliability is strict—agreement within 33 WAS points (one-third of a stage). Percent agreement for the Kohlberg and non-Kohlberg dilemmas employed in each of our studies is shown in Table 6.1.

We quantify consistency in two main ways. First we count the number of subjects whose GSS (on a 9-point scale) on the Kohlberg and non-Kohlberg dilemmas are the same, one substage higher, one substage lower, etc., and we represent this comparison graphically in terms of the difference between Kohlberg and non-Kohlberg stages, with zero representing same substage on the two dilemmas, -1 representing a lower adjacent substage on the non-Kohlberg dilemma, $+1$ representing a higher adjacent substage on the non-Kohlberg dilemma, and so on (see, for example, Fig. 6.1). Second, we compare mean WAS scores on the Kohlberg and non-Kohlberg dilemmas.

As shown in Table 6.1, most of our subjects have been young adults, though we tested teenage girls in two studies. The gender of subjects in each study and sample size also are outlined in Table 6.1. Let us consider each of the studies we have conducted in turn.

STUDIES EMPLOYING MODIFIED KOHLBERG DILEMMAS

Judgments on Kohlberg's test are about hypothetical characters such as Heinz, but moral judgments in everyday life typically involve the self. Other investigations have varied the protagonists of the Kohlbergian dilemmas on Rest's (1986) *Defining Issues Test,* comparing judgments with self-referents ("imagine your wife was near death from a special kind of cancer . . .") to standard judgments about Heinz and other characters. Such studies have produced mixed results—some finding lower moral maturity for judgments about the self (Lonky, Roodin, & Rybash, 1988; Rybash, Roodin, & Lonky, 1981), some finding higher moral maturity (for female subjects) (Lonky et al., 1988), and some failing to find any difference (Rybash, Hoyer, & Roodin, 1983). Another study, which used Kohlberg's dilemmas and an earlier Kohlberg scoring system (Leming, 1978), found that the mean moral maturity in the "self" condition was lower than the mean moral maturity in the "other" condition.

TABLE 6.2.

Interview Judgments	Criterion Judgments

Aids

It is alright to have compulsory testing because the safety of the majority outweighs the right of the few not to be tested, the good of the group outweighs the good of the individual.

A soldier does not have the right to refuse to go on the mission because it is better to sacrifice one man's life for the majority. (Form C, Life (Preservation), CJ #15, Stage 3/4, p. 679)

A doctor shouldn't be permitted to refuse to treat people with AIDS because a doctor is supposed to help people who are sick.

Dr.'s are supposed to care for their patients. (Form B, Life, CJ #10, Stage 3, p. 300)

A doctor has taken an oath to help people, so therefore I feel that they should not refuse to help.

[The doctor should not give the woman the drug] because according to the Hippocratic oath, of the ethics of the medical profession, a doctor should always sustain life and never end it. (Form B, Life, CJ #5, Stage 3/4, p. 357)

Impaired Driving

[Should Jack drive?] No, if by chance he gets into an accident or something, it'll be his fault and he could face a lot of repercussions.

The doctor should not give the woman the drug because he would risk losing his job or going to jail. (Form B, Law, CJ #7, Stage 2, p. 344)

[Are there any circumstances under which Jack should drive?] I say no, because there's a chance that you might kill yourself in the process of trying to help someone.

Heinz or anyone should not steal because he would be taking too great a risk ... or because if he is put in jail that wouldn't help him... (Form A, Law, CJ #8, Stage 2, p. 70)

Because he's going to get a big sentence and a fine and it's not worth it.

Heinz or anyone should not steal because he would be taking too great a risk ... or because if he is put in jail that wouldn't help him... (Form A, Law, CJ #8, Stage 2, p. 70)

Prosocial

...if he knows somebody that can help, suggest it, but if not, just go about your business. If you have no way of helping the person, then just stay out of it ... I would just stay out of it ...

[Louise should keep quiet] because this is none of her business, or she has nothing to do with it; or because she should keep out of her sister's business. (Form B, Contract, CJ #7, Stage 2, p. 531)

I would see a lot of guilt flying around if they didn't help. They wouldn't be responsible but they would feel pretty bad.

[Heinz should steal the drug] because he will feel guilty if he doesn't try to save his wife. (Form A, Life, CJ #17, Stage 3, p. 30)

If I help somebody and they help somebody else, somebody's gonna eventually help me when my turn comes.

[A promise should be kept] so that the other person will keep a promise to you or give you something in return. (Form A, Contract, CJ #6, Stage 2, p. 198)

(Continued)

TABLE 6.2.
(*Continued*)

Business Sale

Why should he be the martyr by losing what he's worked hard for all his life.	Joe should refuse to give his father the money because Joe earned, worked for, or saved the money. (Form A, Contract, CJ #4, Stage 2, p. 196)
They'd probably lie to him if the circumstances were reversed.	Heinz should steal for his wife because if you were in Heinz's shoes you'd steal too or you'd do the same thing. (Form A, Life, CJ #4, Stage 2, p. 15)
[He should tell the truth because] if he does not, he might get sued.	[Louise should keep quiet] because, if she tells, she may get into trouble with her sister and/or mother. (Form B, Contract, CJ #8, Stage 2, p. 532)

Free Trade

He has a duty to his employees and his dependents.	As a captain it's his job or his duty to protect his men. (Form C, Life (Quality), CJ #16, Stage 3, p. 633)
Another consideration is his personal image.	Heinz or anyone should not steal in order to leave a good impression in the community; or so that others won't get the wrong impression. (Form A, Law, CJ #15, Stage 3, p. 78)
As a member of society Mr. Greene should feel an obligation to oppose free trade, because even though it would bring him personal profit it would also bring suffering to many other people.	One has an obligation to the welfare of society in general; or because one's potential contributions should outweigh one's personal problems or unhappiness. (Form B, Law, CJ #26, Stage 4, p. 368)

Prostitution

It's her body, she can do what she wants with it.	[The doctor should give the woman the drug] because it's her life and she can do whatever she wants with it. (Form B, Life, CJ #2, Stage 2, p. 291)
[It's] understandable if the person is absolutely desperate for money and they can't find any work anywhere.	[Heinz should steal the drug if he is desperate; or because he wouldn't have much choice. (Form A, Life, CJ #8, Stage 2/3, p. 19)
[The judge] should give her some time so that she knows that it's wrong, because the longer amount of time the better it is for her so that she learns that it's not o.k.	[The judge should punish the doctor] in order to teach him that mercy killing is wrong,...[or] to make him realize he did wrong... (Form B, CJ #20, Stage 3, p. 478)

Real-life

(*Continued*)

TABLE 6.2.
(Continued)

I think I did the right thing because now I am happier with the siutation and I am not hurting other people by forceful, negative comments.

It is important to keep a promise because if you don't you hurt the other person's feelings or show you don't care about the other person.
(Form B, Contract, CJ #23, Stage 3, p. 545)

Issues of this nature [a previous relationship] should be open and subject to free discussion if the present relationship is to remain intact with any degree of concreteness. To not explain the previous situation is being unnecessarily deceitful.

It is important to keep a promise in order to have a good or lasting relationship; or because you should not destroy the other person's trust or faith in you, or harm the relationship.
(Form B, Contract, CJ #24, Stage 3, p. 546)

I felt that I could not break the trust and responsibility that comes with my job.

The judge should punish lawbreakers if it is required by law, because a judge's function is to uphold the law.
(Form B, Punishment, CJ #28, Stage 3/4, p. 488)

Interpersonal

[He should have] ... try to see the exam papers ... that he was sure he had passed or even if couldn't pass try to explain his legitimate excuse to the committee.

Heinz should not steal or it's wrong to steal because he should plead or beg for help, explain or talk it over with the druggist, the police, doctors, the authorities.
(Form A, Law, CJ #14, Stage 3, p. 76)

Although I don't disagree with the growing and selling of marijuana, it is considered illegal and if you are caught you get a record ...

The doctor should not give the woman the drug because he would risk losing his job or going to jail.
(Form B, Law, CJ #7, Stage 2, p. 344)

[Do you think he did the right thing?] It was what was best for us and my conscience as I wouldn't have an easy time living with the other alternatives ... I still have a good conscience.

The doctor should give the drug because otherwise how could he live with himself, knowing that he made her suffer needless agony. He would have it on his mind or conscience for the rest of his life.
(Form B, Life, CJ #16, Stage 3, p. 286)

Family

My parents should understand how much work I have.

Joe should refuse to give his father the money because if Joe explains how hard he worked his father will understand.
(Form A, Contract, CJ #15, Stage 3, p. 206)

She thinks that it is her job to stop me and I think it is none of her business.

Louise should keep quiet because it is none of her business.
(Form B, Contract, CJ #7, Stage 2, p. 531)

My job as a parent entails helping my daughter learn to be a mature responsible adult.

The mother is responsible for ensuring that her daughter becomes a responsible, mature person, a good member of society.
(Form B, Authority, CJ #26, Stage 4, p. 601)

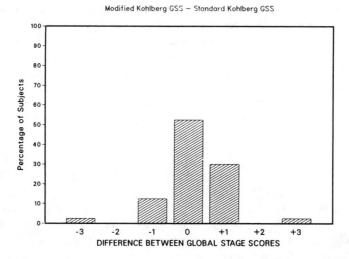

Modified Kohlberg GSS – Standard Kohlberg GSS

FIG. 6.1.   Percentage of subjects scoring at the same and different substages on the modified Kohlberg and standard Kohlberg dilemmas.

In our first study, we compared the maturity of moral judgment on standard Kohlberg dilemmas to the maturity of moral judgment on standard dilemmas modified so the protagonist was the self. The results failed to reveal any significant differences in moral maturity (see Table 6.1). As shown in Fig. 6.1, most subjects (53%) scored at the same substages on the standard and modified versions of Kohlberg's test, and virtually all subjects (95%) scored at adjacent substages. Subjects invoked the same or adjacent substage structures when imaging themselves in Kohlberg's moral dilemmas as they did when making judgments about hypothetical characters.

In the second study, Bush, Krebs, and Carpendale (in preparation) modified Kohlberg's dilemmas so the victims were males with AIDS ("In Europe a man was near death from AIDS . . . the sick man's boyfriend, Heinz, went to everyone he knew to borrow money . . ."). Subjects' attitudes towards people with AIDS, homosexuals, drug users, etc., were assessed, as well as factors such as belief in a just world (Lerner, 1977).

Again, mean moral maturity on the modified and standard dilemmas did not differ significantly (see Table 6.1). Forty-five percent of the subjects scored at the same substages on the modified and standard versions, and 95% scored at adjacent substages. None of the measures of attitude or belief qualified this consistency.

The two studies employing modified versions of Kohlberg's dilemmas supported Kohlberg's structure of the whole assumption, however the dilemmas evoking moral judgments were very similar to those employed by Kohlberg—everything was the same except the identity of the protagonists or victims. We turn now to studies that involved more radical departures from Kohlberg's format.

STUDIES EMPLOYING DILEMMAS OTHER THAN THOSE ON KOHLBERG'S TEST

AIDS

In addition to responding to the Kohlberg dilemma modified to involve AIDS, the subjects in the AIDS study responded to the following open-ended question: "Does the presence of AIDS in our society raise any issues you would consider moral in nature; if so, please outline the issues focusing on why you consider them to be moral." In addition subjects were asked a set of questions based on topical issues such as the following:

1. What is your position on compulsory testing for people with AIDS?
2. Should people with AIDS be quarantined?
3. Should health care professionals . . . be permitted to refuse to treat persons with AIDS?
4. Should a child who has AIDS be allowed to attend the same school as other children?
5. Does the presence of AIDS in our society raise any questions about rights and duties?

Responses to these questions and others were probed extensively for underlying justifications.

The first finding from this study was that the relatively open-ended judgments subjects made about AIDS conformed closely enough to the structure of the criterion judgments in Colby and Kohlberg's (1987) scoring manual to permit reliable matches (see Table 6.2). The second finding was that subjects tended to base their moral judgments about AIDS on the same stage-structures as those on which they based their judgments to Kohlberg's test and to Kohlberg's test modified to involve AIDS. There were no statistically significant differences among the mean moral maturity scores for the three sets of dilemma; 50% of the subjects scored at the same global substages on the open-ended AIDS questions and Kohlberg's test, and 85% scored within adjacent substages. These findings supply much stronger support for Kohlberg's structure of the whole assumption than the previous studies: subjects based their moral judgments about a topical social issue on the same structures they invoked on Kohlberg's test. There were no significant relationships between any measures of attitudes and opinions and moral maturity on open-ended questions about AIDS.

Impaired Driving

A person named Jack is out drinking with his friends. He doesn't keep track of exactly how much he drinks, but when it comes time to go home, he senses that he has had more to drink than the legal limit. His car is outside. What should he do?

Most adults have faced this dilemma. We gave it to 60 subjects, asking half of them to respond to it from the perspective of a hypothetical character and half from the perspective of self. Most subjects said it is wrong to drive impaired, and most subjects justified this decision with judgments that could be scored for stage in Kohlberg's system (see Table 6.2). The question is, did subjects base their judgments about the immorality of impaired driving on the same stage-structures they invoked on Kohlberg's test?

In contrast to the findings from the studies reported above, the answer to this question is a resounding "no." In response to the Impaired Driving dilemma and a dozen probing questions such as "Are there any circumstances under which it is right to drive when impaired?"; "What if Jack promised his friends a ride home?"; "Should the probability of roadblocks affect his decision?"; "What if a close relative had to be taken to the hospital?", subjects obtained significantly lower moral maturity scores (247) than they did on Kohlberg's dilemmas (325). There was no difference between scores of subjects who imagined themselves in the dilemma and those who responded to it from the perspective of the hypothetical character.

The pattern of results in this study was consistent with the idea that high-stage competence on Kohlberg's test is necessary but not sufficient for high stage performance on other dilemmas: no subject who obtained a major Stage 2 score on Kohlberg's test scored higher than Stage 2 on the Impaired Driving dilemma, but 40% of the subjects who demonstrated Stage 4 competence on Kohlberg's test (i.e., scored at stages 3/4, 4, 4/5) made Stage 2 (or 2/3) judgments on the Impaired Driving dilemma.

As shown in Fig. 6.2, 90% of the subjects scored lower on the Impaired Driving dilemma than on Kohlberg's test—60% more than an adjacent substage lower, and 14% more than a full stage lower. A detailed examination of the distribution of stage scores revealed that the modal stage on Kohlberg's test was 3/4 and the modal stage on the Impaired Driving dilemma was 2/3. Clearly, moral judgment was not homogeneous on this dilemma; why not?

It is possible the difference was due to scoring error, but the evidence does not support this possibility. Trained scores matched impaired driving judgments to criterion judgments in the Colby and Kohlberg manual with a high degree of reliability (see Tables 6.1 and 6.2).

A related possibility is that the impaired driving judgments were not adequately probed: If they had been probed more extensively, subjects may have given higher-stage responses. But this also was not the case: trained interviewers

Impaired Driving GSS − Kohlberg GSS

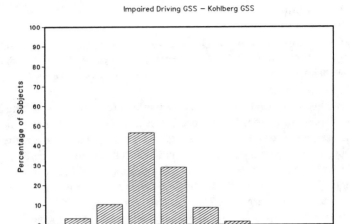

FIG. 6.2. Percentage of subjects scoring at the same and different substages on the Impaired Driving and Kohlberg dilemmas.

probed Kohlberg and impaired driving judgments equally extensively. Indeed, subjects making judgments about impaired driving sometimes became annoyed when responses they considered perfectly adequate were implicitly questioned when probed by interviewers. And, therein, we believe, may lie an explanation for the structures subjects invoked.

Whereas Kohlberg's dilemmas are "open" (see Blatt & Kohlberg, 1975, p. 134) in the true sense of a moral dilemma (upholding one moral norm, such as life, entails violating another, such as law), the Impaired Driving dilemma is more "closed" in the sense that life, law, authority, punishment, and conscience norms tend to favor one choice (not driving impaired). The moral conflict intrinsic in this dilemma is a relatively easy one to resolve: when personal convenience and promises to friends are pitted against the values of upholding life, obeying the law, and avoiding punishment, the latter win an easy victory. Though low-stage in Kohlberg's hierarchy, the types of judgment displayed in Table 6.2 were adequate to resolve the dilemma in question for most subjects in this study. Subjects didn't need to reach any higher; Stage 2 sufficed.

The reasons why people should not drink and drive are often repeated in our culture and salient among our norms. They are part of our "moral order" (Harré, 1983). These reasons, featured in mass media advertisements, usually are based on low-level moral structures. In their various forms, the message is the same: "you better not drive while intoxicated because you might kill yourself or someone else, lose your driver's licence, or go to jail." Thus Stage 2 instrumental, consequence-based, normative justifications for this dilemma are perfectly acceptable and socially sanctioned; nothing more is required.

Although the distribution of judgments to the moral dilemmas in this study supports Kohlberg's contention that his dilemmas supply a better measure of moral competence than other moral dilemmas, it also demonstrates that the moral structures individuals invoke to justify easy, everyday moral choices may differ from those they invoke to justify more complex hypothetical decisions, and, therefore, the stage of moral development displayed by subjects on Kohlberg's test may not supply a representative measure of the moral judgments they make in everyday life. Though moral competence may be structurally homogeneous, moral performance is not. People appear to retain lower-stage structures, and invoke them when they fulfill the purposes at hand. People do not need to be in extreme situations such as the low-level atmosphere of a traditional prison to make low-level moral judgments. The structure of the moral dilemmas, conflicts, and issues people face—even hypothetical ones to which they respond in an academic, arm-chair context—exert a considerable influence on the form of the judgments they evoke. The unanswered question in this study is why some subjects performed at or near their level of competence, whereas others did not.

Prosocial Behavior

In addition to Kohlberg's dilemmas and the Impaired Driving dilemma, subjects in the study reported above responded to the following dilemma about prosocial behavior, patterned after an actual incidence employed by McNamee (1978) in a study on the relationship between moral judgment and moral behavior (discussed at length by Kohlberg and Candee, 1984, pp. 520–523):

A student named Jack promised to participate in a psychological experiment. He shows up at the appointed time, and the experimenter, Suzanne, explains that he is required to fill out a questionnaire, then be interviewed. While Jack is busy working on the questionnaire, another student, Chris, comes to the door and introduces himself. He is obviously in bad shape. Suzanne checks the schedule and informs Chris that he is early for his appointment. He says that he knows that he is early, but he will not be able to participate in the experiment. He explains that he has 'done' some drugs, is feeling sick, and asks Suzanne for help since she is a psychologist. Suzanne explains that she is an experimental psychologist, not a clinical psychologist, and doesn't know anything about drug reactions. She asks Chris to reschedule his appointment, and leaves the office momentarily to get her appointment book. When she comes back, Chris persists, asking Suzanne if she knows of anyone who could help him. Suzanne says she cannot be of any assistance, and excuses herself to turn her attention to Jack.

This dilemma was accompanied by questions such as the following:

1. What should Jack do? Why?
2. What should Suzanne (the experimenter) have done? Why?

3. Were any moral issues raised in the situation? Outline them.

4. In general should people help each other? Why or why not?

5. Would you say people have a moral obligation to help each other? Why or why not? Under what circumstances?

6. Would it make any difference if Chris were one of Jack's friends? Why or why not? What if he were just an acquaintance? Why or why not?

Half the subjects responded to the dilemma from the perspective of a hypo-thetical character, as above; half were asked to imagine themselves in the situa-tion. A sample of judgments to the Prosocial dilemma is shown in Table 6.2.

As with the Impaired Driving dilemma, there were no significant differences between the self and other perspectives, and the mean moral maturity on the Prosocial dilemma (284) was significantly lower than the mean moral maturity on Kohlberg's dilemmas (325). As shown in Fig. 6.3, 65% of the subjects scored lower on the Prosocial dilemma than on Kohlberg's test, with 37% scoring more than an adjacent stage lower. The modal stage on the Prosocial dilemma was 2/3 (and on Kohlberg's test, 3/4). (More than half the subjects received a major Stage 2 [Stage 2 or 2/3] score on the Prosocial dilemma, compared to only 7% on Kohlberg's test.)

These findings surprised us. After Gilligan (1982) and others, we expected the Prosocial dilemma to pull for Stage 3. Inspection of the types of judgment made by subjects suggested that the downward pull in the Prosocial dilemma

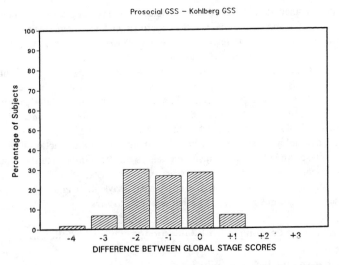

FIG. 6.3. Percentage of subjects scoring at the same and different substages on the Prosocial and Kohlberg dilemmas.

stemmed from its susceptibility to evasion of responsibility through excuses. In Kohlberg's dilemmas, responsibility is focused on the protagonist (Heinz, Dr. Jefferson), and performing a prosocial response is consistent with his role obligations (husband, doctor). However, in the Prosocial dilemma, the primary responsibility for helping is *not* focused on the protagonist, and the role-related responsibilities of both the subject and the experimenter are *in*consistent with helping the victim. In Kohlberg's (1984) terms, the characters in the Prosocial dilemma have "quasi-obligations" to perform their assigned roles, which supply "excuses" for evading the responsibility to help. Subjects who scored at Stage 2 and 2/3, tended to support individualistic judgments such as "he [the victim] got himself into it; he can get himself out" by invoking quasi-obligations and excuses such as, "[the bystander] had a responsibility to fill out for form"; "[People] don't have a moral obligation [to help each other], they can make up their own minds . . . but professional people, I guess you could say they have a moral obligation"; "if he [the bystander] knows someone that can help, suggest it, but if not, just go about your business." Note the consistency between these judgments and the diffusion of responsibility observed in studies on emergency intervention (Piliavin, Dovidio, Gaertner, & Clark, 1981).

Why were moral judgments to the AIDS dilemma, but not to the Impaired Driving and Prosocial dilemmas, homogeneous with moral judgments to the dilemmas on Kohlberg's test? We suspect that the AIDS dilemma elicited more homogeneous judgments than the other two dilemmas because it was more similar to the dilemmas on Kohlberg's test. Like the dilemmas on Kohlberg's test, the AIDS dilemma is extraordinary, academic, and nonconsequential. Unlike driving impaired and helping a stranger in need, subjects had no personal past experience, nor did they anticipate any future experience, with the problem. And, like Kohlberg's dilemmas, the AIDS dilemma was "open"—protecting the rights of people without AIDS tends to entail violating the rights of people with AIDS, and vice versa. The issues raised by AIDS are notably similar to the issues raised in Dilemma V on Form C of Kohlberg's test (a dilemma about who should go on a dangerous mission during war), and both dilemmas tend to evoke similar types of judgment—for example: "It is alright to have compulsory testing because the safety of the majority outweighs the rights of the few not to be tested, the good of the group outweighs the good of the individual," and "A soldier does not have the right to refuse to go on the mission because it is better to sacrifice one man's life for the majority" (CJ #15, p. 679).

The model of moral judgment that emerges from the pattern of responses to the AIDS, Prosocial, and Impaired Driving dilemmas is more interactional than Kohlberg's constructivistic model. Moral judgment seems to be the product of an interaction between the structure of stages and the structure of dilemmas. It is misleading to characterize people as more or less moral on the basis of their stage of moral development on Kohlberg's test. People are more flexible than Kohlberg assumes, and moral judgment is more structurally plastic. Kohlberg's dilemmas, and dilemmas structured in similar ways, pull for the highest level available to people; other dilemmas pull for lower stage-structures, leaving more room for normative defaults and low-level excuses. To predict which structure an individual will invoke, we must attend not only to the structures available to the individual, but also to the structural "pull" or "resistance" of the dilemmas he or she faces, and probably to many other facilitating and inhibiting person-specific and situation-specific factors.

Our interpretation of the source of homogeneity in the AIDS dilemma and stage heterogeneity in the Prosocial and Impaired Driving dilemmas was post hoc; when we designed the studies we did not know whether moral judgment would be consistent or inconsistent. The task demand we varied (perspective of self vs. other) did not exert an effect. In the next set of studies, we explicitly examined two factors we expected to lower the level of moral judgment—the "moral order" embedding the issue in question, and the audience to whom moral judgments were directed.

The ethogenic theorist Harré (1983) argues that "moral orders" in the social environment, not stages of moral reasoning, structure moral judgment. A moral order is an organized "system of rights, obligations and duties obtaining in a society, together with the criteria by which people and their activities are valued" (Harré, 1987, p. 219). According to Harré (1987), a culture may contain a "multiplicity of interacting, overlapping and complementary moral orders" (p. 220): Different social contexts may be governed by different rule-systems, roles, rights, duties, and expectations about appropriate behavior.

Harré believes that Kohlberg's stage-structures describe different moral orders, none any better or more complex than any other. For example, the moral order of business might assume a Stage 2 "dog eat dog" orientation, and the moral order of the medical profession or family might be Stage 3. Harré suggests the reason why children tend to endorse Kohlberg's stages in the sequence identified by Kohlberg is because the sequence reflects the changing form of children's social positions, not the development of their minds. Harré expects moral judgment to be as heterogeneous as the moral orders in a society and, therefore, he expects people to invoke different stage-structures on different types of dilemma. For Harré, people move in and out of moral orders, they are not "in" a moral stage.

In Harré's theory, the audiences to whom moral judgments are directed help define the moral order. Theorists such as Johnson and Hogan (1981) take this line of thought one step further, arguing that Kohlberg's test is susceptible to impression management, and thus, the stages individuals display may depend on the audiences to which they direct their communication (cf. Goffman, 1959).

The positions advanced by theorists such as Harré, Johnson, and Hogan converge with revisions in Kohlberg's approach suggested by cognitive-developmental theorists such as Damon (1977) and Levine (1979). For example, Levine (1979) suggests that moral judgment is "additive-inclusive" in nature ("high stages include components of earlier stages but do not replace these stages,'' p. 155), and acknowledges the importance of "others' evaluations of what constitutes appropriate thought and action" (p. 158) in evoking particular stage-structures.

Business Deals

To examine the effect of moral order and audience, Carpendale and Krebs (under review) asked subjects to make moral judgments to standard Kohlberg dilemmas and to the following two hypothetical dilemmas:

> Mr. Greene, through hard work and devotion, has built up a healthy business from nothing. He has reason to believe that tariffs will devastate his business unless a free trade agreement is reached. Because he is very popular with other business leaders and has a strong public image, he believes he could influence business and public opinion on free trade. A large, well respected group, representing doctors and other concerned citizens, has asked him to lobby against free trade, saying that although free trade may be good for some businesses, including his, it will cause long term social and health care problems for the country. Mr. Greene must decide whether to lobby for or against free trade. What should Mr. Greene do? Why?

> Mr. Greene lobbies for free trade but realizes he will not succeed. Another company has, for several years, wanted to buy his business. This company is willing to pay a good price, but lacks the information Mr. Greene has about the damage that lack of a free trade agreement will do to the business. Should Mr. Greene disclose what he knows about the effects of free trade on the business to the other company? Why or why not?

Subjects were asked what the protagonist facing the dilemma should do, and why, then were asked a series of probing questions designed to elicit the underlying justifications for their judgments. The main probes for the Free Trade dilemma were as follows:

1. What are the main issues involved here? Are there any moral issues involved?
2. Does the protagonist have a duty or obligation to support or oppose free trade? Why or why not?
3. Does he have a right to make a living and pursue his business interests? Why or why not?
4. Should he support or oppose free trade if his business would not be affected?

The main probes for the Business Sale dilemma were as follows:

1. What are the main issues involved here? Are there any moral issues involved?
2. Is it important to tell the truth? Why or why not? How does this apply to the protagonist's decision?

3. In thinking back over the dilemma, what would you say is the most responsible thing for him to do?

Subjects also were asked to reveal their position on the impending free trade agreement between Canada and the United States, and their political orientation (on a scale from 0, conservative, to 5, liberal). Half the subjects believed the study was being conducted by a professor from the Faculty of Business (business audience); the other half believed it was being conducted by a professor from the Philosophy Department (philosophy audience).

A sample of moral judgments to the Business dilemmas is shown in Table 6.2. Although subjects invoked the same or adjacent stages on the two dilemmas from Kohlberg's test, as shown in Fig. 6.4 they invoked significantly lower stages on the business dilemmas. Only 30% of the subjects scored at the same stage on the Kohlberg and Free Trade dilemmas, with 55% scoring a substage or more lower on the Free Trade dilemma (15% scored higher). Only 7.5% of the subjects scored at the same stage on the Kohlberg and Business Sale dilemmas; and the remaining 92.5% scored a substage or more lower.

The mean moral maturity on the Free Trade dilemma was 301 (Stage 3); the mean moral maturity on the Business Sale dilemma was 249 (Stage 2/3); and mean moral maturity on Kohlberg's test was 344 (Stage 3/4). Each mean differed significantly from each of the others. The audience effect was not significant, but there was a significant audience × dilemma interaction: subjects made more morally mature judgments on the Free Trade dilemma (but not on the

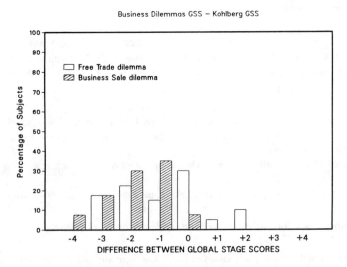

FIG. 6.4. Percentage of subjects scoring at the same and different substages on the Business and Kohlberg dilemmas.

Business Sale dilemma) when directing their responses to the Philosophy Department than when directing their responses to the Faculty of Business Administration. Although subjects also tended to make more mature judgments on Kohlberg's dilemmas when directing their responses to a business audience, the difference failed to reach an acceptable level of statistical significance. The audience did not affect level of moral maturity on the Business Sale dilemma.

It appears the Business Sale dilemma exerted a strong determining effect on moral judgment, overriding the salience of the audience, but the Free Trade dilemma did not. Apparently, when it comes to selling a business, the moral order of the business world—as several subjects summarized it; "buyer beware"—is evoked, whether talking to philosophers or faculty from Business Administration. The Free Trade dilemma was weaker than the Business Sale dilemma in invoking uniform judgments: subjects who presented themselves to a business audience made judgments that corresponded in structure to those they made on the Business Sale dilemma, whereas subjects who presented themselves to a philosophical audience made judgments more similar to those they made on Kohlberg's philosophical dilemmas. For example, when addressing the business audience, subjects made judgments on the Free Trade dilemma such as the "businessman should consider himself first," he should "protect his own investment; no one else will"; whereas subjects addressing a philosophical audience were more inclined to construe the Free Trade dilemma in terms of social welfare and "benefit for society as a whole."

There was relatively little variance in judgments to the dilemmas on Kohlberg's test. As acknowledged by Colby and Kohlberg, self-presentational concerns encourage people to present their highest stage arguments on Kohlberg's test, and most adults are able to construct Stage 3 or Stage 4 moral arguments. Although subjects showed as much competence on the Free Trade dilemma when presenting themselves to a philosophical audience as they did on Kohlberg's test, the results of this study suggest that socially desirable responses are not always cut from the highest stages. People appear, in part at least, to structure their moral judgments in accordance with the perceived expectations of their audiences, which do not always favor high-level judgments. The implicit audience on Kohlberg's test is academic and philosophical—the questions are philosophical in nature, so subjects make philosophical judgments. Put them in a business office, used car lot, army, police force, or family, and they might well speak in a different voice. The effects for the business audience in this study might well have been stronger if the audience were businessmen rather than a professor from the Faculty of Business Administration.

The results of this study also revealed a relationship between moral maturity and political orientation. The higher an individual's moral maturity on Kohlberg's test, the closer to the liberal end he scored on a scale of political orientation (r (40) = .47, p < .001) and the more he was opposed to the free trade agreement between Canada and the United States (r (40) = .59, p < .001)

(The subjects in this study were Canadian; in Canada, the right-leaning political party [the Conservatives] favor free trade, and the left-leaning political party [the New Democrats] oppose free trade.)

The positive correlation between moral maturity and liberal political orientation is consistent with Emler's (1983) argument that Kohlberg's stages are confounded with political values, but they also are consistent with the position advanced by theorists such as Fishkin, Keniston, and MacKinnon (1973) that moral maturity induces individuals to adopt increasingly liberal (indeed left-wing radical) political positions because they match the structure of high-level stages. The design of this study did not enable us to distinguish between these positions (but see Emler et al., 1983; Sparks & Durkin, 1987).

This study supports and extends the conclusions suggested by the study on Impaired Driving and Prosocial Behavior: moral judgment is determined by an interaction between the range of stages available to individuals and the moral orders of the dilemmas they face. In "strong" situations with a clear, unambiguous moral order such as that defined in the Business Sale dilemma, people make highly homogeneous, normative judgments. In more ambiguous situations, the social context or the audience involved may define the moral order and determine both the structure of moral judgment and the content of moral decisions.

Prostitution

In the final study in this series, we investigated a within-person process we expected to influence the stage-structures invoked in a non-Kohlberg dilemma. Following up the suggestion in our research on the Prosocial dilemma that people invoke low-level moral justifications as excuses to evade responsibility, we examined the effect of defense mechanisms on moral judgment. According to Haan (1977), people differ in their susceptibility to excuses and rationalizations when they process moral information, depending on whether they invoke coping or defending mechanisms. Coping involves the undistorted perception and open, rational evaluation of internal processes and external events. Conversely, defending entails distorting information in order to protect the self. People tend to cope well in nonthreatening situations such as taking Kohlberg's test, but those who are susceptible to defensiveness evoke defenses when making judgments about events that threaten their welfare and self-esteem.

Bartek, Krebs, and Taylor (under review) examined the effect of copying and defending on the moral judgments of female juvenile delinquents, aged 14–16. A group of delinquents, half who admitted to engaging in prostitution and half who did not, and a control group matched on age were given Kohlberg's test, Joffé and Naditch's (1977) *Coping and Defending Test,* and the following dilemma:

Jennifer is fourteen years old. She never got along with her father. When her new stepmother moves in, the situation at home becomes worse. Eventually Jennifer's father throws her out of the house. Jennifer looks for a job and is unable to find one. A friend of hers has been going on dates with men and having sex with them for money. Saying that it's "easy money," Jennifer's friend offers to show Jennifer "the ropes" if she's interested.

The dilemma was followed by questions such as the following:

1. Should Jennifer take her friend up on the offer? Why or why not?
2. Would Jennifer be doing anything wrong if she had sex with men for money? Why or why not?
3. Does Jennifer's age make any difference? Why or why not? What if she were an adult?
4. Under what circumstances is it right to accept money for sex? Why?

As with the other dilemmas, prototypical judgments to the Prostitution dilemma are shown in Table 6.2. Consistent with past research, juvenile delinquents (both prostitutes and nonprostitutes) scored lower on moral maturity than control subjects on both Kohlberg's test and the Prostitution dilemma (see Table 6.1). The juvenile delinquents also scored significantly lower than the controls on coping (and significantly higher on defensiveness). Of particular interest, however, was the finding that there was no different between the Kohlberg and Prostitution moral maturity scores for "copers" (subjects who scored above the median on coping-defending) both in the sample as a whole and within the delinquent group. However, the defensive delinquents (but not the defensive controls) obtained significantly lower moral maturity scores on the Prostitution dilemma (218) than on Kohlberg's test (250). We interpret these findings as support for the idea that defense mechanisms tend to lower the level of moral maturity in defensive individuals making judgments about issues that activate their defence mechanisms. We originally expected this effect to pertain only to the prostitutes making moral judgments about prostitution, but found that prostitution was a threatening issue to the other delinquents as well.

AN INTERACTIONAL MODEL OF MORAL JUDGMENT

We opened this chapter by characterizing Kohlberg's model of moral development as structural, consistent, and constructivistic. Our data support the assumption that a substantial portion of moral judgment is structured in terms of the stages outlined by Kohlberg—we were able reliably to match enough prescriptive judgments to all non-Kohlberg dilemmas with criterion judgments in Colby and Kohlberg's scoring manual to give subjects Global Stage and moral maturity

(WAS) scores. Our data do not, however, support the assumption that moral judgment is highly consistent—organized in structures of the whole. Our data are more consistent with Levine's (1979) additive-inclusive model of moral development than with Kohlberg's assumption that new stages "transform and displace" old stages. The types of moral judgment people make to non-Kohlberg dilemmas frequently are different from those they make to the dilemmas on his test; most people evoke different stages in response to different situations.

Our data also fail to support a strong situational model of moral judgment: different people invoked different stages in response to the same dilemma. Clearly, an interaction model is implied, but of what ilk?

The model that fits our data most comfortably assumes (a) that most adults possess a distribution of stage-structures—their latest stage and all the stages below it (note, however, that virtually none of our adult subjects scored at modal Stage 1), and (b) that moral issues, dilemmas, situations and contexts differ in their receptiveness or "resistance" (see Piaget, 1971) to the stage structures available. Moral judgment is the product of an interaction between interpretive structures and the interpretability of the information they process.

People differ in the extent to which they construct situations in terms of one stage. Somewhat counterintuitively, the most highly constructive and homogeneous of all individuals are those at Kohlberg's lowest stages; they base all their judgments on Stage 1 or Stages 1 and 2 because those stages are the only ones available to them. As Kohlberg (1969) notes, adults "fixated" at Stage 2 are pure types:

> As children move into adulthood, then, those who remain primarily at Stages 1 and 2 crystallize into purer types, an extreme being some delinquents with an explicit Stage 2 con-man ideology. (p. 389)

Similarly, Perry and Krebs (1980) found that a sample of mentally retarded girls made highly homogeneous Stage 2 judgments on Kohlberg's test.

Are there "pure types" of highly consistent individuals at Kohlberg's highest stages? We cannot really comment on Stage 5—none of our subjects scored at this stage. However, not one of our Stage 3, 3/4, 4, or 4/5 subjects based all of his or her judgments on one stage-structure, and the range of global stage use was as large for our twelve 4/5 subjects (mean 2.5 substages) as for those who scored at Stages 3, 3/4, and 4. In the Prostitution study, we found that coping and defending affected the consistency of moral judgment. Other sources of individual difference that might be expected to affect the structural homogeneity of moral judgment are "exchange" vs. "commitment" orientation (Murstein & MacDonald, 1983), self-monitoring (Snyder, 1979), self-awareness (Duval & Wicklund, 1972), need for consistency (Bem & Allen, 1974), and cognitive rigidity (Goldstein & Blackman, 1978).

Consistency in moral judgment may be viewed in either a positive or negative light, depending on the context. Highly consistent individuals may seem rigid in situations where flexibility is required; inconsistent individuals may come across as adaptable in situations where different types of moral judgment are valued. Conversely, consistency may reflect moral integrity, and inconsistency hypocrisy in situations in which, for example, judgments of others are compared to judgments about the self.

Our data suggest that moral dilemmas may pull for or lend themselves to interpretation by way of certain stage structures, and resist or fail to fit with others. Further, situations appear to differ in the strength of their pull for particular structures. In this respect "strong" situations may be defined as those that pull uniformly for one interpretive structure, and "weak" situations as those that are constructable in terms of more than one structure (cf. Snyder & Ickes, 1985). Factors that contribute to the strength or pull of a situation would include its moral order (Harré, 1983), normative structure (Backman, 1976), and role-expectations (cf. our study on judgments about business deals). Ambiguous, pluralistic, "open" situations such as the dilemmas on Kohlberg's test, the AIDS dilemma, and the Free Trade dilemma appear to be more constructable in terms of people's modal stages than more "closed" situations such as the dilemmas about impaired driving and business sale. Another factor contributing to the strength of a situation might lie in the extent to which self-interest may be maximized through a particular course of action and type of justification (see Gerson & Damon, 1978). Associated with this, as shown in the prosocial study, is the availability in a situation of excuses for self-interested choices. As shown by de Vries and Walker (1986), the choices people endorse in moral dilemmas may affect the structures they invoke to justify them.

In considering the nature of stage-context interactions, the structural pull of Stage 2 seems particularly important. The central moral conflict experienced by subjects in the Impaired Driving, Prosocial, and Business dilemmas was between self-interest and social responsibility. In this sense, the conflicts in the dilemmas appeared to be experienced by subjects as Stage 2 vs. Stage 3 and Stage 2 vs. Stage 4 conflicts. (Issues raised by questions such as "would it be right to violate the law to help a friend?" tend to evoke Stage 3–4 conflicts.)

The nature of the interaction between structure and content is apparent in the "resistance" of individuals at different stages on Kohlberg's test to the pull of "Stage 2" dilemmas (i.e. dilemmas that evoke a Stage 2 modal stage). As shown in Fig. 6.5, the proportion of subjects who scored at Stage 2 on the Impaired Driving, Prosocial, Business Sale, and Free Trade dilemmas decreased systematically as their Kohlberg stage increased. The higher an individual's Kohlbergian moral competence, the less likely he or she was to make low-level moral judgments. As shown in Table 6.1, there is a weak tendency for individuals to maintain their rank order in moral maturity across Kohlberg and non-Kohlberg dilemmas even though they score significantly lower on the non-Kohlberg dilemmas.

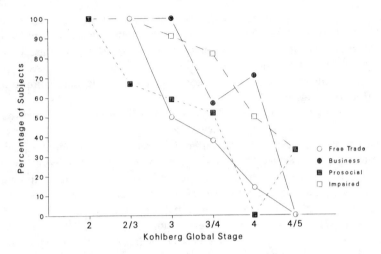

FIG. 6.5. Percentage of subjects obtaining Global Stage 2 scores on non-Kohlberg dilemmas as a function of their Global Stage on Kohlberg's test.

CURRENT DIRECTIONS: MORAL JUDGMENT IN EVERYDAY LIFE

As mentioned earlier, our ultimate goal is to understand the nature of moral judgment in everyday life and its relationship to moral behavior. The most obvious and probably most important way in which real-life dilemmas differ from Kohlberg's dilemmas is that real-life dilemmas involve real consequences for the individuals involved. The most recent direction of our research involves asking subjects to describe moral dilemmas in which they currently are, or recently have been, involved. We score the moral judgments they make about their real-life dilemmas for stage, and compare them with the stages they obtain on Kohlberg's test. (See Table 6.2 for a sample of judgments from real-life dilemmas.)

At present, three studies of this sort are in progress. In the first study, we ask people to describe a moral conflict they are experiencing or have experienced in their everyday lives, and to answer a set of probing questions, such as: "What options did you consider?" "Do you think you did the right thing? Why?" "What makes the conflict a *moral* one?". Many of the moral dilemmas our subjects describe are interpersonal in nature—they involve moral conflicts with other parties. In the second study in this series, we get both sides of the story. We solicit pairs of people who are experiencing or recently have experienced a moral conflict, and ask them independently and anonymously to describe it. We ask each partner to identify the moral issues involved, to state his or her point of view and the partner's point of view, and to evaluate both positions. In the final study, we are examining moral conflicts between teenage girls and their parents. We give the mother, father, and daughter a questionnaire in which they anonymously and independently describe and make moral judgments about a moral conflict they are experiencing or have experienced in the family. The questionnaire contains items such as: please describe the conflict, stating your point of view, your daughter's (parents') point of view, and the aspects of each that are (were) in conflict; what do (did) you see to be the issues involved?; what makes (made) it a moral conflict?

We have obtained preliminary results from these three studies, based on approximately 50 subjects in each, and have a pretty good sense of the direction of the effects (see Carpendale & Bush, 1989; Vermeulen, 1989; Vermeulen, Denton, Zanatta, & Krebs, 1989). The types of real-life moral conflict experienced by subjects are outlined in Table 6.3. Subjects in all three studies made enough scoreable interview judgments to enable us to assign them global stage and moral maturity scores in Kohlberg's system (see Table 6.2). An analysis of global stage and moral maturity scores revealed that subjects tended to score one substage lower on the real-life conflicts than they did on Kohlberg's test (see Table 6.1). However, interestingly, the females in the study on moral conflicts between partners tended to score at the same stage on the Kohlberg and interpersonal dilemmas (mean WAS = 308 and 300 respectively), but the males tended to score lower on the interpersonal conflicts (WAS = 277) than on Kohlberg's dilemmas (WAS = 331). Mothers also tended to be more homogeneous than fathers across the two types of dilemma in the family study.

TABLE 6.3.
Frequency of Real-Life Conflicts

Type of Conflicts	Interpersonal	Real-Life	Family	Total
Marital relationships	2	2	0	4
Dating relationships	2	6	0	8
Premarital sex	2	3	0	5
Personal values/integrity	19	8	0	27
Friendship	6	11	6	23
Honesty, cheating, illegal activity	5	9	5	19
Substance use	4	0	4	8
Conflicting rights	8	0	2	10
Conflicting obligations	4	8	7	19
School performance	2	0	2	4
Obedience to rules	0	0	3	3
Chores	0	0	11	11
Curfew	0	0	6	6
Concern for daughter's conduct	0	1	11	12
Other	0	2	6	8
Total	54	50	63	167

The majority of adults (63% across the three studies) scored at Stage 3 on the real-life dilemmas. Most of the real-life dilemmas involved a violation of role expectations, especially those related to the bonds of friendship. Such dilemmas appear to pull for Stage 3 structures. In the relatively infrequent cases where subjects invoked low stage-structures, the dilemmas seemed to pull for them. For example, one subject who scored at Stage 2 experienced a dilemma in which he lied to the police to avoid getting arrested; another "Stage 2 dilemma" involved buying a used car from an owner who did not know what it was worth.

Although the modal stage for daughters in the family study on the Kohlberg dilemmas was Stage 3, the majority of the daughters (76%) scored at Stage 2 or 2/3 on the family dilemmas. Because most family dilemmas involved parent and daughter conflicts, it is possible the daughters, who were in a subordinate position in the family, experienced constraints on their perspective-taking akin to (but not as severe as) the constraints experienced by convicts on prison dilemmas (Kohlberg, Scharf, & Hickey, 1972).

The "partner" study produced two interesting findings: (a) that each partner in a moral conflict often construes it quite differently, and (b) that conflicts in which both parties invoke Stage 3 structures are more likely to be resolved than conflicts in which one party invokes Stage 2 and the other Stage 3: the respective percentages for resolution are 60% vs. 7% (N = 44).

SUMMARY

To summarize, our research demonstrates that moral judgment tends to be structured in terms of Kohlberg's stages, but individuals retain their old stage structures after they acquire new ones, and invoke them in certain situations. Kohlberg's test tends to assess moral competence, but people do not always perform at their level of competence. Moral performance is determined by the interaction between the stage structures available to individuals, personality factors, and the structural pulls and resistances of the moral dilemmas and moral situations they encounter. Particularly significant is the pull of self-interest and the amenability of the structure of Stage 2 to excuses and rationalizations. The higher an individual's level of moral competence, as assessed by Kohlberg's test, the less likely he or she is to invoke Stage 2 moral justifications.

ACKNOWLEDGMENTS

The research reported in this chapter was supported by Grants #410-87-1115 and #410-89-0649 from the Social Sciences and Humanities Research Council of Canada.

REFERENCES

Backman, C. (1976). Explorations in psycho-ethics: The warranting of judgments. In R. Harré (Ed.), *Life sentences: Aspects of the social role of language* (pp. 98–108). Toronto: Wiley.

Bartek, S., Krebs, D. L., & Taylor, M. (under review). *Moral development and prostitution.*

Baumrind, D. (1978). A dialectical materialist's perspective on knowing social reality. In W. Damon (Ed.), *Moral development: New directions for child development, No. 2.* San Francisco: Jossey-Bass.

Bem, D. J., & Allen, A. (1974). On predicting some of the people some of the time: The search for cross-situational consistency in behavior. *Psychological Review, 81,* 506–520.

Blatt, M., & Kohlberg, L. (1975). The effects of classroom moral discussion upon children's level of moral judgement. *Journal of Moral Education, 4,* 129–161.

Brown, R., & Herrnstein, R. (1975). Moral reasoning and conduct. In *Psychology,* (pp. 289–340). Boston: Little Brown Company.

Bush, A. J., Krebs, D. L., & Carpendale, J. I. (in preparation). *Moral judgment and AIDS.*

Candee, D., & Kohlberg, L. (1987). Moral judgment and moral action: A reanalysis of Haan, Smith, and Block's (1968) free speech movement data. *Journal of Personality and Social Psychology, 52,* 554–564.

Carpendale, J. I., & Bush, A. (1989). *Real-life moral judgment.* Paper presented at the Canadian Psychological Association, Halifax.

Carpendale, J. I., & Krebs, D. L. (under review). *Situational variation in moral judgment: In a stage or on a stage?*

Colby, A., & Kohlberg, L. (Eds.). (1987). *The measurement of moral judgment.* (Vols. 1–2). Cambridge, MA: Cambridge University Press.

Colby, A., Kohlberg, L., Gibbs, J., & Lieberman, M. (1983). A longitudinal study of moral judgment. *Monographs of the Society for Research in Child Development, 48.* Chicago, IL: University of Chicago Press.

Damon, W. (1977). *The social world of the child.* San Francisco, CA: Jossey-Bass.

de Vries, B., & Walker, L. J. (1986). Moral reasoning and attitudes toward capital punishment. *Developmental Psychology, 22,* 509–513.

Duval, S., & Wicklund, R. A. (1972). *A theory of objective self-awareness.* New York: Academic Press.

Eisenberg, N. (1982). The development of reasoning regarding prosocial behavior. In N. Eisenberg (Ed.), *The development of prosocial behavior.* New York: Academic Press.

Emler, N. (1983). Morality and politics: The ideological dimension in the theory of moral development. In H. Weinreich-Haste & D. Lock (Eds.), *Morality in the making: Thought, action, and the social context* (pp. 47–71). Chichester, England: Wiley.

Fischer, K. W. (1983). Illuminating the processes of moral development. In A. Colby, et al. *Monographs of the Society for Research in Child Development, 48,* 97–107. Chicago, IL: University of Chicago Press.

Fishkin, J., Keniston, K., & MacKinnon, C. (1973). Moral reasoning and political ideology. *Journal of Personality and Social Psychology, 27,* 109–119.

Flavell, J. H. (1971). Stage-related properties of cognitive development. *Cognitive Psychology, 2,* 421–453.

Flavell, J. H. (1982). On cognitive development. *Child Development, 53,* 1–10.

Gerson, R. D., & Damon, W. (1978). Moral understanding and children's conduct. In W. Damon (Ed.), *Moral development: New directions for child development* No. 2 (pp. 41–49). San Francisco: Jossey-Bass.

Gilligan, C. (1982). *In a different voice.* Cambridge, MA: Harvard University Press.

Gilligan, C., & Belenky, M. F. (1980). A naturalistic study of abortion decisions. *New Directions for Child Development, 7,* 69–90.

168   KREBS, VERMEULEN, CARPENDALE, DENTON

Gilligan, C., Kohlberg, L., Lerner, J., & Belenky, M. (1971). *Moral reasoning about sexual dilemmas: The development of an interview and scoring system.* Unpublished technical report of the Commission on Obscenity and Pornography (Vol. 1).

Goffman, E. (1959). *The presentation of self in everyday life.* New York: Doubleday.

Goldstein, K. M., & Blackman, S. (1978). *Cognitive style.* New York: Wiley.

Haan, N. (1975). Hypothetical and actual moral reasoning in a situation of civil disobedience. *Journal of Personality and Social Psychology, 32,* 255–270.

Haan, N. (1977). *Coping and defending: Processes of self-environment organization.* New York: Academic Press.

Haan, N. (1978). Two moralities in action contexts: Relationship to thought, ego regulation, and development. *Journal of Personality and Social Psychology, 36,* 286–305.

Harré, R. (1983). *Personal being: A theory for individual psychology.* Cambridge, MA: Harvard University Press.

Harré, R. (1987). Grammar, psychology, and moral rights. In M. Chapman (Ed.), *Meaning and the growth of understanding* (pp. 219–230). Berlin: Springer-Verlag.

Higgins, A., Power, C., & Kohlberg, L. (1984). The relationship of moral atmosphere to judgments of responsibility. In W. Kurtines, & J. Gewirtz (Eds.), *Morality, moral development, and moral behavior* (pp. 74–106). New York: Wiley.

Joffé, P., & Naditch, M. P. (1977). Paper and pencil measures of coping and defense processes. In N. Haan (Ed.), *Coping and defending: Processes of self-environment organization.* New York: Academic Press.

Johnson, J., & Hogan, R. (1981). Moral judgment and self presentation. *Journal of Research in Personality, 15,* 57–63.

Kohlberg, L. (1969). Stage and sequence: The cognitive developmental approach to socialization. In D. A. Goslin (Ed.), *Handbook of socialization theory and research.* Chicago, ILL: Rand McNally.

Kohlberg, L. (1984). *Essays on moral development* (Vol. 2): *The psychology of moral development.* San Francisco: Harper & Row.

Kohlberg, L., & Candee D. (1984). The relationship of moral judgment to moral action. In L. Kohlberg (Ed.), *Essays on moral development* (Vol. 2): *The psychology of moral development* (pp. 498–581). New York: Harper & Row.

Kohlberg, L., Scharf, P., & Hickey, J. (1972). The justice structure of the prison: A theory and intervention. *Prison Journal, 51,* 3–14.

Krebs, D. & Miller, D. T. (1985). Altruism and aggression. In G. Lindzey and E. Aronson (Eds.), *Handbook of social psychology* (3rd Ed., Vol. 2). New York: Random House.

Latané, B., & Darley, J. M., Jr. (1970). *The unresponsive bystander: Why doesn't he help?* New York: Appleton Century-Crofts.

Leming, J. (1978). Intrapersonal variations in stage of moral reasoning among adolescents as a function of situational context. *Journal of Youth and Adolescence, 7,* 405–416.

Lerner, M. J. (1977). The justice motive: Some hypotheses as to its origins and forms. *Journal of Personality, 45,* 1–53.

Levine, C. G. (1979). Stage acquisition and stage use: An appraisal of stage displacement explanations of variation in moral reasoning. *Human Development, 22,* 145–164.

Linn, R. (1984). Practising moral judgment within the day care center: A look at the educator's moral decision under stress. *Early Child Development and Care, 15,* 117–132.

Linn, R. (1987a). Moral disobedience during the Lebanon war: What can the cognitive-development approach learn from the experience of the Israeli soldiers? *Social Cognition, 5,* 383–402.

Linn, R. (1987b). Moral reasoning and behavior of striking physicians in Israel. *Psychological Reports, 60,* 443–453.

Lockwood, A. L. (1975). Stage of moral development and students' reasoning on public policy issues. *Journal of Moral Education, 5,* 51–61.

Lonky, E., Roodin, P. A., & Rybash, J. M. (1988). Moral judgment and sex role orientation as a function of self and other presentation mode. *Journal of Youth and Adolescence, 17,* 189–195.

Martarano, M. A. (1977). A developmental analysis of performance on Piaget's formal operations tasks. *Developmental Psychology, 13,* 666–672.

McNamee, S. (1978). Moral behavior, moral development, and motivation. *Journal of Moral Education, 7,* 27–32.

Milgram, S. (1963). Behavioral study of obedience. *Journal of Abnormal and Social Psychology, 67,* 371–378.

Murstein, B. I., & MacDonald, M. G. (1983). The relationship of 'exchange-orientation' and 'commitment' scales to marriage adjustment. *International Journal of Psychology, 18,* 297–311.

Nisbett, R. E., & Ross, L. (1980). *Human inference: Strategies and shortcomings of social judgment.* Englewood Cliffs, NJ: Prentice Hall.

Perry, J. E., & Krebs, D. (1980). Role-taking, moral development, and mental retardation. *The Journal of Genetic Psychology, 36,* 95–108.

Piaget, J. (1971). The theory of stages and cognitive development. In D. G. Green and M. P. Ford (Eds.), *Measurement and Piaget.* New York: McGraw-Hill.

Piaget, J. (1972). Intellectual evolution from adolescence to adulthood. *Human Development, 15,* 1–12.

Piliavin, J. A., Dovidio, J. E., Gaertner, S. L., & Clark, R. D. (1981). *Emergency intervention.* New York: Academic Press.

Rest, J. (1979). *Development in judging moral issues.* Minneapolis: University of Minnesota Press.

Rest, J. (1986). *Moral development: Advances in research and theory.* New York: Praeger.

Rybash, J. M., Hoyer, W. J., & Roodin, P. A. (1983). Responses to moral dilemmas involving self versus others. *International Journal of Aging and Human Development, 18,* 73–77.

Rybash, J. M., Roodin, P. A., & Lonky, E. (1981). Young adult's scores on the defining issues test as a function of a "self" versus "other" presentation mode. *Journal of Youth and Adolesence, 10,* 25–31.

Snyder, C. R., Higgins, R. L., & Stucky, R. J. (1983). *Excuses: Masquerades in search of grace.* New York: Wiley.

Snyder, M. (1979). Self-monitoring processes. In L. Berkowitz (Ed.), *Advances in Experimental Social Psychology* (Vol. 12, pp. 85–128). New York: Academic Press.

Snyder, M., & Ickes, W. J. (1985). Personality and social behavior. In G. Lindzey and E. Aronson (Eds.), *The handbook of social psychology* (3rd Ed.). New York: Random House.

Sparks, P., & Durkin, K. (1987). Moral reasoning and political orientation: The context sensitivity of individual rights and democratic principles. *Journal of Personality and Social Psychology, 52,* 931–936.

Vermeulen, S. C. (1989). *Moral reasoning, family dynamics, and real-life versus hypothetical conflicts.* Unpublished Master thesis. Simon Fraser University.

Vermeulen, S. C., Denton, K., Zanatta, R., & Krebs, D. (1989). *Moral judgments to interpersonal conflicts.* Paper presented at the Canadian Psychological Association, Halifax.

Walker, L. J., de Vries, B., & Trevethan, S. D. (1987). Moral stage and moral orientations in real-life and hypothetical dilemmas. *Child Development, 58,* 842–858.

Wason, P. C., & Johnson-Laird, P. N. (1972). *Psychology of reasoning: Structure and content.* Cambridge: MA: Harvard University Press.

Zimbardo, P. G., Haney, C., Banks, W. C., & Jaffe, D. A. (1973, April 8). Pirandellian prison: The mind is a formidable jailer. *The New York Times Magazine,* pp. 38–60.

7

First Moral Sense: Aspects of and Contributors to a Beginning Morality in the Second Year of Life

Sharon Lamb

ABSTRACT

The following chapter reviews and examines the work that has been done with toddlers that suggests their capacity for early moral awareness and feelings. There are a number of studies indicating prosocial behavior, empathic responding, and awareness of standards in 1- to 2-year-olds. There is also research on individual cognitive, linguistic, and affective accomplishments of the second year which suggest a capacity for empathic responding and understanding right and wrong. Two observational studies which examine a combination of these acquisitions and behaviors are discussed: Judy Dunn's study (1987, 1988) which examines the social interactional contexts that support moral awareness and Sharon Lamb's (1988) which examines the issue of maturational preparedness.

Although many theorists in the moral development field agree that children in the second year of life show signs of beginning morality, the emergence of a moral sense has only rarely been examined as a phenomenon in and of itself. In order to understand how a child this young might begin to appreciate her mother's prohibitions, pat another child who is crying, and show distress to a crack in a table, a torn piece of clothing, or failure to meet a standard of performance, we need to pull together the research on aspects that may at first seem only tangentially related.

In this chapter I consider research that examines specific aspects of moral development in the second year. This research follows two strands, one focusing on prosocial behavior and empathy, the other on awareness of standards. One can even conceptualize these two kinds of early behaviors as precursors to the two forms of adult moral reasoning proposed by Gilligan (1982), a morality primarily concerned with care and responsibility and a morality primarily concerned with justice, rights and standards of behavior. I also consider those areas of development in the second year of life that are possible contributors to a moral sense, the cognitive, linguistic, and affective accomplishments that may support empathic responding and an understanding of right and wrong. And finally, I summarize two research projects that examine the emergence of moral sense in the second year in relation to these social, linguistic, and cognitive developments. Both, Judy Dunn's (1987, 1988) and my own (Lamb, 1988; in press), are observational studies with somewhat small samples. Dunn's studies focus on the social interactional contexts that support and promote moral concern at this age. My own study examines the issue of maturational preparedness.

PROSOCIAL BEHAVIOR AND EMPATHIC RESPONDING

Sharing, helping, protecting, and nurturing are among the most frequently noted prosocial behaviors in this age group. In one study a 23-month-old helped to put a sock on a younger child and a 24-month-old adjusted a ladder for a playmate while saying "not fall down" (Rheingold & Hay, 1980). In an experimental situation, all 24 18-month-old subjects shared a variety of objects with mothers, fathers, and strangers, regardless of their mother's response or lack of response to the sharing and without her prompting or praise (Rheingold, Hay, & West, 1976). In fact, the percentage of helping acts (out of total number of contacts with a peer) was higher for 18- to 30-month-olds than for any other age group up to 5½ years (Bar-Tal, Raviv, & Goldberg, 1982). Children in the second year also help their mothers care for their baby siblings (Dunn, Kendrick, & Mac-Namee, 1981).

While most studies have examined caregiving unidirectionally, mother to child, mothers often perceive their children as extremely nurturant. Research suggests, in fact, that all children nurture their dolls and animals. They bed, caress, feed, groom, and talk to them. In one study all 18- to 30-month-old children performed nurturing acts, however, the latter half of the second year was an important period. During these 6 months the increase in nurturing acts was much greater than between 24 and 30 months (Rheingold & Emery, 1986). If the motive for nurturing is related to empathic feelings and comforting behaviors, the second year may be a period in which a new competence or sensitivity develops.

Although these prosocial behaviors can be seen as components of or precursors to empathy, they are not equivalent. Some researchers have concentrated on prosocial behaviors as indicators of the beginnings of empathic responding, simply because empathy has been so difficult to define and even more difficult to observe. For example, one could infer that empathic affect motivates prosocial behavior (Aronfreed, 1970). If one conceptualizes empathy as primarily a cognitive achievement one would look to perspective-taking abilities as an indication that the more internal empathic response was actually occurring. One would then necessarily measure empathy by accuracy of predicting another's emotion (e.g., Borke, 1971) and be left with a concept that has little theoretical utility beyond looking at cognitive functioning (Stotland, et al., 1975).

For many years observers have remarked about what seems to be empathic affect of the 1 to 2-year-old calling these signs "gentle feelings," "sympathy," and "tenderness" for others (Murchison & Langer, 1927; Murphy, 1937; Valentine, 1938). In the late 18th century, Tiedemann wrote of his young son who was 14½ months and wept when someone refused his hand which he had offered as a sign of affection. Later, at almost 17 months, he "wept with his sister when she cried" and soon after "objected against having either (his dog or sister) suffer certain harm" (Murchison & Langer, 1927). Gessell and colleagues described children this young as essentially "self-interested" yet also documented the emergence of "symptoms" of pity, sympathy, modesty, shame, and guilt around the second year. By age two, they claimed, the child has "great complexity, depth, and sensitiveness" (Gesell, et al., 1940).

The discussion of empathy as an emotional experience raises interesting questions. Some researchers have looked to evolutionary theory for an explanation of empathy as an instinctual and/or involuntary response (Campbell, 1965; Church, 1959 in Rushton & Sorrentino, 1981; McDougall, 1908; Sullivan, 1953). Hoffman (1982) supports this view, noting that empathy is overdetermined, self-reinforcing, largely involuntary, requiring little cognitive processing, and thus of survival value in human evolution.

Only a handful of studies document the emergence of empathy in the second year of life but the observational data on related behaviors are compelling evidence for the assumption that these children feel empathically towards others in distress. Between 12 and 20 months children will respond to distress by orienting to another (Eisenberg-Berg, 1982). They will make tentative approaches to victims, sometimes attempt to comfort people in distress (Hoffman, 1982), and even try to make upset siblings laugh (Dunn & Kendrick, 1979).

The most extensive work on toddlers' responses to people in distress has been done at the National Institute of Mental Health by Zahn-Waxler and associates. They have shown that during the second year children become sensitive to the distress of other family members (Zahn-Waxler, Yarrow, & King, 1979) and that after 18 months respond with prosocial behavior to about one third of all distresses they witness (Zahn-Waxler & Radke-Yarrow, 1982). In the latter study they used mothers and visitors as recorders of the child's behaviors and found that prosocial acts and imitations of the victim's distress increased with age while self distress decreased with age. They also found that the greatest increase of prosocial behavior to distress situations was between 16 and 24 months.

These observations again raise the question of whether prosocial responses can be understood as expressions of empathic affect. Imitation of the victim's distress seems to express an attempt to understand or feel what the victim is feeling whether or not this imitation is voluntary or involuntary. If some degree of affect matching is necessary in order for a response to be truly empathic the imitative response can be considered an attempt to match affect and would then indicate a connection between empathy and prosocial responding. In any case, those who have observed tender feelings of sympathy as well as those who have researched the area more systematically have suggested that these behaviors first emerge in the second year of life and occur more frequently after 18 months.

AWARENESS OF STANDARDS

The claim that the young child has some capacity for forming judgments about right and wrong that develops or even emerges in the second year offends some who would believe that such a capacity depends primarily on higher cognitive functioning and/or parental socialization practices. And indeed, until recently, most research concentrated on the learning of values and self-control which encourage children to live by accepted social rules and rarely on the child's beginning ability to make morally related evaluations.

For over 2 decades psychologists have investigated maternal control techniques and have shown that differences in technique have an effect on preschool children's socialization (Olim, Hess, & Shipman, 1967) as well as the fact that mothers differ in the techniques they use with their 2-year-olds depending on the gender of their child and the mother's degree of education (Minton, Kagan, & Levine, 1971). In the latter study, 27-month-old children made approximately nine violations per hour and most violations had to do with the protection of household objects. Mothers generally spoke in a mild tone to their children unless the children did not comply, and the forcefulness of the mother's intervention depended on the most recent interaction between mother and child.

Other studies focus on the child's increasing ability to inhibit his or her actions and comply with parental desires (Erikson, 1963; Flavell, 1977; Gesell & Amatruda, 1945; Vaughn, Kopp, & Krakow, 1984). The ability to comply with one's caregiver, to start or stop an activity according to situational demands, to modulate intensity, frequency, and duration of acts in social settings, to postpone the pursuits of goals, and to generate socially approved behaviors in the absence of external monitoring are all aspects of self-regulation. During the second year the integration of cognitive, social, and communicative abilities, as well as the beginning of representational thinking and recall memory may enable children to begin to control themselves (Kopp, 1982); however, a study by Vaughn et al. (1984) shows 18-month-olds restraining themselves only fleetingly in experimental tasks.

Kagan (1981) agrees that children's self-control may have internal motivation apart from caregivers' demands and that they may have a natural (maturationally motivated) interest in standards. His research on standards involved presenting 1- to 2-year-olds with an object that violated a standard adults regard as normative. Over one half of the 19-month-olds in his sample showed distress over a broken toy or a torn piece of clothing, while no 14-year-old did. Children in the latter half of the second year also expressed distress after an examiner modeled an act that was too difficult for the child to imitate. Kagan suggests that these children were aware of a standard of performance and were upset because they could not meet it. Largo and Howard's (1979) work supports this assumption of Kagan's and demonstrates children over 15 months judging whether a task is "too easy" for them. When completing a difficult task, children in the second year will sometimes smile whether or not an adult is watching them (Kagan, 1981; Stipek & McClintic, 1989) thus suggesting an understanding that they have met a standard of performance.

Taken together the studies showing the emergence of prosocial and empathic behavior, along with research that indicates an awareness of standards, suggest that something amounting to a moral sense emerges in the second year of life. We are left with the question of why the second year? What developmental accomplishments mediate, prepare, or encourage children in this year to act prosocially and respond with emotional distress to discrepant events and to failure to meet a standard?

DEVELOPMENTAL CHANGES IN THE SECOND YEAR AND THEIR RELATION TO EARLY MORAL DEVELOPMENT

Changes in Language

The research on language development in the second year points to some interesting changes which may be related to the emergence of empathic affect or prosocial responding as well as awareness of standards. In Kagan's study (1981) children's speech first referred to standards after 19 months. And children first use moral language, words such as "good," "bad," "naughty," and "nice" (Bloom, Lightbown, & Hood, 1975; Kagan, 1981) at this time.

Kagan (1987) suggests that a sensitivity to right and wrong can not appear until children are able to consciously infer possible causes and feeling states in others. It is difficult to assess, however, when a child is "actively" inferring another's internal state or intentions. While children first use internal state words in the latter half of the second year and label the agents of acts, there has been considerable debate over whether this indicates that they are now reflectively inferring the internal states and intentions of others. Because children sometimes acquire the forms of language before fully grasping the meaning, emergence of certain words can not alone suggest a new capacity. Huttenlocher, Smiley, and Charney (1983) argue that it is questionable whether a child in the second year of life can infer intentionally in that the naming of an agent in the context of watching a person act does not necessarily indicate the child is *categorizing* a person as an agent. Slobin (1985), however, argues that understanding a simple act such as one's mother filling a bottle with juice would automatically *require* understanding that the agent is acting intentionally. While labeling may indicate reflective inferences about an agent's intentionality it doesn't necessarily have to and babies and toddlers continue to act as if others have intentions whether or not they reflect on this fact.

Still it does appear significant that around the same time as the emergence of morally related acts children begin to use internal state words even though their mothers may not be promoting such learning by providing them with many examples. Although some researchers have described mothers using a fair number of internal state words to their 1½- to 2½-year-olds (Beeghly, Bretherton, & Mervis, 1986; Dunn, *et al.*, 1987), Huttenlocher, Smiley, and Prohaska (1988) who counted only emotion words and not behavior words (e.g. "crying") found an extremely low frequency of usage. They also found that when mothers use emotion words they usually refer to the *child's* internal state rather than their own, thus hardly directing the child to infer another's feelings (Smiley & Huttenlocher, 1989).

Children do not equally select from all word categories when they first produce speech but before 24 months children begin to use emotion and internal state words to describe mostly themselves but also other people (Bretherton, McNew, & Beeghly-Smith, 1981). Bloom et al., (1975), had a 22-month-old girl in their sample who stated "lamb tired" and "girl hungry." Hood and Bloom (1979) report a 24-month-old saying "crying/wantMommy" about another child. However, Huttenlocher et al. (1988) found that although children used emotion words such as "happy," "afraid," "mad," and "sad," children under 26 months never used these words for others, only for themselves.

One could argue that while children rarely use internal state words to describe others, the fact that they use these words to describe their own internal states may indicate an attention to internal phenomena, a kind of attention that could promote empathic responding upon reflection of one's own internal response. If empathic affect is involuntary it would not necessarily require an accurate or reflective understanding of the other's emotion and distress cues nor a capacity to label them. Moreover, the capacity to label does not in and of itself indicate an understanding of a concept or emotion and may indeed follow comprehension. Although the language data do not overwhelmingly suggest a reflective awareness of another's intention or internal state, the fact that children are beginning to use these words to label emotions suggests greater attention and even a possible new alerting to emotional states.

Affective Changes

According to some theorists (Emde, Kligman, Reich, & Wade, 1978; Malatesta, 1982), the second year is a time of great emotional development and lability. Infants appear adaptively to be insensitive to aversive information (La Barbera, Izard, Vietz, & Parisi, 1976) which suggests that as canalized behavior decreases, the child may be confronted or "flooded" with aversive emotional experience (Izard, 1978). This flooding may help explain infants' increased attention to emotional states suggested by their acquisition of emotion words.

There is a peak in the imitation of affect in the second year which also indicates a focus on others' feelings (Kuczinski, Zahn-Waxler, & Radke-Yarrow, 1987). Kagan (1987) discusses research on young monkeys' brains, suggesting that synaptic density in human limbic structures, structures that regulate the experiencing of emotion, may reach a peak during the second year. This may heighten a child's emotional responsivity to distress cues emitted by victims. If empathy is a state of "unpleasant affect" as Hoffman (1975) and Kagan (1984) suggest, it may motivate a child to respond to another in distress in order to be more personally comfortable.

This new focus on affects and the capacity to take in more affective information could also heighten the toddler's awareness of parental prohibitions. Kagan (1984) claims that all moral standards are based on fundamental affective states, three of which are anxiety in response to social disapproval, a feeling of uncertainty that accompanies encounters with discrepant events, and discomfort in hearing or seeing someone in distress. These emotions, salient as they are for the child in the second year, may form the basis of morality (Kagan, 1981, 1984).

Cognitive Contributions

The capacity to form and use symbols appears to emerge around the middle of the second year (McCall, 1979; Piaget, 1952). It is at this time that toddlers begin to use symbols to refer to absent objects. In pretend play they begin to symbolize the interactions between two people (Nicolich, 1977). Symbolization may be necessary for the categorization of acts as right and wrong. And with regard to awareness of parental standards, it is possible that a broken toy or a torn shirt can represent for a child a "bad" or destructive act that someone else committed.

The capacity for making inferences has also been implicated as a contributor not only to empathy but also to awareness of standards. Kagan (1981) suggests that the child who shows distress at a flawed object makes an inference that another child did something that violates a parental standard. However, even in Kagan's own tasks measuring relational and linguistic inferences, children's competence in this area is neither obvious nor demonstrated consistently across tasks, even as late as the latter portion of the second year. Similarly, when Masangkay, *et al.* (1974) asked two-year-olds to make inferences regarding the affects of dolls who kissed, hugged or fought, they also did poorly. Still, Rheingold and Emery (1986) note that in symbolic play children even under the age of two treat their dolls as if they were animate beings with internal states. Once again, it would seem that acting as though a person or thing has an internal state may be quite different than reflecting on the intentions or internal states of others.

THE SOCIAL CONTEXT OF MORAL DEVELOPMENT IN THE SECOND YEAR

In her longitudinal studies of British toddlers and their mothers over the toddlers' second and third year of life, Dunn (1987; 1988) was interested in how an understanding of standards and moral feelings develop within the context of family relationships. In particular, she was concerned with incidents of conflict, verbal communication about conflict incidents, and affective behaviors in relationships including a mother, toddler, and older sibling.

Teasing behavior increased over the second year and was increasingly sophisticated showing that toddlers were able to infer and understand what might bother their siblings and mothers. They also showed the capacity to infer or anticipate their mothers' reactions to acts of aggression or teasing. They made appeals to their mothers after a sibling aggressed on or teased them but not after they teased or aggressed on their siblings.

As language development increased, the children in Dunn's study began to refer to the responsibility of their siblings when discussing conflicts and to make references to social rules. In pretend play they would even negotiate rules with their older siblings.

With regard to awareness of standards, Dunn's toddlers drew attention to a previously forbidden act as they were committing the transgression. They also, on occasion, laughed when doing something their mothers had previously forbidden them to do. Dunn notes that most theorists have studied the negative emotions that accompany transgressing: shame, guilt, anxiety, fear. In contrast she observed children's amusement, pleasure, and joking about rule violations as well.

Dunn also kept track of children's responses to flawed objects in their households. Measuring their interest solely by their communications about such objects, she found their interest to steadily increase over the second year. While it is possible her measure confounds increasing language ability with increasing interest, it is still important that the children continue to use their increasing language to draw attention to flawed objects. In other words, their language directed towards flawed objects reflects, if not an *increasing* interest, still a strong one.

The children in Dunn's study became more emotionally "expressive" over the second year. She found that after 18 months the children were more agitated, angry, and distressed by conflicts. She also noted more destructive acts and more aggression towards their mothers as well as towards themselves.

Dunn beautifully describes the developments of the second year and the socializing context, of sibling and mother, in which they occur. She begins with the premise that morally related behavior is predominantly socialized behavior and is thus not terribly interested in teasing out various alternative contributions, save for language development.

THE EMERGENCE OF A MORAL SENSE

My own study (Lamb, 1988; in press) is a longitudinal, naturalistic, observational attempt to look at morally-related behaviors as they appear together and in relation to other developmental accomplishment of the second year. Like Dunn, I went into the homes as a participant observer, recording conversations between the mothers and their children as well as a continuous description of the child's activities and facial responses. I followed four children and their mothers over the child's second year, observing every 2 to 3 weeks for 2½-hour sessions each time.

There were three primary aims to the study. The first was to aggregate acts that others had previously suggested were morally related in order to see if there was a pattern to their emergence and to see whether the appearance of such behaviors was dependent on mothers' increasing socialization comments about such acts. While these acts may emerge and be shaped in social-interactional contexts such as the ones described by Dunn, the contexts do not necessarily *explain* the emergence of these acts. The second aim of the study was to examine the relationship between the appearance of morally-related acts to language development and the capacity for making inferences. The third aim was to examine the quality of the interactions around prohibitions between mothers and their children to determine whether there were any systematic changes over the second year.

The Aggregation of Morally-Related Acts

Although mothers were unaware of the purpose of the study, (the running commentaries attempted to include *all* actions of the child), I coded the transcripts of each session for 6 general areas of acts and communications relating to awareness of standards:

1. *awareness of transgressing:* Sophie, for example, at 17 months, showed awareness of transgressing when she crumpled up a piece of tape, held it in front of her mouth touching her lips, turned to her mother, and smiled.

2. *uh oh's:* Again at 17 months, Sophie colored on her mother's guitar with a crayon. Her mother said, "No, no. I don't want you to draw on it." Sophie then looked at the crayon and said, "Uh oh, uh oh, uh oh," and brought it over to the observer to look at it.

3. *interest in flawed objects and discrepant events:* Shane, at 15 months, saw that a bit of felt was torn from the bottom of a music box. Full of concern he brought it to the adults in the room saying, "Look, look, look."

4. *awareness of achievement standards:* Proud looks and achievement smiles were counted in this category. Sasha's mother, for example, asked Sasha who was 19 months if he wanted to ride his hippo. He climbed on and she said, "You can push it by yourself." He pushed it by himself and smiled broadly.

5. *labeling, using moral vocabulary, reciting rules:* Hazel, at 21 months, responded to her mother's directive "We don't throw things" with "And we don't hit people." At 17 months she was very much interested in labeling things found on the playground as "good" and "bad," "garbage," and "yukky."

6. *pointing out something dangerous in the environment:* Hazel, at 20 months, picked a tack up off the floor and gave it directly to her mother.

Acts of prosocial responding were so infrequent that they were not included in the aggregation and were analyzed separately.

Every child expressed awareness of standards in every category except for Sophie who never was observed to point out danger. The differences among the four children in the areas in which they manifested their awareness of standards are presented in Table 7.1. While Shane expressed his awareness primarily through interactions around transgressions and "uh oh"'s over accidents, Sasha manifested his awareness through "uh oh"'s about accidents and achievement standards. Sophie's awareness was primarily manifested in reactions to trans-

TABLE 7.1.
Comparison of Four Subjects in Major Categories of Awareness of Standards

| | *Percentages* | | | |
Type of Incident	*Shane*	*Sasha*	*Sophie*	*Hazel*
1. Awareness of transgressing	34	9	31	15
2. Uh oh's	26	35	15	11
3. Interest in flawed objects	17	17	25	18
4. Awareness of achievement standards	9	30	19	24
5. Using moral vocabulary	13	2	11	26
6. Points out danger	1	2	0	6

gressions and in an interest in flawed objects. Hazel's most salient categories were the labeling of incidents and objects as "good," "bad," "yukky," or "dirty" and awareness of standards of achievement.

Each child expressed his or her awareness of standards in different areas; however, when behavioral and verbal expressions of awareness in the six categories were aggregated to obtain total incident scores for each session, the number of morally related incidents peaked at the same age, between 17 and 18 months, for all four children. While other researchers have observed different behaviors relating to moral development steadily increase over the second year, the aggregation of these specific behaviors shows an increase and then a decrease around the middle of the second year. (See Fig. 7.1.) This finding was not confounded by language development in that language, (as measured by number of words acquired) steadily increased, even after the peak in awareness of standards. Moreover, the greatest increase in word acquisition occurred after the peak in awareness of standards for each child.

Mothers' socializing comments relating to the six areas of interest were counted to determine to what extent they may be promoting this interest in the second year. (See Lamb, 1988 for a fuller description of the methodology.) While mothers made socializing comments in most areas throughout the second year, these comments did not increase or peak before the children's peaks in awareness of standards. In fact, the mothers' comments seemed more to follow the children's interest rather than lead it, supporting the children's attempts to understand, explore, and/or respond to morally related events in their lives. In that morally related events have special salience for children in the middle of the second year somewhat independent of mothers' socializing comments, there may be maturational factors mediating the peaking of such interest at precisely this time.

Empathic Responding

Situations that called for empathic responding were extremely rare during the observations sessions, and because this was anticipated, mothers were asked after every session a series of questions about their child's development over the past few weeks. One question asked mothers whether they had seen their child show concern for or comfort someone in distress. According to their mothers, the first incident of empathic responding occurred between 16 and 19 months, before the peak in awareness of standards for two children and after the peak for the other two children. Again, the children varied in their modes of expressing empathy. One child pretended to weep when hearing his mother read a story of a bunny who was hurt. Another child hugged his mother as she cried following an argument with the child's father. Another child smiled and said "hi" to his mother, "as if to cheer (her) up," when she was crying during an argument with the child's father. It is interesting that although their responses vary, the emer-

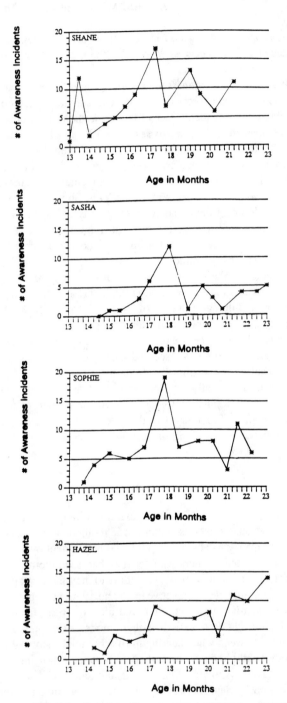

FIG. 7.1. Number of awareness incidents per session for each child

gence of these seemingly empathic responses appear in a relatively brief window of time in the second year, some time around the middle.

The Appearance of Internal State Words

Mothers completed a bisession checklist of new words their children had acquired and used over the past few weeks. By the end of the study no child had a sophisticated vocabulary of internal state words. They used the following internal state words occasionally but mothers were not asked to record whether the word was used to describe self or other: happy, sad, hungry, thirsty, nice, sleepy, tired, mad, and scared. For three of the four children the largest increase in number of internal state words came at or right after the peak in awareness of standards. What is interesting is that this increase in internal state words came before these children's largest increase in vocabulary acquisition. In the 2 months after Shane's peak, he acquired three internal state words; he had none at 17 months. Sophie also had none at the time of her peak in awareness of standards but acquired 4 in the next 2 months. Hazel had one and acquired three more over the next 2 months. And Sasha had one internal state word in his vocabulary at 18 months but did not begin to acquire more until after 21 months at which time he acquired eight more. Over the course of the second year mothers rarely used internal state language. In fact the highest percentage of "turns" of speech that included an internal state word, (out of total number of speech turns for an observation) only reached .02 of one percent. It seems likely that the children themselves are differentially sensitive to internal state words available to them at the time, needing little experience with them to acquire them. This may reflect a heightened awareness of their own emotional or internal states, or a sensitivity to the states of others.

The Capacity for Making Inferences

The children were given a series of inference tasks at the end of every other observation session. One task was designed to examine inference of wrongdoing. The child was shown two objects (two dolls, shoes, or cups); one was broken and soiled; the other was fine. The child was then asked to hand the examiner the "bad" one. This task may have been confounded by language development, however, the child with the slowest development was the child to pass this task consistently the earliest. Three of the children began to pass this task consistently before the peak in awareness of standards which suggests that the task may be tapping an inferential capacity in an area that would soon become a major interest.

Another task that was administered was designed to measure the child's ability to infer, from a visual clue, another's intention. I announced that I was going to hide an attractive toy under one of two boxes and then, out of sight from the child, hid the toy in a box. I then placed both boxes in front of the child and asked, "Where's the (attractive toy)?" repeatedly while staring very intently at and leaning towards the correct box. I repeated the task three times with different toys for each task session. Only one of the children passed this task consistently (three out of three times) before the peak in awareness of standards suggesting that the children were not yet able to use this kind of visual clue to infer where the examiner had placed the toy.

Flawed Objects

Unlike Kagan (1981) but like Dunn I found that the four children I observed expressed enormous interest in flawed objects and little actual distress. It was interesting that the mothers in the study did not even once express interest in a flawed object or discrepant event. This was an interest that appeared to be entirely child motivated; however, one quarter of the mothers' prohibitions they directed to their children were about destruction of property. While they may not be drawing attention to this area, they are certainly making it known that destruction of property is wrong. This may mean that the children's interest in flawed objects may derive from their inference that somebody had transgressed by destroying property, rather than discomfort at a standard of form being violated.

QUALITATIVE CHANGES OVER THE SECOND YEAR

Many of the morally related interactions between the four children and their mothers were focused on the children's transgressing. A child would commit a transgression knowingly or unknowingly and his or her mother would respond by saying "no" with varying degrees of forcefulness, giving reasons, and stating "house" rules. They also distracted their children, substituted one toy or activity for another, or simply removed the child or the object. There were no trends in mothers' responses over time except that as the child became more verbal the mother talked more about what she was doing and why. There was, however, a change in the children in their understanding of and emotional response to transgressing and their mothers' prohibitions. Qualitative analyses of the conversations about transgressions revealed a three phase pattern.

Interaction in the early phase is about conflicting wants. The children seem to understand "no" but only restrain themselves for a moment. When they proceed transgressing it is as if they forgot the prohibition.

During this phase the children show little affect when transgressing or when their mothers prohibit something they are doing. If they show affect at all it seems to be about being restrained or not being able to play with an item their mothers' removed from their possession. When a mother raised her voice, her son simply stared at her. This could be due to the child's limited facial "vocabulary'' at this time. It also suggests a lack of interest in standards or in pleasing mother. One doesn't get the feeling these children in the early part of the second year are grappling with "right" and "wrong"; they are simply frustrated. They do not "disobey"; they merely try to return to what they would like to be doing.

Shane, at 13½ months had been playing in some dirt and his mother told him, "No, no, no, no, no." He then said "No no no" to himself and continued to play with the dirt with no change of expression. He only seemed interested in the dirt. Hazel at 14 months was helping her mother wash dishes. Her mother kept asking her not to spill it on the floor, to "spill it in the sink" instead. Hazel would momentarily spill it in the sink but minutes later would begin to pour it on the floor again showing no expressive sign that she knew what she was doing had just been prohibited.

During the transitional phase, between 15 and 19 months, standards become a focus. It is a time when children experiment with standards; they are questioning, playful, and even willful. During this phase the children smile when they disobey and tease their mothers like the children in Dunn's study. When they confront their mothers it is as if they are testing her; there is little negative affect and full-blown confrontations are rare.

Hazel, during this phase, had been told not to put gravel from the playground on her coat. Moments later she put some on my coat and said "coat, no no" and then brushed the gravel off. Shane at 17 months was riding his toy car dangerously close to the street. His mother said, "No no" but Shane continued to advance closer to the street with a smile on his face, staring at his mother, and saying, "Noooooo."

Sometimes after an act was prohibited the children would stand in front of their mothers and almost repeat it, poising in mid-act, smiling, waiting for a response. Sometimes they would transgress in front of her and wait expectantly for a response. They were mostly happy to challenge their mothers and rarely distressed.

The third phase is marked by an understanding of standards in relation to other people. The children not only begin to understand their mothers' wishes and desires with regard to standards, but also show a desire to do what their mothers want them to do. They begin to make reparations for transgression; they "tattle" on themselves and ask for praise then they show restraint; they hide wrongdoings from their mothers; and they even show signs of inner conflict when their mothers' wishes conflict with their own.

When Sophie was 23 months she spent a good part of the observation session trying to wipe crayon off the coffee table, saying to herself as she scrubbed, "uh oh, uh oh, uh oh." She looked quite concerned.

Hazel provides a nice example of a child wanting to do what her mother tells her to do. At 20 months she threw a book across the room. Her mother asked, "Did you throw a book?" Hazel replied "Yes" and smiled. Her mother said, "Don't throw books." and Hazel asked, "Don't throw books?" quite seriously.

Her mother replied, "Yes, it might hurt people and me." Hazel then asked, "Hurt people and me?" Her mother replied, "Yes, hurt you." Hazel then went to play in a different area. At 22 months Hazel pointed to a straight pin in her mother's quilt and announced proudly, "I'm leaving this in."

Shane at 21 months had been fighting with his mother about putting crayons in his mouth. In the middle of the conflict she left the room. He stared after her, lifted a crayon to his mouth, paused a moment, and then put it back down and went to find his mother.

The emotion in this phase is varied: concern, distress, devilish glee. Children are pleased to be doing what their mothers want and anguished when they are torn between what they want to do and what their mothers want them to do. In the transitional phase they were nonchalant although sometimes willful about transgressions; in the third phase they occasionally even get distressed about the violation of a standard. By the end of the second year these children are varied and more intense in their emotional reactions to situations in which a standard is being violated; they are curious about standards; and they may also begin to understand responsibility.

THE MORALLY CONCERNED TODDLER

Previous research examined independent aspects of the emergence of morality in the second year. Studies on behaviors that may be related to empathic responding saw very young children sharing, helping, nurturing, and comforting others in distress. Other studies, more relevant to awareness of standards, looked at the developing child's ability to restrain herself when a limitation was imposed from without; the child's emerging pride when meeting a parental standard of performance; and the child's interest in flawed objects and discrepant events.

Judy Dunn discovered the 1- to 2-year-old's moral concern within the social context of the family as the child inferred what might work to tease her sibling or as he provided his mother with a stuffed animal to comfort her when she was distressed. She observed distress at flawed objects, emotional intensity, and internal state language increasing as the child became more cognitively, linguistically, and socially competent.

I also discovered the moral sense of the 1- to 2-year-old but only examined the social-interactional context secondarily. While Kagan observed these young children showing distress at flawed objects, like Dunn I mainly observed overwhelming interest, even excitement, and only sometimes concern. Unlike Dunn's mothers, the mothers in my study mentioned internal state words only rarely. This could be a cultural difference in "motherese." Like Dunn's toddlers, the toddlers I observed showed much more affect after and around 18 months.

My most intriguing finding came from aggregating data on behaviors that were related to an awareness of standards. The similar timing of the peaks in awareness of standards for all four children suggests that while mothers socialize for moral concern throughout the second year it is around 17 to 18 months that this concern is salient for the child. This sudden increase in things morally related may be mediated by maturational processes relating to cognition, language, and/or affect: the emotional lability or inability to shut out discomforting affect after the middle of the second year; the onset of symbolization; the start of two word utterances; the understanding of intentionality and/or causality. Future research should look at these influences more carefully around the middle of the second year to determine possible influences and interactions.

It is clear that many have previously underestimated the interests, if not the capacities, of the very young with regard to morally related events. While it is unlikely that 18-month-olds can "know the good" and "choose the good" consistently, they show remarkable concern for knowing about, doing, and not doing "good." Perhaps in these early years lies the seeds of our motivation to help and to live up to the standards of others as well as ourselves, to care for others and to live justly and fairly, to, essentially, do the right thing.

REFERENCES

Aronfreed, J. (1970). The socialization of altruistic and sympathic behavior: Some theoretical and experimental analyses. In J. Macaulay & L. Berkowitz (Eds.), *Altruism and helping behavior.* New York: Academic Press.

Bar-Tal, D., Raviv, A., & Goldberg, M. (1982). Helping behaviors among pre-school children: An observational study. *Child Development, 53,* 396–402.

Beeghly, M., Bretherton, I., & Mervis, C. (1986). Mother's internal state language to toddlers. *British Journal of Developmental Psychology, 4,* 247–261.

Bloom, L., Lightbown, P., & Hood, L. (1975). Structure and variation in child language. *Monographs of the Society for Research in Child Development, 40.*

Borke, H. (1971). Interpersonal perception of young children: egocentrism or empathy? *Developmental Psychology, 5,* 263–269.

Bretherton, I., McNew, S., & Beeghly-Smith, M. (1981). Early person knowledge as expressed in gestural and verbal communication: When do infants acquire a "theory of mind"? In M. E. Lamb & L. R. Sherrod (Eds.), *Infant social cognition.* Hillsdale, NJ: Lawrence Erlbaum Associates.

Campbell, D. T. (1965). Ethnocentric and other altruistic motives. In D. Levine (Ed.), *Nebraska Symposium on Motivation, 13,* Lincoln: University of Nebraska Press.

Dunn, J. (1987). The beginning of moral understanding: Development in the second year. In J. Kagan & S. Lamb (Eds.), *The emergence of morality in young children.* Chicago: University of Chicago Press.

Dunn, J., Bretherton, I., & Munn, P. (1987). Conversations about feeling states between mothers and their young children. *Developmental Psychology, 23,* 132–139.

Dunn, J. (1988). *The beginnings of social understanding.* Cambridge, MA: Harvard University Press.

Dunn, J., & Kendrick, C. (1979). Interaction between young siblings in the context of family

188   LAMB

relationships. In M. Lewis & L. A. Rosenblum (Eds.), *The child and its family*. New York: Plenum Press.

Dunn, J., Kendrick, C., & MacNamee, R. (1981). The reaction of first-born children to the birth of a sibling: Mothers' reports. *Journal of Child Psychology and Psychiatry, 22,* 1–18.

Eisenberg-Berg, N. (1982). *The development of prosocial behavior*. New York: Academic Press.

Emde, R. N., Kilgman, D. H., Reich, J. H., & Wade, T. D. (1978). Emotional expression in infancy: I. Initial studies of social signaling and an emergent model. In M. Lewis & L. A. Rosenblum (Eds.), *The development of affect*. New York: Plenum Press.

Erikson, E. (1963). *Childhood and society*. New York: W. W. Norton.

Flavell, J. H. (1977). *Cognitive development*. Englewood Cliffs, NJ: Prentice-Hall.

Gesell, A. L., & Amatruda, C. S. (1945). *The embryology of behavior: The beginnings of the human mind*. New York: Harper.

Gesell, A., Halverson, H., Ilg, F., Thompson, H., Castner, B. M., Ames, L. B., & Amatruda, C. S. (1940). *The first five years of life: The pre-school years*. New York: Harper.

Gilligan, C. (1982). *In a different voice*. Cambridge, MA: Harvard University Press.

Hoffman, M. (1975). Developmental synthesis of affect and cognition and its implications for altruistic motivation. *Developmental Psychology, 11,* 607–622.

Hoffman, M. (1982). The development of prosocial motivation: Empathy and guilt. In N. Eisenberg-Berg (Ed.), *The development of prosocial behavior*. New York: Academic Press.

Hood, L., & Bloom, L. (1979). What, when, and how about why: A longitudinal study of early expressions of causality. *Monographs of the Society for Research in Child Development, 44,* (6, serial No. 181).

Huttenlocher, J., Smiley, P., & Charney, R. (1983). Emergence of action categories in the child: Evidence from verbal meanings. *Psychological Review, 90,* 72–93.

Huttenlocher, J., Smiley, P., & Prohaska, V. (1988). *Origins of the category of person: Evidence from speech*. Unpublished manuscript.

Izard, C. (1978). On the ontogenesis of emotion and emotion-cognition relationships in infancy. In M. Lewis & L. A. Rosenblum, (Eds.), *The development of affect*. New York: Plenum Press.

Kagan, J. (1981). *The second year: The emergence of self-awareness*. Cambridge, MA: Harvard University Press.

Kagan, J. (1984). *The nature of the child*. New York: Basic Books.

Kagan, J. (1987). Introduction. In J. Kagan & S. Lamb (Eds.), *The emergence of morality in young children*. Chicago: University of Chicago Press.

Kopp, C. B. (1982). Antecedents of self-regulation: A developmental perspective. *Developmental Psychology, 18,* 199–214.

Kuczynski, L., Zahn-Waxler, C., & Radke-Yarrow, M. (1987). Development and content of imitation in the second and third years of life: A socialization perspective. *Developmental Psychology, 23,* 276–282.

La Barbera, J. D., Izard, C., C. E., Vietz, P., & Parisi, S. A. (1976). Four and six month-old infants' visual responses to joy, anger, and neutral expressions. *Child Development, 47,* 535–538.

Lamb, S. (1988). The Emergence of Morality in the Second Year of Life. Harvard Graduate School of Education. Unpublished doctoral dissertation.

Lamb, S. (in press). The beginnings of morality. In A. Garrod (Ed.), *Emerging themes in moral development. New York: Teacher's College Press*

Largo, R. H., & Howard, J. A. (1979). Developmental progression in play behavior of children between nine and thirty months. *Developmental Medicine and Child Neurology, 1-2,* 299–310.

Malatesta, C. Z. (1982). The expression and regulation of emotion: A lifespan perspective. In T. Field & A. Fogel (Eds.), *Emotions and early interactions*. Hillsdale, NJ: Lawrence Erlbaum Associates.

Masangkay, Z. S., McCluskey, K. A., McIntyre, C. W., Sims-Knight, J., Vaughn, B. E., &

Flavell, J. H. (1974). The early development of inferences about the visual percepts of others. *Child Development, 45,* 357–366.

McCall, R. B. (1979). Qualitative transitions in behavioral development in the first three years. In M. H. Bornstein & W. Kessen (Eds.), *Psychological development from infancy.* Hillsdale, NJ: Lawrence Erlbaum Associates.

McDougall, W. (1908). *An introduction to social psychology.* London: Methuen.

Minton, C., Kagan, J., & Levine, J. A. (1971). Maternal control and obedience in the two-year-old. *Child Development, 42,* 1873–1894.

Murchison, C., & Langer, S. (1927). Tiedemann's observations on the development of the mental faculties of children. *Pedagogical Seminary and Journal of Genetic Psychology, 34,* 204–230.

Murphy, L. B. (1937). *Social behavior and child personality.* New York: Columbia University Press.

Nicolich, L. McC. (1977). Beyond sensorimotor intelligence: Assessment of symbolic maturity through analysis of pretend play. *Merrill-Palmer Quarterly, 23,* 89–99.

Olim, E. G., Hess, R. D., & Shipman, V. C. (1967). Role of mothers' language styles in mediating their preschool children's cognitive development. *School Review, 75,* 414–424.

Piaget, J. (1952). *The origins of intelligence in children.* New York International Universities Press.

Rheingold, H. L., & Emery, G. N. (1986). The nurturant acts of very young children. In D. Olwevs, J. Block, & M. Radke-Yarrow (Eds.), *Development of antisocial and prosocial behavior: Research, Theories, and Issues.* Orlando, FL: Academic Press.

Rheingold, H. L., & Hay, D. F. (1980). Prosocial behavior of the very young. In G. Stent (Ed.), *Morality as a Biological phenomenon: The Presuppositions of Sociobiological Research,* Berkeley: University of California Press.

Rheingold, H. R., Hay, D. F., & West, M. J. (1976). Sharing in the second year of life. *Child Development, 47,* 1148–1158.

Rushton, J. P., & Sorrentino, R. M. (1981). Altruism and helping behavior: An historical perspective. In J. P. Rushton & R. M. Sorrentino (Eds.), *Altruism and helping behavior: Social, personality, and developmental perspectives.* Hillside, NJ: Lawrence Erlbaum Associates.

Slobin, D. I. (1985). *The crosslinguistic study of language acquisition. Volume 2: Theoretical issues.* Hillsdale, NJ: Lawrence Erlbaum Associates.

Smiley, P., & Huttenlocher, J. (1989). Young children's acquisition of emotion concepts. In C. Saarni & P. L. Harris (Eds.), *Children's understanding of emotion.* Cambridge, England: Cambridge University Press.

Stipek, D., & McClintic, S. (1989, April). *Factors affecting toddlers' reactions to completing tasks.* Paper presented at the Society for Research in Child Development Conference, Kansas City, Missouri.

Stotland, E., Matthews, K. E., Sherman, S. E., Hansson, R. O., & Richardson, B. Z. (1978). *Empathy, fantasy, and helping.* Beverly Hills: Sage Publications.

Sullivan, H. S. (1953). *The interpersonal theory of psychiatry.* New York: W. W. Norton.

Valentine, C. W. (1938). A study of the beginnings and significance of play in infancy. *British Journal of Educational Psychology, 8,* 285–306.

Vaughn, B. E., Kopp, C. E., & Krakow, J. B. (1984). The emergence and consolidation of self-control from eighteen to thirty months of age. *Child Development, 55,* 990–1004.

Waxler, C. Z., Yarrow, M. R., & King, R. A. (1979). Child rearing and children's prosocial initiations towards victims of distress. *Child Development, 50,* 319–330.

Zahn-Waxler, C., & Radke-Yarrow, M. (1982). The development of altruism: Alternative research strategies. In N. Eisenberg-Berg (Ed.), *The development of prosocial behavior.* New York: Academic Press.

8

Professional Morality: A Discourse Approach (The case of the teaching profession)

Fritz K. Oser

ABSTRACT

Morality in professional acting becomes more and more an important issue. This chapter outlines a new understanding of professional morality.

Ethical dimensions in teachers' professional decision making are illuminated. It is argued that considering these dimensions does not contradict the professional (i.e., instructional) success, as is often thought, but actually is a precondition for good teaching. In contrast to solely normative concepts, for listing the virtues a good teacher is supposed to possess, this approach focuses on an orientation that can be learned but requires fundamental changes in teachers' concepts of their authority. This orientation is called the discourse position. The criteria for a discursive stance towards decision making and interpersonal problem solving are elaborated.

It is demonstrated that moral conflicts in educational settings arise when three types of moral claims cannot be met at the same time: justice, care, and truthfulness. Professional morality emerges in strategies of coordinating these moral dimensions in the search for an adequate solution of a problem.

Central to the theory of professional morality, as it is outlined in this chapter, is the hypothesis of qualitatively different forms of decision making strategies. Five types, or models, of balancing moral claims against functional standards of professional acting and against each other (when they conflict) are described, called "avoiding," "delegating" or "security seeking," "unilateral" or single handed decision making," "incomplete discourse," and "complete discourse."

In a further section, some consequences of this approach for programs in teacher education are elaborated.

Finally, an overview of the empirical research is presented that has been conducted in Switzerland and Austria during the last four years. The core study was interventional, addressing the issue of changeability of the teachers' "ethos." In fact, changes towards a discursive position could be stimulated. Major results of this and other studies are reported, and some methodological issues are addressed.

A MORALLY "GOOD" TEACHER

After coming back from the war, Düischen, the young teacher, establishes a school in a little village in North-Kirgisistan. He devotes his life to the children, he fights for them—against the parents, if necessary. He helps the poor and the orphans. He protects a girl from being misused at work. And while lacking much teaching experience, he insists in instructing the children—despite the resistance of the village residents who think that learning is not work and who think this young man must be crazy to make such an effort for nothing. These are some of the main events in a story of old Russia, written by the contemporary novelist Tschingis Aitmatov.

His little book, "The First Teacher," is one of the very first pieces of literature my beginning student teachers are asked to read. This novel doesn't tell them anything about curriculum formation, or subject matter, or instructional methods. Instead, it gives them something else. It confronts them with a teacher who is deeply committed to his students, in his lessons and outside of school, who lives with them and teaches them to live together, to organize their social life, to control themselves; a teacher who shares their sorrow and helps them in their misery.

Education students are always moved by this person, especially by his interpersonal and moral commitment. This includes his willingness to share the children's thoughts, his ability to accept the children as personalities and to respect their dignity—even when they are dirty and helpless, even when they display stupid or insolent behavior.

Aitmatov's novel is not only about a "good human being" but about a good *teacher*. Let me try to put this story's message into a more theoretical and more general framework. I think it nicely represents a psychological construct we call "professional responsibility" or, broader, "professional ethos" (professional morality).

Normally we presuppose that teachers have something like a professional ethos, just like craftsmen have their ethos, without further analysis or questioning. But looking at real school life gives reason for a more skeptical view. It is not difficult to notice that (a) teachers (as well as researchers) have different views regarding the meaning of those notions ("responsibility," "ethos"). Everyday experience tells us (b) that individual teachers may show varous degrees of quality in professional responsibility, i.e. have a higher or lower professional ethos. One may assume (c) that the particular quality of what I call ethos will influence everything else, so that, for instance, a teacher with high didactical competences but a low professional ethos will be much less successful than a colleague with a high ethos with only average instructional performance.

Now, let us delve further. What does the notion of a "teacher's ethos" mean more exactly? How can it be distinguished from other variables like the classroom climate or teachers' subjective theories of instruction or teacher expectations toward the students, or teacher personality traits that also affect teacher's professional behavior? How might this notion of expertise relate to Berliner's (1986) differentiation between subject matter knowledge and knowledge of organization and classroom management? Is the notion of professional ethos one that integrates these other areas of professional capacity, or is it something different from both? Obviously, we need some clarity regarding the meaning of the construct before we can start planning efforts to ensure that most of the teachers act with a high ethos in most practical situations.

Let me offer a preliminary definition. We conceive of the ethos of the teacher as a general tendency to consider moral standards in a specific realm, namely the teaching profession. It is, like Aristotle would say, a "well-achieved practice," or what can be generalized from this "well-achieved practice," respectively. Stated in modern terms, it is a cognitive structure with three procedural elements: (a) awareness of responsibility, (b) balancing of conflicting variables, and (c) commitment to the act. We assume that this general and deeply rooted structure is connected to moral judgment competence, though it surely is not identical with moral judgment competence in a Piagetian sense since there is always a functional or product-oriented component. Nonetheless, allow me to talk of the ethos as a competence, since in our view it doesn't have much in common with the social-psychological concept of "attitude," or related notions of personality.

To further explicate this notion of teacher ethos, we turn to an examination of the types of cognitive moral capacities.

THREE TYPES OF COGNITIVE MORALITY

There is much discussion about the judgment-action gap in morality. Common sense knowledge says that many people do not do what they preach. Moral psychology has made some progress in this area. A number of researchers (cf. Blasi, 1980, 1983; Kohlberg & Candee, 1984; Rest, 1983; Oser, 1987, among others), have been able to identify at least some spheres where the level of moral judgment appears partly to determine particular courses of action. But such findings are still far from being able to explain inconsistencies between moral reasoning and situational acting.

I suggest that part of the problem is the lack of clear distinctions with respect to the notion of moral judgment. I think there are at least three types of moral cognition relevant to the issues under discussion here. I call these three types "normative morality," "situational morality," and "professional morality."

Normative Morality

"Normative morality" refers to reasoning about hypothetical courses of action in moral decision making situations. A major characteristic of this type of moral reasoning is that it is insufficient in itself to generate action in a concrete situation. This type of hypothetical reasoning tends to be justified by the subject's most optimal cognitive means, and is characterized by its presciptivity (i.e., reference to moral norms). Perhaps this normative morality is best thought of as moral cognitive "competence." Kohlberg's research dilemmas—like the famous "Heinz-Dilemma" that poses the question of whether a man should steal a life preserving drug—typically aim at uncovering this type of moral thinking.

Conditions for identifying a competence (normative) morality are, further, characterized by the fact that subjects do not experience limits of time for problem solution, that they can abstract from certain situational factors (which actually may make it very difficult to break into a drugstore and steal the medicine), and that subjects may control their inner dispositions in an easy way. They do not have to integrate action decisions under complicated conditions. That would require coordination within their personality structures and their self-concepts.

All of this does not mean, however, that emotionality is unimportant and is necessarily neglected in competence morality. Everyone who is pushed to his or her cognitive limits in an interview is concerned, maybe even intimidated or pleased with one's own courage. But everything happens in a sphere of indulgence and relative relaxation. Memories of morally wrong decisions may emerge and then have to be coped with, but concurrent there is no danger of acting once again in the same way. Often times in interviews we hear the statement: One should, or even one *has to* act in this or that way, for one reason or the other— "but I don't know whether I would myself be able to act that way in the concrete situation." Thus the normative aspect ("one should") is in the foreground, because the action alternatives always include classical contrary moral norms like stealing versus not stealing, lying, destruction of intimacy, humiliation of persons, and the respective moral contraries. One could state the main features like this: in the case of normative morality the action is somehow imagined ideally and then ignored, whereas the judgment (that justifies the action) is the dimension to be explored and exhausted by the individual.

This judgment has a particular structure. This structure is holistic, it transcends content, and it always refers to the same set of elements. Progress eventually must include a fundamental transformation. In the case of the

Kohlberg-scheme this accounts for the hierarchy of stages and the developmental process of stage transformation.

Situational Morality

The second type of morality I call "situational morality." This type is crucial in real life situations where the individual is required to act. Conduct has a particular form: *moral* action is action with respect to certain normative standards (again: do not lie, do not hurt, do not destroy life, etc.). Every concrete course of action has to be justified—especially in the case of normative transgressions. Now this justification is much more complicated than in hypothetical dilemmas because situational facts (social, psychological, political, economic aspects) play their role and influence moral reasoning.

Something strange happens to normative judgment under pressure to act. The judgment is netted in these social or psychological variables and is completely re-evaluated. For example, the poverty and sickness of a person may become a reason for certain moral actions against the law without further reasoning. In normative judgments this poverty might also be taken into consideration, but it may be much easier to abstract from its real significance in the light of the law's normative demands. Abstraction from the contextual conditions makes the reasoning susceptible to moral segmentation.

To put it quite clearly, even with respect to concrete actions, as well as to actions already performed situational moral judgment generally differs from "pure" normative judgment.

Examples in the research literature abound (though normally not presented under this heading). See, for instance, the variety of studies on concrete moral behavior—studies on cheating (starting with the Hartshorne & May, 1928 investigation) or on conformity behavior (Asch- and Milgram type); illustrative studies have been conducted, e.g., on tax cheating (Althof, Garz, & Zutavern, 1988) or on driving in a drunken state. Other relevant research has been done in the Just Community approach to schooling. What, for instance, characterizes children's reasoning when they are included in democratic decision-making processes on school matters (cf. Power et al., 1989)? In studies like these, not only the moral judgment stage is measured but also moral motivation, sensitivity, responsibility, etc. (see Schläfli, 1986, for a comprehensive type of interventional study).

Empirically, to get a clear picture of situational morality, the action itself must be assessed, beginning with the quantitative probabilities of its occurrence. A most important question is what connects moral judgment and action. A measurement instrument is needed that grasps the readiness to act, e.g., the preparedness to take personal responsibility or to identify with a normative standard. Furthermore, the difference between contexts has to be taken into consideration, contexts which make it more or less likely that this particular action will take place. Research in this domain is one of the most difficult things a social scientist can encounter.

Professional Morality

The third type of morality is professional morality, which is connected to non-moral, functional, professional acting. When a teacher assigns grades, when an apprentice has to tell the customer that he didn't fill out a form correctly, and that for this reason he may not pay the requested amount of money, when a farmer uses (probably problematic) fertilizers, when a salesperson offers a certain musical instrument, when a craftsman renovates the front of a building, when a dentist fills a tooth—all these situations are instances for types of action that refer to *professional* standards and that, at first sight, don't touch *moral* standards. All these situations, however, are also potentially conflictual by their very nature. The teacher must assign a bad grade if the student's performance was too poor—though the student might have strived very hard. The apprentice has to refuse payment—though he may be confronted with an elder, or other powerful person. The farmer thinks he should use some fertilizer in order to survive with his little farm and his bad soil, though he might notice that most bees have left his ground, bees necessary for pollinating the blossoms. The salesman has to sell though maybe he would never purchase this product for this price himself. Quite similarly, the teaching profession normally is oriented to children's academic success and to supporting learning conditions (class climate, etc.) above all. But as soon as teachers have to give grades and to select students (which means to affirm or to deny shortterm and longterm career chances), as soon as they face critique or resistance by the students, as soon as they make an effort to integrate a handicapped child in their class (or fail to make that effort), as soon as they have to decide whether to act against the parents' will; in other words, as soon as the normal routines of instruction are interrupted, it becomes blatantly apparent that ethical standards have their significance for the teaching profession, too. In many conflict situations teachers must be mindful of some sort of comprehensive principle that helps establish appropriate criteria for solving problems of this type. The type of principle teachers implicitly or explicitly refer to defines a major features of what we call their **professional responsibility.** Professional responsibility manifests itself in professional acts, it refers to the consequences of this acting for the people involved. The notion, however, is not primarily directed to general moral duties that are characterized by their nonspecific nature.

Professional morality is more than expertise and correctness in fulfilling the average requirements of a job. People who solicit the help of a professional (lawyers, physicians, etc.) trust that somebody will act in their best interests. Expertise must be framed by professional responsibility or by a lived value system (cf. Peters & Waterman, 1983).

I proposed this distinction among three types of morality for one major reason. I do believe that the professional ethos is a particular competence leading to particular types of action which cannot be covered by the traditional constructs of "moral judgment" and "moral action." Our view of the world is always via cognitive structures, and cognitive structures are constructed in dealing with meaningful experiences and circumstances. There is good reason to suggest that professional experiences call for and establish domain specific attitudes and cognitions. If this is true, professional morality needs a particular explanatory theory and, of course, specific measurement devices—not just adaptations of the "traditional" Kohlbergian approach.

A Brief Review of the Literature: Paradigms

What does the research literature contribute to the understanding of professional morality? Are there any basic research paradigms reflecting the issues described, and how close are they to the construct as we use it? I would like to mention four approaches that might be able to claim paradigmatic status. (The notion of "paradigm" as introduced by Kuhn certainly is not precise, but it is undoubtedly useful as a tool for classification.) These four "paradigms" are: the virtue conception of professional ethos; personality conceptions, commonly used as a substitute for a notion of ethics; conceptions that view moral judgment as extending to the professional act (professional performance as a domain of application of general moral consciousness), and a procedural ethical conception as a basis for professional morality.

Before outlining these four approaches let me first answer the question "What does the research literature tell us about professional morality?" in a general way. The answer can be given quickly: Not much. There are not many research projects that have dealt with that question. I'll mention those that exist as I describe each of the four approaches.

In this regard it is worth noting that the "International Encyclopedia of Teaching and Teacher Education" (Dunkin, 1987) includes only two small chapters on the personality of the teacher, and only in Coulter's contribution (pp. 589–598) is the word "commitment" used. In the last edition of the "Handbook of Research on Teaching" (Wittrock, 1986) the professional morality of teachers is not explicitly mentioned. To take one final example, in Sprinthall and Sprinthall's excellent textbook on "Educational Psychology" (4th ed., 1987) you find a chapter on the personal dimension of teaching, but again this writing deals with expectations, with self-concept and with affective dimensions, but not with professional morality. The impression is even worse when you look closely at the methodology and results of educational productivity research (see Fraser et al., 1987): Not only do the outcome variables focus entirely on learning (and students' development, identity, personal courage, respectively), but the ethical dimension of teachers' actions is completely missing.

Let me return, then, to what I call the four paradigms for understanding teachers' professional morality.

The teacher's ethos has for a long time been considered to be a normative topic. This is especially true in Europe, where there was kind of a consensus that teachers be required to show certain characteristics. As an example, I would like to quote a list of presumably necessary virtues from a widely distributed book on teacher education issued in 1966. According to this book, people who believe that they want to be a teacher should possess the following attributes:

They should have an ethical character with the following virtues: be religious, just, lenient, loving, and cheerful.

These should be gifted with: a high intelligence; a reliable, extensive, and quick memory; a rich imagination; a deep sentiment, and the ability to suppress any involuntary expression of unpedagogical emotions.

They should be of high activity and initiative, have a quick psychic tempo combined with inner tranquility.

These characteristics should be crowned with educational talents in the narrower sense, such as the disposition to deal with children, to teach them, to lead them to the good, such as undisturbed youthfulness and communicativeness; they should be familiar with the art of presentation and have to ability to catch the children's individuality; they should have educational delicacy and the ability to manage a class, which again includes in particular: personal energy, a sense of superiority, and distributive attention.

These attributes should be combined with special personality features. The good teacher is impressive, open for all good and beautiful things, fundamental, with the golden basis of a deep religiosity.

Not to forget the physical attributes. Our teacher should be healthy, have a strong body, be resistant against ailments of the profession, which means he should possess: healthy nerves, strong respiratory organs, a normal shape, an impressive physical presentation, easiness and appropriateness in all movements, and, last but not least, pleasant social manners (cf. Schneider 1966, p. 50).

One could add a series of similar (though most of the time slightly more modest) definitions of the teacher's ethos from a normative point of view. One of those more modest concepts is stated in the "Code of Ethics of the Education Profession," as adopted by the 1975 NEA Representative Assembly (Strike & Soltis, 1985). Like similar codes of other professions, this code consists of two sets of should-statements: commitment to the student (client), and commitment to the profession. "Shall not intentionally expose the student to embarrassment or disparagement" is an example of a rule referring to the first principle; the second principle is illustrated by: "Shall not assist a noneducator in the unauthorized practice of teaching." This ethical code's authors emphasize such norms as a necessary element of ethical inquiry on the one hand. On the other hand they view them as a concentrated form of general ethical guidelines for professional acting.

In this traditional normative approach, the teachers knew what characteristics they should be provided with, they knew what they were expected to do (or omit), at least on a very general level, and why. Operational definitions of the teacher's ethos contained a catalogue of ''must''-statements, often times with reference to some higher order norms that themselves were not further justified.

In its pure form this approach describes an ideal teacher who, in reality, can never exist. I think, fortunately so: I find it an interesting fact that if one asks laypeople to describe their notion of an ''ideal teacher'' the answers are much less utopian than the indications of some educational scientists or philosophers. In a large scale study we conducted, we found that the ''ideal teacher'' is in no way perceived differently from the ''best teacher I ever had'' (cf. Oser, Klaghofer et al., 1987).

The normative approach was concerned with the question of what teachers *should* be or do. What is completely neglected here, however, is how teachers actually *are,* and second how they can *become* what they are supposed to be. Consequently, this approach did not address the issue of how the teacher's ethos influences his or her way of teaching. Of course, this approach also does not offer any measurement devices.

PERSONALITY CONSTRUCTS OF THE ETHICAL TEACHER

This body of research mainly deals with personality characteristics like identity, self-concept, ego strength, decision making capacity, etc. Levis (1987) recently presented a good overview of this research tradition, beginning with Allport's and Vernon Lindzay's test of values, and Getzel's and Jackson's (1963) assessments of teacher personality. Levis mentions the Kuder Preference Record, the Strong Vocational Interest Blank, measures of adjustment and needs such as the Minnesota Multiple Personality Inventory (MMPI), and others. But Merz (1980) critically states that in most studies no correlation was found between personality traits and student's success. A new branch of this approach is represented by Shavelson and Stern (1981) who depicted teachers' pedagogical thoughts, judgments, decision making, and behavior from a cognitive point of view. Their model of teachers' interactive decision making especially concerns those situations when the teacher leaves his or her classroom routines to deal with a problem calling for immediate reaction.

Mostly, in this movement the professional morality aspect is hidden in other variables and is not explicitly mentioned. It seems that researchers often compound personality traits with morality.

PROFESSIONAL MORALITY AS A SUBDOMAIN OF NORMATIVE MORALITY

A third approach to the professional ethos focuses on normative morality as measured by Kohlberg's scheme, relating it to moral sensitivity or success, respectively, in the professional sphere. The most extensive research has been done by a University of Minnesota group at Minneapolis, under the cooperation of Jim Rest and Muriel Bebeau. Bebeau (1985; Bebeau & Brabeck 1985; Bebeau et al. 1987) assessed the moral judgment stage of dental students (using Rest's instrument) and their moral sensitivity, by using a new instrument called DEST (Dental Ethical Sensitivity Test, 1985). This sensitivity measure shows the number of dentists' considering their clients pain in decision making. Bebeau also did some interventional work: She successfully trained students, promoting their moral reasoning level as well as their moral sensitivity. Similar work has been carried out by Scandinavian researcher Trygve Bergem (1988) with respect to teachers. He starts from the assumption of a moral component in teachers' behavior. Teachers are moral agents, but their own moral judgment changes as a function of professional development. Bergem's studies of the moral component in teaching indicate that individual differences in social sensitivity are significantly related to differences in teacher ratings, while individual differences in moral reasoning are not.

Both lines of research seem to be important for our main issue, even though neither of them deal with professional morality in itself. In both cases global moral judgment competences are taken as the assumedly main component of the ethical side of teaching. This is a major shortcoming of this approach, since it does not take into account the fact that professional morality is always in a complex set of relations to aspects of expertise and functional success.

PROCEDURAL MORALITY: THE THEORY OF A LIVED VALUE-SYSTEM

If a physician has the complicated duty to tell his patient that s/he has cancer he must be very much aware of the patient's capacity to cope with such a threatening situation. If the doctor primarily cares about the patient (and his/her *mental* health), he might not tell the truth. On the other hand, in doing so he may be considered unjust because the patient has a right to know the truth. If, instead, his primary concern is to be truthful, his actions may become less empathic and perhaps upsetting (e.g., in case where the patient actually is unable to cope with the perspective of a lethal disease). This set of alternatives looks like a hopeless dead end. How can the physician find a way out? This is a well-known example of the need to weigh important moral issues against each other and to find a balance between them.

Professionals have to learn that behind professional acting there is a value system that has to be balanced against functional standards. This is, professional acting must not only be evaluated solely in terms of functionality and factual expertise but also in terms of moral expertise and reliability. Furthermore, there must be a practicable strategy of dealing with the moral (i.e., interpersonal) aspects of professional problem solving. The most appropriate strategy we call "discourse." Through ethical discourse the ethical point of view can be *integrated* in professional decision making. Procedural concepts of determining this ethical point of view, as proposed in post-Kantian ethics, gives hints as to what the discourse strategies could be like (see, e.g., the work of philosophers Höffe, 1985, on political problem solving, or Rawls, 1971, on constitutional decision making, or Habermas and Apel, 1988, on what they call "discourse ethics"). Discourse ethics suggests that the procedure of justification of norms and evaluation of claims does not only require the willingness to take the role of each party involved, but also the actual possibility of each party involved to make itself heard. The discourse has to be undertaken in reality, not only in the head of the individual decision maker. One of the implications is that in searching for a consensus the individual actors must presuppose that the others are equally open to practical reason; that they are equally able to decide what course of action is most justified, and to take responsibility for following it through. That is why professional morality is procedural morality and why there can't be a solution strictly planned in advance—before the discursive process has taken place.

But how is this procedure structured? What are the important elements of it? To answer this question, we conducted extensive interviews with teachers on their perception of pedagogical ethos related to important situations of interpersonal conflict. Looking closely at their statements, *one can reduce what they said about the ethos of the teacher and about teaching problems to three fundamental variables, namely care, justice, and truthfulness. This reduction is the result of a long process of analytical attempts to group the elements of the problem solving processes. In all conflict situations teachers have to coordinate these three dimensions.* This coordination is the internal side of procedural tasks in professional morality.

Let us take the example: "pedagogical grading."

Mrs. G. is teaching 4th grade math. Twice a year she doesn't give her marks on the basis of a score or the mean performance of the class (as usual) but assesses the increases of achievement as compared to the previous tests. She has explained and justified this approach to students and parents. When she did, parents were not enthusiastic about that idea, but they didn't object to it, either.

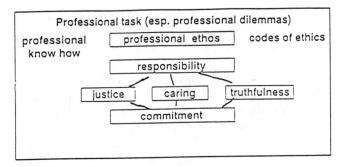

FIG. 8.1.   Dimensions of the teachers' ethos model.

Now, it is the third time she makes use of this procedure. Peter, who normally is bad in math, attains quite a good grade because in this test he clearly made fewer mistakes than in the weeks before. Of course, Peter is very pleased, and he tells Jim, his classmate. However, Jim can't share Peter's happiness. He is one of the best in math. Like always, his performance in the test has been much better than Peter's, but this time both of them got the same mark. Jim perceives this as an injustice, and in talks with his parents and with teacher G., he complains angrily. Other students, too, join in these complaints, and a father has a phone call with the teacher the next day, insisting that Mrs. G. renounces her unconventional style of grading.

This is a dilemma that we confront our subjects with in our research. What should the teacher do? Does she feel responsible for the weaker students in her class? If she really does, she'll find it hard to please the better students, given that justice is understood as parity. If she grades in the sense that the best students will have the best grade, she can hardly say that she cares about the weak students. How can the weak students feel she was impartial even if they are disappointed? So care and justice seem to be in opposition, and the teacher has to find some kind of equilibrium. How can one be just, caring, and truthful at the same time? How can a teacher stay true to his or her convictions and still be open to some kind of compromise? What form can a discursive solution (integration of all parties concerned in the decision making procedure) take?

Types of Equilibrium Between Justice, Care and Truthfulness

In our work on teachers' ethos the coordination among dimensions of justice, care and truthfulness emerged as the critical issue in professional decision making. Naturally, a lot more factors come into play in determining teachers' behavior, such as social norms and role expectations, personality facets, knowledge and expertise, and situational aspects. But none of these factors define the ethos, the particular understanding of responsibility as a professional. The equilibration of justice, caring, and truthfulness does, and our data show that differences between individuals' professional morality are in fact differences of teachers' strategies in coordinating these dimensions.

Empirically we found five types of establishing such an equilibrium in concrete decision making situations. We call them avoiding, delegating, unilateral or "single handed" decision making, incomplete discourse ("discourse I"), and complete discourse ("discourse II"), respectively. I believe that these five types can be assigned values in a rank order from 1 through 5. "Avoiding" is the least responsibly course of action, while the "discourse II" mode of acting is the most responsible orientation.

Having outlined the five types of professional ethos, I turn now to a more detailed discussion of these issues.

Avoiding

In this orientation the teacher tries to "solve" the problem by not facing it. Obviously, in these cases someone else would have to find the balance of justice, care and truthfulness.

Let me give an example. This is a part from an interview with a statement of a science teacher (from a secondary school):

> If a student has a normal level of intelligence, but is lazy and just does what is absolutely necessary, I can certainly give him a B. When I have to write an evaluation, I'll say that he's just lazy and uneager and that he should put more effort into school work. But parents have a hard time understanding such messages (. . .). I always find it difficult to deal with such parents. Parents accept a "B-" when they see it in black and white. But when you transform the grades verbally and tell them about your everyday observations of their child's behavior, they can't handle it. I've had countless phone calls regarding that evaluation sheet.
> *Question:* So now you do without that sheet?
> *Answer:* Yes, because of the considerations I mentioned. I can save myself the trouble, I don't want to get myself into hot water.

This teacher knows that he should be engaged in a deeper decision making process, but he just steps outside of his responsibility. To create a balance of the important dimension mentioned would be "to step into hot water."

Delegating

The teacher, who prefers delegating as a problem-solving strategy basically accepts that he or she has some responsibility for dealing with the situation. However, in an attempt to maintain security, s/he tries to adjourn the decision making and to share the burden or shift the responsibility to some authority (the principal, a psychologist, etc.).

Here is an illustrative example from an excerpt of an interview with respect to the same dilemma (pedagogical grading):

> If the student's father does not want to calm down, I would tell him that I'd like to talk to the district inspector. I would also insist that I have the right to grade the endeavor of a student once a term. If the father disputes my right to do so, we can ask the inspector if it is justified or not. So I would obtain backing. The district inspector would take the responsibility.
>
> *Interviewer:* Wouldn't the district inspector have the last word in this matter anyway?
>
> *Answer:* I would say that we have qualified people to coordinate those things. It is his job to make sure that grading is equivalent. He could tell the teachers in a conference how they can grade student work. So one could have a unified grading policy at least in the same school building.

This teacher refers to the inspector's responsibility to solve the problem. He knows in fact that there is a specific problem. But the act of balancing the variables justice, care and truthfulness is delegated to a school authority.

Single Handed Decision Making

The third type of coordinating justice, care, and truthfulness in professional conflict solving is called "single handed decision making." In this case, the teacher tries to settle the problem by assertively taking it into his or her hands. Decision making in this case does not engage the interested parties but is generated by the teacher (as "expert"), quickly and often-times in an authoritarian manner. Decisions by the teacher are final and stand without additional justification.

Here is a statement of a vocational teacher that nicely illustrates single-handed decision making.

> I would say that this (the grading) is probably a question of scaling. How much does a teacher count the pedagogical objectives besides the level of performance. Basically, if I was convinced of this approach, I would certainly continue to give these marks. This is a matter of finishing an adequate of scale, which weight do I give which aspect. Either I fit my grading to the situation, or I change the situation, so there wouldn't be any complications. For a while I might value the pedagogical aspect more than the actual performance. Then, at another time the performance may become more significant. If the latter is the case, it's possible that I would cancel the initial decision and correct it. But again, if the teacher is convinced that he is doing the right thing, he should stick to it.

Discourse I

The next type is called "discourse I" (incomplete discourse). In this case, the teacher accepts his/her personal responsibility for settling the problem, and s/he subscribes to the task of balancing justice, care, and truthfulness in each new situation. S/he justifies his/her viewpoints and commits him/herself to a good life (as a legitimate interest on behalf of the students) and a just environment.

Example: Yes, I am convinced that the students should not have been treated exactly the same way, and none the less I don't think I am an unjust teacher."
Interviewer: And you think the students will understand that?
Answer: This has to be regulated by way of explanation and discussion. We talk about things until each student understands. And if there's somebody who doesn't and goes home, I would experience this as my failure, I would be disappointed.

Here the teacher explains what he/she means, gives reasons, takes the burden of responsibility on his/her shoulders. He/she knows that students are able to understand a well reflected balance of justice, care and truthfulness.

Discourse II

The final type is what we refer to as complete discourse, "discourse II". In discourse II, the teacher acts similarly to one with a "discourse I" orientation. But there is, however, something additional: S/he presupposes that each student and every other person who is concerned and involved is—in a deep sense—a rational human being who is also interested in and capable of balancing justice, care, and truthfulness. This holds, for such teachers, even in critical or aggressive situations.

Interviewer: Why do you maintain this form of grading?
Answer: Because I have to help those students who are less capable and less motivated. If I can stimulate their motivation, and if they show a better performance afterwards, this is the prove that there was a foundation to build on. (. . .) It's important to discuss the matter with the parents. They should show the same engagement as their child does . . . I am sure they can do so.

A Research Program

To examine the utility of our theory of procedural morality for the teaching profession, we engaged in a series of research projects all of them dealing with the same "hard core": the discourse orientation. Our approach accepts Lakatos' (1970) statement that the research program should not allow itself to be distracted by all the possible anomalies. It highlights the belief that "there are no such things as crucial experiments, at least not if they are meant to be experiments which can instantly overthrow a research programme" (p. 173). Thus, this program deals first with the description of the professional ethos of the teacher—subjectively and objectively. In a second part, it reveals possible explanations through interventional studies. In a third part it assesses the effectiveness of teachers with "high ethos" compared to teachers with "low ethos." In the last part, external validity and reliability questions were to be considered.

The whole program was designed to provide bases of assessing critical aspects of the ethos construct. We wanted to find out in depth what really characterizes teachers' ethos (diagnostical task) and to be able, in the long run, to change teachers' professional ethics towards a more discursive attitude.

DESCRIPTION OF THE CONSTRUCT:
EMPIRICAL RESULTS

Study I

Attitudes Towards Norms. In a first attempt at probing the construct we asked 210 teachers (female/male, all types of schools, all ages) about their subjective theories concerning the notion of "ethos." We used a sentence completion format in which subjects were asked to finish the following statement: "A teacher has a high ethos if s/he . . ." . The following features emerged. Caring attitudes were given the highest priority (cf. Fig. 8.2). Truthfulness and commitment were also mentioned fairly often, in contrast to justice which appeared less frequently as a teacher concern. Obviously, the teaching profession is not very much different from the helping professions in the emphasis on care.

Should-would Discrepancies

We also asked 192 teachers (both sexes, all types of schools, all ages) to judge a couple of "should"-statements. Each item was rated twice: with respect to the degree subjects' thought the norm was justified and with respect to the degree subjects' thought they actually lived up to it in their classroom behavior. To give some examples: "A teacher should integrate all students into the class community"; or: "A teacher should teach the students all necessary knowledge and competences." The following norms were included in these statements: (1) integration of students; (2) discipline and order, (3) support of the students, (4) participation, (5) flexibility in terms of curricular requirements, (6) opportunities for students to improve their academic performance, (7) ability to admit faults, (8) justice in classroom management, (9) discussion of problems with colleagues, (10) teachers' knowledge and competence, (11) motivation of students, (12) caring for students outside of school, (13) helping the student with their homework, (14) readiness and efforts to provide time to talk about students' personal problems.

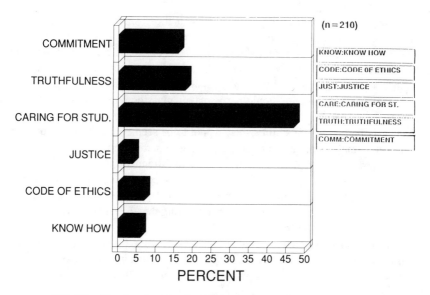

(n = 210)

KNOW:KNOW HOW	
CODE:CODE OF ETHICS	
JUST:JUSTICE	
CARE:CARING FOR ST.	
TRUTH:TRUTHFULNESS	
COMM:COMMITMENT	

FIG. 8.2.   Teachers' subjective theories about ethos.

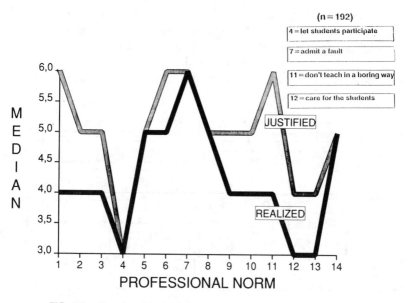

(n = 192)

4 = let students participate	
7 = admit a fault	
11 = don't teach in a boring way	
12 = care for the students	

FIG. 8.3.   Teachers' attitudes regarding professional norms.

Figure 8.3 shows the differences between these should- and would-statements. In most cases actual differences between normative conviction and everyday behavior become apparent. Obviously, teachers sense the tension between ideals and reality themselves. One exception is participation, a variable that defines a crucial element of the "discourse II" perspective. Most teachers oppose the idea that students should participate in classroom decision-making and, consequently, they don't practice participation. Learning to participate—that is to take individual responsibility—seems not to be seen by teachers as a requirement for human autonomy (at least not in the classroom context).

The same tendency results when we use a questionnaire on ethos orientations (as described in the types mentioned above). Subjects prefer items representing discourse I or II orientations, but in their normal practice they would choose nondiscursive ways of problem solving, expecting this to be the typical course in regular school life, too (cf. Fig. 8.4).

The tension between ideals and reality provides a basis for interventional efforts in teacher education and in-service training. Such interventions don't only seem necessary but also promising—since teachers are themselves aware of this tension.

DECISION MAKING AND ETHOS: AN INTERVENTIONAL STUDY

Teachers are aware of the tension between ideals and actual practice, but they are not aware of the structure of their cognitions in decision making. Thus in studying the ethos structure we do not try to directly access subjects' cognitive organization, but instead we confront them with situational content. In a pilot study we presented professional decision-making situations to 60 teachers, asking them to

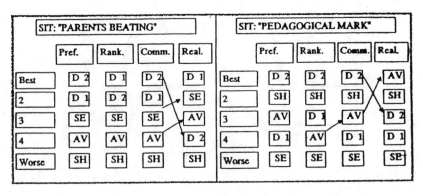

SIT: "PARENTS BEATING"					SIT: "PEDAGOGICAL MARK"			
	Pref.	Rank.	Comm.	Real.		Pref.	Rank.	Comm.	Real.
Best	D 2	D 1	D 2	D 1	Best	D 2	D 2	D 2	AV
2	D 1	D 2	D 1	SE	2	SH	SH	SH	SH
3	SE	SE	SE	AV	3	AV	D 1	AV	D 2
4	AV	AV	AV	D 2	4	D 1	AV	D 1	D 1
Worse	SH	SH	SH	SH	Worse	SE	SE	SE	SE

FIG. 8.4. Different preferences for ethos orientations.

reflect on how they would act and why. These situations dealt primarily with an actor's relationship to different people affected by decisions. Table 8.1 gives an overview.

The interview format also included questions concerning subjects' own experience with situations like the ones described and concerning the subjective importance of such situations.

Our first strategy employed in analyzing this interview material was a very open attempt to judge the type of ethos on the basis of the whole interview transcript or of a summary of most important statements. However, this strategy didn't yield very precise results, there was no satisfying interrater reliability. Thus in a second step we developed a much more structured scoring format. The procedure of analysis includes elements like the subject's dominant action tendency, his or her normative orientation, his or her strategy of justification and proposed solutions to the conflict. Most importantly, we tried to grasp subjects' conceptions of an adequate decision making process (are other people involved,

TABLE 8.1.
Ten Situations Stimulating the Decision-Making Process of Teachers
Under the Aspect of Professional Morality

QUESTIONNAIRE OF TEACHERS' PROFESSIONAL ACTING;
SITUATIONS 1-10

Situation 1: Relation between parents and teacher I.
Divergent behavior of parents when their child has bad grades.

Situation 2: Relation authority - teacher.
Decisions of administration without talking to the teacher.

Situation 3: Relation student - teacher I
How does a teacher deal with discipline problems related to labeling as got by students.

Situation 4: Relation student - teacher II.
The quality of teaching is questionned by students.

Situation 5: Relation parents - teacher II.
Discussion of the teaching style without the teacher knowing about it.

Situation 6: Relation student - teacher III.
Some students laugh about others, which is a problem of interpersonal respect.

Situation 7: Relation student - teacher III.
Selection opposed to the so called pedagogical grades.

Situation 8: Relation student - student II.
Some students fight and the teacher has to intervene.

Situation 9: Relation teacher - teacher II.
A colleague is often late and this is a challenge to the order in the school.

Situation 10: Relation teacher - teacher II.
A teacher is asked by his/her colleague for particular information about a student who is a big troublemaker for this teacher.

	participation	presupposition	responsibility	commitment
DISCOURSE 2 (D2)	YES	YES	YES	YES
DISCOURSE 1 (D1)	partly	partly	YES	YES
SINGLE-HANDED (SH)	NO	NO	partly	YES
SECURITY (SE)	NO	NO	NO	YES
AVOIDING (AV)	NO	NO	NO	NO

FIG. 8.5. Layout of the scoring sheet.

do they participate in the decision making, who is to take responsibility, etc.; see Fig. 8.5). Further, we considered subjects' statements in terms of the probability of actual conflict occurrence and the likelihood of the proposed conflict solution in real school life.

Each interview was coded by at least two raters. Preliminary reliability calculations were promising (between 80 and 95% agreement). After the period of construction and testing the evaluation method we switched to a coordinated analysis. In this procedure, the raters are to discuss differences and reach the most plausible consensus in interpretation.

In the meantime, we dispose of a broader basis of interview material. Results showed that, although most teachers judge different situations differently, the strategy of first choice is unilateral ("single handed") decision making. Discursive strategies, especially "discourse II" solutions, are far more seldom.

There are also differences in rating the difficulty of situations (see Fig. 8.6).

For future research it will probably be reasonable to use only the three situations estimated most difficult.

DECISION MAKING AND ETHOS TYPES:
A QUESTIONNAIRE

On the basis of our conception of 5 types of professional morality we also constructed a questionnaire. The questionnaire takes the following format. Subjects are confronted with 10 short descriptions of situations and asked to evaluate statements (constructed in accordance to the five decision making types). They are asked to judge the correctness of statements and to rank order their importance. Finally, they are asked to state which item they find the most realistic and for which solution they themselves would make special efforts.

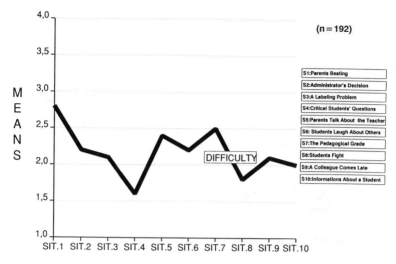

FIG. 8.6.   Ratings of situation difficulties.

This questionnaire was tested in a pilot study with 64 teachers and later used in an interventional study (see below) with 84 teachers.

For the different decision making types the following reliabilities were found:

—for the pilot study (64 teachers): alpha between .57 and .67;<

—for the participants to the Salzburg courses (interventional study; 84 teachers): alpha between .53 and .69.

These reliabilities are not very high. This is in fact a confirmation of our understanding that the ethos types to a large amount are not *personality types* but types of situational decision making. That means that a teacher may react in a comparable way to comparable situational instances, but no one reacts the same way all of the time.

Since the instrument does not meet the classical test-theoretic conditions (although it is in agreement with our theory), we have to use other techniques to evaluate the interventions than are typically used. In particular, it is not possible to pretend to have a "discursive" scale for each participant. Rather, we have to judge the impact of an interventional course on a situation-to-situation basis, (i.e., we have to assess whether there is progress of the participant with respect to each separate situation of the questionnaire).

Some interesting comparisons show the relationship between the interview data and the questionnaire data on the one hand, and preference, readiness for commitment and "real life" expectations on the other hand. While the questionnaire data always shows preferences for higher discourse levels, the interview data represent a more realistic state of affairs. We hardly found a discourse orientation in the interview data wherein teachers have to express their thinking based on their experiences. Now looking at the preferences for the different categories in the questionnaire the commitment gap appears. We find a preference for the discourse 1 and discourse 2 items over the nondiscoursive categories. The least important items are avoiding categories. This finding supports our theoretical considerations.

The next figure shows the rank order of the different categories based on the sum of the ten situations in a sample of 124 female and male teachers predominantly from the primary and secondary level (grades 1 through 9/10; see Fig. 8.7).

The differences between discourse 1 or 2, respectively, and each of the nondiscourse categories were significant at the 1% level.

The impression of the dominance of discourse 1 and discourse 2 is confirmed by an analysis of the single situations and it is also confirmed by a look at the rank ordering of the items. But again the view changes when we arrive at the question for which categories the teacher would make an effort. Now nondiscursive orientations are put into first place. Similarly, when we asked for the most likely solution subjects expect the teachers to use in school, nondiscursive solutions appeared more probable.

Problematic situation for a teacher with following persons involved:	PREFER most	RANK highest	would ENGAGE for	EXPECT most
S1:Parents/Student	D 2	D 1	SH	SE
S2:Administrator	D 1	D 1	D 1	SH
S3:Student / Class	D 1	D 1	SE	SH
S4:Student / Class	D 1	D 1	AV	SH
S5:Parents	D 1	D 1	SH	AV
S6:Student / Class	D 1	D 2	SH	AV
S7:Stud./Par./Adm.	SH	SH	SE	SH
S8:Students	D 1	D 1	D1	D 2
S9:Colleague/Class	D 1	D 1	D 2	SE
S10:Colleague/Stud	SH	SH	SE	SE

ETHOS ORIENTATIONS, Teachers ... (n = 124)

AVOIDER (AV) SECURITY (SE) SINGLHAND. (SH) DISCOURSE 1 (D1) DISCOURSE 2 (D2)

FIG. 8.7. Rank order of different categories across situations: Preference and commitment.

In terms of research methods, the questionnaire thus must be used in such a way that the differences between an ideal and the perception of the subject's own commitment becomes apparent.

VALIDATION STUDIES: STUDENT QUESTIONNAIRE

If there is reality to our notion of "teacher ethos" it must possess some power to guide action. It should also be visible for students. We suggest that children would feel most accepted and integrated into classroom life if the teacher practices a "discourse II" orientation in different situations. This is because "complete discourse" implies that students have equal rights in contributing to the solution of a problem. That is, it is supposed that the children argue reasonably and that they are willing to cooperate and to take responsibility.

Data from our pilot study show that in this domain teachers seem to have problems. Schwartz (1981) reported large differences between students' perspectives on teachers' acting and the teachers supposition about the students' views. Therefore students' assessment of teacher acting seem to be a critical indicator for the relevance of teacher ethos model. We performed two studies with a sample of 30 teachers with their classes (about 500 students), drawn from the same group as had provided the teacher questionnaire data.

The first questionnaire is based on Schwartz's (1984) scale of interpersonal respect and Achtenhagen's (1979) student questionnaire (e.g., classroom atmosphere, teachers commitment), combined with teacher ethos items, questions of didactical competence and situation oriented questions like in the FFL (teacher questionnaire). The student is asked to keep in mind a particular teacher's behavior and estimate the statements on a 6 point scale where "1" means that the statement is entirely true, "6" that it is extremely false. The teachers, too, answered the student's questionnaire guessing what the students perspective would be.

In general, there is fairly high agreement between students' ratings and teachers' estimations of students' perception. However, teachers judge their own commitment higher than students do. Figure 8.8 shows some of the differences with respect of the subscales "interpersonal respect," "teacher's commitment," "teacher's fairness," "didactical competence," and two particular items on "well-being" and "teacher's truthfulness."

It is interesting that students' estimation of classroom atmosphere and their view of teachers' didactical competence correlates highly with the teachers avoiding and discourse 2 -orientation. We set some of the subscales (which all have a reliability about alpha= .80) in relation to teachers orientations. The following figure shows that for the 30 classes high correlations result between the avoiding ethos and students view of feeling well in the class, the didactical quality of the teachers, their truthfulness and fairness. Same correlations are also

Perspective of the class and   (N = 30 classes)
TEACHER's expectations
on ...

	TEACHER	STUDENTS	Diff. (T-Test)
Interpers. RESP.	2.09	2.57	**
COMMITMENT	2.21	2.66	**
DIDACT. COMP.	2.28	2.41	n.s.
FAIRNESS	2.50	2.82	*
TRUTHFULL	1.43	1.90	*
WELL-BEING	2.16	2.76	**

* p < = 0.05
** p < = 0.01

(Scale: 1 = "very good " / 6 = "very bad")

FIG. 8.8.   Gap between students' and teachers' perspectives.

found between the discourse 2 orientation and the students view with the exception of the truthfulness item. No correlations results regarding the other ethos
orientations (Fig. 8.9).

It seems that teachers who try to ignore problems and in some respect let the
kids do what they want are as popular as those who try to establish democratic
ways of problem solving.

correlated with teacher's orientations of ethos:

Students view of:	AV	Sign.:	SE	Sign.:	SH	Sign.:	D 1	Sign.:	D 2	Sign.:
Interpers. RESP.	.18	n.s.	-.02	n.s.	.03	n.s.	-.05	n.s.	.38	*
COMMITMENT	.30	*	.00	n.s.	.11	n.s.	.05	n.s.	.39	*
DIDACT. COMP.	.38	*	-.07	n.s.	.11	n.s.	.07	n.s.	.39	*
FAIRNESS	.30	*	-.10	n.s.	.09	n.s.	.06	n.s.	.30	*
TRUTHFULL	.56	**	.00	n.s.	.09	n.s.	.00	n.s.	.03	n.s.
WELL-BEING	.42	**	-.19	n.s.	.31	*	.01	n.s.	.36	*

(N = 30 classes)   * p < = 0.05   ** p < = 0.01

FIG. 8.9.   Students' perspectives and teachers' ethos orientation.

THE INTERVENTION STUDY

The most important study we conducted deals to a large part with the question: "Is it possible to 'learn' a 'discourse II' orientation?" Certainly, everybody is convinced that teachers are able to learn how to teach (i.e., how to use routines, higher order questions, sound combinations of didactical strategies, give meaningful feedback, etc.). But does the same hold true for their deeply rooted pedagogical attitudes? Is it possible to create a setting where the importance and the feasibility of discursive problem solution is learned? We believe it is. And our intervention study shows at least some success in this direction.

This interventional study had a quasi-experimental character with a course treatment on ethos-related issues; the ethos of teachers, teachers courses of action and the perception of these actings were conceived as dependent variables.

What are the underlying ideas in this study? In which way can it be expected to contribute to our understanding of the ethos construct?

First of all, it is assumed that the teacher's ethos is not completely independent of any other variable. In particular, we think that the ethos is quite close to, yet not identical with, professional teaching competence (expertise), since both concern the teachers' actions. However, there are considerable theoretical differences between those two concepts. In teaching competence, the normative impetus is of little importance. Here, normative decisions must be made prior to any decision on instructional techniques. Typically, those decisions are not made deliberately but are standardized and often times given in the curriculum. On the other hand, the normative aspect is central to ethos since normatively based decisions usually are not anticipated, but have to be made ad hoc, just about in the same minute as the act has to be executed. Usually, there are no general rules that can be adopted; as we have seen the "catalogue of virtues" mentioned in the beginning is both too general and too utopian to be useful in concrete situations.

A second aspect is of special importance for the intervention. While we can assume that teaching competence can be acquired through communication of the respective abilities and by way of practice (i.e. trying to act according to expert standards), the same cannot be said for the ethos. Given the close relationship of the ethos to moral judgments, we suggest—as mentioned before—that the ethos has certain deeply rooted structural features. This means that a teacher has a series of ethical convictions which, up to now, have more or less worked. Just telling him or her how to do better will certainly not change the structure. Rather, what is needed is the critical experience that the available structure is insufficient to solve certain conflicts. Thus, the main interventional approach had to be what in the Piagetian tradition is called "disequilibrium." Subjects try to solve certain dilemmas with the structures they have (i.e. by means of assimilation); they fail to find an appropriate solution, and thus they try to integrate new elements into their structure (accommodation) so that they can solve the problems more appropriately.

To give an example, I want to recall the ethical dimensions in decision making as discussed before. Consider the case of when someone has always tried to solve problems only by reference to standards of justice. When this person is in a real conflict situation and discusses the problem with colleagues, he or she may find out that justice rules don't go far enough, that their application might result in new problems. Just telling him or her that caring and truthfulness are other relevant principles will not be sufficient. These concepts, so far, have not been integrated into the system of this teacher. But in the process of serious problem solving, s/he may actually experience the fact that further concepts are needed and s/he may begin to reconceptualize his or her view of such conflicts and of appropriate ways of settling them. Thus, in the intervention the creation of such desequilibria was understood as crucial for the development of teachers' ethos, while it was not seen as the primary method for the didactical—teaching ability—course.

All in all, the interventional study was designed to clarify several points:

a. Can the ethos be influenced by a treatment as conceived (convergent validity; we suppose that this is true)?

b. If the ethos is changed, what is the influence on the teachers' actual behavior?

c. If the behavior is changed, what is its influence on the students, i.e. how is it perceived, and does it change anything in the children's attributes?

Some complementary questions can be answered by introducing additional measures (in particular, moral judgment) and additional treatment variables, as for instance a treatment designed for improvement of didactical competence.

a. Does a treatment in didactical competence influence the ethos (use of a control treatment which differs only in specific aspects from the ethos treatment)? (Discriminant validity; our hypothesis is that this is not the case.)

b. Does the ethos treatment also influence other variables than the ethos, e.g., didactical competence on one hand and the moral judgment on the other hand? (Discriminant validities; our hypothesis is that this is not the case.)

c. Does a treatment in didactical competence influence the didactical competence? (Convergent validity; we suppose that this is true.)

d. What is the relationship between the ethos and moral judgment (additional correlational study)?

84 teachers of all levels (elementary school teachers, secondary level I and II teachers, teachers of special classes) participated in the experiment. Most of these teachers were attached to a teacher training institution and frequently had student teachers visit their classes. In a first meeting, to which all teachers

attached to the teacher training institution were invited, they were informed about the procedure and asked if they would volunteer to participate. The course was acknowledged as part of the compulsory in-service teacher training.

Four experimental groups were formed, according to the following scheme: Group 1 had a purely didactical treatment, group 3 a purely ethos-related treatment. Group 2 had a combined treatment; all these treatments were of equal duration (10 weeks with 3 hours weekly) and given by the same staff members. The fourth group was a delayed treatment control group. In this case subjects were tested at the end of the 10 week period course with the same measures as the other groups. After the post measure, subjects in group 4 were given a 3-day-course, and some of the assessments were done again. The subjects were assigned to the groups according to their schedule possibilities; a perfect randomization turned out to be impossible, but as far as possible, assignment was done randomly.

Treatments

The ethos-treatment consisted of discussing situations with professional dilemmas of teachers. Each session focused on a particular aspect of ethos (e.g., responsibility, justice, care, truthfulness), and discursive approaches to problem solving. In each meeting, it was emphasized that there must be some equilibrium between these different values, and that the teacher has to act in a way that such an equilibrium—which might be different from situation to situation—is established again and again. Throughout we tried to create cognitive disequilibrium in the teachers by showing them that with their actual cognitive structure, they could not deal appropriately with the given situation. Additional information and discussions of proposed solutions brought most subjects to agreement on procedural approaches for problem solving based on a discursive orientation. The main topic was values; the method of influence disequilibrium and equilibrating discussions.

The didactical treatment provided subjects with means for action-oriented

	Ethos-Treatm.	Didact.-Treatm.	N =
Ethos-Course	YES	NO	17
Didactics-Course	NO	YES	16
Mixed-Course	YES	YES	24
Control-Group	NO	NO	21

FIG. 8.10. Design of the interventional study.

teaching (i.e., the teachers were shown how to activate the student so that he or she learns actively, instead of waiting to be fed with information). The premise was that such an activity oriented teaching (including differentiation, learning to learn, learning how to build up self control, etc.) is more successful than the passive learning which still dominates in many of our schools. Values were not discussed. The main topic was how to teach effectively, and the method of influence was knowledge acquisition.

In the combined group, both contents and methods of influence were used. The ethos approach and the didactical approach were shown to be related to each other. The course lasted exactly as long as the other courses, and the single contents and methods were dealt with less deeply, with less examples and in less detail; some contents had to be left out.

Measures

Many variables were assessed, but some of them could only be measured with a subset of subjects. The following measurements were used:

a. Ethos questionnaire (with all subjects); the responses to this questionnaire were used to select the subjects to be given additional measures. Subjects were rank ordered within groups according to their discourse score.

b. Observations of the teachers by video (first two and last two of each rank order), some with additional interviews on the taped lesson;

c. Ethos interviews and moral judgment interviews (first five and last five of each rank order);

d. Students' questionnaire regarding the teaching climate and related variables (8 classes in each group); the teacher answered the same questionnaire regarding how she thought the students would respond;

e. Students' questionnaire on their locus of control (8 classes in each group).

Assessments were made before and after the course (in the control group: approximately at the same time). A follow-up measure is planned, but not yet done. Each measurement period lasted about two weeks with a staff of three to eight people. The questionnaires and some additional measures have been analyzed so far, but the observations and the analysis of many of the interviews still remain to be done.

Results

One of the first results stemming from this intervention study confirms the optimistic view that we obtained with respect to the student data. Sensitivity to teachers' professional ethos is changeable. Assessments after the course show that in the ethos and the mixed course intervention effects can be stated. Let us choose two examples for effects across situations and two examples for situation specific effects.

Teachers of the ethos course show a significant increase in the display of discourse-II-orientation (see Fig. 8.11a). Teachers of the mixed course demonstrated a significant removal of avoiding preferences. On the other hand, the didactic course *enhanced* the avoiding preferences. This last effect is probably due to the fact that the participants of the didactic group were not only unaware of the ethical implications of the course content but became increasingly insecure in terms of their daily concept of effective instruction (see Fig. 8.11b).

Teachers in the ethos course also showed a decrease in "single handed" ethos orientation (see Fig. 8.11c). This effect seems to show that given conflicts are not to be "managed" but instead should be used for learning purposes. On the other hand, the security orientation of these teachers showed a remarkable decrease. (All these effects are of an interactional nature; controlled for differences at the first testing time.

A deeper analysis was done for each single subject with respect to the interviews (pre and post). Figure 8.12 shows that the clearest changes of the decision making types resulted from the ethos course. All cases analyzed for the time being, changed from the single handed decision to the discourse I or II orientation.

There are also some irregular results to be reported (see Fig. 8.13). In situation no. 10 a teacher was asked to give an evaluation of a student who is applying for an apprenticeship. The teacher had had a lot of trouble with this particular student. Most participants of the ethos course (just like subjects in the didactics course) stated a much more explicit preference for the avoidance decision, compared to their pretest answers. It is possible that a first change toward a higher sensitivity for "single handed decision makers" goes via avoiding complicated decisions.

There are more results to be reported: One third of the 60 (30 pre and 30 post) "Moral Judgment Interviews" have been scored so far. Except for three persons who are at stage 4 all these teachers are at stage 3 or 3/4. As we have expected no changes are observable between the pre- and post-assessments.

Regarding the students' questionnaire data one can state an interventional effect in the fairness subscale. In particular, students of the "Mixed Course" tended to give "better grades" to their teachers on this subscale following the course period.

We hope further and more detailed analyses of the interventional data, especially the observations, will help to find even more hints of how to fulfill the main task; to sensitize teachers for the ethos point of view in classroom activities. Fuller and Bown (1975) have proposed a model of professional development of teachers which ends with the "routine stage." Not before reaching this stage is a teacher able to fully recognize the students' needs and individual perspectives and to act accordingly. Hopefully, the orientation to developmental processes

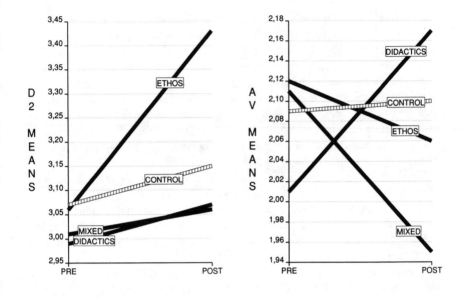

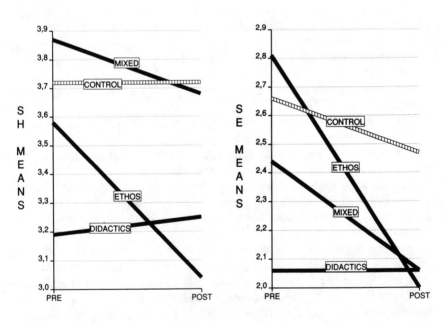

FIG. 8.11a–d. Interventional effects of different ethos orientations.

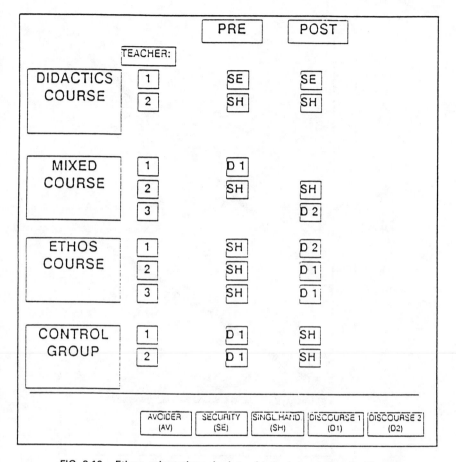

FIG. 8.12. Ethos orientations in interviews: Interventional effects.

and cognitive structures which is and has been the basis for some teacher—researcher cooperation (e.g. Sprinthall and Bernier, 1979) are able to accelerate the development to this pedagogical point.

FURTHER STUDIES

Several further studies are planned in our research program. The relationship between school climate (cf. Moos, 1974) and decision-making types will be investigated. The influence of these types (that is, of the respective teachers' actions) on students' level of self control will be analyzed. There will also be an

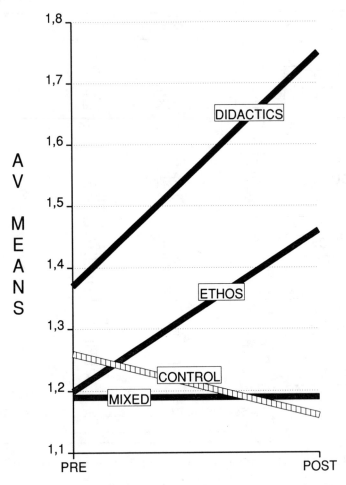

FIG. 8.13.   Interventional effects of avoiding orientation (Situation 10).

investigation into the role ethos dimensions play in the teacher training programs at the university level.

We have already conducted a biographical study of the developmental processes and conditions that result in specific variations of professional morality. Further research is needed here, but the study gives some good suggestions for further inquiry.

The main question was, "How is it that certain teachers have a given ethos, while others have completely opposite beliefs?" One cannot reasonably expect beginning teachers to have value systems that are as explicit and well-reflected as those of experienced teachers (cf. Fuller & Bown, 1975). Rather, it is only in the process of socialization that teachers acquire a system of values of increasing complexity. In particular, it is supposed that the personal experiences in conflict situations have an influence on a teacher's belief system. Further, we assumed that professional socialization can lead to an increased tendency to solve problems in the discursive way (under conditions that need to be specified). While young teachers often are directly or indirectly forced to use autocratic teaching styles (cf. Dann et al., 1978), experienced teachers can (or could) be more democratic.

Hence we analyzed how teachers perceive their own professional career and how they link their professional ethical belief systems to this career. Of special interest was the experience of events that were particularly conflictual and which could have triggered changes in the belief system. Six teachers participated in this in-depth study. Each of them was interviewed extensively, and their responses were analyzed by use of qualitative methods to identify the main phases of professional socialization and the ethical belief systems during these phases as well as the events that were recalled as leading to changes.

Five of the six teachers indicated they had evolved during their professional career with respect to ethical belief systems. However, this evolution was not always in the direction of discursive solutions, as we had hoped. Rather, most of these teachers became quite utilitarian. Further, it turned out that major critical events had an influence on the ethical socialization for only one of the six teachers. For the others, there were a series of events of lesser importance all leading essentially in the same direction. These problem situations and the respective reflections eventually led to changes in ethical orientations.

Of course, these conclusions are based on the teachers' post-hoc interpretations of their lives, with all the problems of such a retrospective approach. However, this study turns out to be quite informative with respect to potential sources of professional development. At least it is a worthy starting point for further research.

CONCLUSION. TEACHERS' "DISCOURSE II" ORIENTATIONS: STANDING THE TEST

I do not want to finish this presentation without addressing some normative issues. I am convinced that the development of what I called the "discourse II" concept of professional interaction should be a primary goal in teacher education, and beyond. I belief this goal not only has a high value in itself but, rather, that it would imply better teacher-student relations and an improvement of the school culture. "Discourse II teachers" do not simply "manage" interpersonal conflicts but take them as a starting point for social learning, for getting familiar with what responsibility and justice actually can mean. "Discourse II teachers" are committed teachers. Professional ethos is more than the acknowledgement of moral norms, it is more than general moral judgment competence in the Kohlbergian sense. In my view, teacher education doesn't do enough when it leaves out preparation for responsible solution of professional conflicts.

I would like to present one example that may illustrate why a "discourse II" attitude is also a necessary condition for vital school reform.

Let me take the school reform movement I'm most familiar with. The so called "Just Community" idea, based on Dewey's (1916) thinking and elaborated by Lawrence Kohlberg, has led to a number of programs in American and European schools (cf. Codding, 1987; Kohlberg, 1987; Kohlberg et al., 1974; Oser, 1989; Power, 1979; Power et al., 1989; Wasserman, 1980). I myself am the scientific supervisor of a project including four schools in the west-german state of Northrine-Westfalia.

In this context, consider the following. In the Gutenberg School in Langenfeld (West-Germany) all the 90 5th graders and their 20 teachers assemble every 2 or 3 weeks for democratic decision making in order to settle issues concerning school policy, behavior in school, community life, and matters of fairness and responsibility.

The topic of one community meeting was: "What obligations do we have to the school as a community?" There was a special motive for this discussion. A lot of students had not participated in a sports meeting which was of high importance for the school as a whole. Schools in the region take turns in organizing this event, and only once in 30 years does a school have the opportunity to host that sports meeting.

The course of the Just Community assembly was extremely controversial. Many kids viewed a sports meeting as obligatory for the participants but not for those who are restricted to the role of spectators. Their moral point of view was that nobody should have a right to proscribe duties except with regard to purely academic issues (including attending class, etc.). This argument is stage 2, according to the Kohlberg scheme. Others argued this standpoint. They believed that there should be an obligation, because, in their words, "we are a community." This use of the word "we" indicated a stage 3 position. Even among the teachers there was vehement opposition of views. Part of them publicly apologized for not having given clear information about the (indirect) obligation to participate in the meeting. Others believed the children were overly suppressed by the teachers' demand to participate and thus had no inner relationship to what was requested. Some students reproached their peers with being untruthful. Interestingly, in their peer group they had complained about the pressure to participate in a "boring" event, while openly, in the community meeting, they adopted their teachers' standpoint.

Toward the end of the discussion one child posed the question: "So what are we doing now? What will be the consequences?" It was decided that in the next occasion there should be a real discussion *before* the event would reach the planning stage, so that everybody would have the chance to figure exactly whether or not there was an obligation to attend. As to the general issue of the community meeting, "What obligations do we have to the school community?", there was not much more than a general consensus, that on the one hand, students actually *have* duties. On the other hand, the next step to establish a deeper sense of community was done immediately. The participants decided to organize a Christmas event for the whole school, and to plan cooperatively and ahead of time, so that everybody would know which part to take.

The theoretical model underlying the Just Community approach puts forth a number of important goals. In establishing these kinds of community processes students begin, first, to identify more and more with the rules and norms of the school. People who are invited to participate in something significant will feel part of it. Second, the students develop a higher stage of moral reasoning, because they are provided with opportunities to reflect on moral matters. Third, the students learn to coordinate and integrate moral judgment and action. Fourth, they are provided with experiences in democratic procedures; and the school setting is small enough to overview the direct consequences of democratic decision making. Fifth, students are provided with experiences regarding the limits of societal regulations: not everything can be changed only because it is wanted by one group of concerned people. Sixth, as a part of these processes students learn to take the role of the other, and gradually they understand that the other is an equally autonomous being who can play a constructive and responsible role in conflict resolving negotiation processes.

In terms of these goals, the long-term results of the Langenfeld Just Community experiment are impressive. But in my view, the most astonishing effect after two Just Community years is not on the side of the students. The teachers developed in a most dramatic way. There is a considerable evidence indicating that their cognitive ethos structures changed. Teachers interacted much more with one another, provided more help for one another, and made more efforts to help troubled students. Obviously, teachers began to realize that a "discourse II" orientation helps provide all the necessary support for the project's success. Every systematic analysis of the goals and the chances of this model of school reform leads to the acknowledgement that only a "discourse II" perspective allows for a full commitment to the project. The fundamental belief in children's reason makes it absolutely necessary for teachers to develop the attitude of respect for children's reasoning and to appeal to it. The only practical alternative is to quit the job. There is no other choice in this context.

The development of teachers in this Just Community project is all the more remarkable given that in the beginning they were no extraordinary educators. In conflict situations they tended to delegate or avoid the responsibility or to make unilateral decisions. Their moral reasoning stage was not more than average (stage 3 or 3/4). These teachers changed considerably. They started to take children seriously, and they began to employ those strategies that we call "discourse II."

Certainly, a "discourse II" teacher is not a saint, nor should he have to be.

226   OSER

She or he need not be a person with extraordinary virtues. But s/he must create situations in which everybody uses his or her practical reason, balancing truthfulness, justice, and care. S/he must be someone who believes in the positive potential of children, who sees them as human beings with dignity and reason, and who presupposes, even in cases of severe conflict, that they are able to share their part.

In the beginning of this presentation, I talked about Düischen, the young teacher in Aitmatov's novel. Düischen is a very humane, though often times very weak discourse II-teacher. Aitmatov describes the fascinating development of the children learning with this teacher. There's truth in that.

ACKNOWLEDGMENTS

I wish to thank Wolfgang Althof for helpful comments on earlier versions of this chapter. Research reported here was supported by the Swiss National Science Foundation (Grant No. 1.188-0.85) and was conducted together with Richard Klaghofer, Jean-Luc Patry, Roland Reichenbach, and Michael Zutavern. This chapter was originally presented to the annual convention of the American Educational Research Association in April 1989. Thus, it does not represent final results and the current state of research.

REFERENCES

Achtenhagen, F. et al. (1979). Die Lehrerpersönlichkeit im Urteil von Schülern: Ein Beitrag zur Aufklärung "naiver" didaktischer Theorien. *Zeitschrift für Pädagogik, 25,* 191–208.
Aitmatow, T. (1980). *Der erste Lehrer.* 5th Edition. München: Weisman.
Allport, G. W. (1973). *Personality: A psychological inter-pretation.* New York: Holt.
Allport, G., Vernon, P., & Lindzey, G. (1960). *Study of values (3rd ed).* Test booklet and manual. Boston: Houghton Mifflin.
Althof, W., Garz, D., & Zutavern, W. (1988). Heilige im Urteilen, Halunken im Handeln? Lebensbereiche, Biographie und Alltagsmoral. In *Zeitschrift für Sozialisationsforschung und Erziehungssoziologie (ZSE),8* (3), pp. 162–181.
Apel, K.-O. (1988). Diskurs und Verantwortung. *Das Problem des Übergangs zur postkonventionellen Moral.* Frankfurt M.: Suhrkamp.
Bebeau, M. J., Rest, J. R., Yamoor, C. M. (1985). Measuring dental students' ethical sensitivity. *Journal of Dental Education, 49,* No. 4.
Bebeau, M. J., & Brabeck, M. M. (1987). Integrating care und justice issues in professional moral education: A gender perspective. *Journal of Moral Education, 16,* No. 3.
Bergem, T. (1988). Teachers thinking and behavior. An empirical study of the role of social sensitivity and moral reasoning in the teaching performance of student teachers. *Scandinavian Journal of Educational Research.*
Bergem, T. (1988). *The teacher as moral agent; A Scandinavian perspective.* Invited paper presented at the 13th Annual Conference of the Association for Moral Education, Pittsburgh.
Berliner, D. C. (1986). In pursuit of the expert pedagogue, *Educational Researcher, 15,* No. 7.
Blasi, A. (1980). Bridging moral cognition and moral action: A critical review of the literature. *Psych. Bulletin, 88*(1), 1–45.

Blasi, A. (1983). Moral cognition and moral action: A theoretical perspective. *Developmental Review, 3,* 178–210.

Codding, J. (1987). Education for democracy: The Just Community approach to secondary education. Bronxville, NY. Unpublished paper.

Coulter, F. (1987). Affective characeristics of student teachers. *The International Encyclopedia of Teaching and Teacher Education,* (pp. 589–598). University of Sydney. New York: Pergamon Press.

Dann, H. D., Müller-Fohrbrodt, G., Cloetta, B. (1981). Sozialisation junger Lehrer im Beruf: "Praxisschock" drei Jahre später. *Zeitschrift für Entwicklungspsychologie und Pädagogische Psychologie, 13,* 251–261.

Dewey, D. (1916). *Democracy and education.* New York: Macmillan.

Dunkin, M. J. (Ed.). (1987). *The international encyclopedia of teaching and teacher education.* University of Sydney. New York: Pergamon Press.

Fuller, F. F., & Brown, O. H. (1975). Becoming a teacher. In K. Ryan (Ed.), *Teacher education. 75th Yearbook of the NSSE* (pp. 25–52). Chicago.

Fraser, B. J., Waldberg, H. J., Wayne, W. W., & Hattie, J. A. (1987). Syntheses of educational productivity research. *International Journal of Educational Research,* Vol. II, pp. 145–252.

Getzels, J. W., & Jackson, P. W. (1963). The teacher's personality and characeristics. In N. L. Gage (Ed.), *Handbook of research in teaching: A Project of the American Educational Research Association* (pp. 506–582). Chicago: Rand McNally.

Hartshorne, H., & May, M. A. (1928–1930). *Studies in the nature of character.* Columbia University Teachers College. Vol. 1: Studies in Deceit. Vol. 2: Studies in Service and Self-Control. Vol. 3: Studies in Organization of Character. New York: Macmillan.

Höffe, O. (1985). *Strategien der Humanität. Zur Ethik öffentlicher Entscheidungsprozesse.* Franfurt: M.: Suhrkamp.

Klaghofer, R., Oser, F., & Patry, J.-L. (1987). Der Lehrer—Besser als sein Ruf. Bericht über die PRP 1986 im Kreis VII zum Thema "Das Bild des Lehrers aus der Sicht der 20-Jährigen". Fribourg (CH): University.

Kohlberg, L. (1984). *Essays on moral development, Vol. 1: The philosophy of moral development.* San Francisco: Harper & Row.

Kuhn, D., Langer, J., Kohlberg, L., & Haan, N. (1977). The development of formal operations and moral judgments. *Genetic Psychological Monographs, 95,* pp. 95–188.

Lakatos, I. (1970). Falsification an the methodology of scientific revolutions and the history of science. In I. Lakatos & A. Musgrave (Eds.), *Criticism and the growth of knowledge.* Cambridge University Press.

Levis, D. S. (1987). Teacher's personality. In M. J. Dunkin (Ed.): *The international encyclopedia of teaching and teacher education.* University of Sydney. New York: Pergamon Press.

Merz, J. (1980). Die Lehrerpersönlichkeit als Variable im Unterrichts- und Erziehungsgeschehen. In H. Gröschel (Ed.), *Die Bedeutung der Lehrerpersönlichkeit in Erziehung und Unterricht.* Munich: Ehrenwirt.

Moos, R. H. (1974). *The social climate scales—An overview.* Palo Alto: Consulting Psychologists Press.

Oser, F. (1987). Das Wollen, das gegen den eigenen Willen gerichtet ist: Über das Verhältnis von Urteil und Handeln im Bereich der Moral. In H. Heckhausen et al. (Hrsg.), *Jenseits des Rubikon* (pp. 255–299). Berlin: Springer.

Peters, T. J., Watermann, R. H. (1982). *In search of excellence—Lessons from America's best-run companies.* San Francisco: Harper & Row.

Power, C. (1979). *The moral atmosphere of a Just Community high school: A four year longitudinal study.* Unpublished doctoral thesis, Harvard Graduate School of Education.

Power, C., Higgins, A., & Kohlberg, L. (1989). *Lawrence Kohlberg's approach to moral education.* New York: Columbia University Press.

Rawls, J. (1971). *A theory of justice.* Cambridge, MA: Belknap Press.

Rest, J. R. (1983). Morality. In J. H. Flavell & F. M. Markmann (Eds.), *Cognitive development manual of child psychology*, 4th ed., P. H. Mussen, (Ed.). (Vol. 3). New York: Willey, pp. 556–629.

Schläfli, A. (1986). Förderung der sozial-moralischen kompetenz. Frankfurt/M.: Lang.

Schläfli, A., Rest, J. R., Thoma, S. (1987). Does moral education improve moral judgment? A meta-analysis of intervention studies. *Review of Educational Research, 55*, 319–352.

Schneider, F. (1966). Methodik des Volksschulunterrichts. Hochdorf (CH): Martinusverlag.

Schwartz, S. H. (1984). *Value self-confrontation to increase behavior showing interpersonal respect.* Jerusalem: Internal Paper.

Shavelson, R. J., & Stern, P. (1981). Research on teachers' psychological thoughts, judgments, decisions and behavior. *Review of Educational Research, 51*, No. 4.

Sprinthall, N., & Bernier, J. (1979). Moral and cognitive development for teachers: A neglected arena. In T. Hennessy (Ed.), Value/Moral education: The schools and the teachers. New York: Paulist.

Sprinthall, N. A., & Sprinthall, R. C. (1974). *Educational psychology. A developmental approach.* 4th Edition. New York: Random House.

Strike, K. A., & Soltis, J. F. (1985). *The ethics of teaching.* New York: Teachers College Press.

Wassermann, E. (1980). An alternative high school based on Kohlberg's just community approach to education. In R. L. Mosher (Ed.), *Moral education. A first generation of research and development* (pp. 259–278). New York: Praeger.

Wittrock, M. C. (1986). *Handbook of research on teaching.* A Project of the American Educational Research Association. New York: Macmillan.

9 The College Experience and Moral Development

James Rest
Darcia Narvaez

ABSTRACT

Research using the Defining Issues Test of moral judgment on the effects of college upon moral judgment development is reviewed. Three kinds of studies show a "college effect": cross-sectional comparisons of students at various educational levels, longitudinal follow up of subjects who attend or don't attend college, and the association of involvement in college with degree of change. Then studies on more specific life experiences (the conditions and mechanisms whereby the "college experience" has its effect) are reviewed, highlighting the role of variables such as "Continued Intellectual Stimulation" and "Academic/Career Orientation." Moral education programs are reviewed. Then the larger question of moral development (of which moral judgment development is part) is discussed in terms of a Four Component Model of moral development.

MORAL DEVELOPMENT AS AN OUTCOME OF THE COLLEGE EXPERIENCE

In his widely-read book, *The Closing of the American Mind,* Allen Bloom (1987) writes that "higher education has failed Democracy and impoverished the souls of today's students." For Bloom, the decade of the 60s was particularly disastrous for colleges and universities, for it was then that higher education was vulgarized by the excesses of student activities and their ideology. In contrast, as much as Bloom detests the student activists, Arthur Levine admires them. In *When Dreams and Heroes Died* (1980), Levine states that the decade of the 60s was the high water mark of student idealism. Antithetically, Levine laments that the goals of today's students have degenerated into an obsession with "meism" and the pursuit of privatism and materialism. In either case, however, Bloom and Levine suggest that colleges currently are doing a poor job in facilitating the moral development of students. This chapter disputes such a view. The research evidence reviewed and discussed here indicates that, by and large, the college experience *does* promote at least some aspects of moral development in today's youth.

Moral development has long been considered one of the important outcomes of a liberal education. Today, many educators who are concerned with the reconceptualization of what it means to be liberally educated also advocate an important place for moral development as an outcome of higher education. For instance, Derek Bok, President of Harvard University, has written often on the college experience and moral development (cf. 1976, 1988). He points out that, in the first 200 years of American higher education, a concern for student character was at least as strong as a concern for student intellectual development. While not recommending a return to the institutions of the early years, Bok nevertheless posits that colleges "have a responsibility to contribute in any way they can to the moral development of students" (1976, p. 26).

The Age of Accountability has arrived for colleges and universities (Hartle, 1985). This means that colleges and universities must produce evidence and document that students really are benefiting from the college experience in the ways that are claimed in college bulletins and promotional materials. As the costs of higher education rise and as the competition for scarce resources by rival societal goods increases, higher education must be able to demonstrate—and not just claim—that students are changing as a consequence of the college experience and in ways that society values. Amazingly, obtaining the data to document this outcome has proven to be a very arduous task. The difficulties in measuring the effects of the college experience upon the student are many and vexing. Furthermore, the data that are available thus far have not been too encouraging. For instance, Howard Bowen in the late 1970s summarized hundreds of studies dealing with the benefits of college (*Investment in Learning,* 1978). Bowen is clearly an apologist on behalf of higher education and would like to make colleges look good. Yet even his conclusions suggest quite modest effects for the college experience. Table 9.1 is reproduced from a summary chapter in his book. From this table we note that, according to the evidence available to him in the late 1970s, no effect of college exceeds an effect size of 1.0 (considered to be a "very large" effect size), and most effects of college are rather modest (if not meagre). Also, we note in Bowen's review that the effect on moral development cannot be ascertained. Although Bowen's review is dated now, no other report of this scope has since been published. The largest, most funded, most frequently cited studies also concur with Bowen's conclusions. For instance, the massive

TABLE 9.1.

Summary of Estimated Average Changes in Individuals Resulting
from College Education

Descriptive Term	Personality Dimension	Estimated Overall Change Expressed in Standard Deviation Units
Not ascertainable	Intellectual integrity, wisdom, morality	
Negative change	Religious interest	-.10 or less
No change	Human sympathy toward individuals	-.09 to +.09
Small increase	Mathematical skills, rationality, creativity, refinement of taste and conduct, consumer behavior, leisure	.10 to .39
Moderate increase	Verbal skills, intellectual tolerance, esthetic sensibility, life-long learning, psychological well-being, human sympathy toward groups, citizenship, economic productivity, health	.40 to .69
Large increase	Substantial knowledge, personal self-discovery, family life	.70 to .99
Very large increase or over	None	1.00

study by Astin (1978) of 200,000 students at 300 institutions also shows that the college experience contributes little to the variance of scores of students postgraduation once their precollege characteristics are taken into account. That is, in multiple regression analyses, if precollege scores are entered first, the during-college effects increase the predictability to postcollege scores only about 1% (see the data tables in the back of Astin's book, 1978, pp. 267–269). Such findings do not engender a quiet confidence and optimism among those responsible for documenting the benefits of higher education.

However, we contend that researchers who indicate that college does not have a significant impact on moral development have not had access to or have not attended to recent findings regarding moral judgment development. Moral judgment research takes an approach to assessment different from most of the earlier studies assessing college outcomes, where variables are constructed according to a developmental strategy rather than according to an individual difference strategy. Most of the findings about moral judgment development in college students are too recent to have been included in the cited reviews of the higher education literature. Moreover, the investigators in moral judgment are not usually identified with higher education research but more often belong to the field of developmental psychology. Nevertheless, this research area should be of considerable interest to higher education researchers.

WHAT COUNTS AS A "COLLEGE EFFECT"?

It is not a simple matter to demonstrate the benefits of college. One difficulty is essentially a problem of study design. Namely, how can the researcher collect data that would build a case for inferring that college was causing some effect? A little reflection reveals a basic limitation in study design: Researchers in higher education cannot randomly assign subjects to experimental and control groups. Since we don't have control over people's decisions to go to college or not, a straight experimental design is not possible. Therefore, less compelling designs are used. There seem to be three major ways for setting up a study to be used for inferring college effects, each with its own special problems. (1) The first design is the simplest and also the most difficult from which to draw unambiguous inferences. It is to test a group of freshmen and a group of seniors on some measure; if senior scores are higher, one may infer that the college experience must be causing student scores to increase. Of course, there are many possible sources of invalidity here; nonetheless, it is reasonable to do this kind of study initially, before engaging in more costly or complicated designs. (2) Another design is to conduct a longitudinal study of adolescents going to college and those not going to college. Measurements are taken before and after the college years. Then, contrasts are made between the groups on the posttest scores, *statistically* adjusting for certain pretest characteristics. The hope in this design is that it be possible to use the same subjects as their own controls pre- to posttest (thus obtaining true gain scores), and to equalize the college and noncollege groups statistically, even if one cannot control by design to ensure equalization by randomization. (3) A third design is to study only the college group, to look at the degree of involvement in the college experience, and to relate involvement with gains during college. The basic idea here is that different students actually receive different "doses" or amounts of college; those who receive bigger "doses" of college should gain more than those who receive smaller "doses" (if college is indeed causing the effect). Studies of this type attempt to operationalize "dosage" in various ways, usually by time and effort spent in participation or by measures of psychological involvement and commitment.

These are the kinds of studies that are used to assess whether college is having some effect or not. Each of these types of studies has been reported when using moral judgment (more specifically, the Defining Issues Test) as the outcome measure. To anticipate a little, the following sections review these sorts of studies and show positive results for each type, that is, that college seems to be having a positive effect in promoting moral judgment development. We estimate that over 100 colleges and universities have used or are currently using the

Defining Issues Test (DIT) as part of their assessment program. This is probably due to the fact that results are usually positive and that the DIT can be administered and scored easily.

WHAT IS MORAL JUDGMENT AS MEASURED BY THE DIT?

Before moving on to a discussion of the college studies, some brief comments on the variable under consideration here, the DIT, seem in order.

The DIT is derived from the work of Lawrence Kohlberg (cf. 1984) and the cognitive developmental tradition of research in moral judgment. Moral judgment is understood to be one of the major components in moral development and one of the major determinants of moral behavior. However, moral judgment is not the *only* component of moral development or moral behavior. (More is said later about the other components of moral development.) Essentially, moral judgment refers to the process of deciding which course of action within a specific dilemma is the morally ideal one—that is, what ought the person to do? The DIT follows Kohlberg in asserting that there are six basic problem-solving strategies that people use in making moral judgments, and further, that the six strategies can be fruitfully characterized in terms of six basic conceptions of justice ("justice" being described here in terms of what is fair or what are the requirements of reciprocity given different conceptions of how cooperation can be organized—see Rest, 1979, chap. 2 for further discussion).

Not only are there differences among people in the basic problem-solving strategy used to arrive at a moral judgment, but, also reflecting Kohlberg, the six orientations are said to be developmentally ordered such that the first orientation shows up early in a person's development while the other orientations show up afterwards, in the order described by the theory. The sequencing of the stages comes about because the early orientations are logically simpler and the later orientations are elaborations of the earlier orientations—in other words, the ordering principle is such that simple precedes complex.

The DIT uses hypothetical stories—stories patterned after the Kohlberg dilemmas, such as Heinz and the Drug—to engage subjects in moral problem solving. Unlike the Kohlberg procedure where subjects are asked to talk about their solutions to the dilemmas, subjects on the DIT are presented with 12 items and asked to rate and rank these items. The items present different versions of what might be the crucial issue or most important concern of someone making a decision about the story. Subjects are not asked to furnish these, but to indicate which of the 12 items is the most important issue to them. The items are designed to represent different stages of reasoning. On the basis of how they rate and rank these, a developmental score is calculated. This procedure does not call for individual interviewing, but can be group administered. The subjects' responses can also be scored by computer. Optical scan forms for computer scoring are available.[1]

A variety of scores result from the DIT, but the most frequently used is the "P" score ("Principled" moral thinking). The P score indicates the extent to which the subject considers the "Principled" items (items from stages 5 and 6) as most important. Because moral philosophers have the highest P scores, one way to interpret the DIT's P score is the extent to which the subject makes moral judgments like a moral philosopher. Test–retest reliability in several studies is in the .8 range, and Cronbach's alpha is also around .8.

A *developmental* approach to instrumentation entails that the investigator be more interested in how people change over time and less interested in how individuals are different from each other at one point in time. In other words, developmentalists are interested in how a group of 10-year-olds differ from a group of 15-year-olds; developmentalists are less interested in how 15-year-olds are different from each other. Of course both types of differences exist. But as developmentalists devise methods of assessment, they highlight the changes that occur over time in people generally, minimizing differences among subjects in the same cohort. In contrast, researchers in the individual difference tradition highlight differences among individuals in a cohort and minimize differences over time. In fact, the development of many trait measures involves choosing items that show stability over time and situations.

There is an important consequence of the differences in basic strategy in developing instruments. Most measures in higher education research have been developed primarily with an individual difference approach and not with a developmental approach. Yet the critical question of assessing the impact of higher education logically seems more congenial to an interest in changes in the individual over time, not in stable differences among people that persist over time.

EVIDENCE THAT THERE IS A "COLLEGE EFFECT" ON THE DIT

Recall that the first line of evidence (from the three discussed before) for a college effect is to find that more educated subjects have higher scores than less educated subjects. There have been many studies of this sort reporting contrasts between subjects grouped by age and/or education. Perhaps the most impressive evidence to report are two secondary analyses that combine subjects from dozens of studies into samples of over 5000 subjects. In a secondary analysis reported in 1979 (Rest), formal education accounted for almost 50% of the variance of DIT

---

[1]For information about scoring procedures and the availability of printed forms of the DIT, write to The Center for the Study of Ethical Development/ 206-A Burton Hall/ 178 Pillsbury Drive SE/ University of Minnesota/ Minneapolis, MN 55455 (612-624-0876 or 612-624-4540).

scores. In a secondary analysis by Thoma in 1986 (in Rest, 1986, chapter 2), formal education also accounted for about 50% of the variance. (Incidently, by way of contrast, sex of subject accounted for less than half of 1% of the variance, education was 250 times more powerful than gender, therefore gender as a variable in DIT scores is a trivial variable.) Therefore it is quite common to find that the DIT scores of seniors are higher than those of freshmen.

The second line of evidence for a college effect on the DIT is produced by longitudinal studies. Here the subject is retested a number of times and hence can serve as his or her own control. The question is, with repeated testings, do scores increase? The most recent longitudinal study of the DIT is reported by Deemer and Rest (in Rest, 1986) on 102 subjects who were followed from high school and reassessed 10 years later. (In Fig. 9.1, "HS" indicates DIT scores in high school, "HS+2" indicates high school plus 2 years afterward, and 1983 represents 10 years after high school.) Some of this group graduated from college (the "high" education group), some did not go to college at all (the "low" education group), some went for a short time (the "moderate" education group). As Fig. 9.1 shows, the general pattern is that those who completed college degrees continued to gain in DIT scores, those who had no college education dropped in scores, and those who had some college education gained while in college but their scores tended to plateau when they left college. Evidently, there is a strong college effect and not just an age or maturational effect. College attendance accounts for 38% of the variance in posttest DIT scores, and the college effect is still strong after initial high school scores are statistically partialed out.

The findings with the DIT parallel the trends in Kohlberg's longitudinal data (Colby, Kohlberg, Gibbs, & Lieberman, 1983). Using the Moral Judgment Interview, the adult subjects in that sample showed correlations of moral judgment with education in the .50s and .60s.

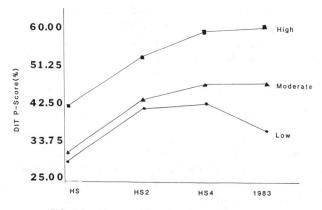

FIG. 9.1. Query author for short FC.

The third line of evidence for a college effect is to look only at those attending college, contrasting highly involved students with students less involved. Deemer's dissertation (1987) presents evidence of this sort. She coded a variable called "Educational Orientation." Students high on Educational Orientation were those who worked hard at their studies, enjoyed academic life, the world of ideas and the activities of reading and discussing, and who chose friends who were similarly serious students. The highly involved students gained more on the DIT than students with low involvement. In multiple regression analyses, Educational Orientation accounted for 12.6% of the variance after high school DIT scores were statistically controlled. (This 12.6% is relatively high compared with the 1% accounted for in the large-scale studies by Astin, and others cited earlier.) Therefore, there is evidence that those students who receive a larger *dose* of college (by virtue of being more involved) show greater gains in DIT scores.

WHAT IN THE COLLEGE EXPERIENCE CAUSES DEVELOPMENT?

The findings presented so far suggest that there is a "college effect"—that is, that gains in moral judgment are associated with going to college. But what is it about college that produces growth? Do the gains in moral judgment reflect material that is learned from assigned readings and lectures? Do the gains come from extracurricular activities? Do the gains come from the social mixing that takes place in college? Do they come from characteristics that students bring to college themselves, and, as such, are not caused by anything pertaining to college at all?

The researcher might look for answers to this question in different ways. The way that one asks the question affects what one finds. Research is pointing to both general and specific features of the college experience that affect moral judgment development. Different kinds of experiences may be important for different people. In addition, both the college environment and personal predispositions appear to interact to produce measurable gains in moral judgment.

The first research strategy was a rather straightforward one, but simpleminded. We might call this the "checklist" approach. At least nine studies have used this approach (see Rest, 1986, chapter 2 for a more detailed review). The researcher starts out with a list of "life experiences" (such as certain readings, religious activity, personal stress, new work responsibilities, social experiences of various sorts, etc.). Subsequently, each item on this list is related to development in moral judgment. The point of such a study is to look for those items that are highly related to gains in order to conclude that those particular kinds of experiences are producing moral judgment development. Clearly highlighting the importance of the environment—individual interaction is the evidence that an experience could be characteristic of some people whose scores increased and also characteristic of some people whose scores did not. Interestingly, none of the items was strongly and consistently related to gain. According to the logic of the checklist approach, one might conclude that the findings show that there is nothing in the college environment that facilitates growth.

With hindsight, we now see that there are several problems with a checklist approach. One difficulty stems from the assumption that one particular kind of activity is generally conducive to growth among all subjects. Instead, what we now conclude is that moral judgment is stimulated in different people by different activities. What is favorable for growth in one person may not work for another. In fact, combinations of activities may spur development in some individuals, rather than a single activity.

Furthermore, in characterizing life experiences, it is important not only to record the environmental stimuli impinging upon a subject but also the subject's response to and assimilation of that event. For instance, imagine two students who take a trip to Europe. One student might be struck by the different conditions in which people live, which might trigger reflections upon the human condition more generally, and in turn, affect moral judgment development. In contrast, another student going to Europe might experience the trip as essentially going from one restaurant to another, and the trip would not affect moral judgment development at all. In other words, the same kind of stimuli events might not have the same meaning or impact on different students. Therefore, in characterizing life experiences we need to take into account both the stimulus event and the person's reaction to it. To paraphrase John Dewey (1916), experience is not what happens to you, it is what you do with what happens to you (p. 140).

Spicklemier (1983) and Deemer (1987) have devised a better strategy for studying the life conditions that lead to gains in moral judgment. Instead of analyzing narrow, specific events (e.g., travel, reading certain books, certain living arrangements) they look at broad conditions. Their way of characterizing life experience is in terms of categories such as "Educational Orientation" and "Continued Intellectual Stimulation." As described earlier, "Educational Orientation" codes students who work hard at their studies, who enjoy learning, and who seek out friends who are also serious students. Table 9.2 provides examples of interview excerpts that were used to code high or low on this variable.

"Continued Intellectual Stimulation" characterizes in a very general fashion the extent of intellectual stimulation provided by one's environment. For instance, a person who leaves high school, goes to college, and secures a professional job involving many challenges would be coded high; a person who went to college but then worked in a stifling job would be coded lower; a person who worked in a routine job in a factory or was chronically unemployed would

TABLE 9.2.
Code Examples for "Educational Orientation"

Examples of High Codes

I really enjoyed the academic support groups, and the professors. I liked many of my classes. I liked to be in the academic atmosphere. You would go and you would talk to interesting people about interesting things. Life just seems higher pitched. I like that atmosphere.

I was in the honors program. That was really good training. I had good grades, about a 3.7 approximately. I studied real hard especially right before a test. I enjoyed living on campus because there were always people around to do something with, something to talk about.

With my roommate, we got extremely close. We'd talk about all sorts of things, like should we be organ donors? What happens when you die? Does God exist? We had fantastic talks, it was terrific.

Examples of Low Codes

I was always undecided. I never had a major. Somebody would tell me, "Hey, this is an easy course," and I'd take it. I took a little of everything, mostly entry level classes. I never applied towards anything. (Interviewer: How did you spend your time?) I didn't do much. I worked a little. I was living at home and probably worked half the week. I was doing a lot of drugs at the time. And I did a lot of partying. Hence the effect on my GPA. They weren't particularly happy or productive years. There isn't anything that sticks out in my mind that was really enjoyable.

I went to college right after high school. I was sort of forced to by my folks. I didn't particularly want to but parental pressure dictated. I went to a college close to my home. I figured that's as good a place as any. I never had a major. I eventually dropped out. I'd go for a quarter or two, then take a quarter off, and then go back the next quarter. All the time I was going to college I didn't really have an interest in it, and I was just more or less buying time, and I didn't study. (Interviewer: What did you like most about school?) I don't know what I enjoyed most. Dating. Partying. Summers.

receive very low scores on this code. Examples of high codes are not difficult to imagine: some of the previous excerpts in Table 9.2 convey the excitement of college and later work. Also included are some noncollege subjects whose work has been challenging. For intermediate scores on this code, people are included whose work may not be particularly stimulating, but whose community involvements are rich, or whose circle of friends and spouse are enlivening, or who have made family life stimulating. Examples of low scores on this code are given in Table 9.3.

Note these features about this type of approach to characterizing life experience: (1) Many different kinds of specific experiences can contribute to a per-

TABLE 9.3.
Examples of Low Codes for "Continued Intellectual Stimulation"

I get bored easy. Most of the jobs that I had were for a couple of months here, a couple of months there. I get bored real easy with what I'm doing. I don't like to get stuck in a rut. All those places I worked until I couldn't go no higher.

All I do is stay home with the baby. With a small baby you don't get a chance to meet people. I don't go out except to the grocery store.

son's general level of intellectual stimulation or educational orientation. For example, some people find that what makes life stimulating is what they read, while for others, it is their friends. (2) These characterizations presuppose a complex reciprocal interaction of personal characteristics and environment. People help make their own environments and often self-select themselves into situations of challenge and opportunity. At the same time, in order to develop, people need certain environmental supports and advantages. Development proceeds most favorably with the best of both aspects, when the person seeks to develop and when the situation fosters and supports development. It is not assumed that all people would profit from college if all were encouraged to go. Nor it is supposed that all people with the potential to profit from high intellectual stimulation do in fact receive the stimulation necessary for development. It would be interesting for future research to trace out how this reciprocity between personal characteristics and the environment interacts in specific cases.

Deemer's study (1987; also discussed in Rest, 1986) used 10-year longitudinal data to ascertain the relation of these experience codes with gains in DIT scores. DIT scores were available for 102 subjects when they were seniors in high school and 10 years later. Deemer conducted multiple regression analyses, entering first the high school DIT scores, then the experience variables, and predicting to DIT scores 10 years later. In effect, this procedure relates gains in DIT scores to the experience codes and statistically controls for initial differences in DIT scores in high school. She found highly significant effects: the Academic Orientation code accounted for 12.6% of the post test DIT scores, and Continued Intellectual Stimulation accounted for 22% of the variance (after controlling for high school DIT scores). Therefore, in contrast to the first strategy (the "Checklist" strategy, which produced little predictability or consistency), this second strategy produced considerable predictability and consistency in both the Spickelmier study (1983) and in the Deemer (1987) study.

We conclude, then, that one of the influences of the college experience is that it provides general intellectual stimulation that causes students to overhaul and rethink the basic ways in which they make moral judgments. We stress the *general* nature of this influence. It was striking in the Deemer study that subjects did not attribute growth to specific moral leaders or special moral crises or distinctively moral experiences. Instead, moral development in these subjects seems to progress along with social development on a wide front, promoted by a broad range of experiences. Furthermore, the college effect is about the same for humanities and liberal arts students as for science and technology students (Rest, 1979; Schomberg, 1978). This finding suggests that the college effect is not curriculum specific, or at least does not seem to follow academic majors. In general, college's impact on moral judgment development does not seem to be mediated primarily through specific readings or through the learning of particular academic content. The extracurricular milieu of the college may be as important as the general stimulation that is provided in course work.

SPECIFIC MORAL EDUCATION COURSES

If development in moral judgment is a general phenomenon, then does it make any sense to conduct moral education courses? Can educational interventions be designed to specifically target development in moral judgment?

Although our longitudinal studies indicate that most students do not participate in moral education courses, and that the general stimulation of college promotes moral judgment development, research on moral education courses evinces that such experiences are also beneficial. In short, the college experience can promote moral judgment development in both general ways and in specifically targeted ways.

A review and meta-analysis of over 50 moral education programs is reported in Schlaefli, Rest, and Thoma (1985; also see Rest, 1986, chapter 3). All of these programs used the DIT to evaluate the effectiveness of the program in promoting development in moral judgment. One analysis grouped the 50+ programs into four treatment types: (1) Dilemma discussion, (2) Personality development, (3) Academic courses, and (4) Short-term interventions. In this four-way classification, the attempt was made to characterize the major educational method for instituting change. Although within each of the four types there were many differences in curriculum, there were some important family resemblances.

In the *Dilemma discussion* group of moral education programs, subjects were presented with moral dilemmas and were asked to volunteer their thinking about possible solutions. The participants generated solutions and critiqued each other's thinking. In the *Personality development* programs, subjects were involved in a social service project, in reading developmental psychology materials, and in a seminar which was intended to integrate personal experience with the readings in academic developmental psychology. Moral development was intended to be fostered as one strand in general personality development. In the *Academic course* interventions, regular didactic courses were tested for their effectiveness in promoting moral development. Courses included church history, various literature and humanities courses, and art appreciation. Mastery of academic content was the focus of the course, and the format was the usual combination of lecture, discussion, and examination. The *Short term* programs were so designated by the length of the intervention rather than by the activity of the intervention. Programs meeting for several hours for no more than 2 weeks were grouped in this category.

Table 9.4 shows the effect size of the experimental group ("E") under each treatment type along with the control group ("C") used to compare pre- and posteffects. The larger the difference between the effect size for the E group in contrast to the C group, the more powerful is the educational effect. The last column in the table displays the 95% confidence interval for the effect size. (If the range of the *d* statistic does not encompass the value of "0", then the effect size is statistically significant.) Table 9.4 indicates that Dilemma discussion had

TABLE 9.4.
Effects of Different Types of Treatments

Treatment Type	Number of Samples	Effect Sizes	95% C.I.
Dilemma discussion			
E	23	.41	(.28<d<.56)
C	17	.09	(-.11<d<.28)
Personality development			
E	38	.36	(.20<d<.52)
C	17	.09	(-.09<d<.27)
Academic Courses			
E	9	.09	(-.09<d<.27)
C	7	-.11	(-.15<d<.33)
Short-term			
E	15	.09	(-.15<d<.33)
C	3	-.11	(-.74<d<.52)

the most powerful impact, followed by the Personality development interventions. The Academic courses and the Short-term interventions did not show significant effect sizes. Therefore, there is evidence that particular types of moral intervention programs are effective in promoting development of moral judgment.

In both the Dilemma discussion interventions and the Personality development interventions, the role of the teacher is more as facilitator than as information-giver. Typically, educators influenced by the Piagetian or cognitive-developmental theory have emphasized student activity in the learning process and have deemphasized didactic teaching. A salient feature of these Dilemma discussion and Personality development programs in our meta-analysis is that the educative activities are designed to get the student active in discovering problem-solving strategies rather than designed to inform the student about useful strategies that have been developed in the past. The message of this meta-analysis seems to be that the teacher should desist from didactic teaching and instead function as a process facilitator. Presumably, what is wrong with didactic teaching is that the student learns the ideas on a superficial verbal level and does not integrate them into his or her own operative decision-making process. Although this seems to be the message of the meta-analysis, it is important to realize that a review of past studies can only summarize what has worked in the past; a review cannot say what will be most effective in the future.

Recently a study reported by Penn (1989) challenges the view that effective moral education is best accomplished by nondidactive methods. Penn's most convincing argument is to cite data that show that his didactic approach repeatedly produces effect sizes over twice that of the Dilemma discussion method and of the Personality development method.

Table 9.5 shows five different classes with different intervention elements. All five involve experience in solving moral dilemmas (application of methods to social issues). Groups 1–3 involve didactic teaching of concepts from moral philosophy. Group 1 includes a component in the didactic teaching of formal logic. As the bottom part of Table 9.5 shows, the biggest effects were with Groups 1–3, those containing the didactic teaching of concepts of moral philosophy. We note that in Groups 1–3, the effect sizes of 1.00, .94, and .84 are over double the effect sizes in Table 9.4 for the Dilemma discussion and Personality development groups (.41 and .36, respectively). The argument can be made that getting students active in their own learning does not entail that the teacher be passive (see discussion, for instance, by Anderson, 1989). Penn argues that the instruction of physics does not proceed by just placing the student in a lab and letting the student discover anew the laws of physics. There are past discoveries

TABLE 9.5.
Five Educational Interventions

Group (N)	1 (57) U. Ethics ID 1	2 (31) MBA Ethics ID 2a	3 (114) U. Ethics ID 2b	4 (19) U. Ethics Non ID	5 (97) Non Ethics
ELEMENTS	Formal logic				
	Dev. theory, stage typology	Dev. theory, stage typology	Dev. theory, stage typology	Dev. theory stage typology	
	Philos. methods of ethical analysis	Philos. methods of ethical analysis	Philos. methods of ethical analysis		
	Applic of methods to social issues	Applic of methods to social issues	Applic. of methods to social issues	Applic. of methods to social issues	Applic. of methods to social issues
P Score Pretest					
X	35.25	39.78	36.61	37.41	35.93
SD	15.2	13.45	14.22	13.06	15.58
Posttest					
X	50.41	52.42	48.52	41.29	39.95
SD	17.01	17.72	15.84	19.89	17.21
EFFECT SIZE	1.00	.94	.84	.30	.19

worth telling to the student. (Of course, this must be done in a way that the student can comprehend.) Similarly, Penn argues, there are important tools of thought that moral philosophers have discovered, and these need to be presented didactically in a way that the student can follow and understand. Properly taught, students can appropriate discoveries of the past and use them in operative moral decision-making.

In sum, moral education programs are effective. There is still debate over which method works best with whom, and there is much room for future research and educational development in the field. What seems clear, however, is that college can be efficacious in providing general stimulation that results in moral judgment development. Moreover, specific types of college courses in moral education are effective in promoting development of moral judgment.

THE FOUR COMPONENT MODEL

A nagging question persists: If colleges are doing such a good job at moral development, why is the world in such lousy shape? More and more people are going to college, so things should be getting better and better—or so it seems to follow from our discussion thus far. But are they?

The idea that civilization is inevitably progressing and that education will create a material and spiritual utopia on earth was severely challenged by the World Wars. The experience of seeing the most educated and civilized countries of the world in the struggle to inflict harm upon each other has disabused people of such quixotic notions.

If the college experience has such a positive influence on moral judgment, what, then, is the evidence that people are morally better?

This paradox unravels once we realize that moral judgment is but one of four basic components in moral development. There are four major internal processes that produce moral behavior; moral judgment is only one of these (see Rest, 1984, 1983). The four components are (1) moral sensitivity, (2) moral judgment, (3) moral motivation, and (4) ego strength or moral character. Briefly, the characteristics of each process follow.

1. Moral sensitivity is the process by which a subject interprets a social situation, figures out what lines of action are possible, identifies who has a stake in what is done, figures out how each line of action would affect the welfare and interests of each party; moral sensitivity involves being aware that there is a moral problem, involves role taking and empathy.

2. Moral judgment, as we have said, concerns the process by which a person selects one course of action as the morally best course of action.

3. Moral motivation concerns the processes whereby a person prioritizes

moral values such that other personal values do not preempt or compromise what the moral line of action should be.

4. Ego strength or moral character concerns those processes by which a person persists in pursuing the moral course of action, overcomes distractions and fatigue, exercises courage in following through on one's moral convictions.

In sum, moral behavior is the result of this ensemble of inner processes, not the result of just one psychological construct or variable.

Moral failure can come about by deficiencies in any one of these components. The four processes are like links in a chain: the chain is only as strong as the weakest link. Therefore even if we see rampant moral failure in behavior among our college graduates, this does not contradict the findings that colleges are effective in facilitating moral judgment. Development in moral judgment means that at least people are not failing to behave morally due to inadequate, simplistic reasoning about what constitutes a moral course of action. If people have developed defensible ways of reasoning about moral dilemmas, their moral failures must lie in other deficiencies.

What good is development in moral judgment if people still behave immorally? Not surprisingly, there is research evidence for a significant positive correlation between development in moral judgment and moral behavior (Blasi, 1980; Rest, 1986, Chapter 5). Development in moral judgment makes a significant difference, but it is not nearly enough to powerfully determine behavior by itself. Mature moral judgment means that *it* cannot be the source of moral failure and that there must be another cause for moral inefficacy.

A comprehensive moral education program would attend to all four components of moral behavior. Currently, such a program does not exist. Regardless, we ought not deny the positive impact of the college experience upon even one of these major components of moral behavior. To quote Derek Bok (1976) once again, colleges "have a responsibility to contribute in any way they can to the moral development of students" (p. 26). As we have seen, one of the ways college does contribute is in fostering the development of moral judgment. Current work in moral education programming suggests the possibility of fostering development in the other components as well. Perhaps we shall learn how to do that.

REFERENCES

Anderson, L. M. (1989). Learners and learning. In M. C. Reynolds (Ed.), *Knowledge base for the beginning teacher* (pp. 85–101). New York: Pergamon.

Astin, A. W. (1978). *Four critical years.* San Francisco: Jossey-Bass.

Blasi, A. (1980). Bridging moral cognition and moral action: A critical review of the literature. *Psychological Bulletin, 88,* 1–45.

Bloom, A. (1987). *The closing of the American mind.* New York: Simon and Schuster.

Bok, D. (1976). Can ethics be taught? *Change Magazine,* 26–30.

Bok, D. (1988). Ethics, the University, and Society. *Harvard Magazine, 90,* No. 5, 39–49.

Bowen, H. R. (1978). *Investment in learning.* San Francisco: Jossey-Bass.

Colby, A., Kohlberg, L., Gibbs, J., & Lieberman, M. (1983). "A longitudinal study of moral judgment. *Monograph of the Society for Research in Child Development, Vol. 48,* (1–2) (serial no. 200).

Deemer, D. (1987). *Life experiences and moral development.* Unpublished doctoral dissertation, University of Minnesota.

Dewey, J. (1916). *Democracy and education.* New York: Free Press (reprinted in paperback, 1986).

Hartle, T. (Ed.). (1985). *Assessment in higher education.* Washington, D.C.: Office of Educational Research and Improvement.

Kohlberg, L. (1984). *The psychology of moral development.* San Francisco: Harper & Row.

Levine, A. (1980). *When dreams and heroes died.* San Francisco: Jossey-Bass.

Penn, W. (1989). *Teaching ethics—A direct approach.* Unpublished manuscript, submitted for publication.

Rest, J. (1979). *Development in judging moral issues.* Minneapolis: University of Minnesota Press.

Rest, J. (1983). Morality. *Manual of child psychology* (ed. by P. Mussen). *Vol. 3: Cognitive Development,* edited by J. Flavell & E. Markham (pp. 556–629). New York: Wiley.

Rest, J. (1984). The Major Components of Morality. In W. Kurtines & J. Gewirtz (Eds.), *Morality, Moral Behavior, and Moral Development* (pp. 24–40). New York: Wiley.

Rest, J. (1986). *Moral development.* New York: Praeger.

Schaefli, A. Rest, J. R., & Thoma, S. J. (1985). "Does moral education improve moral judgment? A meta-analysis of intervention studies using the Defining Issues Test. *Review of Educational Research, 55*(3), 319–352.

Schomberg, S. F. (1978). *Moral judgment development and freshman year experiences.* Dissertation Abstracts International 39: 3482A (University microfilms no. 7823960).

Spickelmier, J. (1983). *College experience and moral judgment development.* Unpublished doctoral dissertation, University of Minnesota.

10 An Information-Processing Model of Retributive Moral Judgments Based on "Legal Reasoning"

Thomas R. Shultz
John M. Darley

ABSTRACT

An information-processing account of retributive moral judgments is presented which draws heavily on conceptual analyses of moral issues in jurisprudence. In contrast to the more familiar Kohlbergian approach, the information-processing theory focuses on the mechanisms of moral decision making rather than on postdecisional rationalizations. Empirical evidence relevant to the theory is discussed, and implications of this new perspective are drawn for the future study of moral development. Drawing on observational research, several specific socialization contexts for the learning of moral rules are suggested.

It is fair to say that the major influence on research on moral judgments has been the work of Lawrence Kohlberg (1969, 1981; see Rest, 1984, and Kurtines & Gewirtz, 1989 for recent presentations). The work of Kohlberg and his associates and students is vast, and has been continued by those who were originally his students and later made their own independent and original contributions to the field. Even when they came into significant disagreement with him on one or two aspects of moral reasoning, researchers often implicitly accepted many other aspects of his general theory of moral reasoning.[1] In the present paper, we advocate a quite different approach to conceptualizations of moral judgments. Given the prevalence of Kohlbergian perspective to the field, we need to begin

---

[1]Much as many of the neo-Freudians disagreed with one or more aspects of Freudian theory, while appearing, at least to outsiders, to have implicitly accepted many aspects of the theory.

by characterizing the two approaches, so that the contrasts between them can be seen clearly.

Kohlberg was influenced by the stage theory perspective of Piaget. In outline, Kohlberg held that moral judgments progress through a unvarying series of stages. Although it is interactions with peers that provides the impetus for this progression (rather than developments in the cognitive sphere), the progression is unidirectional and one that can genuinely be described as upward, in that each stage is more morally sophisticated and "right" than the stage that precedes it. In earlier versions of the theory, one progressed through all of the stages; more recently, Kohlberg has concluded that not all people progress to the highest stages of moral development.

Influenced also by moral philosophers, Kohlberg and his associates have added several other meta-theoretical postulates to the stage-driven one. By his choice of research tool, Kohlberg has at least implied that the stage of moral development of a person is best detected by a trained coder's examination of the persons' justifications for their decisions on a series of ethical dilemmas that have been designed so that a reasonably compelling moral case can be constructed for each conflicting action alternative. Thus the person is asked to reach a decision about what to do, and then to elaborate the reasons for that decision. But it is an examination of the justifications alone that reveals the individual's stage of moral development, not the decision on the course of action that the individual comes to. Thus, a person's stage of moral development is discovered by the coding of his or her justifications for, for example, whether Heinz should break into a drugstore to obtain expensive medicine that would ameliorate his wife's illness, but not by the decision of whether or not to break in. This has meant that the major orientation to the study of moral decision making has seemed to have taken the position that any decision made about a moral issue can be an equally moral one.[2]

This strikes us as wrong because it implicitly focuses our attention away from the fact that moral rules, like other human rule sets, do conclusively decide some cases; that is, there are some constraints on moral reasoning all reasonable people adhere to. Two strange limits are interposed by this on our study of morality. First, to imply that the moral decision itself is noncentral in the study of morality is to trivialize the aspect of the moral question that most people find critical. Second, to avoid recognizing the rule structure that exists, and examining its content and articulation, is to miss seeing the connections between the child's learning of moral rules and the other rule sets that it learns. By missing these connections, the theory of morality fails to draw on the modern movement in

---

[2]Whether or not one should saddle Kohlberg with taking this position is a complex question that we do not propose to settle. What we do argue is that the weight of the Kohlbergian enterprise, and probably above all the fact that he produced a research instrument of the sort described, seems to have led to other researchers treating him as if he made this claim.

cognitive psychology to examine the mental representations of various knowledge domains. This seems to us to be a fair criticism of the Kohlbergian research program; there has been no examination of how the alteration of the elements of a moral dilemma alter the internal representations of that dilemma in the dilemma-deciding individual. Instead we simply infer that the dilemma—any dilemma—is internally represented according to the principles prevalent in the deciding individual's prevailing stage of moral development. By implication, the morally relevant facts of the case do not receive any representation—or at least any representation that requires our attention.

It is the elucidation of the moral rules of our culture, and the assessment of the degree to which children converge toward the judgments represented in these rules, that we address in this chapter. The present review is guided by current information-processing perspectives, and focuses on the specific principles that individuals use to come to judgments of causation, responsibility, blame, and punishment for moral transgressions. As the focus on responsibility linked questions implies, we emphasize that subarea of morality known as retributive justice, that domain in which judgments of blame and punishment, rather than moral praise or positive obligation, are studied.

MORAL THEORIES DRAWING ON LEGAL REASONING

A number of contemporary investigators of the psychology of retributive justice (Darley & Zanna, 1982; Jaspars et al., 1983; Shaver, 1985; Shultz & Schleifer, 1983) have found theoretical inspiration in philosophical analyses of morality or law (Austin, 1956; Feinberg, 1968; Harper & James, 1956; Hart, 1968; Hart & Honoré, 1959). These philosophical treatments are typically conceptually rigorous, and designed to be logically consistent. The psychologists who have drawn on the philosophers' systematizations might be referred to as ''legal reasoners'' if we can use that as a shorthand phrase for those who argue that the legal system provides several subsets of integrated rules that are useful for modeling the information and inference rules that ordinary people use in their judgments of harm doing. It is these ordinary people's judgments that the psychological theories that have been inspired by these philosophical analyses have been primarily interested in representing. In contrast to Kohlberg's concentration on rationalization of past moral decisions, the emphasis here is on the processing of case information by rules of reasoning. Thus, it is appropriate to apply the term *information processing* to these theories. Such information processing is thought to actually generate moral decisions, regardless how these decisions might be justified later.

Given the strong cultural tradition in North America to find the legal system flawed, inadequate, corrupted, or frequently arriving at outrageously immoral outcomes, it requires some explanation as to why the legal reasoners think that the legal system will give any insights on the ordinary person's moral judgments or any other kind of morality. Much of the plausibility of the proposition is understood if one examines exactly what component of the legal system is focused on by the legal reasoners. It is not the criminal justice delivery system, with all of its acknowledged inadequacies, that is looked to. Nor is it the elaborate codifications of the often arcane rules, e.g., concerning the exact number and status of witnesses required to execute a valid will in a particular jurisdiction. Instead it is the systematizations of the general principles that underlie legal decisions, that have been formulated by those trained in jurisprudence and philosophy, to which the legal reasoners look for their inspiration. Lloyd-Bostock (1983) has provided an extended rationale for drawing on common law principles. However, an example may clarify the point. If one were to read the introductory sections of, for instance, LaFave and Scott's (1972) text on criminal law, one could easily become confused as to whether one were reading a law book or one in moral philosophy. There are cases about what crime is committed if A shoots at B and accidentally kills C, what it means to "intentionally" take the property of another, which "state of mind" is critical to converting an act into a criminal one, and other discussions that are characteristic of a philosophical examination of morality.

After reading such analyses, one recognizes one component of what the authors are attempting to do, and a good deal of the mystery of why one thinks that their codifications of the legal system have anything to do with ordinary moral reasoning is dispelled. The authors are trying to systematize the often disparate (and no doubt occasionally biased or corrupted) decisions of judges and juries into some coherent whole. As they do this, they are clearly responding to a felt pressure to make those systematizations make moral sense. In other words, at the most general level at which they are working, they converge toward those common-sense notions of morality that they have available to them as normally socialized members of the society. What is obvious is that the writers are feeling an imperative to make moral sense out of the legal results that they have in front of them, while not denying that in certain ways, the legal and the moral systems diverge. However, even when they do diverge, it is often the case that the two systems may not do so to any great extent. Indeed, if law were not based in common sense moral reasoning, it would not be possible to identify particular legal practices as incorrect, faulty, or unjust. After considering the question of why, in Anglo-Saxon law, the law does not impose a general duty to rescue others, LaFave and Scott (1972) comment that "we do not view death-causing omissions in the same way as death-causing acts, so that what is in fact a distinction on moral grounds is appropriately also a distinction in the criminal law" (p. 191).

As we commented earlier, it is important here to notice the level at which the legal system generalization is said to match the moral one. It is not at the level of detail, e.g., the exact wording of a sign warning passers-by of danger, on which specific cases often turn, but rather the principles that lie behind the specifics with which the judge or the jury struggle; in this case the principle of the duty to warn others when they might stray into a danger that you have created.

Still, there is an argument to be made for the eventual moral properties of even the legal code at this lower level of detail. Once "what counts" as, e.g., an adequate number of disinterested witnesses to a will, has been decided within the legal system, then this knowledge, publicly shared, can shape members' of the culture's understanding of what does constitute an adequate number of witnesses to the informal equivalent of contracts. Putting this more generally, the legal system, as its rules and procedures are publicly disseminated to the population, can influence the population's perceptions of what counts as substantive justice and what procedures are appropriate to bring about just outcomes. As an example of this, consider the way every informal organization, faced with the possibility of a member's transgression, "instinctively" forms a court, with roles of judge, defendant, prosecutor, and jurors. As readers who have been parents will have noticed, even remarkably young children proceed in this fashion, an observation that we will later suggest has considerable significance.

A final remark on the convergence between the legal system and the moral system. Earlier, we commented on the tendency of the legal system to affect thinking about morality; here we want to make the point, once again, that there are forces on the legal system to converge with the moral one. As LaFave and Scott (1972) comment in their authoritative treatment of the criminal law, "There is no doubt that society's ideas of morality, to the extent that they are held by those members of society who are legislators . . . and judges . . . have had much to do with formulating the substantive criminal law" (p. 95). There is a tendency within the legal system to treat this as a naive contention. Apparently it is often the first task of an attorney to explain to a client that, although (at least from the client's point of view) justice and morality demand the outcome that the client advocates, that fact may have startlingly little to do with the outcome of the legal system. Perhaps because this is so, a standard joke among lawyers involves the tag line "but if its justice you want, the minister (priest, rabbi) is down the hall." However, it would be unwise to generalize from this reaction to the conclusion that a legal system that embodies moral principles that significantly deviate from those of the culture is a long-term viable system. As well as the fact that those who formulate the laws share the general moral understandings of their culture, there is a continuing pressure to keep the legal system from drifting away, either procedurally or substantively, from the ordinary moral understandings of the culture. The legal system that does not represent the culture's conceptualizations of justice is a system that creates pressures for its replacement by a system that does embody society's notions of justice. As societal analysts have noted, a system for fairly governing conduct is a central and essential part of a cultural system. Law must embody the moral understandings of the society.

This observation has special force in the year 1990. Looking back at the recent events in eastern Europe, one cannot deny that a considerable contribution to the forces leading to the overthrow of governments came from the workings of legal systems that the citizens of the country found oppressive and morally outrageous.

The process by means of which the legal system converges toward the moral standards of the community is often subtle, and need not involve alterations in the legal code at the exact point that the moral code would suggest. One of the most well worked out demonstrations of this is given by a legal historian (Green, 1985). In 13th-century England, the legal rules concerning what counted as self-defense were strikingly restrictive; one almost literally had to have one's "back to the wall," and be in immediate danger of one's life to fend off an attacker. This meant that jurors would have to convict, and hang, many who fatally injured their attackers, even when the jurors encoded the killing as self-defense according to ordinary community standards. It was not within the power of local legal systems to alter this general rule. Green shows how the juries re-coded, distorted, or occasionally blatantly altered the facts of the case to make the action of the defendants fit the restrictive court's standards of self-defense. Hedges, ditches, and dikes were found to exist for the defendants to be backed up against. So, because of power considerations, the legal code did not alter at the point that the moral code pressed it most hard. Instead, it altered in a procedural fashion, in the power it gave to juries to determine the facts of the case, and later by putting the deliberations of the jury out of reach of corrective actions by the legal authorities.

One suspects that this is a very general phenomenon when authority-promulgated systems are coming into convergence with the moral and practical understandings of people who are governed by that code. Because the authoritatively imposed code is just that, imposed by a powerful authority, "face saving" considerations dictate that the code be preserved at a visible, formal level. However, the wise authority may allow the sub rosa accommodations that we suggest, and the unwise authority may not be powerful enough to prevent them. Anthropologists studying the imposition of "colonial law" on "native" systems have numerous examples of the way the law of the conquerors is modified to include aspects of the moral judgments of the conquered population.

A LEGAL REASONER'S THEORY
OF MORAL JUDGMENT

For all of these reasons, several scholars have suggested that it would be profitable to begin the process of developing an information-processing theory of the moral judgments of ordinary people in our culture by looking to moral principles that analysts of the legal system have extracted from that system. (The legal system being understood as expounded earlier.) A number of individuals initially seemed to have this insight at roughly the same time, sometimes applying it to different domains of moral reasoning. Jaspars and Fincham (Fincham & Jaspars 1980; Jaspars, Fincham, & Hewstone, 1983) have reviewed and contributed to much of this legally inspired psychological literature. Darley and Zanna (1982) have conducted psychological experiments on the moral acceptability of certain defenses drawn from legal philosophy, and have suggested that these are relevant to ordinary people's conceptualizations of "intent." Shultz and his colleagues (Shultz & Wright, 1985; Shultz, Wright, & Schleifer, 1986) have carried out a series of studies that demonstrates the relevance of principles of moral and legal reasoning in modeling the moral judgments of ordinary individuals. Rule and her colleagues, (Rule, Nesdale, & McAra, 1974: Rule, Dyck, McAra, & Nesdale, 1975) assessing the moral judgmental principles of children, have found a number of convergences with adult principles of moral judgments, which in turn can be put in correspondence with principles drawn from the legal system. Shaver, in an important recent book (1985), has reviewed and summarized much of the relevant philosophical and psychological work and has proposed a psychological theory of blame and responsibility.

One such philosophically inspired psychological theory was developed by Shultz and Schleifer (Shultz & Schleifer 1983, Shultz, Schleifer, & Altman, 1981). Other researchers have developed parallel sorts of ideas to that model, overlapping with the Shultz–Schleifer model in a number of respects. Shultz (1989) has recently taken the step of specifying a computational model of moral reasoning. Although the model is implemented on a computer, this is not so important as is the fact that the principles are systematized and their interrelationships to each other are specified. This model, then, is more complete in that it incorporates a comprehensive set of the principles that many researchers have articulated; and it is more rigorous in that it explicitly specifies the ways that the various rules in that set are interrelated. It is one of the themes that we stress in this chapter that the theorist's task is not completed when she has listed the various rules that evidence shows can guide the moral judgments of individuals. It is also necessary to specify the ways that these rules interrelate and link with each other before one can claim to have a complete theory of moral reasoning.

A recent paper reviews the empirical evidence for the computational version of the theory, by comparing the decisions reached by the computational model with the decisions reached in actual legal cases, and finds a satisfactorily high rate of correspondence (Shultz, 1990). Future research will be needed to test the convergence of the model with the actual moral judgments of individuals; however, the research cited earlier and in the following section of the chapter gives some confidence that those tests will provide support for the model. In the next section we turn to the task of explaining the model, and making clear the psychological principles that it embodies.

THE INFORMATION-PROCESSING MODEL

The information-processing theory focuses on cases in which a person may have done harm to someone else. The theory highlights major decisions such as whether that person is the cause of the harm, is morally responsible for the harm, is deserving of blame, and how much punishment should be administered. Each of these major decisions uses information on previous major decisions, and the relations among these major decisions can be described in terms of presupposition. The box and arrow diagram in Fig. 10.1 shows some of the main concepts involved in these decisions.

Presupposition Relations

A judgment of responsibility, for example, presupposes a positive prior decision on causation. These two concepts of responsibility and causation have frequently been confused in the literature since Heider's (1958) influential treatment of them in *The Psychology of Interpersonal Relations.* Heider proposed a stage

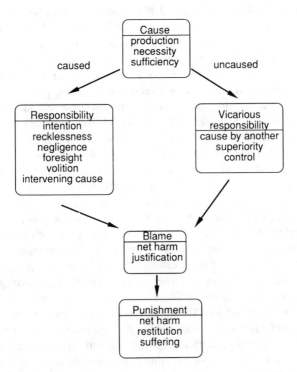

FIG. 10.1. Overview of an information-processing model of moral reasoning.

model in which "responsibility" varies with the relative contribution of environmental influences. His stage 2 defined responsibility as impersonal causality. A person here would be seen as responsible for anything that he or she caused. At Heider's stage 4, responsibility was defined as personal causality, which required the presence of intention, equifinality, and local cause. The notion of equifinality involved the idea that an invariant end could be produced by a variety of different means. The term local cause referred to the idea that a person is not only the initial source of some effect, but remains the persistent cause of it.

This confusion between responsibility and causation persisted in much of the early attribution research that was conducted within the Heiderian framework. The confusion was both theoretical and methodological. Theoretical statements used the terms cause and responsibility interchangeably. Methodologically, they were often measured with a single response scale.

In jurisprudence, however, it has long been common to distinguish responsibility from causation. And to specify clearly that a judgment of responsibility presupposes a positive judgment of causation. For example, Harper and James (1956), in a discussion of negligence, wrote that "Negligence is not a ground of liability unless it causes injury or damage. . . . The establishment of the requisite causal connection is . . . an element of a plaintiff's case to be pleaded and proven by him. And . . . the question of causal connection will determine the scope of liability" (p. 1108).

This presupposition relation between responsibility and causation is more general than tort law or negligence. An example case was contained in the lead story in the Montreal Gazette of 16 May 1985, under the headline "Bus driver absolved in death of rider he punched." The story described a 57-year-old passenger who died after a fist fight with a bus driver who had kept about 20 passengers waiting in the rain while he adjusted the mirrors on the bus. The victim had argued with and spat on the driver before receiving several punches to the face. In this case, the coroner concluded there was no causal connection between the punches and the death of the victim. Instead, it was ruled that the victim died as a result of a ruptured blood vessel at back of his head. The pathologist testified that facial bruises were "of a discreet nature" and too slight to cause the weakened blood vessel wall to break. It was argued that such ruptures occur, not because of physical blows, but during moments of high stress when the blood rate has increased. And so the coroner's inquest concluded that there was no need for a trial to establish legal guilt. In the model, blame is roughly equivalent to legal guilt.

Another presupposition relation in the model is that a judgment of blame presupposes a prior positive judgment of responsibility. This distinction, between the concepts of responsibility and blame, is perhaps even more subtle than the distinction between responsibility and cause. The distinction between responsibility and blame is indeed made by very few psychological researchers, Shaver (1975) being a notable exception. The distinction was formally noted by Austin

(1956) who stressed the corresponding difference between excuses and justifications. Austin observed that, when one is accused of doing something wrong or harmful, there are essentially two choices in mounting a defense: (1) Admit that one did cause the harm, but argue that it was a good thing to have done, or (2) Admit that it was not a good thing to have done, but argue that one did not do it baldly. The first tack would be in the nature of providing a justification, the second an excuse. Any of the various entries in the responsibility box of Fig. 10.1 might qualify as legitimate excuses. If one provides an excuse, this constitutes an admission that the action and consequence was bad, but at the same time, it represents a refusal to accept responsibility for the harm. If the excuse is in fact accepted, then the issue of blame does not even arise.

By providing a justification, in contrast, one accepts responsibility for the harmful consequence, but at the same time, denies that the harmful consequence was bad on balance. If the justification is accepted, one successfully avoids blame, and may even earn credit (the opposite of blame). Obviously, this can only be accomplished in the context of being responsible for the harm that one caused.

An interesting example of this is provided by Hart (1968) who cites the 1811 case of a Mr. Purcell of County Cork, Ireland. Purcell, a septuagenarian, was actually knighted for killing four burglars with a carving knife. More mundane cases are provided daily in the course of surgical intervention.

Note that both of these categories of defenses (excuse or justification) presuppose a positive judgment of causation.

Psychological evidence that ordinary reasoners honor this distinction between blame and responsibility was reported by Shultz and Mitnick (1990). They found, as predicted from Austin's analysis, that ratings of responsibility were affected by excuses but not by justifications, and that ratings of blame were affected by justifications but not by excuses.

Still another presupposition relation in the model is that a judgment of punishment presupposes a prior positive decision on blame. Blame is a decision that a person is at fault (given positive decisions on causation and responsibility). Punishment is a decision about what consequences should befall the person as a result of being held blameworthy. If person is not at fault, then no decision needs to be taken about punishment. In the law, one notes that courts do sentencing last, and then only after a guilty verdict has been reached.

Much of the psychological evidence for these presupposition relations in the moral reasoning of ordinary subjects is fairly indirect using the statistical technique of path analysis. Figure 10.2 portrays the results of path analyses of judgments of causation, responsibility, and punishment (Shultz et al., 1981). Statistics showed that a restricted model with paths from cause to responsibility and responsibility to punishment accounted for as much variance in punishment as did a saturated model with an extra path directly from cause to punishment. In other words, the relations from cause to responsibility and from responsibility to

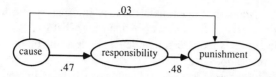

FIG. 10.2. Path analysis of judgments of causation, responsibility, and punishment. From Shultz et al. (1981).

punishment are direct, whereas the relation from cause to punishment is indirect, mediated by responsibility. This is a result that has been replicated several times (e.g., Fincham & Shultz, 1981).

More recently, similar studies have included judgments of blame in the path analyses. Figure 10.3 presents path results among ratings of responsibility, blame, and punishment (Shultz & Rose, 1990). Statistical tests indicated strong relations between judgments of responsibility and blame and between judgments of blame and punishment. In contrast, the relation between judgments of responsibility and punishment were much weaker, suggesting a less direct relationship, largely mediated by the concept of blame. This result has been replicated at least once (Shultz & Mitnick, 1990).

Somewhat more direct evidence for the presupposition relations between cause, responsibility, and punishment was obtained in a study with children (Shultz, Wright, & Schleifer, 1986). Children as young as 7 years sorted the major events in a case of harm-doing according to the expected temporal order: find out who caused the harm, find out if they did it on purpose, and decide how to punish them. Moreover, children as young as 5 years recognized that one need not consider the mental state of those who do not cause harm, nor consider punishing those who have acceptable excuses.

Causation

Returning to the overall picture of the model in Fig. 10.1, note that the first major decision to be made concerns causation of the harm. How is causation determined? Heider (1958) had suggested looking at intention, equifinality, and

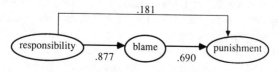

FIG. 10.3. Path analysis of judgments of responsibility, blame, and punishment. (From Shultz and Rose (1990).

local cause, but this is not much help because equifinality and local cause are themselves both causal notions (thus presupposing what one is trying to decide) and because intention is more directly relevant to deciding on responsibility than to deciding on causation.

Jurisprudence suggests two principal techniques for deciding on causation that would appear to be more useful: the *but for* test and the differentiating factor analysis. The *but for* (or sine qua non) test focuses on the necessary conditions of the harm (Harper & James, 1956). It specifies that a person's behavior is a cause of harm if and only if the harm would not have occurred without the person's behavior. A classic example concerns a boat captain who does not install life-saving floats on his boat and a passenger who falls overboard and drowns (Morris, 1961). The question being, did the captain's omission cause the drowning? The answer depends critically on whether this drowning would have occurred even if the captain had installed the life-saving floats. If no one had seen the drowning, then the captain's behavior is not a necessary condition for the harm; the harm would have occurred anyway. On the other hand, if a crew member had seen the drowning and had searched in vain for a life-saving float, then the captain's behavior would constitute a necessary condition for the harm. Experiments with this item and others like it found strong evidence that ordinary subjects use the *but for* test in determining causation (Shultz et al., 1981).

In contrast to *but for*, the differentiating factor analysis focuses on sufficient conditions for the harm. Sufficient conditions for harm have been regarded by many researchers, in both jurisprudence and psychology, as being critical for judgments of causation (Gorovitz, 1965; Hart & Honoré, 1959; Hilton & Slugoski, 1986; Kahneman & Miller 1986). In brief, a person's behavior is considered to be the cause of some harm if and only if that behavior differentiates the harm from some appropriate standard. If the behavior can be singled out as the one relevant difference between the current harmful situation and other, harmless situations, then the behavior is a sufficient condition for the harm. In the case of the boat drowning, for example, the critical question would be whether it was typical for life-saving floats to be installed on boats. If it was typical, then the captain's omission could be construed as the cause of the drowning. But if few boats are so equipped, then the captain's omission would not be a cause of the drowning. Empirical support for the differentiating factor analysis in causal judgments has been equivocal. Some experiments found no support for it (Schroeder & Linder, 1976; Shultz et al., 1981), while others have found that subjects do use it (Hilton & Slugoski, 1986; Kahneman & Miller 1986). Consequently, we have decided to leave it in the model, although we still wonder about the sources of empirical discrepancies in the literature.

The *but for* principle on its own has a number of problems in determining causation. One problem, identified by Hart and Honoré (1959), is that there may be many necessary conditions for some harm, only a small number of which may be relevant to issues of responsibility and blame. Another problem for the *but for* principle is created by cases in which two or more perpetrators independently cause harm. An example is the case of Corey vs. Havener (Commonwealth of Massachusetts, 1902) in which two defendants on motorcycles passed the plaintiff's horse, one riding on either side, and so frightened the horse by their speed, noise, and smoke that the horse ran away, injuring the plaintiff in the process. The plaintiff successfully recovered damages against both defendants in spite of the obvious probability that either motorcycle alone would have produced the result and the fact that each was sued separately. The actions were tried together in the same case. This is a case in which the actions of each defendant would have been judged not to cause harm on the *but for* test. But the intuitively correct result is the one actually obtained.

Thus, the *but for* test does need to be supplemented with something else. Some have argued that it is sufficient to supplement *but for* with the differentiating factor analysis (Gorovitz, 1965; Hart & Honoré, 1959). Our view is that conditional analyses of causation fall short of dealing with the essence of causality, i.e., the production of one state of affairs by changes in another. This generative or realist position on causation holds that an analysis of actual causal mechanisms can often reveal the presence or absence of causal connections. The aforementioned case of the bus driver could be cited as one such example. Physical and physiological mechanisms were analyzed in support of the hypothesis that the punches of the driver could not have caused the death of the victim. The generative view of causation uses information on the causal properties of objects, i.e., the kinds of transmissions that objects can emit, the kinds of transformations objects can undergo, and how such transmissions and transformations are related. Psychological evidence from both children and adults supports the view that the generative or mechanisms approach to causation predominates over less direct approaches (Shultz, 1982). In this sense, conditional analyses, whether focusing on necessary or sufficient conditions, may best be regarded as fall back systems to deal with cases in which the underlying causal mechanisms are unknown.

Responsibility

The next major decision in the model, shown in Fig. 10.1, is that of responsibility. Given that it has been decided that someone has caused the harm, is this person morally responsible for it? According to the model, the answer would be positive unless the harm was caused accidentally, or the harm could not be foreseen, or the person did not act voluntarily, or there was an intervening cause that exacerbated the harm.

Accidentality is a default decision made if it can be determined that the actor did not act with the mental states of intention, recklessness, or negligence. Intentionality can be determined either directly or indirectly. Direct evidence of intention is provided by knowledge that the harm was part of the actor's plan and was caused as planned (Davidson, 1973; Goldman, 1970; Woodfield, 1976). The latter condition is necessitated by cases of so-called deviant causal chains, in which the intended event is produced, but not in the intended manner. One such hypothetical case, presented by Chisholm (1966) involved a person who, in deciding to kill his uncle, became so upset and distracted from his driving that he struck and killed a pedestrian. As luck would have it, the pedestrian turned out to be the uncle, the intended victim. Although the actor's intention matches the outcome, and indeed causes the outcome, the manner of causation deviates sufficiently from the actor's plan that most observers would probably consider the outcome to be unintentional.

An even more puzzling case of deviant causal chains, also hypothetical, was discussed by Davidson (1973) and Searle (1983). This involved a person who tries to kill someone by shooting him. As it happens, the shot misses, but alarms a herd of wild pigs which then tramples the victim to death. In this case, the actor's plan became quite detailed and was even enacted much as planned. But the causal chain is still deviant enough to make observers question the intentionality of the killing.

Indirect evidence of intention can be marshaled if the actions are neither reckless nor negligent, and one or more of the following is true: the possibility of the accused's intending the harm cannot be discounted, the accused monitored his actions, or the harm benefitted the accused. Any direct evidence for the alternative mental states of recklessness or negligence overrides an indirect conclusion of intentionality. The discounting heuristic (Kelley, 1973) specifies that internal causes, such as intentions, can be discounted insofar as sufficient external causes are known to be operational. There is substantial evidence, not dealing exclusively with intentions, that suggest that discounting is used as young as about 4 years of age (Lepper, Sagotsky, Dafoe, & Greene, 1982; Wells & Shultz, 1980).

The monitoring heuristic specifies that an event is likely to be intended if the actor monitors the relation between his action and the event. The valence heuristic specifies that outcomes that are positive for the actor are likely to be intended, whereas those that are negative for the actor are likely to be unintended. Subjects from 5 years to adults have been observed to use valence and monitoring in their assessment of an actor's intentionality (Smith, 1978). Where sources of evidence on intention are in conflict, the more direct evidence, based on matching and manner of cause, dominates over the indirect evidence supplied by valence, monitoring, and discounting (Shultz & Wells, 1985).

Experimental evidence that intentional harm is judged to be more culpable than unintentional harm, even by young children, is extensive (Berndt & Berndt, 1975; Darley & Zanna, 1982; Ferguson & Rule, 1983; Karniol, 1978; Keasey, 1978).

The alternative mental state of recklessness is defined as acting without due care coupled with relatively high foreseeability of the harm, unless the harm has already been judged to be intended (Williams, 1953). If a person throws a brick at his enemy, who happens to be standing in front of a plate glass window, and unintentionally breaks the window while missing the enemy, the throw could well be considered as reckless with respect to the damage.

Negligence ordinarily involves an omissive act (i.e., not doing something) coupled with a relatively low foreseeability of the resulting harm (D'Arcy, 1963; Prosser, 1955; Williams, 1953). If I set a fire on my property in calm weather which then blows over to your property, my lack of subsequent action may be construed as negligent with respect to the damage to your property.

If a harm-producing action is not judged to be intentional, reckless, or negligent, it can be judged, by default, to be an accident. Consistent with legal practice, ordinary observers have been found to judge responsibility to be highest for intentional harm, lower for reckless harm, still lower for negligent harm, and lowest for accidental harm (Karlovac & Darley, 1989; Shultz & Rose, 1990; Shultz & Wright, 1985; Shultz et al., 1986).

In jurisprudence, an actor is held responsible only for consequences that are considered to be reasonably foreseeable in the circumstances (Harper & James, 1956; Hart & Honoré, 1959). An example is provided by a 1949 South African case, Workmen's Compensation Commissioner vs. DeVilliers (Hart & Honoré, 1959). Although a defendant was held negligent for backing a lorry against a door, he was not held liable for injuries to a plaintiff who was working on a ladder, unseen, behind the door. Many experiments have reported evidence that a lack of foreseeability successfully mitigates judgments of responsibility in ordinary subjects (Darley & Zanna, 1982; Nelson-LeGall, 1985; Schroeder & Linder, 1976; Shultz et al., 1981).

Lack of voluntariness in acting is also a mitigator of responsibility for caused harm (Feinberg, 1968; Fitzgerald, 1961; Harper & James, 1956; Hart & Honoré, 1959). Actors are held responsible only for actions that they freely choose to perform without coercion or pressure. Note that voluntariness is quite distinct from intentionality, since actions may be performed intentionally under pressure and thus involuntarily. The classic "gun to the head" situation may be cited as providing many relevant examples. The bank manager who cooperates in the robbery of his own branch because his family is being held hostage does so with definite intentionality. But his responsibility for the robbery is excused on account of the lack of voluntariness in his actions. Experiments indicate that ordinary observers are strongly influenced by manipulations of voluntariness information (Shultz et al., 1981).

An intervening cause is an event that occurs between an action and some resulting harm that contributes to or exacerbates the harm (Harper & James, 1956; Hart & Honoré, 1959). The basic idea here is that since the intervening event breaks the causal chain between the action and resulting harm, the actor's responsibility for the harm must be mitigated. Because some studies had failed to find evidence for the mitigating effectiveness of intervening causation (Brickman, Ryan, & Wortman, 1975; Shultz et al., 1981), it has been necessary to clarify the conditions under which intervening causes operate.

From jurisprudence, two qualifications seemed to be particularly relevant. Prosser (1955) held that an intervening cause will be viewed as mitigating only insofar as its occurrence is not foreseeable in the circumstances. For example, if I light a fire that spreads over to your property, a sudden high wind would constitute an acceptable intervening factor only if the wind could not be foreseen. Otherwise my action might merely take advantage of other causal factors which I can reasonably expect to occur. The second qualification stems from Hart and Honoré's (1959) argument that an intervening cause mitigates only when it comprises a voluntary human action, i.e., by a different party than the accused. Hart and Honoré cite many difficult and troublesome causes in which the victim does something to exacerbate harm. In the 1943 New York State case of People vs. Goodman (Hart & Honoré, 1959), the accused persuaded the victim to get in his car and thereafter attempted to sexually assault her. She immediately opened the door of the car and jumped, fatally fracturing her skull. In this case, the accused was found guilty, but many other such cases have gone the other way when the victim did something contributing to her own demise.

Experimental evidence has confirmed that ordinary subjects mitigated responsibility judgments in the presence of an intervening cause more when the intervention was voluntary than when it was involuntary, and more when the intervention was unforeseeable than when it was foreseeable (Fincham & Roberts, 1985; Fincham & Shultz, 1981).

Blame

If none of these excuses apply, a person who caused harm will be held responsible for the harm. This naturally raises the issue of whether this person is also worthy of blame for this harm. In the model, blameworthiness is determined by a joint consideration of the presence of net harm (i.e., more harm than benefit) and a lack of justification for the harm. Harm can be justified if it achieves some goal that is judged to be more valuable than the state created by not doing the harm, provided that this goal could not be achieved in some other, less harmful way.

A good example of justification is provided by the well-publicized Goetz case. Goetz often carried a loaded revolver when riding the New York City subway. He had been a victim of mugging and had concluded that he needed a gun to protect himself. At one point, Goetz thought he was being mugged again when three young men asked him for money in a threatening tone on the subway. It was later discovered that the men were carrying weapons, but had no guns. Goetz pulled out his gun and shot each of them, some of them more than once, even as they lay motionless on the floor of the subway car. One of the victims was left paralyzed from the shooting. This case, we would argue, turns on the issue of whether the harm caused by Goetz was justified. There is no question but that he caused the harm and is responsible for it.

The harm caused by Goetz probably achieved the goal of protecting himself from being robbed and perhaps injured or killed. Depending on how much threat to Goetz there actually was, it may even be that this goal could be judged as more valuable than the state of the men's well being prior to the shooting. But it is difficult to imagine that this goal could not have been achieved in a less harmful manner. Given that the men had no guns, Goetz may well have been able to defend himself simply by drawing his gun, but never firing it. Contrary to this analysis provided by our model, the actual outcome was an acquittal on the shooting charge. His only conviction was for illegal possession of a firearm.

Self-defence, of course, is not the only way in which harm can be justified. Revenge, particularly in the heat of anger, can sometimes at least partially justify doing harm. The prevention of greater harm is also often offered as a justification for harm, as in the recent U.S. invasion of Panama.

Darley et al. (1978) found that children as young as 6 years were sensitive to various kinds of justifications, including necessity, public duty, and provocation.

Vicarious Responsibility

So far, we have been discussing holding someone blameworthy for harm that he directly caused, as illustrated in the left hand path of the box and arrow diagram of Fig. 10.1. It is also possible to blame someone who did not directly cause the harm. Generally, this comes under the heading of vicarious, rather than direct, responsibility since one may be held vicariously responsible and possibly blameworthy for harm actually caused by someone else (Feinberg, 1968; Hart & Honoré, 1959). This possibility is illustrated by the right hand path in Fig. 10.1.

Examples would include a parent who is held vicariously responsible for harm caused by his child or an employer who is held vicariously responsible for harm caused by one of his employees to another while on the job. At least three different lines of justification for vicarious responsibility have been offered in the literature on moral philosophy. On one view, in order to be vicariously responsible, a person must be in a superior relation to the person who caused the harm. This notion of social superiority accounts for most of the noncontractual types of vicarious responsibility discussed by Feinberg (1968). The importance of social roles in the attribution of responsibility has also been noted by Hamilton (1978). Another view is that, to be assigned vicarious responsibility, one must have had the power to prevent the other person from causing the harm. The importance of this sort of control is thought to derive historically from the concept of suretyship, wherein one's kin (and later in history, one's social group) was considered to control, and thus be vicariously responsible for, one's actions (Feinberg, 1968). A third view is that a person is assigned vicarious responsibility because of a greater ability to pay compensation to the victim (Feinberg, 1968). In support of this deeper-pocket idea, Lloyd-Bostock (1983) reported evidence that fault in road and industrial accidents was likely to be attributed to someone who was insured.

A systematic test with ordinary subjects of these three hypotheses for the basis of vicarious responsibility revealed support only for the superiority and control views, but not for the deeper pocket view (Shultz, Jaggi, & Schleifer, 1987).

Punishment

If someone has been found blameworthy for harm, then the issue of punishment arises, the main decision being how much, if any, punishment should be applied. Adhering to the retribution theory of punishment (Hart, 1968), the model holds that punishment should be directly proportional to net amount of harm (harm − benefit), appropriately scaled down by the amount of blame. Consistent with this view, many psychological experiments have found that severity of the harm is a major determinant of punishment (e.g., Dejong, Morris, & Hastorf, 1976; M. E. Shaw & Reitan, 1969).

Punishment may be further mitigated by either the proportion of harm for which restitution has been made or the degree to which the perpetrator has suffered as a result of having caused the harm. Restitution is very widely used to mitigate punishment in quite sophisticated ways in many traditional cultures (e.g., Pospisil, 1958). Our own culture, with its long-standing emphasis on prisons, is only recently returning to the view that direct restitution by the perpetrator, either to the victim directly or to society in general, is an acceptable substitute for punishment. Hommers and Anderson (1985) found strong effects of restitution on the punishment of judgments of children as young as 4–5 years. Apologies, a particular form of restitution, have also been found to be effective in mitigating punishment by children from 6–7 years (Darby & Schlenker, 1982; Leon, 1982).

The notion of punishment being mitigated by suffering of the perpetrator may sound strange, but it does have support in legal practice. A famous example is the Patty Hearst case, in which the punishment of this convicted society girl turned terrorist-bank robber was mitigated by the fact that she and her family had already suffered enormously. Moreover, supporting evidence for the mitigating effects of perpetrator suffering has been reported in ordinary observers (e.g., J. I. Shaw & McMartin, 1975).

Computational Modeling

As psychological theory becomes more precise and more complex, the possibility of doing useful computational modeling naturally arises. A computer program was developed to stimulate how the ordinary person (down to about 5-years-old) reasons about harm-doing (Shultz, 1989). The program is called MR, for Moral Reasoner. MR provides a convenient way of rigorously specifying the information-processing theory reviewed above and a technique for having the theory generate conclusions that can be compared with those produced by human subjects. The MR program accepts a case described in terms of categorical values on a number of features (e.g., foreseeability of the harm is high) and produces a series of conclusions on any of the other critical concepts in the model needed or requested.

The model was tested on two large sets of actual cases of harm-doing. One set was based on legal cases in English and American law; the other set on cases recorded among traditional cultures that possess no codified legal system. On both sets of cases, the overall proportion of agreement on MR's decision of blameworthy with a judicial decision of guilty was quite high. The success with the cross-cultural cases suggests that the model implemented in MR does have some claim to cultural universality. Cultures undoubtedly vary widely in their value judgments about what constitutes what degree of harm, but they do not appear to differ much in the rules they apply to moral judgments about harm-doing. This universality could have important implications for explaining the development of these moral judgment rules.

Systematic damaging of rules in MR revealed which rules were critical to these high levels of agreement and which were capable of being compensated for by other rules in the program.

The simulations revealed that the MR program is computationally sufficient to qualitatively match human reasoning about harm-doing. The construction of the MR program was extremely useful in forcing a rigorous specification of an increasingly complex psychological theory. This was particularly true in terms of specifying how different parts of the theory ought to interact. Early simulations identified a number of inconsistencies and anomalies in the rule base. Corrections of these problems were then tested in subsequent simulations. It would have been extremely difficult to identify and test these issues without the benefit of a working computational model.

THE DEVELOPMENTAL TASK: CONCEPTUALIZING CHILDREN'S MORAL JUDGMENTS

A good many research studies, including some studies done by both of the present authors, concern the moral judgments of children. In terms of the present presentation, the concern is with how the moral judgments of children might deviate from the just described model. We do not attempt a complete description of the moral judgments of children here. Instead, we simply comment on how those differences might be conceptualized within the present scheme, and more generally, within any information-processing approach. First, children may have information-processing substructures that differ from those used by adults. For instance, as Piaget once argued (we translate his contention into the terms of the present model), the degree of punishment assigned to the perpetrator of an act is not a function of the intentionality of the act, but rather of the degree of damages done by the action. If this is so, then it should be representable within the present model by causing the output of the rule subsystem that determines intentionality for adults to register that any act is, on one hand, to be regarded as intentional, or more generally, as some fixed level intermediate between intentional and unintentional. To test whether this were an accurate description of the children's decision-making structure, within an experiment, children's actual punishment-assignment decisions would be compared to the output of the appropriately modified model. The modeling could be carried out at the individual level; if examination of the intermediate judgments of a child revealed that she were judging intentionality in a way that was deviant from the standard way, then the subset of rules deciding intentionality could be modified to fit her judgments. Her judgment of intentionality would form one of the inputs to later subsystems of rules, modeling decisions that were logically later in the moral decision making structure. Thus if her variant decision of intention, carried forward in the decision making system led to an outcome that was congruent with her actual punishment judgment, this outcome would support the conclusion that it was only in the intentionality sub-system that she differed from the adult system of moral judgments.

We would suggest that the emergence of a mature moral code is driven by several processes. First, children are likely to learn those moral concepts that are less complex before they learn other, more complex concepts. In support of this idea, Zanna, Darley, Hilton, and Shultz (1990) found that children acquired the concept of intention before that of negligence. Negligence could be considered a more difficult concept to acquire than intention because it represents an absence, rather than the presence, of a particular mental state. Moral philosophers have typically defined negligence as a lack of due care in either acting or failing to act (D'Arcy, 1963; Hart, 1968; Mackie, 1977). The relative complexity of dealing with negative, as opposed to positive, information has been well documented (Trabasso, Rollins, Shaughnessy, 1971; Wason, 1959).

Second, a concept that is an elaboration of another concept should appear after that other concept in development. Zanna et al. (1990) also found support for this principle in that the concept of justification followed that of intention. Justification elaborates on the notion of intentional harm by arguing that the intentional harm served some higher purpose.

Third, it seems intuitively likely that many of the young child's moral rules are initially less differentiated versions of adult rules. For instance, the young child may have a rule that holds with "IF somebody does harm, THEN he deserves to be punished." The adult version is more differentiated. "IF somebody does harm, AND has no excuse, THEN he deserves punishment." In the discussions and arguments that go on when parents are adjudicating harm doings, and punishment is being assigned, it is likely that the discussion will center around these differences in rules, fairly efficiently leading the child to *rule discrimination*.

What is *rule discrimination?* The moral judgment model we present here usually employs a production system architecture. An important component of production systems is a set of if–then rules (or productions) that model the set of decisions that the individual makes. Researchers employing production system models have been experimenting with a variety of techniques for learning production rules. Rule discrimination strikes us as a particularly good candidate for being a transition mechanism in the development of moral judgment. Rule discrimination increases the specificity of a rule's conditions, usually by adding condition elements (Anderson, 1983; Langley, 1987). Adding a condition element, in the foregoing example, involves adding the clause specifying that only unexcused intentional harms are punished. There is mounting evidence that children's knowledge does become increasingly differentiated as they mature (Smith, Carey, & Wiser, 1985).

Within a stage-driven model, there is a tendency to suggest that a person functioning at a different stage level holds a genuinely different decision-making structure of rules. As we suggest earlier, a production system model invites the consideration that a child holds a decision-making rule structure that is similar to but less differentiated that an adult system. A second possibility is latent within the notion of rule discrimination just presented. Recall that the production system model suggests that moral decision making is a matter of processing both rules and what empirical states of affairs count as instantiating different concepts. Concretely, it will be recalled that many rules output their decisions as inputs to other rules. Once it is decided, for example that an act of harm-doing was intentional, the next decision to arise is whether the intentional harm-doing was excused, justified, or not. This then causes the decision maker to consider which, if any, of a new set of possible empirical states of affairs is actually true. Is it the case that some playground person punched another because of "self-defense?" Obviously, there is the possibility that children make different inferences from facts to concepts than do adults; have different notions about what counts as "self-defense." In terms of an older vocabulary of science, that children have different "coordinating definitions." Thus if we were to examine only the if–then rules within the child's moral reasoning production system, it might be identical to the rules held by an adult. It is perhaps only in a different set of production system rules, those involving what facts count as instantiating what concepts within the rule set, that the child differs from the adult. For instance, a child might have the same rule for dealing with an act once it was seen as intentional, but have different readings of what sorts of acts were intentional, or at a more interpersonal level, have different rules for decoding intentionality from other person's descriptions of actions. For instance, whereas an adult might be aware of a possible difference in intentionality between the child "hit" and the child "bumped into" the other child, a child might read both as intentional.

Putting this problem into cognitive modeling terms, we are asking how information gets encoded in ways that cause the production rules to fire or not fire. One possibility would be that the perceiver builds a mental model of the situation from the description available of it, and then applies the inference rules of the type presented in the current account to the representations in that mental model (cf. Johnson-Laird, 1983, pp. 52–53). The fact that different people build different mental models of the same problem insures that there will be variation in conclusions, even in people with the same rule base (i.e., the rule base in our current model). Some of these differences in mental models may be associated with developmental differences.[3]

We can now return to a question implied earlier. Within the present system, it is possible to ask whether the child's moral judgment deviates from the adult for interesting or uninteresting reasons. "Uninteresting" in this context, would be that the child did not understand that some fact that it was told should trigger some obscure but valid excuse, but could understand this if it the information that revealed the excuse was delivered with more force or vividness, or in a different modality. An interesting child–adult difference would arise, for instance, if children temporarily but genuinely hold different conceptualizations of what counts as an excuse. On the moral jungle of the playground, for instance, a name calling provocation might count as an excuse for physical retaliation, while it might not do so in the more effete world of teacher and parent. Similarly, it strikes us as relatively uninteresting if a child's deviant moral judgment arises because they did not construct a mental model of events matched in complexity to that of the adult's, but could do so if the modeled information was presented more clearly.

Clearly, though, there are a number of things that a child needs to learn about morality, and the learning processes the production system researchers refer to as rule discrimination seem relevant to this learning, and the dialogue between child and adult is likely to efficiently focus on this learning.

To summarize, these are a number of possibilities for representing the moral decision-making systems of children of different ages within an information

---

[3]The astute reader will have noticed that where only one problem existed before, now two problems exist. That is, we now need an account not only of how the production rule set gets learned, but how the mental model gets formed. Cognitive modelers are addressing this problem, suggesting that there are model-building production systems. A good current example of one is a program called NL-Soar, which takes a natural language account of some situation or problem and builds a mental model of it. That mental model provides "front end" inputs to a reasoning program such as "Immediate Reasoning Soar" (Lewis, Newell, & Polk, 1989; Polk, Newell, & Lewis, 1989).

To carry this discussion yet one step further, it is possible that much of the knowledge employed in model building is of the background "declarative" sort. That is, not procedural knowledge, as is involved in productions. A more natural representation for declarative knowledge, i.e., knowledge of what is true of the world, would be *frames*. *Frames* are hierarchically organized data structures that enable storage, retrieval, default inference, and inheritance inference for declarative knowledge (cf. Minsky, 1975). Frames could be a vehicle for model building, but we would not want to rule out the possibility of production type inferencing carrying some of the load.

processing approach. Notice that an information processing approach enables us to model where children deviate from adult judgments; not in terms of stages, but in terms of deviant inference patterns, mental models, or rule organizations at different points within the production system model. Thus developmental research could examine, and recently has examined, how children work with various subsets of rules within the general inferencing system. Once this is clear, it would be possible to see whether we could reproduce children's final blame and punishment judgments by replacing the standard adult subsystems in the computational model with subsystems more faithful to the children's patterns of inferences. If so, then the model would be shown to have utility in representing development within the realm of moral judgments.

In our presentation so far, one obvious element of the child's learning of moral reasoning has been studiously avoided. Morality is not always, or perhaps even often learned in a hedonically neutral context. Children are likely to most quickly learn those moral principles that will work to their advantage in actual moral disputes. They are most likely to learn those defensive claims that will eliminate or mitigate their own punishments after they have committed harmdoing actions. Lying behind these comments, of course, is a theory of how the moral rules are learned, a topic that we address more extensively in the next section of the paper.

THE LEARNING OF MORAL JUDGMENTS WITHIN A CULTURE

Several major observational studies have been done that provide evidence about how children learn the moral rules of our culture. Walton and Sedlak (1982) have observed peer interactions and peer–teacher interactions within a day care setting. Dunn and her colleagues (Dunn & Dale, 1984; Dunn & Munn, 1986a, 1986b) have observed sibling and parent-child interactions in homes of two-children families. Edwards (1987) has contrasted data sets from Kenya and the United States. Reviewing these observational studies, one is struck by in how many instances they support a *social constructionist* account of the learning of morality. Moral questions arise in social interactions, not because some objectively immoral act has been committed, but because some other interactant gives a signal of disapproval of the actor's conduct (Dunn & Munn, 1986a; Edwards, 1987; Much & Shweder, 1978; Walton & Sedlak, 1982). It is then the task of the challenged interactant to deal with the challenge; to engage in, in Goffman's useful phrase, a "remedial exchange." As the complexity of the propositional model that we propose suggests, there are a great many points that the "accused" child can raise in answer to the accusation. Blame, responsibility, or even causality can be denied. Justifications and excuses can be made.

Walton and Sedlak (1982) examined moral disputes taking place in elementary school open classrooms. First, and in agreement with the point made above, they observed that the dispute almost always began with raising of the moral challenge by a second party. In the ensuing interaction between the perpetrator and the accuser the meaning of the morally dubious act is determined. These exchanges seemed best to fit a social constructionist account in which the interpretation of the situation, and therefore the assignment of responsibilities within it, was negotiated via dialogue between the participants. Second, the dialogue followed a set sequence; one that articulated in an interesting way with the decision model we suggest. It generally began with a challenge from the accuser which asserted, often implicitly, that an act had occurred for which the perpetrator was blameworthy. The challenged individual then could move back through the chain of reasoning, disputing the facts that suggested causality, or providing an excuse that might eliminate or reduce responsibility, and thus cause the question of blame to disappear. Alternatively, the individual could move forward through the chain of reasoning, responsibility could be accepted, but a justification could be provided, such as "public duty"—one pushed another child because that child was butting into line and thus violating a school rule.

A second, procedural aspect of the metaphor from legal reasoning is now highlighted. Particularly if the incident involved or had come to the attention of a teacher, a set of exchanges between child, teacher, and accuser then ensued that resembled a courtroom trial. (A child accused only by another child was more likely to respond defiantly, thus simply asserting power and sidetracking the punishment-assigning procedures.) Within this "trial," under direction of the adult, the child learns that a moral challenge is an occasion for negotiating the meaning of the incident, and that there are a number of specific claims, that group under general rule headings, that are the basis for this negotiation. Guided by the adult, the child learns the rule set we described earlier; the child learns to differentiate and elaborate his or her rules to come into concord with those of the adults. The child learns this for the best of reinforcement reasons. Getting the rules right avoids punishment; getting them wrong leads to punishment.

The question arises about whether the child learns to abide by these moral rules, or simply to use them. That is, whether the child internalizes the rules, and uses them prospectively to govern his or her behavior, or instead learns to use them, after the fact, to put the best face on transgressions he or she has committed. (This latter possibility is the one that is suggested by an account that emphasizes social construction and negotiation.) Certainly the transcripts provided by Dunn and others provide vivid examples that reveal that surprisingly young children can carry out these negotiations with a wily regard for their own self-interest, and at least occasionally a wily disregard for truth. However, if we were to conclude that the social construction process was an essentially free negotiation process, we would fail to extract all that the observational studies tell us. Observing actual interactions, it is clear that reality constrains the situation in two related ways. In the "trial" situation, if a child makes an excuse or a justification, or a claim about facts, that claim needs to be both *valid* and fit the facts as they are known to the various participants. Oversimplifying slightly, the excuse needs to be *true*.

In terms of validity, it has been widely recognized that denials, excuses, and justifications have limited scope. "I forgot and left the bath run" may mitigate the punishment for water on the bathroom floor. It won't do for drowning a sibling. More generally, the sorts of rules and distinctions identified by the information-processing theorists are not and, indeed cannot, be ignored in the negotiating process.

In terms of factualness, on first approximation, denials, excuses, and justifications had better be true. That is, if I claim that I didn't know a teacher's rule, I better be able to show that I was absent when it was promulgated. If I claim that "he hit me first," then it needs to be true that he hit me first. Because we are all aware of the possibility of fabricating excuses, adults in the judging role are careful to make clear to the excuse maker that the factual basis for the excuse can be checked, and often will be checked. A transcript published by Walton (1985) shows a teacher ruthlessly pressing a line of questioning that makes clear to a child that its original excuse of "I wasn't there" (when directions were given) is untenable, and concludes with the teacher assigning the then-miserable child punishment. Much and Shweder (1978) report similar exchanges. Therefore we would insist that the moral negotiation process is one that is constrained by the recognition by all participants that many of its terms refer to accepted rules and matters of fact that are asserted to be true and often can be verified.

Thus while it is true that the process of learning moral rules is a social constructionist one, in which the child has considerable leeway to construe the meanings of the complex and ambiguous sanctions that he or she observes, it is also a process that has cognitive and cultural constraints on validity, fact, and culturally-created authoritative judges to rule on these matters. What it is important for the reader to see is the ways in which the social interaction setting of moral negotiation lends itself to learning the complex relationships between the various sub-process of making moral judgments, the differing sorts of facts relevant at different points in the judgmental sequence, and the resulting punishment judgments.

The reader may have noticed something else, which is that these adult-driven inquisitions are usually terribly painful for the child. This is likely to motivate the child to discover the rules by paying careful attention in other settings in which the rules can be learned, without risk of his or her own punishment. Observations of disputes in which third parties are the accuser, accused and judge provides one such lower-risk setting. Certainly, the presence of other peers, as in a day care or kindergarten classroom, creates an important setting for the observational learning of moral rules. The other children, age matched, are likely to be committing the same transgressions that the observing child might, and the exchanges between supervising adult and child that Sedlak and Walton described can be observed without threat of punishment to self.

To Dunn's research we owe the discovery of two other contexts in which children learn moral reasoning by participating in moral negotiations. In both of those situations, the child plays an active role in a moral negotiation, generally as accused, and yet, because of certain overarching agreements, is not at risk of punishment. The first is "pretend play." Beginning about 18 months, children who have a close and affectionate relationship with an older sibling are drawn into "let's pretend we are . . ." play by the older sibling (Dunn & Dale, 1984; Dunn & Munn, 1986b). In these settings, moral incidents of considerable complexity are often represented. In them, younger and older children often take on various social role sets, e.g., "daddy and mommy, mommy and child," and the older child often responds to moves by the younger child with comments about the validity of those moves and with announcements of punishments for the "transgressions" of the younger child, punishments which are not actually delivered in the play context. This gives the younger child the possibility of making "transgressions" and observing their effects without risking punishment, making the various fact, excuse, and justification claims that might be relevant, and getting feedback on their actual relevance, and also receiving enacted but not real versions of the punishments that the "trial" system regards as valid.

While mothers in Dunn's sample do not engage in this sort of pretend play with 2-year-olds, they do something closely related that provides a second protected context for the learning of moral rules; they create or allow a joking context, in which the child's threatened (and occasionally actual) transgressions are responded to with threatened punishments, but it is clear to both participants that this is all in fun. Further, parents sometimes playfully threaten to or actually commit domestic transgressions, and 2- and 3-year-olds will seize on these opportunities to announce the punishments they will give to the parents. The parent's response to these imagined punishments, and the facts, justifications, and excuses they imaginatively put up, can instruct the child about moral rules. Here the child is brought to cast him or herself in the role of decider of the validity of the claims, certainly a useful exercise in mastering the complexity of the rule set, and one, guided by the claims the adult is making, that is likely to provoke differentiation and elaboration of the moral rule set.

A final comment about the learning of moral rules. As is generally true of rule-based accounts, there are a number of degrees of attachment individuals can have with the rule set, ranging from pragmatic use of it without any commitment to it, to a deeply felt embracement of it. Certainly one of the characteristics that typifies a moral rule set is a high degree of commitment to its principles. Putting this another way, certainly the normal individual in our culture does not experience the moral rule set as a set to be manipulated for personal advantage, but as a structure that embodies principles that are—we know no other way of saying this—moral ones. Universal in that they govern the conduct of all people, and embodying our notions of justice and rightness.

Although we cannot make more than fragmentary remarks about how the moral rule system comes to have this latter character, it is interesting to contemplate the following possibility: The moral rule structure is originally experienced by the child as an externally imposed one, that does not represent his or her underlying feelings. As Kagan (1981, 1987) has remarked, about age three, there seems to be a tendency for the child to be receptive to the learning of general rule sets, whether those be of a grammatical, moral, or logical nature. So the child may come to learn the moral rule set without experiencing it as having imperative properties that differ from other rule sets. However, through a roughly parallel set of experiences, the child also comes to learn the special quality of the moral rule set. Through the development of skills at taking the role of the other, the child comes to realize that his or her own emotions of anger, hurt, and distress when transgressed against are felt by others when they are transgressed against. The actions of others in the various learning contexts support this learning. For instance, in pretend play, the older child often responds to moves by the younger child with expressed feelings of pleasure and pain, sadness, and distress, and articulates the cause of these as being the younger child's pretend transgressions. In the case of actual transgressions, a teacher or parent is often likely to explicate that one of the important aspects of a moral transgression is the way that it makes the victim feel. It is this sort of training, as well as similar training that the child receives in the other moral learning contexts, that may eventually come to give the special character to the moral rule set that is assumed to be characteristic of it.

Reinforcing the learning of moral principles, and likely aiding them taking on this special character, are the other cultural institutions that convey moral messages. Stories and, more likely now, television shows convey moral messages to children in overt and subtle ways. Now only are moral transgressions identified, but if the transgressor is portrayed sympathetically, feelings of remorse and sorrow for those transgressions are modeled. This cannot but help to contribute to the learning of moral rules and to the development of the emotions that are the particular concomitant of moral transgressions.

A further point needs to be made. As is well known, many believe that moral rules are ones that humans are naturally disposed to hold. The level at which this generalization is thought to hold is critical to specify. (For Christians, taking off a hat is the proper mark of respect in church, for Jews, putting on a head covering is proper on entering synagogue.) Still, operating with a more abstract set of rules, it strikes us that moral teachers would have a tough time of it convincing youngsters that people who do not cause harm, or people who have valid excuses should be punished. It seems to us to be quite possible that children have strong moral intuitions, although the source of these intuitions remains an unsolved problem.

CONCLUSIONS

We have suggested that it is now possible to present a theory of moral judgments that consists of a set of moral principles, specifies what empirical knowledge is relevant to moral decision making, and draws those principles together into a systematized whole. The goal of the model is to specify what decisions will be made by ordinary individuals in moral decision making cases. We suggested that, although the dominant position of Kohlberg's orientation has served to mask this point, predicting moral decisions is a primary task of a theory that aims to explain moral judgments. The principles for the theory are drawn from the legal system, but for a number of reasons that system has a serious claim to contain many principles useful in conceptualizing ordinary moral reasoning.

Second, we have suggested how developmental differences can be conceived within such a system, and specified how one would test the accuracy of such conceptualizations. While by no means doing a complete review, we have cited some evidence that uses the methodology that we would suggest is appropriate for developmental studies. The empirical results of such studies supports the conclusion that it is fruitful to conceptualize younger children's moral judgments in the ways that we have suggested.

Third, drawing on the procedural component of the legal system analogy, we have suggested how these moral judgmental principles are learned. They are learned, we suggest, in a social interactional context, and we have pointed out four specific social interactional contexts in which it seems likely to us that they are learned. Two consequences arise from the fact that moral judgments are learned in a social interactional context. First, it provides the opportunity for authority figures, who ordinarily play the role of accuser and judge, to model the form of the rules, the order in which the rules are applied, and particularly the ways in which the rules often contain reference to empirical states of affairs that can be shown to be true or false, and thus the way that moral judgments can be said to be in considerable part fact-based. Second, though, it gives the child the opportunity to learn that the resulting moral judgments are to a considerable extent negotiated between the various participants, and so to learn that moral rules, like the rules of games and other interpersonal endeavors, are to some extent flexible, and that that flexibility can be exploited by interested parties. We have suggested that children naturally first learn to exploit this flexibility on their own behalf, but later, as empathic and sympathetic processes develop, and skills at taking the perspective of the other mature or are learned, a set of rules that is originally learned to advantage the self can turn into a moral representational system in which the welfare of others is genuinely represented.

ACKNOWLEDGMENTS

Preparation of this chapter and some of the original research cited in it was supported by grants from the Social Sciences and Humanities Research Council of Canada and the McGill-IBM Cooperative Project to the first author; and grants from the National Science Foundation (BNS#87-07412 and BNS#80-11494) and the John D. and Catherine T. MacArthur Foundation to the second author.

REFERENCES

Anderson, J. R. (1983). *The architecture of cognition.* Cambridge, MA: Harvard University Press.

Austin, J. L. (1956). A plea for excuses. *Proceedings of the Aristotelian Society, 57,* 1–30.

Berndt, T. J., & Berndt, E. G. (1975). Children's use of motives and intentionality in person perception and moral judgment. *Child Development, 46,* 904–912.

Brickman, P., Ryan, K., & Wortman, C. B. (1975). Causal chains: Attribution of responsibility as a function of immediate and prior causes. *Journal of Personality and Social Psychology, 32,* 1060–1067.

Chisholm, R. M. (1966). Freedom and action. In K. Lehrer (Ed.), *Freedom and determinism* (pp. 11–44). New York: Random House.

Darby, B. W., & Schlenker, B. R. (1982). Children's reactions to apologies. *Journal of Personality and Social Psychology, 43,* 742–753.

D'Arcy, E. (1963). *Human acts: An essay in their moral evaluation.* Oxford: Clarendon.

Darley, J. M., Klosson, E. C., & Zanna, M. P. (1978). Intentions and their contexts in the moral judgments of children and adults. *Child Development, 49,* 66–74.

Darley, J. M., & Zanna, M. P. (1982). Making moral judgments. *American Scientist, 70,* 515–521.

Davidson, D. (1973). Freedom to act. In T. Honderich (Ed.), *Essays on freedom of action* (pp. 139–156). London: Routledge Kegan Paul.

DeJong, W., Morris, W. N., & Hastorf, A. H. (1976). Effect of an escaped accomplice on the punishment assigned to a criminal defendant. *Journal of Personality and Social Psychology, 33,* 192–198.

Dunn, J., & Dale, N. (1984). I a Daddy: 2-year-olds. Collaboration in Joint Pretend with Sibling and with Mother. In I. Bretherton (Ed.), *Symbolic play: The development of social understanding.* New York: Academic Press.

Dunn, J., & Munn, P. (1986a). Sibling quarrels and maternal intervention: Individual differences in understanding and aggression. *Journal of Child Psychology and Psychiatry, 27,* 583–595.

Dunn, J., & Munn, P. (1986b). Siblings and the development of prosocial behaviour. *International Journal of Behavioral Development, 9,* 265–94.

Edwards, C. P. (1987). Culture and the construction of moral values: A comparative ethnography of moral encounters in two cultural settings. In J. Kagan & S. Lamb (Eds.), *The emergence of morality in young children.* IL: The University of Chicago Press.

Feinberg, J. (1968). Action and responsibility. In A. R. White (Ed.), *The philosophy of action.* (pp. 95–119). Oxford: Oxford University Press.

Ferguson, T. J., & Rule, B. G. (1983). An attributional perspective on anger and aggression. In R. G. Green & E. I. Donnerstein (Eds.), *Aggression: Theoretical and empirical reviews,* (Vol. 1, pp. 41–74). New York: Academic Press.

Fincham, F. D., & Jaspars, J. M. (1980). Attribution of responsibility: From man the scientist to man as lawyer. *Advances in Experimental Social Psychology, 13,* 81–138.

Fincham, F. D., & Roberts, C. (1985). Intervening causation and the mitigation of responsibility for harm doing. *Journal of Experimental Social Psychology, 21,* 178–194.

Fincham, F. D., & Shultz, T. R. (1981). Intervening causation and the mitigation of responsibility for harm. *British Journal of Social Psychology, 20,* 113–120.

Fitzgerald, P. (1961). Voluntary and involuntary acts. In A. G. Guest (Ed.), *Oxford essays in jurisprudence.* Oxford: Clarendon.

Goldman, A. I. (1970). *A theory of human action.* Princeton, NJ: Princeton University Press.

Gorovitz, S. (1965). Causal judgment and causal explanation. *Journal of Philosophy, 62,* 695–711.

Green, T. (1985). *Verdict According to conscience: Perspectives on the English criminal trial jury, 1200–1800.* Chicago: University of Chicago Press.

Hamilton, V. L. (1978). Who is responsible? Toward a social psychology of responsibility attribution. *Social Psychology, 41*, 316–328.

Harper, F. V., & James, F. (1956). *The Law of Torts*, (Vol. 2). Boston: Little, Brown.

Hart, H. L. A. (1968). *Punishment and responsibility: Essays in the philosophy of law*. Oxford: Clarendon Press.

Hart, H. L. A., & Honoré, A. M. (1959). *Causation in the law*. Oxford: Clarendon Press.

Heider, F. (1958). *The psychology of interpersonal relations*. New York: Wiley.

Hilton, D. J., & Slugoski, B. R. (1986). Knowledge-based causal attribution: The abnormal conditions focus model. *Psychological Review, 93*, 75–88.

Hommers, W., & Anderson, N. H. (1985). Recompense as a factor in assigned punishment. *British Journal of Developmental Psychology, 3*, 75–86.

Jaspars, J., Fincham, F. D., & Hewstone, M. (1983). *Attribution theory and research: Conceptual, developmental and social dimensions*. London: Academic Press.

Johnson-Laird, P. (1983). *Mental models: Towards a cognitive science of language, inference and consciousness*. Cambridge, MA: Harvard University Press.

Kagan, J. (1981). *The second year*. Cambridge, MA: Harvard University Press.

Kagen, J. (1987). Introduction. In J. Kagan & S. Lamb (Eds.), *The emergence of morality in young children*. Chicago: University of Chicago Press.

Kahneman, D., & Miller, D. T. (1986). Norm theory: Comparing reality to its alternatives. *Psychological Review, 93*, 136–153.

Karlovac, M., & Darley, J. M. (1989). Attribution of responsibility for accidents: A negligence law analogy. *Social Cognition, 4*, 287–318.

Karniol, R. (1978). Children's use of intentional cues in evaluating behavior. *Psychological Bulletin, 85*, 76–85.

Keasey, C. B. (1978). Children's developing awareness of intentionality and motives. In C. B. Keasey (Ed.), *Nebraska symposium on motivation*. (pp. 219–260). Lincoln: University of Nebraska Press.

Kelley, H. H. (1973). The processes of causal attribution. *American Psychologist, 28*, 107–128.

Kohlberg, L. (1969). Stage and sequence: The cognitive-developmental approach to socialization. In D. A. Goslin, (Ed.), *Handbook of socialization theory and research*. New York: Rand McNalley.

Kohlberg, L. (1981). *The philosophy of moral development: Moral stages and the idea of justice, Vol. 1 of essays on moral development*. San Francisco: Harper & Row.

Kurtines, W., & Gewirtz, J. (1989). *Moral development through social interaction*. New York: Wiley.

LaFave, W. R., & Scott, A. W. (1972). *Criminal Law*. St. Paul, MN: West Publishing.

Langley, P. (1987). A general theory of discrimination learning. In D. Klahr, P. Langley, & R. Neches (Eds.), *Production systems models of learning and development* (pp. 99–162). Cambridge, MA: MIT Press.

Leon, M. (1982). Rules in children's moral judgments: Integration of intent, damage, and rationale information. *Developmental Psychology, 18*, 835–842.

Lepper, M. R., Sagotsky, G., Dafoe, J., & Greene, D. (1982). Consequences of superfluous social constraints: Effects of nominal contingencies on children's subsequent intrinsic interest. *Journal of Personality and Social Psychology, 42*, 51–65.

Lewis, R. L., Newell, P., & Polk, T. A. (1989). Toward a Soar theory of taking instructions for immediate reasoning tasks. *Proceedings of the Eleventh Annual Conference of the Cognitive Science Society* (pp. 514–521). Hillsdale, NJ: Lawrence Erlbaum Associates.

Lloyd-Bostock, S. (1983). Attributions of cause and responsibility as social phenomena. In J. Jaspars, F. D. Fincham, M. Hewstone (Eds.) *Attribution theory and research: Conceptual, developmental and social dimensions*. New York: Academic Press.

Mackie, J. J. (1977). *Ethics: Inventing right and wrong*. New York: Penguin.

Minsky, M. (1975). A framework for representing knowledge. In P. H. Winston (Ed.), *The psychology of computer vision* (pp. 211–277). New York: McGraw-Hill.

Morris, H. (1961). *Freedom and responsibility: Readings in philosophy and law.* Stanford: Stanford University Press.

Much, N. C., & Shweder, R. A. (1978). Speaking of rules: The analysis of culture in breach. In W. Damon (Ed.), *New directions for child development: Social cognition.* San Francisco: Jossey-Bass.

Nelson-LeGall, S. A. (1985). Motive-outcome matching and outcome foreseeability: Effects on attribution of intentionality and moral judgments. *Developmental Psychology, 21,* 332–337.

Polk, T. A., Newell, A., & Lewis, R. L. (1989). Toward a unified theory of immediate reasoning in Soar. *Proceeding of the Eleventh Annual Conference of the Cognitive Science Society* (pp. 506–513). Hillsdale, NJ: Lawrence Erlbaum Associates.

Pospisil, L. (1958). *Kapauku Papuans and their law.* New Haven, CT: Yale University Press.

Prosser, W. L. (1955). *Handbook of the law of torts.* St. Paul, MN: West.

Rest, J. R. (1984). Morality. In *Handbook of child psychology* (Vol. III, Ed. P. H. Mussen, pp. 556–629). New York: Wiley.

Rule, B. G., Dyck, R., McAra, M. J., & Nesdale, A. J. (1975). Judgments of aggression serving personal versus pro-social purposes. *Social Behaviour and Personality, 3,* 55–63.

Rule, B. G., Nesdale, A. R., & McAra, M. J. (1974). Children's reactions to information about the intentions underlying an aggressive act. *Child Development, 45,* 795–798.

Schroeder, D. A., & Linder, D. E. (1976). Effects of actor's causal role, outcome severity, and knowledge of prior accidents upon attributions of responsibility. *Journal of Experimental Social Psychology, 12,* 340–356.

Searle, J. R. (1983). *Intentionality: An essay in the philosophy of mind.* Cambridge, England: Cambridge University Press.

Shaver, K. (1985). *The attribution of blame, causality, responsibility, and blameworthiness.* New York: Springer-Verlag.

Shaw, J. I., & McMartin, J. R. (1975). Perpetrator or victim? Effects of who suffers in an automobile accident on judgmental strictness. *Social Behavior and Personality, 3,* 5–12.

Shaw, M. E., & Reitan, H. T. (1969). Attribution of responsibility as a basis for sanctioning behavior. *British Journal of Social and Clinical Psychology, 8,* 217–226.

Shultz, T. R. (1982). Rules of causal attribution. *Monographs of the Society for Research in Child Development, 47*(1, Serial No. 194).

Shultz, T. R. (1990). A rule based model of judging harm-doing. *Proceedings of the Twelfth Annual Conference of the Cognitive Science Society* (pp. 229–236). Hillsdale, NJ: Lawrence Erlbaum Associates.

Shultz, T. R., Jaggi, C., & Schleifer, M. (1987). Assigning vicarious responsibility. *European Journal of Social Psychology, 17,* 377–380.

Shultz, T. R., & Mitnick, A. (1990). *The distinction between responsibility and blame.* Unpublished manuscript, McGill University.

Shultz, T. R., & Rose, G. (1990). *Concepts of negligence, recklessness, and intention in moral judgments.* Unpublished manuscript, McGill University.

Shultz, T. R., & Schleifer, M. (1983). Towards a refinement of attribution concepts. In J. Jaspars, F. D. Fincham, & M. Hewstone (Eds.), *Attribution theory and research: Conceptual, developmental and social dimensions* (pp. 37–62). London: Academic Press.

Shultz, T. R., Schleifer, M., & Altman, I. (1981). Judgments of causation, responsibility, and punishment in cases of harm-doing. *Canadian Journal of Behavioural Science, 13,* 238–253.

Shultz, T. R., & Wells, D. (1985). Judging the intentionality of action-outcomes. *Developmental Psychology, 21,* 83–89.

Shultz, T. R., & Wright, K. (1985). Concepts of negligence and intention in the assignment of moral responsibility. *Canadian Journal of Behavioural Science, 17,* 97–108.

Shultz, T. R., Wright, K., & Schleifer, M. (1986). Assignment of moral responsibility and punishment. *Child Development, 57,* 177–184.

Smith, C., Carey, S., & Wiser, M. (1985). On differentiation: A case study of the development of the concepts of size, weight, and density. *Cognition, 21,* 177–237.

Smith, M. C. (1978). Cognizing the behavior stream: The recognition of intentional action. *Child Development, 49,* 736–743.

Trabasso, T., Rollins, H., & Shaughnessy, E. (1971). Storage and verification stages in processing concepts. *Cognitive Psychology, 2,* 239–289.

Walton, M. D. (1985). Negotiation of responsibility: Judgments of blameworthiness in a natural setting. *Developmental Psychology, 21,* 725–736.

Walton, M. D., & Sedlak, A. J. (1982). Making amends: A grammar-based analysis of children's social interaction. *Merrill-Palmer Quarterly, 28,* 389–412.

Wason, P. C. (1959). The processing of positive and negative information. *Quarterly Journal of Experimental Psychology, 11,* 92–107.

Wells, D., & Shultz, T. R. (1980). Developmental distinctions between behavior and judgment in the operation of the discounting principle. *Child Development, 51,* 1307–1310.

Williams, G. L. (1953). *Criminal law: The general part.* London: Stevens Sons.

Woodfield, A. (1976). *Teleology.* Cambridge, England: Cambridge University Press.

Zanna, M. P., Darley, J. M., Hilton, J. L., & Shultz, T. R. (1990). *Concepts of intention, foreseeability, and justification in the judgment of harm.* Manuscript submitted for publication.

11

Faith Development, Moral Development, and Nontheistic Judaism: A Construct Validity Study

John Snarey

ABSTRACT

Kohlberg advocated expanding the scope of the study of moral judgment and behavior to include religious reasoning, and he also inspired James Fowler's subsequent model of faith development. In this chapter, the validity of Fowler's construct is evaluated from the nontheistic perspective of three groups of Jewish nontheists who were the original founders of an Israeli kibbutz. Four broad theoretical assumptions underlying faith development theory were operationalized as tenable psychometric hypotheses and then tested: Stages of faith development are not reducible to or solely determined by stages of moral development; stages of faith development are structural wholes; variations in level of faith development significantly predict relevant outcomes (e.g., consequences or characteristics defined by psychological, sociological, and religious criterion); and stages of faith development are cross-culturally universal. The composite findings provide tentative support for the legitimacy of Fowler's model and indicate that the degree of construct validity is adequate for research purposes.

During the last 2 decades of his life, Lawrence Kohlberg increasingly revealed a strong interest in faith, that is, in how men or women find meaning or purpose in their lives, often within the context of a religious tradition. Kohlberg was impressed with the fact that people who have exemplified mature (Stage 6) moral reasoning and behavior, such as Socrates, Gandhi, Martin Luther King, Jr., and Mother Theresa, have usually been people of "deeply religious" faith (Kohlberg, 1974, p. 11). In writing about Socrates and Martin Luther King as two great moral exemplars, for instance, Kohlberg (1981) comments:

Indeed, it is doubtful that either King or Socrates would have calmly faced his own death, or sacrificed his life for principles of justice, if his principles did not have some religious support. Their willingness to die for moral principles was partly based on their faith in moral principles as an expression of human reason and partly on their faith in justice, which had religious support. (p. 318)

Kohlberg maintained that though both men saw the principles of justice as the only equitable way to resolve conflicts in civil society, they also saw the principles of justice as a reflection of and supported by a transcendent or cosmic order. Without this connection of moral reasoning to the larger order, to their construction of the ultimate purpose of life, it is doubtful that King or Socrates would have acted, solely on rational and logical principles of justice, to the extent of sacrificing their lives.

Kohlberg, over the years, also pursued a second line of inquiry bearing on the relationship between moral development and religious development (Kohlberg, 1967, 1974, 1981). First, he clarified the distinction between moral and religious reasoning: The function of moral reasoning is to resolve competing claims among people on the basis of a norm or principle; the function of religious reasoning is "to affirm life and morality as related to a transcendent or infinite ground or sense of the whole" (1981, p. 321). He then struggled with the question, "Why be moral in a world that is largely unjust?"—a question that is metaethical and points towards the domain of faith. He writes,

If we continually ask for the reasons why a particular norm should be upheld (such as keeping a promise), we will, after a time, exhaust the possible moral reasons supporting the norm. We will find ourselves asking "Why be moral at all?"—a question that can no longer be answered strictly on moral grounds. The "Why be moral?" question appears at the limit of moral inquiry and raises a new problem for consideration—the fundamental *meaningfulness* of human activity. (1981, p. 321)

At this level, the question "Why be moral?" entails the parallel questions, "Why live?" and "How should I face death?", questions that have to do with the ultimate meaning of life and that are not resolvable on purely rational or logical grounds. Kohlberg implies that moral *maturity,* as distinct from moral reasoning, rests upon the answers to these ultimate questions of life, questions that lie in the domain of religion. According to Kohlberg, moral maturity requires both the capacity to reason about values in conflict from a principled perspective, and the conviction or faith that one should and must live according to these larger principles. Complex moral reasoning is not sufficient for genuine moral maturity.

Kohlberg's writings also provide another justification for expanding the scope of the study of moral development to include faith development. He implies that although a strict Piagetian structural stage model is sufficient for charting the logic of justice development in childhood and adolescence, it is unable to capture the experientially seasoned logic and wisdom of adulthood. He suggests that further study of adult development will depend on the use of more holistic, inclusive, and integrative models that attempt to define aspects of human personality and development that are more intangible and dynamic. Kohlberg (1974, 1981) offered James Fowler's model of faith development as an example of a more holistic stage model in human development. Fowler builds on aspects of the Piagetian and Kohlbergian models, but also outlines a series of qualitatively different stages in the self's reflection about, and construction of, the meaning of life. The issues Fowler includes in a Faith Development Interview are the same issues Kohlberg raises in attempting to address the problem "Why be moral in a world that is often unfair?"

Fowler's perspective has been regarded by Kohlberg (1981) and other developmental psychologists (e.g., Kegan, 1980; Parks, 1988) as a potentially helpful organizing theory. While the theoretical conversation has been lively (cf. Dykstra, 1981; Dykstra & Parks, 1986; Fowler, 1980; Nipkow, Schweitzer, & Fowler, 1988), empirical research has lagged far behind. An objective of this present study is to evaluate the validity of Fowler's construct from the perspective of the founding members of an Israeli kibbutz who, based on their current residences, represent three expressions of nontheistic Judaism (kibbutz Judaism, Israeli city Judaism, and North American Judaism). The study, thus, addresses a question that lies in the path of future faith development research: Is the degree of construct validity adequate for research purposes? To answer this question, we briefly summarize faith development theory and relevant kibbutz studies, present the research methods and results, and discuss the study's conclusions and caveats.

Faith Development

Faith, according to Fowler (1981), is a manner of being-in-relation that is at least triadic in form; it involves trust in and loyalty to self, others, and shared causes or values that are, in some sense, "beyond" us. Faith as a way of being-in-relation constructs a context that Fowler refers to as our "ultimate environment." Faith, then, is a person's way of being in relation to an ultimate environment and of being ultimately concerned. Faith, as such, refers to the total composing-understanding activity of the person as he or she constructs a holistic conception or image of an ultimate environment (Fowler, 1977). Every time of life is held together by a form of faith, thereby supplying everyday life, past and future, with meaning.

Faith *development* refers to qualitative changes in the constructing and attributing of ultimate meaning that may occur during childhood, adolescence, adulthood, and later life. Fowler's model of faith development, summarized in Table 11.1, describes the organizational or structural characteristics of faith that evolve through an invariant sequence of stages, each of which represents a

TABLE 11.1.
Stages of Faith Development According to Fowler

<u>Stage 1 Intuitive-Projective Faith</u>

Intuitive-projective faith is a fluid, magical, fantastic construction of a final environment that constitutes a person's first conscious efforts to give meaning to experiences. It typically characterizes the thinking of children younger than 6 years.

Because children lack stable logical operations, coupled with their limited abilities to differentiate and coordinate their own perspective from and with others, their imagination has free reign and their experience has an episodic character. In this stage (which orients to mystery and to visible signs of power) deep and significant images are constituted, which may fund, for better or worse, future faith constructions.

Stage 1 images of God have a mixed anthropomorphic and animistic focus; the person imagines God as arbitrary, powerful, magical. Intuitive-projective children are fascinated by the magic of a God introduced to them an invisible and living in an inaccessible realm, but who is also everywhere.

<u>Stage 2 Mythic-Literal Faith</u>

Mythic-literal faith is a story-telling or myth-employing type of meaning-making, often found during the years 6 to 12.

New logical operations make possible more stable forms of conscious interpretation of experience and meanings. Concrete cause and effect relations are now understood, and one's own perspective can be differentiated from those of others. One does not yet, however, construct the internal feelings, attitudes, and guiding process of oneself or others. The young person constructs the world in terms of a new "linearity" and predictability. In the effort to gather meanings in their interrelatedness, persons at this stage employ narrative, but the person's use of symbols and ideas remains largely concrete and literal. Persons at this stage regularly rely on the external structures of simple fairness; goodness is rewarded and badness is punished.

The emergence of a fully anthropomorphic God-image characterizes persons at Stage 2; they must construct some basis for discerning predicability and pattern in the behavior of God as they do for other persons. God is often composed, for example, on the analogy of a stern, but fair or caring, ruler or parent. God, the rule giver, is also bound by quid pro quo reciprocity. Stage 2 atheism may be manifested when thoughtful children come to terms with their observation that ours is not a quick-payoff or necessarily fair world; the good guys do not always get rewarded and the bad guys do not always get punished.

<u>Stage 3 Synthetic-Conventional Faith</u>

The stage of synthetic-conventional faith is characterized by unreflective conformity to one's religious tradition's synthesis of reality and by the structuring of an ultimate environment in primarily interpersonal terms. It is regularly found among both adolescents and adults.

In this stage, mutual interpersonal perspective-taking emerges. "I see you seeing me; I see the me I think you see." And, conversely, "You see you according to me; you see the you you think I see." Identity and interiority, one's own and others', become absorbing concerns. Personality, both as style and substance, becomes a conscious concern but self-worth is heavily based on relationships and the approval and affirmation of significant others. In trying to become what will be found worthy by those--present and future--who matter, the person seeks values and beliefs that call forth trust and direct loyalties. The person at this stage tries to express a way of being, forming from within, while also trying to maintain connections and exchanges with all those with whom he or she feels integrally connected. Beliefs and values that link the person with others take form in a tacit, largely unexamined unity. From within this stage the person constructs an ultimate environment in terms of the personal.

Common images of God at Stage 3 include a friend, life-line, companion, and protector of harmonic relations. God, at this stage, is often understood as one who knows us better than we can know ourselves-- knows who we are and who we are becoming. In connecting deeply with others, we are somehow linked with the depth, or height, of ultimacy. A sense of alienation from, or the nonexistence of, God at this stage is often closely related to a person's feelings of estrangement with persons from his or her circle of family, lovers, friends, or work associates.

(Continued)

TABLE 11.1.
(Continued)

<u>Stage 4 Individuative-Reflective Faith</u>

The stage of individuative-reflective faith involves the individual construction of an explicit, systematic conceptualization that is unintentionally reductionistic. It is the modal stage of mature adults.

At Stage 4 a person's tacit system of beliefs, values and commitments must be critically examined and replaced or reorganized into a more explicit meaning system. The sense of self, derived from one's important roles and relationships, must be re-grounded in choices (and exclusions) and in a qualitatively new authority and responsibility for oneself. Roles and relations, that once constituted identity, now being chosen, become expressions of identity. "System" becomes a generative metaphor for this stage. Control becomes its goal. In its new-found power to bring so much that is constitutive of self, others, and world to consciousness and presumed control, this stage of faith is vulnerable to the self-deception that forgets mystery, including the mystery of its own unconscious.

A person at this stage approaches images of God with a strategy of demythologization, critically examining symbol and myths and converting their "meanings" into conceptual formulations. Images of God at Stage 4 are conceptually mediated, that is, based on conscious ideation and conscious aspects of experiences and choices. Theism, if present, may be lost in the process.

<u>Stage 5 Conjunctive Faith</u>

Faith at Stage 5, seldom found before midlife, involves a reworking of what Stage 4 made firm, conscious, and explicit into a more porous, permeable, and paradoxical construction of ultimate reality that usually reembraces and reinterprets one's faith tradition.

This stage arises from an awakening to polar tensions within oneself and to paradox in the nature of truth. The person at Stage 5 knows that symbols are symbols, and is capable of reducing them to abstract meanings, but he or she also knows that truth, as mediated by symbol and myth, must be given the initiative if it is going to correct and transform us. Therefore faith, in this stge, learns to be receptive, to balance initiative and control with waiting and seeking to be part of the larger movement of spirit or being. It develops a second or willed naivete, an epistemological humility in face of the intimacy and richness of mystery. Moreover, it comes to prize a certain givenness to life, as opposed to always choosing one's way or the way of one's group. It comes to value the stranger as one by whom new truth--or liberation from self-deception--may come.

The person at this conjunctive stage uses multiple names and metaphors for the Holy in order to avoid idolatry and to honor paradox. Such a personal-systematic understanding of a transcendent-immanent reality has little use for the tribalism of homogeneous groupings, and no use for ideological holy war. Whether theistic or nontheistic, there is an awareness of that which is both disclosed and concealed, which supports a deepened appreciation of the otherness and nonavailability of that which gives ultimate meaning.

<u>Stage 6 Universalizing Faith</u>

Stage 6 involves a transcendence of the paradoxical awareness and the embrace of polar tensions of the previous stage. Universalizing faith is an activist incarnation of unifying love, ultimate justice, and an inclusive regard for all of humankind or Being. A person at this rarest of stages tends to jolt our standard of normalcy.

The structuring of Stage 6 is grounded in the completion of a radical process of decentration from self as the epistemological and valuational reference point for construing the world. The self is now seen explicitly as a subjective construct having an unconscious foundation. A person at Stage 6 has begun to manifest the fruits of a powerful emptying of self. Often described as "detachment" or "disinterestedness," this process is the fruit of having one's affections powerfully drawn beyond the finite centers of value and power that bid to offer us meaning and security.

A person at this stage lives in communion with the commonwealth of Being. An identification with or participation in the Ultimate brings a radical transformation in which one begins to love and value from a centering located in the Ultimate.

Note. Adapted from Fowler (1977, 1981, 1984). The model also includes Stage 0 and five transitional stages (1/2, 2/3,...5/6).

different mode of being in relation to an ultimate environment. Faith may be religious, but it is not necessarily religious (Fowler, 1981). The stages are applicable to the materialistic atheist and the religious theist, to those for whom the term "God" suggests a concrete authority, a myth based on pure projection, or the ultimate wholeness of meaning (Fowler, 1983; Nipkow et al., 1988). Movement through the stages is promoted by religious role-taking or symbolic-functioning opportunities. Faith Development, that is, is rooted in the changing ability to distinguish one's own symbolic constructions and religious perspectives from those of others and to be able to assume the perspective of these others.

Fowler's theory has been the subject of scholarly critiques. Reviewers have questioned whether faith development is a distinct and unified developmental theory or simply an eclectic conglomerate of several developmental theories applied to issues of faith (cf. Fernhout, 1986; Oser, 1980). The relevance of the theory for nontheistic persons in particular and for non-Christian traditions in general has also been questioned (cf. Broughton, 1986; Hennessy, 1976; Kwilecki, 1988; Power, 1988). Still others have characterized the model as a system of fascinating, but untested, assumptions (McBride, 1976; Smith, 1983; Webster, 1984). These critical perspectives, together, correctly highlight the need for empirical studies that address the validity of Fowler's construct.

Israeli Kibbutzim

Kibbutzim are intentionally created communities in Israel characterized by collective economic production, direct participatory democracy, and varying degrees of collective childrearing. Each kibbutz is a self-contained community, but nearly all kibbutzim are also a part of one of the three kibbutz movements (the United Kibbutz Federation, the National Kibbutz Federation, and the Religious Kibbutz Federation). Kibbutzim in all three federations mark most Jewish holidays, but this is accomplished in the two nonreligious federations by secularizing the rituals so that they focus exclusively on nontheistic values, seasonal themes, and Jewish historical events. The kibbutz under study is a member of the National Kibbutz Federation, the federation whose ideology has been more consistently atheistic and socialistic and whose practices have been relatively loyal to traditional communalistic patterns of structuring a kibbutz living environment.

Previous studies of kibbutzim have shown that kibbutz members are generally functioning at a relatively high level of moral and ego development (Altman, 1978; Bar-Yam & Abrahami, 1982; Kohlberg, 1971; Snarey & Blasi, 1980; Snarey, Reimer & Kohlberg, 1985). Faith development, however, has not been previously assessed among kibbutz members. Kibbutz scholars interested in the study of religion have noted that the kibbutz represents a culture of *Jewish* unbelief in that kibbutz atheists are still clearly Jewish atheists (cf. Bowes, 1982; Buber, 1949; Landau, 1966; Rubin, 1986). They also have noted several areas of concern, however, ranging from passive or meaningless holiday ritual participation, to antagonistic antireligious attitudes, to the long-term viability of kibbutz values if they remain cut off from their religious roots (cf. Leslie, 1971; Lilker, 1982; Reisberg, 1978). Lilker's (1982) landmark study of "Kibbutz Judaism" posed the question of the meaning of Judaism within kibbutzim, primarily in the United Kibbutz Federation. Lilker concluded his observations of a "quality of religion," "kibbutz theology," and "kibbutz faith" with the assertion that, "despite its insistence upon calling itself secular, the kibbutz can be considered a member of the community of faith, even though the object of its faith is man" (p. 233). Lilker, that is, observed a convergence of kibbutz social-political values and Jewish religious values. Yet, Lilker's study also documented tendencies toward barrenness in the metaphysical reasoning of kibbutz members and meaninglessness in the secularized holiday rituals of kibbutz communities. These previous critiques of the secular kibbutz experience of Judaism, in the language of developmental theory, suggest that kibbutzim may be relatively lacking in the diverse religious role-taking opportunities and symbolic-functioning environmental qualities that Fowler's work suggests are stimulants to faith development. Kibbutz studies and Fowler's theory, that is, cast some doubt on the sufficiency of so-called kibbutz Judaism in terms of supporting the development of mature faith. While these observations are quite speculative, they provide faith development theory with a testable hypothesis.

Research Questions

Construct validity is generally considered the most appropriate validity concept for structural stage models of personality development (cf. Kline, 1979). Construct validity considers the degree to which the postulated relationships between concepts specified in the theory are consistent with the empirical relationships between measures of the relevant concepts. Construct validity, thus, also encompasses criterion validity in terms of predicting relevant outcomes (Cronbach & Meehl, 1955). The construct validity of faith development is evaluated by employing conventional psychometric tests to address the question: To what degree does the faith development of nontheistic kibbutz founders empirically satisfy the general theoretical assumptions and claims underlying Fowler's structural-developmental stage theory? Specifically, four broad assumptions underlying Fowler's theory were expressed as tenable psychometric hypotheses and then tested: (1) stages of faith development are structural wholes, (2) variations in level of faith development significantly predict variations in relevant or criterion outcomes (e.g., developmental, social status, and religious characteristics), (3) stages of faith development are cross-culturally universal, and (4) stages of faith development are not reducible to or simply determined by stages of moral development.

METHOD

Sample

Kibbutz Ramat Yedidim (a pseudonym) is located in the northern Galilean hills of Israel. Although Ramat Yedidim's over 500 current residents represent diverse national origins, one unique feature of Ramat Yedidim is that all of its original founders came from North America. A census of these founders was conducted through a search of the kibbutz archives; a total of 120 names were documented, including 99 who had left the kibbutz and 21 who had remained on the kibbutz.

The sample included 50% ($N = 60$) of the total 120 original members. The subjects were divided into three subgroups: (1) those still living on the kibbutz 30 years later ($n = 21$), (2) those who left the kibbutz shortly after its founding and became residents of Israeli cities ($n = 18$), and (3) those who left the kibbutz shortly after its founding and became residents of North American cities ($n = 21$). The 21 kibbutz-residing subjects represented 100% of the founders who had continuously lived on a kibbutz in the National Kibbutz Federation; this included 19 at Ramat Yedidim and 2 who had married and joined their spouse's kibbutz. The 18 Israeli city subjects and 21 North American subjects, together, represented 39% of the founders who had left the kibbutz. All Israeli city and North American subjects were randomly selected. Each subgroup included a nearly equal number of men and women.

Comparisons of the childhood, adolescent, and early adulthood demographic characteristics of the kibbutz founders showed that they came from extremely homogeneous backgrounds: The majority were born into religiously Orthodox families (72%), and were equally likely to be their parents' first- (29%), middle- (35%), or last- (36%) born child. They typically grew up in working class or lower class homes (78%), and nearly all (96%) spent their adolescent years in the Young Guard Youth Movement (89%) or another similar Jewish youth movement (7%). During early adulthood they were typically highly involved supporting the war effort through military service in the U.S. or Canadian armed forces (94% of the men), smuggling, and other activities. Following World War II, the founders regrouped and immigrated to Palestine where they created Kibbutz Ramat Yedidim. At the time the kibbutz was founded, they ranged in age from 21 years to 27 years, with a mean age of 23 years. The three residence subgroups were *not* significantly different in terms of any of these pre-immigration demographic background characteristics. At the time of their interview, the mean age of the subjects in each of the three subgroups was 53 +/- 1 year (age range = 51 to 57 years).

There is a clear difference between the three subgroups, of course, when one compares their length of residence as kibbutz members. The founders who stayed have lived on the kibbutz for nearly all of their adult life, while the mean number of years of kibbutz residence was 3.4 years for those who returned to North America and 7.8 years for those who became residents of Israeli cities. The continuous kibbutz residents were still kibbutz members during later adulthood, while nearly all those who left the kibbutz did so when they were still in their 20s. In addition, their religious role-taking opportunities have differed significantly, subsequent to their decision to remain on or to leave the kibbutz. Kibbutz Ramat Yedidim provides its residents with a relatively homogeneous secular-humanist experience of Judaism; in contrast, North American cities expose their residents to a variety of Jewish as well as other non-Jewish religious traditions, and Israeli cities offer even more diverse varieties of both Jewish and non-Jewish religious experiences.

Procedure

The subjects were interviewed individually in their homes in Israel, the United States, or Canada; each interview was tape-recorded and later transcribed. The research instruments assessed faith development, moral judgment, ego development, demographic background, and the use of ethnic-religious symbols.

Faith Development. To assess faith development, each person was interviewed regarding the centers of meaning and value that guided their life. The structure of the interview followed Fowler's (1978, 1981) standard semiclinical nondirective procedure; the content of the interview was culturally adapted to address the distinctive ethnic-religious context of the kibbutz founders' lives and to encompass the motivational factors underlying their life choices (for discussions of functionally equivalent cultural adaptation, see Mayers, 1974; Snarey, 1985). The first group of questions focused on their retrospective interpretations of why they originally came to Israel and founded a kibbutz. Another set of questions focused on the motivations for their current residence decision, including their satisfactions and dissatisfactions with their life at the present. Finally, they were asked about their hopes or concerns for the future. Topics of implicit religious relevance typically discussed in the interviews included their ethnic-religious background, personal experiences of anti-Semitism, perspectives on the Holocaust, commitments to Zionism, socialism, or the Israeli kibbutz, and appropriation of religious ideas or symbols (cf. Snarey, 1988). If a subject had not raised explicitly religious topics during the interview, however, the topic of religion was directly introduced near the end of the interview by asking them to explain their answers to questionnaire items, completed before the interview, that had asked whether they or their family of origin were religious in any sense.

To ascertain each subject's level of faith development, the interviews were scored using the standard faith development scoring manual (Moseley, Jarvis, & Fowler, 1986). This scoring method yields average stage scores for each of the seven different aspects of faith: (a) Faith Logic, (b) Faith Perspective Taking, (c)

Faith Ethics, (d) Faith Bounds of Social Awareness, (e) Faith Locus of Authority, (f) Faith Cosmology or World Coherence, and (g) Faith Symbolic Functioning. Each aspect contributes equally to the interview's global average score, which may range from 1.00 to 6.00; it, in turn, is converted to a global stage score based on an 11-point ordinal scale (Stage 1, 1/2, 2, . . . 6).

The 60 interviews were scored by an expert scorer who was blinded to the purpose of the study as well as to information about the subjects. To ascertain interrater scoring reliability, 30 (50%) of the interviews were randomly selected and rescored by a second blinded scorer. Comparing the level of agreement between the independently assigned stage scores, in 90% of the cases an interview received a stage score that was exactly the same or within one-half of a stage from both raters, and in 53% of the cases an interview received the exact same stage score from both raters. The interrater reliability coefficient was .88. Fowler's (1981) original study did not assess interrater reliability, but this figure is similar to the mean levels of interrater agreement (.88 to .93) reported in Moseley's reliability study of faith development (Moseley et al., 1986).

Moral Judgment.   Each person was administered Kohlberg's moral judgment interview (Form A), which includes three moral dilemmas. To ascertain the subjects' level of moral reasoning, the interviews were scored using the standardized scoring manual (Colby & Kohlberg, 1987). The 60 interviews were randomly divided between two blinded expert raters who assigned each interview a global moral stage score from Kohlberg's 9-point scale (Stage 1, 1/2, 2, . . . 5). Fifteen (25%) of the interviews were randomly selected and independently scored by both blinded expert raters. Comparing the level of agreement between the independently assigned stage scores, in 100% of the cases an interview received a stage score that was exactly the same or within one-half of a stage from both raters, and in 53% of the cases an interview received the exact same stage score from both raters. The interrater reliability coefficient was .92.

Ego Development.   Each person completed Loevinger's sentence completion test, consisting of 36 incomplete sentence stems; the standard scoring manual (Loevinger, Wessler, & Redmore, 1970) and standard ogive scoring algorithm (Loevinger & Wessler, 1970) were used to assign each protocol a global stage score from Loevinger's 9-point scale (Stage 2, Delta, Delta/3, . . . 6). All tests were scored blind by an expert rater, and 15 randomly selected protocols were rescored by a second blinded expert rater. The interrater reliability coefficient was .85.

Background Information.   Each subject completed a basic data questionnaire and a related occupational interview. Information was obtained on a range of demographic variables including the following: age, educational level, and occupational level (Hollingshead, 1975), level of work complexity (Kohn & Schooler, 1983), and parents' religious orientation.

Jewish Artifact Observations.   During the course of interviewing the founders, the presence of ethnic-religious Jewish artifacts in the entrance to and living areas of their homes was observed (Webb, Campbell, Schwartz, & Sechrest, 1966). Each home was assigned to one of the following three categories: (a) absent—no ethnic or religious artifacts were evident; (b) primarily conspicuous-literal—Jewish ethnic-religious artifacts for which the meaning is conventionally symbolic (such as explicit Jewish subjects in paintings, photos, or posters; or traditional Jewish artifacts; or books on explicitly Jewish topics conspicuously displayed); or (c) primarily unobtrusive-metaphorical—unobtrusive Jewish ethnic-religious artifacts for which the meaning is multifaceted and genuinely symbolic (such as partially hidden or subtle Jewish topics in paintings, photos, or other works of art; subtle but identifiable materials from Israel's natural environment; books, records, or photos by Jewish authors but not on exclusively Jewish topics).

RESULTS

Very few founders considered themselves religious in any theistic sense (5%). Yet, faith development stage scores ranged from Stage 3 (18%) to Stage 5 (15%). Stage 4 (43%) was the mean, mode, and median; transitional stages 3/4 (8%) and 4/5 (15%) were also represented. Analyses of the data are presented as they relate to each of the four theoretical assumptions underlying the construct of faith development.

Structural Wholeness

Structural wholeness is one of the most critical empirical criteria of construct validity for stage models like Fowler's because such theorists claim generality of stage usage across content issues or aspects being measured. The primary evidence for a model's structural wholeness is homogeneity or internal consistency—the degree to which a subject reasons at the same stage on all interview items at any one interview time. Structural wholeness predicts, for instance, that when a subject makes use of more than one stage structure, the additional structures in use should be from adjacent rather than nonadjacent stages. Structural wholeness is assessed by (a) examining the correlations among the seven aspect scores that make up the global faith development stage score, (b) applying a coefficient that measures the internal consistency of item scores, Cronbach's alpha, to estimate reliability, and (c) using factor analysis to evaluate the degree to which one major force or multiple factors account for the major portion of the variability. In addition, (d) the assumption is evaluated by examining the percentage of stage usage by each subject for each stage. These four procedures, combined together, tentatively evaluate the assumption that faith development is a unified dimension.

According to Fowler, the seven faith aspects in his theory are windows on a unified whole. Let us begin by examining the relationships among the stage scores for each of the seven aspects that make up the global or total interview score. A correlation matrix for all aspects is presented in Table 11.2. Consistent with Fowler's assumptions, the correlations are all positive, moderately strong, and highly significant.

Applying Cronbach's alpha, the reliability was estimated to be .93. This finding is also consonant with the theoretical assumption that a single construct was being measured.

If the structural-wholeness hypothesis is correct, one would also expect to find one major factor, not several factors, accounting for the major portion of the variability. The factor loadings and principal components analysis for the seven aspects were thus examined. One factor accounted for 73.7% of the variance, with an eigenvalue of 5.16. The second factor's eigenvalue was less than 1. Because only one factor, loading on all faith aspects, emerged, the analysis provided evidence that only one common developmental domain was being measured.

A final indication of structural wholeness is the degree to which any particular individual reasoned at the same stage at any one interview time. Subjects' stage usage in percentage was examined across all six stages. The 60 interview profiles included 47 subjects (78.3%) for whom all aspect scores were at one major stage or in transition between two adjacent stages such that the difference between the highest and lowest assigned stage scores never exceeded one stage (e.g., Stage 3/4 mode with all other aspect scores at or between Stage 3 and Stage 4). In

TABLE 11.2.
Correlations Among Seven Faith Aspects

Aspects[a]	A	B	C	D	E	F	G
A. Faith logic	–						
B. Faith perspective taking	.885	–					
C. Faith ethics	.595	.616	–				
D. Faith boundaries	.856	.867	570	–			
E. Faith authority locus	.796	.813	.534	.750	–		
F. Faith cosmology	.910	.874	.551	.834	.822	–	
G. Faith symbolization	.503	.498	.580	.436	.479	.535	–

Note. For all correlation coefficients, p value < .001.
[a]Alternate aspect names for precisely the same aspect categories have been used in previous publications (cf. Moseley, Jarvis, & Fowler, 1986).

addition, there were 13 subjects (21.7%) for whom aspect scores were at three adjacent stages and for whom the difference between the highest and lowest aspect stage scores never exceeded one-and-a-half stages (e.g., Stage 3/4 mode with all other aspect scores falling at or between Stage 2/3 and Stage 4). None of the subjects were scored at nonadjacent stages.

In sum, the composite picture created by the above four analyses suggests that the structural-wholeness theoretical claim cannot be rejected; the findings support the understanding that there is a general dimension of faith development that is not aspect-specific.

Criterion Validity

As for any developmental measure, one would want to know if faith development accurately estimates a relevant criterion outcome, whether the criterion outcome is measured before the assessment of faith development (postdictive), simultaneously with the assessment of faith development (concurrent), or after the assessment of faith development (predictive). This study will address the postdictive and concurrent criterion validity of faith development theory by asking if variations in (a) developmental criteria, (b) social status criteria, and (c) ethnic-religious criteria covary with faith development in a theoretically coherent manner.

Developmental Criteria.   Stage change in faith development, as in other structural-developmental theories, is hypothesized to be consecutive and upward in sequence. Faith development is further expected to be associated with other theoretically related domains of development. The expectation is that the level of association will be moderate; if the correlation between stage scores for faith development and for another domain of development is extremely low, one would tend to conclude that they are not really related; if the correlation between stages scores for faith development and for another domain of development is extremely high, one would tend to conclude that they are not really different. This study examines the association between subjects' faith development stage scores and their scores on two theoretically related and concurrently administered developmental criterion measures: moral development as defined by Kohlberg (1984) and ego development as defined by Loevinger (1976).

The correlation of faith development with moral development was .597, and with ego development .467. Both sets of correlations are positive, moderately strong, and statistically significant ($p < .001$). These findings compare well with the strength of the correlation between moral development and ego development themselves in this same sample ($r = .54$) and in prior studies ($r = .65$; Lee & Snarey, 1988). It is also noteworthy that faith development stage scores were not significantly correlated with age in this study ($r = .03$, $p = $ ns), due to the fact that the sample only included adults and the age range was narrow.

Social Status Criteria.   Construct validity is also assessed by examining the relationship between faith stage and relevant social status variables with which psychological development usually covaries: educational level, occupational level, and work complexity level. The relationship between faith development and gender is also considered.

Significant correlations were found between faith stage and levels of education ($r = .49, p < .001$), occupation ($r = .45, p < .001$), social class ($r = .43, p < .001$), and work complexity ($r = .49, p < .001$). Multiple regression analysis was used to separate out the contribution of the social status variables to explaining variance in faith development. When faith development was entered as the dependent variable in a stepwise regression procedure, work complexity and then education accounted for 24.0% and 6.2% of the variance successively, for a total of 30.2%, $R = .549$, $F(2, 57) = 12.36$, $p < .0001$. To ascertain if work complexity and education would still make a significant contribution to explaining variance in faith development after controlling for other domains of psychological development, the regression analysis was repeated: When moral development was forced to enter the model first, it explained 35.7% of the variance in faith development, and the contribution was significant (F change $= 32.16, p < .001$); yet work complexity still entered the equation after controlling for moral development and explained an additional 7.0% of the variance, and the contribution was significant (F change $= 6.90, p < .05$; $R = .653$, $F(2, 57) = 21.17, p < .001$); education did not enter the equation after controlling for moral development. Similarly, when ego development was forced to first enter the model, it explained 21.9% of the variance in faith development, and the contribution was significant (F change $= 15.10$, $p < .001$); yet work complexity again still entered the equation after controlling for ego development and explained an additional 9.8% of the variance, and the contribution was significant (F change $= 7.56, p < .01$); education also then entered the equation and accounted for an additional 2.7% of the variance, and the contribution was significant, F change $= 2.15, p < .05$; $R = .586$, $F(3, 52) = 9.05, p < .001$. In sum, the association between faith development and social status variables was maintained even after controlling for other domains of development.

Besides the expected associations between the foregoing indices of social status and faith development, the possibility of gender differences in faith development was also considered. The claim that structural-developmental theory applies to both males and females is generally considered to mean that *inherent* gender differences (i.e., gender differences that cannot be attributed to social experiences) should not be found in the structure of faith development, although gender differences based on different educational and occupational backgrounds are to be expected.

The correlation coefficient between faith development and sex (coded as femaleness) was weak and nonsignificant ($r = -.08, p = $ ns). A cross-tabulation of sex by faith stage for all subjects further showed that the association was weak

(Cramer's V = .14) and not significant (X^2 (4, N = 60) = 1.31, p = ns). Similarly, when men's and women's mean level of faith development were compared, there were no significant differences, t (58) = 0.61, p = ns. Furthermore, when the possibility of sex differences in level of faith development was considered separately for each of the three residence groups, the analyses did not reveal any significant differences among the kibbutz residents (t (19) = 0.10, p = ns), Israeli city residents (t (16) = 0.26, p = ns), or North American residents (t (19) = 0.70, p = ns).

In sum, as expected, faith development proved to be generally effective in distinguishing between variations in social status, and there was no evidence of significant gender differences.

Ethnic-religious Criteria. This part of the study provisionally addresses the ethnic-religious postdictive and concurrent criterion validity of faith development theory by asking whether variations in level of faith development can be differentiated by: (a) the orthodoxy of the subjects' past childhood families of origin, (b) their current adulthood communities of residence, and (c) their current use of ethnic-religious symbolic artifacts in their homes. These three indices are relevant to construct validity because faith development theory tentatively predicts that one's environment, broadly defined in terms of providing opportunities for religious role-taking and symbolic-functioning, will be positively associated with level of faith development. Role-taking and symbolic-functioning opportunities, that is, fund or promote faith development, which, in turn, enables one to more effectively incorporate symbols and other aspects of faith in the process of constructing meaning (Fowler, 1984; Kohlberg, 1984; Simmonds, 1986).

TABLE 11.3.
Ethnic-religious Variations in Founders' Level of Faith Development

Group I	M	Group II	M	t value	p value
Childhood Family's Religious Orientation					
Orthodox	4.03	not orthodox	3.85	0.76	ns
Adulthood Community of Residence					
Kibbutz	3.83	Israeli city	4.19	1.78	< .05
Kibbutz	3.83	North America	4.00	0.88	ns
Israeli City	4.19	North America	4.00	0.96	ns
Adulthood Home's Jewish Artifacts					
Unobtrusive-Metaphorical	4.27	Conspicuous-Literal	3.88	1.88	< .05

Note. ns = not significant; one-tailed test.

Table 11.3 summarizes a series of t tests comparing the subgroups within each ethnic-religious variable in terms of their average level of faith development. The majority of the subjects grew up in Orthodox Jewish families (72%), and the three founder subgroups were not significantly different in this regard. Can adherence to Orthodox Judaism by the founders' childhood families of origin be postdictively predicted, based on the founders' own present level of faith development? As Table 11.3 shows, the mean level of faith development among founders from Orthodox families was not significantly different from that of those from non-Orthodox families.

The three founder subgroups were not significantly different in level of moral or ego development. Can the three residence subgroups be distinguished, based on level of faith development? The mean scores for the three groups were: Israeli city residents, 4.2; North American residents, 4.0; kibbutz residents, 3.8. A series of t tests showed that the kibbutz residents' mean score was significantly lower than the Israeli city residents' mean level of faith development ($p < .05$); the North Americans' mean score was not significantly different from those of either of the two groups (see Table 11.3), supporting the hypothesis that a possible developmental trade-off of kibbutz residence, compared with Israeli city residence, is that it provides relatively less support for faith development.

The third ethnic-religious variable indexes the use of Jewish symbolic materials in each founder's home. Only two categories were observed: primarily conspicuous-literal symbols of ethnicity and religion were noted in 75.5% of the cases and primarily unobtrusive-metaphorical symbols of ethnicity and religion were noted in 24.5% of the cases. The three founder subgroups were not significantly different in terms of their use of ethnic-religious symbols, X^2 (2, $N = 60$) $= 4.38, p =$ ns. Table 11.3 compares the dichotomous symbolic-display categories in terms of the subjects' mean level of faith development. Level of faith development among subjects whose home symbols were rated as primarily unobtrusive-metaphorical was significantly higher than that of subjects whose home symbols were rated as conspicuous-literal ($p < .05$).

Universality

Faith development theory, like other structural-developmental models, is based on the implicit assumption that the model is generally applicable to all people (e.g., all persons will follow the same sequence of structurally unified stages in a step-wise order, provided that their faith development undergoes change). Fowler (1981), however, has been correctly careful not to explicitly claim universality because cross-cultural research on faith development is quite limited (pp. 296–299). While all of the analyses in this study implicitly address this assumption, the universality assumption is explicitly addressed by comparing the stage distribution for the kibbutz founders with the stage distributions for similarly aged subjects from diverse populations previously studied by others. The mean level of faith development among nontheistic kibbutz founders would not be expected to be significantly different from that of comparably aged theistic populations. Simply being nontheistic, that is, should not prejudice level of faith development.

The present findings were compared with the results from representative studies of faith development among adults in 7 other religious groups—Buddhist, Catholic, Greek Orthodox, Hindu, Jewish, Muslim, and Protestant (Bradley, 1983; Fowler, 1981; Furushima, 1983; Kalam, 1981; Mischey, 1976; Shulik, 1979; Simmonds, 1986; White, 1985). These studies are summarized, with the samples listed in rank order by their mean level of faith development, in Table 11.4.

Overall, the scores among the 7 religious groups ranged from Stage 1/2 to Stage 6. The lower scoring groups were typically younger adults or adults who were selected because they represented a deficit characteristic. The higher scoring groups were generally older adults or intentionally selected elites. Protestant, Catholic, Jewish, and other religious groups were otherwise found throughout the ranked list, although there is an apparent tendency for groups of elite Protestants to post somewhat higher mean scores than both elite and non-elite non-Protestants.

The kibbutz founders compare very favorably with adult subjects included in previous studies. Their mean level of faith development, for instance, is similar to that of somewhat older middle class and upper class Protestant, Catholic, and Jewish subjects. The only two groups with a higher mean level of faith development than the overall mean for the 60 founders ($M = 4.00$) were Fowler's original selective Protestant sample ($M = 4.29$) and a selected group of religious leaders ($M = 4.40$) who, somewhat like the founders themselves, had played a leadership role in their congregations.

Faith Development in Relation to Moral Development

Fowler posits that faith development encompasses (but is not dependent upon) moral development. Kohlberg has suggested that the faith development stage sequence is dependent upon a decalage relationship with moral development. In particular, Kohlberg (1974) has hypothesized that "development to a given moral stage precedes development to the parallel faith stage," that is, moral judgment development is a "necessary but not sufficient" condition for the development of the parallel stage of faith development (p. 14; cf. Kohlberg, 1981; Power & Kohlberg, 1980). This thesis creates the expectation that moral judgment scores will always be higher than or equal to faith development scores.

The necessary-but-not-sufficient thesis was tested by comparing the moral and faith stage scores for each subject. As Table 11.5 shows, in 41.6% of the cases ($n = 25$), subjects received the same moral development and faith development stage scores; 26.6% of the subjects ($n = 16$) scored higher in moral than in

TABLE 11.4.
Distributions of Faith Development Stage Scores: Comparisons Between Kibbutz Founders and Other Adult Religious Populations

Samples[a] (Age Range) N (Source)	Global Faith Stage Scores in Percentages									Mean Ranked
	1/2	2	2/3	3	3/4	4	4/5	5	6	
Protestant: selected church leaders (adults) N = 10 (Simmonds, 1986)				10.0	0.0	30.0	20.0	40.0		4.40
Protestant[b] (41-60+) N = 26 (Fowler, 1981)				3.8	7.7	42.3	19.2	26.9		4.29
Nontheists; Israeli city Judiasm (51-57) N = 18 (present study)				11.1	5.6	44.4	11.1	27.8		4.19
Nontheists; North American Judaism (52-57) N = 21 (present study)				19.0	4.8	42.9	23.8	9.5		4.00
Protestant; senior adults (50-80+) N = 16 (Shulik, 1979)				12.5	18.8	43.8	18.8	6.2		3.94
Protestant; primarily upper class (19-60+) N = 64 (Bradley, 1983)				12.5	31.4	35.9	12.5	7.8		3.86
Catholic[b] (41-60+) N = 30 (Fowler, 1981)	3.3	3.3		30.0	3.3	26.7	16.7	13.3	3.3	3.85
Nontheists; kibbutz Judaism (51-56) N = 21 (present study)				23.8	14.3	42.9	9.5	9.5		3.83
Buddhist (Jodoshinushu); Japanese- or Chinese-Hawaiians (28-59) N = 12 (Furushima, 1983)				33.3	16.7	25.0	8.3	16.7		3.79
Jewish senior adults (50-80+) N = 13 (Shulik, 1979)				23.1	30.8	30.8	0.0	15.4		3.77
Catholic and Greek Orthodox, senior adults; (50-80+) N = 11 (Shulik, 1979)				45.5	0.0	27.3	9.1	18.2		3.77
Protestant[b] (21-40) N = 45 (Fowler, 1981)				28.9	24.4	28.9	11.1	6.7		3.71
Catholic[b] (21-40) N = 38 (Fowler, 1981)				31.6	23.7	31.6	5.3	7.9		3.67
Protestant, Catholic, and Jewish; Canadians, most college-educated (20-35) N = 30 (Mischey, 1976)				13.3	13.3	40.0	20.0	13.3		3.53
Catholic; college students (18-22+) N = 33 (White, 1985)				54.5	21.2	24.2				3.38
Catholic; para-professionals (35-45) N = 27 (Bassett, 1985)				61.5	23.1	15.4				3.27
Protestant; para-professionals (35-45) N = 27) (Bassett, 1985)		3.7	0.0	59.3	22.2	11.1	3.7			3.24
Protestant; church nonleaders (adults) N = 10 (Simmonds, 1986)				70.0	20.0	10.0				3.20

(Continued)

TABLE 11.4.
(*Continued*)

Thomas Christian; lower and middle class, Chavakkad, India (22-78) N = 30 (Kalam, 1981)			3.3	0.0	86.7	0.0	10.0	3.07
Hindu; lower and middle class, Chavakkad, India (21-66) N = 30 (Kalam, 1981)			6.7	0.0	76.7	6.7	10.0	3.07
Protestant; halfway-house residents (21-48) N = 23 (Morgan, 1989)		8.7	13.0	74.0	0.0	0.0	4.3	2.93
Muslim; lower and middle class, Chavakkad, India (21-75) N = 30 (Kalam, 1981)	6.7	10.0	13.3	53.3	10.0	6.7		2.85

Note. [a] Unless otherwise indicated, Ss were living in the continental United States.
[b]The figures for Fowler's study are somewhat different than previously reported (1981) because Fowler originally included subjects from other studies that are reported separately in the above table.

faith development; and 31.6% of the subjects ($n = 19$) scored higher in faith development than in moral development.

If one still wished to defend the necessary-but-not-sufficient thesis in spite of these findings, one might argue that the kibbutz findings are inevitable if Fowler's construct confounds moral and religious development. Such an argument would, of course, be inconsistent with the results of the previous analyses regarding structural wholeness, which supported the understanding there is a general dimension of faith development that is not aspect-specific. Nevertheless, to address this possible critique, the faith development scores for all subjects in this study were recalculated without regard to their scores on Aspect C, Faith Ethics. The resulting faith development stage scores were then again cross-tabulated with moral development stage scores. Similar to the pattern previously reported in Table 11.5, 38.3% of the subjects ($n = 23$) received the same moral

TABLE 11.5.
Cross-Tabulation of Subjects' Faith and Moral Stage Scores

	Moral Stages					
Faith Stages	3	3/4	4	4/5	5	N
3	3	5	2	1		11
3/4		4	1			5
4		8	11	7		26
4/5		2	3	4		9
5			3	3	3	9
N	3	19	20	15	3	60

Note. Pearson's $r = .597$; Spearman's rho = .573.

development and faith development stage scores; 25.0% of the subjects ($n = 15$) scored higher in moral than in faith development; and 36.7% of the subjects ($n = 22$) scored higher in faith development than in moral development. The pattern of development among the kibbutz founders, in sum, provided no support for a decalage relationship between moral and faith development.

DISCUSSION

This chapter has evaluated the validity of Fowler's construct. The findings showed that although very few founders considered themselves religious in any theistic sense (5%), all of the founders spontaneously discussed topics of implicit religious relevance. Despite their consistent nontheistic stance, their faith development stage scores ranged from Stage 3 (18%) to Stage 5 (15%). The following discussion summarizes the major findings, places the results in the larger context of prior faith development research findings, and notes a number of caveats.

Structural Wholeness

The structural wholeness assumption was evaluated across four indices of internal consistency. First, the correlations between all seven aspects were positive, moderately strong, and highly significant. Overall, the correlations were not so weak as to suggest that each aspect is measuring a significantly different developmental domain, and they were not so strong as to suggest that the aspects are extremely redundant or that the measure is too narrow. Second, the reliability coefficient was quite high. Third, the eigenvalue and proportion of variance were predominately accounted for by only one general factor. Finally, no subject made use of nonadjacent stages. Although not one of these findings is definitive by itself, the composite picture resulting from all four analyses provides tentative evidence that a single construct, defining one common developmental domain, was being measured. These composite findings are still not conclusive, however. Since Fowler's standard scoring procedure directs the same rater to score all aspects for an interview, and the clinical nature of an interview generally makes it impractical to divide the interview transcript according to aspects for blinded scoring by separate raters, it is possible that the findings reflect raters' prior assumptions about the unity of the self more than they reflect the actual unity of faith. This interpretation is worthy of future research.

Criterion Validity

Do faith development stage scores effectively distinguish between variations in other relevant assessments of development, social status, or ethnic-religious status?

Developmental Criteria.   The correlations between faith development and both ego and moral development were positive and statistically significant. The strength of these correlations is comparable to the statistically significant correlations reported (or obtained by a secondary analysis of the reported data) in previous studies of the relationship between faith development several other theoretically related measures: intrinsic ego motivation ($r = .62$ to $.72$), extrinsic ego motivation ($r = -.41$ to $-.65$), internal locus of control ($r = .71$), IQ ($r = .51$), moral development ($r = .36$ to $.76$), and midlife adaptation ($r = .28$) (Bassett, 1985; Chirban, 1980; Gorman, 1977; Kalam, 1981; Mischey, 1976; Shulik, 1979). There are no known studies that report a correlation between faith development and other theoretically related measures that are in the opposite direction of the theoretical expectations.

Faith development stage scores were not significantly correlated with age in this study, apparently due to the limited age range of the adult sample (51 to 57 years). In contrast, secondary analysis of the less constrained age-by-stage distributions reported by Mischey (1976) showed that faith development was significantly correlated with age ($r = .57$, $p < .01$; stages 2/3 to 4/5 by ages 20 to 35). Similarly, secondary analysis of Fowler's (1981) original sample showed that faith development was significantly correlated with age ($r = .36$, $p < .01$; stages 1 to 6 by ages 4 to 84). In general, faith development and age are very strongly correlated during childhood and increasingly less strongly correlated during the adult years.

A major caveat related to these findings, however, is that the present data cannot directly address the issue of an invariant stage sequence. The claim of invariant sequence was indirectly supported, however, because faith development was significantly correlated with both moral development and ego development for which the claim has been previously longitudinally validated (Colby et al., 1983; Loevinger, 1979; Redmore & Loevinger, 1979). Longitudinal studies are critically needed to address directly the assumption of development through an invariant stage sequence.

Social Status Criteria.   Faith development was significantly and positively correlated with level of education, occupation, social class, and work complexity. Multiple regression analysis indicated that work complexity and education explained the most unique variance in faith development. This suggests that the association between social status and faith development is primarily due to a job's substantive intellectual complexity, rather than to its ascribed social class level. A caveat, of course, is that this study can not determine if education and working in more complex jobs lead to higher levels of faith development or if faith maturity results in one seeking more education and being matched with more complex jobs.

There were no significant differences between men and women in faith development stage scores, as expected.

Ethnic-religious Criteria. The relationship between faith development and three ethnic-religious criteria was considered: childhood family-of-origins' religious orthodoxy, adulthood community of residence, and use of ethnic-religious symbolic materials.

First, the mean level of faith development among nontheists from Orthodox families versus those from non-Orthodox families was not significantly different. However, there was little variation in the subjects' religious backgrounds; 72% came from Orthodox families.

Second, and in contrast, the mean level of faith development among the kibbutz residents was modestly but significantly lower compared with that of the Israeli city residents. The highest mean level of faith development was found among those living in the most religiously complex communities—Israeli cities, followed by those living in North American cities, with the lowest mean level of faith development found among those living in the least religiously complex communities—the kibbutz. This findings provide additional evidence that faith development as a construct should be taken seriously in that the founder residence groups, while differentiated by level of faith development, were not distinguished by level of moral or ego development. A major caveat, however, is that the lower scores of kibbutz residents compared to those of nonkibbutz residents could just as easily be interpreted as reflecting a bias of faith development theory in favor of urban communities (see Snarey & Keljo, Chapter 12 in Volume I). This interpretation is worthy of future research.

The third ethnic-religious variable appraises the symbolic atmosphere of their homes in terms of the use of ethnic-religious symbols. All subjects used artifacts to communicate their ethnic-religious heritage to their house guests. Yet, the mean level of faith development among subjects who primarily used unobtrusive, metaphorical symbols was significantly higher than that of subjects who primarily used conspicuous-literal symbols.

A general caveat here is that all three socioreligious indices in use are not optimal criteria. More adequate criteria for future research would include independent assessments of religious or spiritual maturity or a procedure whereby the larger community would nominate exemplars of mature faith. Nevertheless, the pattern of association between individuals' faith development and their homes' symbolic atmosphere, introduced in the present study, has the important advantage of being based on observed artifacts that are based on outcomes of actual ethnic-religious behavior rather than on self-reported backgrounds.

Universality

The assumption of universality was addressed by asking if the level of faith development among nontheists was significantly different from the level of faith development among theists from other socioreligious groups. The present findings were compared with the results from representative studies of adults from 7 other religious groups. The comparisons showed that sampled individuals who scored lower than the nontheists were always younger adults or adults who represented a deficit characteristic (e.g., nonleaders, halfway-house residents, lower class). Groups scoring higher than the nontheistic kibbutz founders were always older or intentionally selected elites (e.g., leaders, upper-class professionals). The nontheists' scores compared very favorably with similarly aged or older Protestant, Catholic, Jewish, and other theistic religious groups. It appears that Fowler's model and measure is able to capture the thinking of persons whose religious orientation and background is quite different from those of his original sample. In this study, that is, the faith of non-Christians was not undervalued by Fowler's model.

Despite the supportive nature of these findings regarding universality, two caveats must be noted. First, drawing conclusions based on comparisons between small, often nonrandom, and globally defined samples is fraught with difficulties. Second, faith development research has not been conducted in a sufficiently wide range of socioreligious populations to jeopardize adequately this assumption. In general, future research should directly address the primary sociological critiques of faith development theory—that it is biased in favor of subjects from urban communities, advantaged social classes, and liberal Protestant denominations. In particular, as Parks (1988) and Power (1988) have correctly noted, Stage 6 has been a rare empirical phenomena: one Catholic senior adult in the study reported by Fowler (1981), no subjects in any of the other previously published studies, and, of course, no subjects in the present study. Currently, the highest stage in Fowler's model seems to have the same status as the highest stage in Kohlberg's model; it is a philosophical extension of the theory that has not been empirically established. Interviews with religious elites from non-Western religions are particularly needed. The empirical exploration of the highest stage will, no doubt, result in significant expansions. For instance, the claim that persons at Stage 6 extend an "inclusive" awareness or regard to all of "humankind or Being" (Fowler, 1984, p. 68; Moseley et al., 1986, p. 180) could be expanded when confronted with, for instance, an Indian Jain notion of the unity of all of life, humankind or nonhumankind.

Faith and Moral Development

This study evaluated Fowler's thesis that faith development encompasses but is not solely determined by moral development. As previously discussed, Kohlberg has offered the reasonable alternative conjecture that moral judgment development is a necessary but not sufficient condition for the development of the parallel stage of faith development. In this study, level of faith development was associated with but not systematically dependent on level of moral development. Post-hoc analysis, deleting Aspect C or Faith Ethics from the averaging procedure used to calculate global faith development stage scores, did not alter the findings. Among the five previous pilot studies of the relationship between scores on Kohlberg's moral judgment interview and Fowler's faith development interview, four studies (80%) have provided either contradictory evidence (Gorman, 1977; Mischey, 1976) or no support (Kalam, 1981; Shulik, 1979), and one study (20%) has provided modest support (Power & Kohlberg, 1980).

Fowler's (1980) own theoretical response to the decalage thesis was that faith development is a more comprehensive construct that includes (but is not dependent upon) moral development. This thesis creates the expectation that there will be a relatively close relationship between subjects' faith and moral stages but that it will not be characterized by a decalage pattern. Fowler's position is consistent with the present findings.

There are alternatives to both Kohlberg's decalage hypothesis and Fowler's parallel hypothesis, however. One is that a decalage relationship only occurs at the highest stages; this would be consistent with Kohlberg's speculations on the further reaches of moral maturity and on the role of faith development as a replacement for cognitive developmental distinctions during adulthood. In the present sample, for instance, six people achieved Stage 5 in faith development without achieving Stage 5 in moral development, but no one achieved Stage 5 in moral development without also achieving Stage 5 in faith development. The present data, that is, appear to show that Stage 5 faith development may be necessary, but not sufficient, for the achievement of Stage 5 in moral development; this is the opposite of Kohlberg's decalage thesis, but it is consistent with some of his other speculations on the role of religion in moral maturity.

A second alternative is that the relationship between faith and moral development varies across the life span. A similar decalage relationship, for instance, was originally hypothesized for ego and moral development, but an analysis of the combined data from nine previous studies showed that the relationship varied across the life span (Lee & Snarey, 1988): During adolescence, the typical youth scored at a higher stage of ego than moral development; by middle adulthood the levels of ego and moral development were usually parallel; and, during the mature years, stage of moral development was typically higher than that of ego development. Similarly, the existence of a simple decalage relationship between faith and moral development across the entire life span seems unlikely, but a more complex patterning that varies with social age or psychological stage is possible.

Conclusion

When one stops to reflect on the impact of Kohlberg's work, it is striking that "so many scholars in many branches of the social sciences, philosophy, and theology claim that he was the most influential person in their intellectual development" (Rest, Power, & Brabeck, 1988, p. 400). James Fowler (1988) has suggested that "without [Lawrence Kohlberg] it is clear that there would have been no theory of faith development" (p. 3). This study has reported a series of analyses designed to test psychometrically the basic assumptions underlying Fowler's construct. The results, taken together, lend tentative support to the power and generality of the model and indicate that the degree of construct validity is adequate for research purposes. Yet there is no doubt that further examination of the validity of Fowler's construct is clearly needed.

REFERENCES

Altman, M. (1978). *Three kibbutz generations: A comparison of ego development and perception of parenting behavior.* Unpublished doctoral dissertation, Fordham University, New York.

Bar-Yam, M., & Abrahami, A. (1982). *Sex and age differences in moral reasoning of kibbutz adults.* Unpublished manuscript, Boston University, Boston, MA.

Bassett, P. (1985). *Faith development and midlife transition.* Unpublished doctoral dissertation, Baylor University, Waco, TX.

Bowes, A. (1982). Atheism in a religious society: The culture of unbelief in an Israeli kibbutz. In J. Davis (Ed.), *Religious organization and religious experience* (pp. 33–49). New York: Academic Press.

Bradley, L. (1983). *An exploration of the relationship between Fowler's theory of faith development and Myers-Briggs personality type.* Unpublished doctoral dissertation, Ohio State University, Columbus, OH.

Broughton, J. (1986). The political psychology of faith development theory. In C. Dykstra & S. Parks (Eds.), *Faith development and Fowler* (pp. 90–114). Birmingham, AL: Religious Education Press.

Buber, M. (1949). *Paths in Utopia.* Boston: Beacon Press.

Chirban, J. (1980). *Intrinsic and extrinsic motivation in faith development.* Unpublished doctoral dissertation, Harvard University, Cambridge, MA.

Colby, A., & Kohlberg, L. (1987). *The measurement of moral judgment, Volume II: Standard issue scoring manual.* New York: Cambridge University Press.

Colby, A., Kohlberg, L., Gibbs, J., & Lieberman, M. (1983). A longitudinal study of moral judgment. *Monographs of the Society for Research in Child Development, 48*(1–2), 1–124.

Cronbach, L. J., & Meehl, P. (1955). Construct validity in psychological tests. *Psychological Bulletin, 52,* 281–302.

Dykstra, C. (1981). *Vision and character.* New York: Paulist Press.

Dykstra, C., & Parks, S. (1986). *Faith development and Fowler.* Birmingham, AL: Religious Education Press.

Fernhout, J. H. (1986). Where is faith? In C. Dykstra & S. Parks (Eds.), *Faith development and Fowler* (pp. 65–89). Birmingham, AL: Religious Education Press.

Fowler, J. (1977, August). *Faith and the structuring of meaning.* Paper presented at the annual conference of the American Psychological Association, San Francisco, CA.

Fowler, J. (1978). *Faith development interview guide.* Mimeographed manuscript, Harvard University Divinity School, Cambridge, MA.

Fowler, J. (1980). Moral stages and the development of faith. In B. Munsey (Ed.), *Moral development, moral education, and Kohlberg.* Birmingham, AL: Religious Education Press.

Fowler, J. (1981). *Stages of faith: The psychology of human development and the quest for meaning.* San Francisco: Harper & Row.

Fowler, J. (1983). Stages of faith. *Psychology Today, 17*(11), 56–62.

Fowler, J. (1984). *Becoming adult, becoming Christian.* San Francisco: Harper & Row.

Fowler, J. (1988). Meditation. In J. Fowler, J. Snarey, & K. DeNicola (Eds.), *Remembrances of Lawrence Kohlberg* (pp. 1–4). Atlanta, GA: Emory University Center for Research in Faith and Moral Development.

Furushima, R. (1983). *Faith development theory: A cross-cultural research project in Hawaii.* Unpublished doctoral dissertation, Columbia University, New York.

Gorman, M. (1977). Moral and faith development in seventeen-year-old students. *Religious Education, 72*(5), 491–504.

Hennessy, J. (1976). Reaction to Fowler: Stages in faith and stages in commitment. In T. Hennessy (Ed.), *Values and moral development* (pp. 218–223). New York: Paulist Press.

Hollingshead, A. B. (1975). *Four-factor index of social status.* Working paper, Department of Sociology, Yale University, New Haven, CN.

Kalam, T. (1981). *The myth of stages and sequence in moral and religious development.* Unpublished doctoral dissertation, University of Lancaster, England.

Kegan, R. (1980). There the dance is: Religious dimensions of a developmental framework. In J. Fowler & A. Vergote (Eds.), *Toward moral and religious maturity* (pp. 403–440). Morristown, NJ: Silver Burdett.

Kline, P. (1979). *Psychometrics and psychology.* New York: Academic Press.

Kohlberg, L. (1967). Moral and religious education and the public schools: A developmental view. In T. Sizer (Ed.), *Religion and public education* (pp. 164–183). Boston, MA: Houghton Mifflin.

Kohlberg, L. (1971). Cognitive-developmental theory and the practice of collective moral education. In M. Wolins & M. Gottesman (Eds.), *Group care: An Israeli approach* (342–371). New York: Gordon & Breach.

Kohlberg, L. (1974). Education, moral development and faith. *Journal of Moral Education. 4*(1), 5–16.

Kohlberg, L. (1981). *Essays on moral development, Vol. I: The philosophy of moral development.* San Francisco: Harper & Row.

Kohlberg, L. (1984). *Essays on moral development, Vol. II: The psychology of moral development.* San Francisco: Harper & Row.

Kohn, M., & Schooler, C. (1983). *Work and personality: An inquiry into the impact of social stratification.* Norwood, NJ: Ablex.

Kwilecki, S. (1988). A scientific approach to religious development. *Journal for the Scientific Study of Religion, 27,* 307–335.

Landau, H. (1966). Jewish holidays and secularism. *Israel Horizons, 14*(8), 25–28.

Lee, L., & Snarey, J. (1988). The relationship between ego and moral development: A theoretical review and empirical analysis. In D. Lapsley & C. Power (Eds.), *Self, ego, and identity: Integrative approaches* (pp. 151–178). New York: Springer-Verlag.

Leslie, S. C. (1971). *The rift in Israel: Religious authority and secular democracy.* London: Routledge & Kegan Paul.

Lilker, S. (1982). *Kibbutz Judaism: A new tradition in the making.* New York: Herzl.

Loevinger, J. (1976). *Ego development: Conceptions and theories.* San Francisco: Jossey-Bass.

Loevinger, J. (1979). Construct validity of the sentence completion test of ego development. *Applied Psychological Measurement, 3*(3), 281–311.

Loevinger, J., & Wessler, R. (1970). *Measuring ego development I: Construction and use of a sentence completion test.* San Francisco: Jossey-Bass.

Loevinger, J., Wessler, R., & Redmore, C. (1970). *Measuring ego development II: Scoring manual for women and girls.* San Francisco: Jossey-Bass.

McBride, A. (1976). Reaction to Fowler: Tears about procedure. In T. Hennessy (Ed.), *Values and moral development* (pp. 211–217). New York: Paulist Press.

Mayers, M. K. (1974). *Christianity confronts culture.* Grand Rapids, MI: Zondervan.

Mischey, E. (1976). *Faith development and its relationship to moral reasoning and identity status in young adults.* Unpublished dissertation, University of Toronto, Toronto, Canada.

Moseley, R., Jarvis, D., & Fowler, J. W. (1986). *Manual for faith development research.* Atlanta, GA: Center for Research in Faith and Moral Development.

Morgan, P. (1989). *The faith development of women in crisis.* Unpublished doctoral dissertation, University of Houston, TX.

Nipkow, K., Schweitzer, F., & Fowler, J. (Eds.). (1988). *Faith and religious development: Critical and constructive engagements.* Gutersloh, W. Germany: Gutersloher Verlagshaus Gerd Mohn. (German)

Oser, F. (1980). Stages of religious judgment. In J. Fowler & A. Vergote (Eds.), *Toward moral and religious maturity* (pp. 277–315). Morristown, NJ: Silver Burdett.

Parks, S. (1988). A summary of the main points of the North American critique of James Fowler's theory of faith development. In K. Nipkow, F. Schweitzer, & J. Fowler (Eds.), *Faith and religious development: Critical and constructive engagements* (pp. 91–107). Gutersloh, W. Germany: Gutersloher Verlagshaus Gerd Mohn. (German)

Power, C. (1988). Hard versus soft stages of faith and religious develoment: A Piagetian critique. In K. Nipkow, F. Schweitzer, & J. Fowler (Eds.), *Faith and religious development: Critical and constructive engagements* (pp. 108–123). Gutersloh, W. Germany: Gutersloher and Verlagshaus Gerd Mohn. (German)

Power, C., & Kohlberg, L. (1980). Religion, morality, and ego development. In J. Fowler & A. Vergote (Eds.), *Toward moral and religious maturity* (pp. 343–372). Morristown, NJ: Silver Burdett.

Redmore, C., & Loevinger, J. (1979). Ego development in adolescence: Longitudinal studies. *Journal of Youth and Adolescence, 8*(1), 1–20.

Reisberg, J. (1978). *A comparison of attitudes toward personal, social, national, and religious factors of selected non-kibbutz high school students and kibbutz high school students.* Unpublished doctoral dissertation, New York University.

Rest, J., Power, C., & Brabeck, M. (1988). Lawrence Kohlberg, 1927–1987. *American Psychologist, 43*(5), 399–400.

Rubin, N. (1986). Death customs in a non-religious kibbutz: The use of sacred symbols in a secular society. *Journal for the Scientific Study of Religion, 25*(3), 292–303.

Shulik, R. (1979). *Faith development, moral development, and old age: An assessment of Fowler's faith development paradigm.* Unpublished doctoral dissertation, University of Chicago, Chicago, IL.

Simmonds, R. (1986). *Content and structure in faith develoment.* Unpublished doctoral dissertation. Southern Baptist Theological Seminary, Louisville, KY.

Smith, M. E. (1983). Developments in faith. *The Month, 16,* 222–225.

Snarey, J. (1985). Cross-cultural universality of social-moral development. *Psychological Bulletin, 97,* 202–232.

Snarey, J. (1988, August). The faith development of kibbutz founders: Case studies in kibbutz Judaism. Invited address delivered at the 96th Annual Convention of the American Psychological Association, Atlanta, GA.

Snarey, J., & Blasi, J. (1980). Ego development among adult kibbutzniks: A cross-cultural application of Loevinger's theory. *Genetic Psychology Monographs, 102,* 117–157.

Snarey, J., Reimer, J., & Kohlberg, L. (1985). The development of social-moral reasoning among kibbutz adolescents: A longitudinal cross-cultural study. *Developmental Psychology, 20*(1), 3–17. (a)

Webb, E., Campbell, D., Schwartz, R., & Sechrest, L. (1966). *Unobtrusive measures: Nonreactive research in the social sciences.* Chicago: Rand McNally.

Webster, D. H. (1984). James Fowler's theory of faith development. *British Journal of Religious Education, 7,* 14–18.

White, V. (1985). *Faith stages, affiliation, and gender.* Unpublished doctoral dissertation, Boston University, Boston, MA.

12

Social Contexts in Social Cognitive Development

Elliot Turiel
Judith G. Smetana
Melanie Killen

ABSTRACT

This chapter addresses the role of social context in social cognitive development.
It is proposed that analyses of social contexts should include distinctions in social
environmental components corresponding to differentiations in domains of social
judgment. It is shown that global characterizations of the cultural ethos of this
society yield conflicting portrayals. Whereas some assert that the central ethos of
this culture is individualism, others claim that the culture is exemplified by a
bureaucratic mentality of other-directedness. We propose that these opposing
views reflect stereotypes that fail to capture the heterogeneous social orientations
of persons in this culture. We further propose a "domain-specific" view of social
contexts to avoid the stereotyping inherent in global characterizations of culture.
Evidence for these propositions comes from several research traditions. We also
discuss recent supporting research on social interactions in early childhood and on
children's judgments about moral issues and interpersonal relationships.

Individualism is all the rage—in two respects. Many social scientists currently assert that our culture is individualistic at its core. And many social
scientists rage at individualism because they view it as a major source of moral
crisis in the society. It has become commonplace to portray this culture as
characterized by an ethos of individualism and the psychology of persons in the
culture as oriented to self-sufficiency, personal goals, autonomy, and detachment from others. Frequently invoked to illustrate the cultural ethos are the
metaphors of the cowboy and the entrepreneur as lone, rugged, self-sustained

individuals struggling for self-promotion against others or the society (cf. Kessen, 1979). The ethos of individualism is not solely presented as a social scientific description of the culture. Many who believe that the culture is highly individualistic also believe that individualism is largely responsible for what is perceived to be a state of moral decay in the society and collapse of social institutions (Bellah, Madsen, Sullivan, Swidler, & Tipton, 1985; Hogan, 1975; Sampson, 1977, 1978).

The proposition that there is a cultural ethos of individualism follows a tradition of social scientific thought that presumes cultures are largely global and homogeneous contexts from which persons acquire their personal dispositions and social orientations. It is rather telling, however, that in the not too distant past the dominant personal dispositions and social orientations of members of this culture were frequently described in terms opposite to individualism. From the 1940s through the early 1960s it was commonplace to portray American culture as populated by dependent, conformist persons primarily oriented to fitting into their immediate group and society at-large. This theme was evident in literature and the folk wisdom of the time. Probably the best known example is the portrayal of the lack of freedom and originality in the central character of Arthur Miller's *Death of a Salesman*. Similarly, in a folk song made popular by Pete Seeger we hear about the sameness of life in this society:

> Little boxes on the hillside, Little boxes made of ticky tacky. Little boxes on the hillside. . . . And they all look just the same. And the people in the houses, all went to the university; where they were put in boxes, and they came out all the same. And there's doctors and there's lawyers, and business executives; And they're all made of ticky tacky. And they all look just the same.

The portrayals in literature and folk songs were in accordance with those of social scientists, whose writings were popularly embraced. As examples, C. Wright Mills (1956) wrote about white-collar people as interchangeable links in social organization; William Whyte (1956) wrote about the *organization man* whose life revolves around the corporation; and David Riesman (Riesman, Glazer, & Denney, 1953) characterized the other-directed types who are part of *The Lonely Crowd*. In Whyte's view, this society is dominated by those who "take the vows of organization life" and "are the mind and soul of our great, self-perpetuating institutions." He perceived a deification in this society of collectivism that went well beyond the employees of corporations to include those in the church hierarchy, the medical world, the legal system, science, and intellectuals (1956, p. 3).

The paucity of freedom, personal control, assertiveness or creativity—that is, of individualism—in this society was also described by Mills. He suggested that the idea of self-centered, entrepreneurial individualism is more myth than reality. As he articulated it (1956, p. xv):

> By examining white-collar life, it is possible to learn something about what is becoming more typically "American" than the frontier character probably ever

was. What must be grasped is the picture of society as a great salesroom, an enormous file, an incorporated brain, a new universe of management and manipulation.

For social commentators such as Mills, Whyte, and Riesman, individuals, rather than being self-contained, independent, and self-motivated, are impersonal parts of social organizations.

During the 1950s and 1960s, many decried the cultural ethos that placed the organization and society above the individual. It was complained (see especially Whyte, 1956) that the subordination of the individual to the society and its institutions was justified on the false grounds that the collectivity, rather than individuals, is the source of creativity, that individuals derive meaning only through group participation and collaboration, and that individuals can best attain fulfillment through group participation.

Whereas 30 or 40 years ago it was often claimed that the cultural ethos is one of conformity and individual subordination to the group and that it had negative societal consequences, it is now often claimed that the cultural ethos is one of self-contained individualism that produces moral degeneration in the society. Individualism pervades all sectors of the society, including and especially the public media, religious leaders, the scientific community, and those in academic institutions (Sampson, 1978). It is said that the dominant temper of the society emphasizes detachment and self-promotion at the expense of the group and even ultimately the well-being of the individual. It is complained (see especially Hogan, 1975, and Sampson, 1977) that the subordination of the group to the individual is justified on the false grounds that independence and separation are the best routes toward personal fulfillment and the welfare of society.

How can it be that we are presented with such diametrically opposed cultural characterizations within a relatively short time span? The answer is not that contemporary social scientists are describing shifts in the cultural ethos over the past 20 or 30 years. These characterizations are meant to reflect deep-seated, firmly rooted, and longstanding cultural orientations. Moreover, the very idea of cultural orientations that pervade the psychology of its members is tied to a conception of cultural contexts as resistant to rapid shifts. One plausible answer is that these characterizations are stereotypes of cultures which fail to capture the multifaceted orientations of societies and the heterogeneous social concerns of individuals. As discussed elsewhere (Turiel, 1989a, 1989b; Turiel, Killen, & Helwig, 1987), characterizing individuals in global, one-dimensional terms (e.g., individualistic vs. conformist; independent vs. interdependent) fails to account for the mixture of social judgments, actions, and concerns of persons within culture. Individuals hold, as the anthropologist Malinowski pointed out a long time ago (1926), a mixture of social concerns that manifest themselves in individualism and collectivism, as well as independence and interdependence. In addition, individuals make judgments about the necessity to uphold personal rights or freedoms in certain situations, and to subordinate individual goals to the welfare of the group in other situations.

A related reason for the existence of opposing characterizations is that they stem from a conception of the social environment as a homogeneous cultural context from which individuals acquire their equally homogeneous social orientations. A typical manifestation of this approach in empirical research is to compare the moral judgments and practices of persons from different cultural groups. The quest in such studies is for uniformity within groups and variation between groups that could be attributed to individuals' acquisitions through the transmission of a general cultural orientation or ethos (for an example, see Nisan, 1987, and for further discussion of the shortcoming of the approach, see Turiel, Nucci, & Smetana, 1988). A major proposition upon which we elaborate in subsequent sections is that a characterization of culture as a general context is both too global and too restricted a view of social environments to provide the basis for an adequate way of explaining the role of contexts in the development of moral and social judgments. The globality of the construct of a homogenous or unitary "cultural" context renders it too restricted because it fails to account for the variety of different types of social contexts that are experienced by individuals within a society. A more differentiated conception of social context that accounts for within-culture heterogeneity in social experiences needs to be connected to heterogeneity in individuals' social judgments and practices. Before considering these features of heterogeneity in judgments and experiences, we discuss evidence from several sources showing that social contexts are not of one kind.

VARIATIONS IN CONTEXTUAL INFLUENCES

Research from disparate theoretical perspectives provides evidence that context affects individuals' judgments and behavior. However, these research findings also show that it is not broad cultural variations that make for such differences. Rather, variations in behaviors and judgments appear to be based on the individual in interaction with differentiated contexts within culture. A first set of examples come from research from a behavioristic perspective—a perspective that most clearly relies on the proposition that situations or stimuli are the determinants of responses. From the viewpoint of learning theories that explain stimulus–response connections as a function of reinforcement, it might be expected that, once learned, different presentations of a stimulus would produce the same response. As cogently analyzed by Gewirtz, this is not often the case:

> It would be unnecessary to consider the context of stimulus provision if successive presentations of a stimulus were to lead to the same response. However, this

homogeneity in responding is rare, and it is therefore important to consider the conditions under which a stimulus has a certain impact on behavior. (1972, p. 9)

Gewirtz has shown that a variety of social contextual conditions in which stimuli are embedded serve to produce shifts in responses to the stimuli. A few examples of contextual features of stimuli can serve to illustrate the phenomenon. It has been found, for instance, that personal or social attributes of the source of stimulation can alter responses. These include gender, social role, social status, and popularity. For example, reinforcement from an adult has been found to be less effective with children of the opposite sex than of the same sex. As another illustration, it has been found that verbal reinforcement from another child is less effective when that child is popular. An adult's proximity and attentiveness to a child also has a bearing on the child's responses. Specifically, in experimental situations children seek more social contact with an adult who is busy and distant than from one who is attentive and close. Previous experiences also serve as contexts that produce variations in responses to similar stimuli. Children's learning of a task is more positively influenced by verbal approval from an adult when it is preceded by social isolation than when preceded by social contact. Similarly, whether a neutral reaction from an adult experimenter is experienced as positive or negative reinforcement depends on preceding events. It is positive reinforcement when preceded by verbal disapproval and negative reinforcement when preceded by verbal approval.

Along with many other examples of this sort, Gewirtz's review of experiments on processes of conditioning show that variations in the surrounding conditions of a stimulus are associated with response variations. In demonstrating the lack of consistency or homogeneity in responses to successive presentations of a stimulus, Gewirtz revealed a facet of findings from the literature on conditioning that was generally unrecognized. In contrast, social psychological research is often aimed at demonstrating how experimental manipulations of the situation or context result in behavioral shifts (Brown & Herrnstein, 1975; Nisbett & Ross, 1980). A number of such experiments show not only that behavior can vary by context, but also that individuals display both individualistic and conformist or collectivistic orientations. These studies include bystander intervention (or lack thereof) of another in need of help (Latane & Darley, 1970), vandalism (Zimbardo, 1969), roles played in simulated prison settings (Haney, Banks, & Zimbardo, 1973), conformity with group judgments (Asch, 1956), and obedience to authority (Milgram, 1974).

The findings from all these and other research programs demonstrate the influence of context. We consider two examples: The first comes from studies in which subjects were placed into a small-group situation where their task was to compare the lengths of lines (Asch, 1956). Several confederates of the experimenter in the group provided incorrect judgments prior to the actual subjects' judgment regarding the lengths of the lines. It was found that a large number of the non-confederates conformed with the group and themselves gave the incorrect response. However, variations in the experimental conditions produced shifts in the number of subjects conforming with the group. As examples, shifts in subject's responses occurred when there was a change in the number of confederates giving a correct response (one person giving a correct response decreased conformity) and when the difficulty of the task was altered (the more difficult the task, the greater the conformity). An interesting comparison with the type of conformity obtained in the Asch experiments is what occurs in experiments on bystander intervention. In several experimental situations, Latane and Darley (1970) found that a bystander was more likely to help when he or she was alone in observing the event than when a number of other potential helpers were present. It seems, then, that even when the behavior has moral relevance, individual initiative is taken in some situations and not in others.

More serious forms of conformity and seemingly faceless, bureaucratic, organizational mentality and other-directedness come from Milgram's laboratory experiments. These experiments showed large numbers of persons adhering to an experimenter's terse and sharply worded instructions to inflict intense, and presumably dangerous physical harm on another. In the guise of a learning experiment, subjects were told by an experimenter to administer increasing levels of electric shock. In certain well-known experimental conditions (especially Milgram, 1963), the majority of subjects continued obeying the experimenter to the highest intensity of shock available. Equally dramatic, however, are the findings from other experimental conditions with altered situational contexts. In several of those conditions the majority of subjects did not display an organizational mentality and, instead, defied the authority by refusing to inflict harm upon another person. These experimental variations included changes in the proximity of the subject to the victim or to the authority.

Research on very young children's social interactions also shows the influences of contexts. As reviewed elsewhere (Turiel et al., 1987), it has been found that toddlers display varying social competencies in different contexts. Whereas with their parents toddlers manifest early forms of moral behaviors (e.g., helping, sharing), they appear to lack the ability to establish such reciprocal relations in their peer interactions. However, toddlers do show more of these behaviors when they have had a fair amount of previous contact and familiarity with peers.

In one of our recent studies (Killen, 1987) we examined ways in which young children structure their interactions and resolve conflicts in two settings: peer group and free play at school. The peer group settings entailed focused interactions among a few children in the absence of adult supervision, whereas the free play was supervised by adults. Differences in social interactions between the two settings were observed. For instance, there were more conflicts among the children during free play than in the peer-group setting; and the conflicts were resolved in different ways. In the peer-group setting children showed that they were able to, on their own, generate ways of resolving conflicts. In contrast, in the free-play setting the children most often looked to adults to resolve conflicts for them.

It has also been found that naturally-occurring differences in social and physical contexts influence children's cognitive development. Hollos (1987) examined children's performance on measures of social cognition (role-taking and communication) and logical-physical cognition (measures of classification and conservation of quantity). The children were from Norway and Hungary and resided on farms, as well as rural village and town settings. The farm children lived in dispersed rural communities in which little peer interaction occurred since the families were geographically separate. By contrast, the villages and towns were densely settled, with children experiencing a good deal of peer interaction. The comparative findings for the three settings were similar in Norway and Hungary. On the social cognitive tasks of role-taking and communication abilities, the performance of the village and town children was better than that of the farm children. However, the farm children performed as well as or better than the other two groups on the logical-physical tasks. Since the groups were comparable on most social and cultural dimensions, the latter finding indicates that the more socially isolated setting of the farm children included levels of experiences, greater than in the other setting, which serve to stimulate development in the logical-physical realms of thought.

The findings we have reviewed from behavioristic, social psychological, and developmental perspectives document that contextual variations do influence behavior. The findings also demonstrate the coexistence of behaviors that appear individualistic and collectivistic. Interpretation of these findings is not as straightforward as it might appear. The empirical phenomena, in themselves, might seem to indicate that situations or contexts mechanically elicit behaviors. In turn, this can be generalized to mean that individuals accommodate to the social environment and thereby acquire cultural patterns. However, the very findings of shifts in responses by context suggests the alternative interpretation that there is an intersection of the individual and context, which needs to include analyses of how individuals make inferences or construe situational parameters. The findings of response variability suggest that individuals systematically make different inferences about different situations and that individuals do not acquire anything like generalized cultural patterns.

As a means toward explaining these interpretations we first consider another set of studies by Asch (1952) that examined cognitive inferences about stimuli with varying contextual features. The context for Asch's research was a commonly observed phenomenon, documented by research, that positive and negative evaluations of statements made by public figures are affected by the prestige of persons making the utterances. Asch challenged the view that the affective evaluation of the statement is determined by an arbitrary association with the strength of affect linked to the person making it. Instead, through some interesting experimental manipulations and direct study of the meanings attributed by individuals, Asch was able to demonstrate that changes in contexts can change the meaning of the situation. Subjects were presented with a series of statements along with a name of its author and asked to describe the meaning of the statement. One such statement was the following by Thomas Jefferson: "I hold it that a little rebellion, now and then, is a good thing, and as necessary in the political world as storms are in the physical." Some subjects were told that the statement was authored by Jefferson, while others were told it was authored by Lenin. Changing the authorship of the statement changed its context in that subjects interpreted the meaning by assimilating it into their understandings of the more general views and perspectives of the respective authors. One subject for instance, interpreted the Jefferson statement as follows, "by rebellion he means alertness and the exercise of rights." In contrast, another subject interpreted the "Lenin" statement to mean he was "justifying the Russian Revolution and probably all revolutions as a potential source of good." For the majority of subjects the mention of the term rebellion in the statement was taken to refer, in the case of Lenin, to revolution, and in the case of Jefferson, to conflict toward peaceful change in political control.

Using this type of procedure for several statements (e.g., a statement about capitalism attributed to the president of the U.S. Chamber of Commerce or to a union leader; an election platform attributed to the Republican or Democratic party), it was found that subjects actively interpreted the statements by imposing previous knowledge about the author upon its content. As Asch (1952, p. 422) concluded:

> The outstanding fact about the reactions is that the statement is not simply the "same" under the two conditions, at least not for most persons. The effect of changing the authorship has been to *alter the cognitive content* of the statement. The individual has usually assimilated the passage to his understanding of the actual or assumed author. (emphasis in original)

The research by Asch shows that a stimulus is part of a whole. That is, from the perspective of active construction of meaning by the individual a stimulus can take on different definitions by virtue of its place in a larger context. The emphasis on the meaning attributed to the situation should not be taken to imply that judgments of events are entirely subjective. Rather, both cognitive inferences about events and the content of events need to be taken into account. In accounting for this interaction, Asch's findings showed that variations in contexts serve to change the nature of the situation.

Although the conditioning and social psychological experiments discussed earlier only assessed shifts in behavior, it is likely that subjects made interpretations of the situations and that the behavioral shifts by context were associated with shifts in meanings attributed to the different situations (see Asch, 1956, for such an interpretation of his conformity studies). We can illustrate how this may be the case for the Milgram experiments. The Milgram studies actually point to a more complex picture of context than we have presented thus far because most of the experimental conditions included at least two separable contextual elements in conflict with each other. Embedded within the experimental situation is what we have previously (Turiel & Smetana, 1984) referred to as a moral context and a social organizational context. By the moral context we are referring to the issues faced by subjects regarding inflicting harm upon another person (shocking the victim). The social organizational context was established by the implicit rules and explicit authority commands that were part of the social system established in the experimental situation (including the scientific aims and legitimacy of the task).

These two components were placed in conflict in that subjects had to make a forced choice between them. In order to avoid inflicting harm, it would be necessary to disrupt the social organization of the experiment. In order to avoid disrupting the experiment it would be necessary to inflict harm. Indeed, there is good indication that subjects attended to both components or contexts (Milgram, 1974). Subjects who went along with the authority and continued shocking did so with reluctance, vacillation, and they expressed concern with the other person's welfare. Similarly, those who refused to shock did so with reluctance to disrupt the experiment or defy the authority. These two components, therefore, can be seen as two social contexts embedded in one situation about which subjects made inferences. This constitutes a complex coordination problem entailing conflicts between moral judgments (regarding harm) and understandings of social organization (Turiel & Smetana, 1984). Following Asch's analyses, it is plausible to propose that the different experimental conditions produced changes in the situation from the viewpoint of meanings attributed to it by subjects. As an example, some of the changes in the experimental conditions that essentially rendered the social organizational component less central or salient resulted in greater willingness to defy the authority in order to avoid inflicting harm upon another.

CONTEXT AND CULTURAL DETERMINISM

As can be seen in our analysis of the parameters of the Milgram experimental conditions, the evidence on contextual variations suggests that we need to investigate the different types or domains of judgment that individuals bring to bear on situations. This is in keeping with the position put forth by Asch that changes in the context for an event serve to change the event or "object of judgment." In contrast, however, findings of contextual variations often are assumed to support the proposition that children acquire their social judgments and behaviors through cultural transmission. The line of thought in this regard is that shifts in behavior by context demonstrate the force of situational determinants of behavior, which in turn is taken to be part of a more general explanation of children's development as an accommodation to the social environment. Cultures as global and homogeneous contexts are regarded as a primary force for the acquisition or learning of social practices—especially in the realm of moral norms.

The juxtaposition of contextualism or situationalism with cultural determinism of moral development can be seen in the application of principles from operant conditioning (Skinner, 1971), social learning theory (Bandura, 1977; Bandura & McDonald, 1963; Mischel & Mischel, 1976), and most recently in explanations of acquisition through social communication (Shweder, 1986; Shweder, Mahapatra, & Miller, 1987). However, the juxtaposition of contextual or situational determinants with cultural determinism entails putting together two propositions that may be in contradiction with each other. On one side of the equation, contextual variations in social behaviors are expected; they are explained as due to the individual's accommodation to situational contingencies. As stressed by Mischel (1969), from a social learning perspective ". . . one should not expect social behaviors to be consistent unless the relevant social learning and cognitive conditions are arranged to maintain the behavior cross-situationally" (p. 1014). Mischel also stressed the likelihood that children experience changes in situational contingencies:

> For example, what happens when the mother-dependent child finds that his preschool peers now consistently have little patience for his whining, attention-getting bids, and instead respect independence and self-confidence? Generally the child's behavior changes in accord with the new contingencies, and if the contingencies shift so does the behavior—if the contingencies remain stable so does the new syndrome that the child now displays. (1969, p. 1017)

The position is consistent insofar as behavioral specificity is seen to be determined by situational contingencies (though we offer a different interpretation of the findings). The inconsistency comes when situational determinism is combined with the more general proposition that there are cultural patterns or homogeneous orientations acquired by children. As an example, it has been proposed, in keeping with the theme of individualism, that the morality of Western culture is "rights-based," emphasizing individual rights and personal freedoms, while in other, divergent cultures (such as that of India) morality is "duty-based," emphasizing a commitment to the social order, rules, and particular duties (see the social communication view of Shweder, 1986, and his colleagues). These cultural (and cross-cultural) propositions are *consistent* with the proposed mechanism of acquisition as accommodation to the social situation but *inconsistent* with the propositions of behavioral specificity, contextual variations, and changing contingencies. They are also inconsistent with the findings on contextual variations in behavior and judgment. Homogeneity in responses —of the sort Gewirtz (1972) and Mischel (1969) claim is rare—would be required to provide support for the view that there is a general cultural scheme acquired by children.

Furthermore, it is expected that a general cultural scheme would be applied across situations.

It should now be evident that there are empirical and conceptual bases for our earlier assertion that the notion of culture as a homogeneous environmental context is both too global and too restricted to explain the sources of social judgments and behaviors. The concept is too global to account for differentiations in the social environment that make for the types of contextual variations evident in the research discussed thus far. As the evidence clearly shows, we cannot speak of a general cultural context that determines the social orientations of its members. By virtue of its globality, the concept of culture is restrictive in that it does not allow for delineation of the rich variety of social contexts within cultures. The point can be made more concretely with regard to the specific characterizations of this culture as individualistic or bureaucratic and conformist. The evidence indicates that persons in this society hold a mixture of these orientations, which are manifested in different behavioral contexts. The globality of the notion that cultures and persons are individualistic or conformist or collectivistic serves to restrict examination of the heterogeneity of these orientations. That is, a concentration on one set of characteristics may have narrowed the focus, such that the other coexisting characteristics were left unattended. Perhaps it is the very coexistence of different types of behaviors in different contexts that has produced the diametrically opposed characterizations of this culture. On the initial assumption that there is a general homogeneous cultural orientation, researchers may then generalize from only one type of empirically observed behavior.

We are not proposing that individuals respond differentially and mechanically to any shift in the situation. Rather, we propose that there are systematic connections between persons' differentiated conceptual structures and differentiated situational contexts in the environment. As noted earlier, situations as "objects of judgments," to use Asch's terminology, can change when placed in a different context. The idea that the event itself undergoes transformations is sensible only when the person's interpretations and inferences about it are taken into account. Asch (1952) labeled this process as "relational determination." This concept is interactional in that it is premised on the idea that the influence of the situation on behavior cannot be analyzed or specified without reference to the meanings attributed to it. From this "interactional" perspective, therefore, it is necessary to consider the different ways individuals perceive and interpret their environments. That is, there is heterogeneity in judgments as well as in components of the environment. This calls for two types of what can be referred to as domain-specific analyses. The first is the now familiar analyses of domain-specifity in judgments. Our own research has extensively examined domain-specifity in social judgments—with an emphasis on the domains of morality and social convention (see next section). Perhaps less familiar is the possibility that something akin to domain-specificity is applicable to analyses of the social environment. Distinctions in domains of judgment and differentiations in social situations provide a basis for an interactional position on the relationship between the individual and context.

The idea of domain-specificity in the environment has been at least alluded to by several researchers taking a cognitive and interactional approach. The essence of the idea is that systematic distinctions among components of experience can be mapped onto distinctions in types of judgments. Piaget (1970), for example, distinguished among experiences with the physical environment, the social environment, and those that entail relating objects or events. These experiential distinctions were seen to correspond to physical, social, and logical-mathematical knowledge (the Hollos, 1986 findings from Norway and Hungary provide evidence for this position). Moreover, Piaget (1932) distinguished between the roles of peer contexts and adult-oriented contexts in children's moral development. In brief, he proposed that children's peer interactions in the absence of adult authority is a necessary context for the emergence of understandings of cooperation and mutual trust. Piaget expected that, particularly in the context of games, young adolescents would develop concepts of equality and democratic procedures, which would not be evident in their understandings of spheres like governmental or religious systems.

Vygotsky (1962) also made distinctions in categories of experience in his theorizing on the intersection of the development of cognitive structures and cultural contexts. He proposed a major distinction between experiences that produce spontaneous concepts and scientific concepts. Spontaneous concepts (such as knowledge about a brother or falling off a bicycle) stem from children's everyday personal and direct experience, while scientific concepts stem from instruction provided to children. Because scientific concepts entail learning about what cannot be directly seen or experienced, it is necessary for their formation to be based on explicit instruction. In contrast, the spontaneous concepts emerge from the child's "face-to-face meeting with a concrete situation" (p. 108).

From Asch, Piaget, and Vygotsky we obtain some general characterizations of how differentiated conceptual structures map onto different types of experiences. This contrasts to positions of cultural determinism that assume what can be referred to as a "global contextual structuralism." We take the liberty of labeling it a form of structuralism, even though its proponents might wish to avoid that label, because culture is taken to constitute a wholistic system of organization that hangs together in ways that provide coherence to the experiences that determine social and moral development. Thus far we have drawn from a variety of sources to demonstrate that social contexts vary within cultures. We have also shown that some situations include more than one contextual component—as in the conflicting components embedded in the Milgram experimental situations. In the following sections we elaborate upon and further document our domain-specific interactional approach by considering recent studies on social cognitive development.

CONTEXTS OF EARLY SOCIAL INTERACTIONS

Our position is that the common theme, in the interactional approaches considered thus far, that persons attribute different meanings to varying situations should be approached from the perspective of the multiple, organized, and systematic forms of judgment that individuals bring to social contexts. We have examined a delineated set of such domains meant to represent basic epistemological categories in cognitive and social cognitive development (Turiel & Davidson, 1986). Within the social realm we have extensively analyzed the domains of moral and social conventional concepts. A large number of studies have documented that morality, which pertains to issues of welfare, justice and rights, and social conventions, which refer to consensually agreed-upon behavioral uniformities that structure social interactions within social systems, are conceptually and developmentally distinct forms of social knowledge (see Turiel, 1983, for detailed definitions of the domains and Smetana, 1983, and Turiel et al., 1987, for extensive reviews of the research).

The research has also shown that aspects of these domains form distinctively different types of social interactional contexts. A series of observational studies examined whether domain-relevant events produce different types of social interactions. The studies, which were conducted in preschools (Much & Shweder, 1978; Nucci & Turiel, 1978) and elementary schools (Nucci & Nucci, 1982a, 1982b), have shown that behavioral interactions and social communications among the participants differ by the domain of the event. Children and adults respond in different ways to the two events. In general terms, the distinction revolves around communications that focus on authority, rules, and social order (convention), on the one hand, and on welfare, harmful consequences, fairness, and reciprocal rationales, on the other hand.

As a starting point, these observational studies provided evidence that, indeed, systematic patterns of differential social interaction parallel corresponding domains of judgment. The studies were conducted in schools not so much to examine the physical or social features of those institutional settings, but as places in which it was expected that moral and conventional events would occur with some frequency. Having established that distinct domains of judgment can be mapped onto different types of contexts of social interaction, it becomes plausible to examine more specific physical and social contexts. Two recent studies were aimed at accomplishing this task in early phases of ontogenesis. Both studies included toddlers. One study (Smetana, 1989) examined naturally occurring social interactions in the home and the other (Smetana, 1984) in day care centers. Aspects such as the physical setting, the activities that can be performed in that setting, the participants available for social interaction, and the roles of children and adults were examined under the assumption that each would be related to children's social experiences in the moral and conventional domains.

The study of social interactions in the home included naturalistic observations of two types: one in which only mothers and the child were present and one that included the mother, child and a familiar peer (these are referred to as the mother–child and peer sessions, respectively). A total of 36 toddlers, along with their mothers and peers, were observed. There were approximately equal numbers of males and females at 24 and 36 months of age. The peers were within 6 months of the age of the target child. The observational sessions which lasted 45 minutes, were videotaped and subsequently scored for the occurrence of moral and conventional events in accordance with criteria established in prior studies. (Two other types of events were also examined: prudential events, or events pertaining to the health or safety of the child, and psychological events, or events pertaining to emotions, psychological states, motivations for behavior, or personality characteristics.) When an event of one of these types occurred, the participants' activities, types of interaction, and all sequential responses were scored. In previous research on domain differences in social interactions, only responses to transgressions have been examined. However, not all social interactions in the two domains occur in the context of transgressions. Communications regarding behavior may occur in the absence of, in anticipation of, or following a violation. In this study four different types of social interactions were distinguished: transgressions, maternal commands and directives, child commands, and maternal initiations. Furthermore, mothers' and children's activities were classified as occurring during play, food related episodes (eating, cooking, or helping to prepare food), reading or looking at books, or helping with or doing chores.

The study in day care centers provides a comparison of different social settings. Subjects were children in 16 classrooms serving day care centers. In half of the centers, children were 12–24 months old, and in the other, 24–36 months old. In this observational study, coders watched for the occurrence of naturally occurring classroom transgressions and then coded the nature (domain) of the transgression, who responded (caregivers, children, or caregivers in conjunction with children), and the specific responses, using a coding scheme developed for this research. Although the observations in the home study were more extensive, the two studies are comparable on some, but not all, dimensions. Moreover, within the home study, comparisons were made among three aspects of the social context: the presence or absence of peers, the type of activity engaged in, and the form of the social interaction. The results of these studies are complex, but both similarities and differences across the different contexts are found.

In the home study the mother–child and peer contexts resulted in different frequencies of moral and conventional interactions. In the mother–child context, conventional interactions comprised 45% of the total interactions and were more frequent than moral, psychological, or prudential interactions (18%, 14%, and 15%, respectively). In the peer context, moral interactions accounted for 58% of the total interactions and were more frequent than conventional, prudential or psychological interactions (23%, 14%, and 5%).

Not surprisingly, children's activities differed across the two sessions. The primary activity in both sessions was play, accounting for 63% of the scorable interactions in the mother–child session and 82% of the scorable interactions in the peer session. However, activities in the mother–child session were more varied, with 15% of the activities involving eating or food preparation, 14% entailing chores, and 8% entailing reading. These same activities occurred but were more infrequent in the peer session. Clearly, the availability of a peer increased the likelihood of play and decreased the likelihood of other activities occurring.

Children's activities were further differentiated by social-cognitive domain. In both sessions, nearly all moral interactions occurred in the context of play, accounting for 90% of the moral interactions in the mother–child session and 93% of the moral interactions in the peer session. In both sessions, conventional interactions occurred across a broader range of activities, with approximately half of the conventional interactions occurring during play, another 20% to 25% occurring during eating and food preparation episodes, and another 15% to 25% occurring during chore-related episodes.

Children's social interactions were found to be more varied when they were alone with their mothers than when they played with peers. In the mother–child session, the frequency of the four types of social interactions did not differ, whereas in the peer session, transgressions were more frequent than the other forms of social interaction. The results become more complex when social-cognitive domain is taken into consideration. When children were alone with their mothers, conventional transgressions and maternal conventional commands were the most frequent types of interactions observed. With peers present, children's moral transgressions and moral commands were the most frequent types of interactions observed.

Choice of activities or forms of social interactions were not assessed in the day care study and thus cannot be compared with the home study. However, responses to transgressions can be compared across homes and day care centers. In both studies, responses to events were analyzed as to who responded (caregivers, children, or caregivers in conjunction with children) and the specific form of the response. First, there were some differences between day care centers and homes as to who responded to transgressions in the two domains. In day care settings, caregivers in conjunction with children more frequently responded to moral transgressions than caregivers alone or children alone, whereas in home settings, mothers were more likely to respond to moral transgressions than mothers in conjunction with children or children alone. Upon further investigation, however, we find that children, typically the victims of the transgressions, responded to 61% of moral transgressions in the home and to 70% of moral transgressions in day care centers. Therefore, differences between the two settings pertain to the likelihood of adult, not child response and are most likely due to the different adult–child ratios in the two settings. Mothers may simply have been more vigilant and more available to respond than caregivers in day care centers.

The comparisons in these two settings, then, provide a picture both of contextual variability and contextual stability in moral and social interactions. Contextual variation was found in that certain types of interactions were more likely in certain settings than in others. Moreover, in the home, toddlers' social experiences differed when alone with mothers from when with mothers and peers. For instance, with peers present, interactions were more frequently moral and were more likely to involve transgressions than when peers were not present. More generally, children's activities were structured by different types of social interactions in different domains. For instance, episodes entailing eating and food preparation were more likely to give rise to conventional than moral interactions, although discussions regarding sharing (or even moral events pertaining to welfare, such as the child biting the mother) also arose during such activities. Peers were more likely to structure their interactions in terms of play, where issues pertaining to the coordination of rights arose, although children's play also provided a context for conventional interactions (for instance, saying "please" when asking for a toy). Differences were in terms of relative frequency, with considerable overlap occurring across contexts. Thus, while certain experiences may be more likely during some activities than others, they were not restricted to those activities.

In conjunction with these variations in types of activities and interactions by settings, the moral and conventional categories also constituted stable patterns of social interactions and communications. Basic types of interactions and communications were similar in the home and day care settings and consistent with earlier studies. In both day care centers and homes, caregivers responded in similar ways to conventional transgressions. Their responses included commands and statements pertaining to aspects of social organization, such as sanctions, statements of rules, and statements pertaining to the disorder the act created. However, these responses were found to be age-differentiated (and context-dependent) in the homes but not in day care centers. Statements of rules and sanctions were found to be associated with mothers' responses to 3-year olds' but not 2-year olds' conventional transgressions in the mother–child context. Statements pertaining to social order were significantly associated with maternal responses to conventional transgressions in the peer context. In addition, emotional reactions and physical retaliation, which were both associated with child responses to moral transgressions in peer and day care contexts, were found to be associated with children's responses to conventional transgressions when children interacted with their mothers.

Children's statements focusing on the intrinsic consequences of acts for others' rights and welfare (e.g., emotional reactions, statements of injury or loss, and physical retaliation) were associated with children's responses to moral transgressions in both the day care and peer contexts. In these contexts, caregivers and mothers responded to moral transgressions in ways that focused the victim on the intrinsic consequences of their acts for others' rights and welfare (e.g., with evaluations of rights and requests for the transgressor to take the victim's perspective). Differences between home and day care centers were found primarily in the use of undifferentiated responses, such as commands. Both mothers and children issued commands in response to moral transgressions in the homes, but not in day care settings. Mothers also issued rationales and commands in response to moral transgressions, whereas those responses have been found to be associated with conventional transgressions in day care centers.

These findings show that, once initiated, responses to children's moral and conventional interactions were highly similar across contexts and differentiated from each other. Moral interactions focused on the intrinsic consequences of the acts for others' rights and welfare, and conventional interactions focused on social organization and social regulation. Thus, although different contexts may affect the likelihood of an event being initiated, responses to events in each domain were similar across contexts and different from each other.

CONTEXT OF MORAL AND NONMORAL JUDGMENTS

The observational studies of early social interactions just detailed, along with prior observations in school settings (Nucci & Nucci, 1982a, 1982b; Nucci & Turiel, 1978) serve to provide further evidence for the viewpoint stressed here and put forth by others (Brownell, 1987; Gelman & Massey, 1987; Saxe, Guberman, & Gearhart, 1987) that contextual variations are influenced by the ways children structure situations, as well as features of the environment. In their structuring of social situations, children make conceptual discriminations reflective of basic domains of judgment. These discriminations are related to differing components of the social world, so that it is necessary to attend to distinctions in the characteristics of situations or contexts. In the realm of social interactions it is also important to note that differentiations in domains of social judgments are likely to be shared by those (peers and adults) with whom the child is interacting. This feature of shared interactions further contributes to the heterogeneity forming part of the child's social environment.

In contrast to the proposition of heterogeneity stemming from domain-specific judgments, the morality of individuals is often portrayed as reflecting a general cultural orientation. However, consensus does not exist regarding the particular characterization of this culture's morality. Just as there are opposing descriptions of the cultural ethos (i.e., individualistic or conformist), we see opposing descriptions of the predominant morality in this society. Earlier we mentioned the proposition of social communication theorists that morality in Western culture is rights-based and, thereby, concerned with maintaining individual rights and personal freedoms (Shweder, 1986; Shweder et al., 1987). From that perspective, there are contrasting traditional cultures which are duty-based and concerned with maintaining tradition, social order, rules, and particular duties and interpersonal obligations. However, other commentators who view morality as based on the formation of character traits, maintain that the morality of Western society *is* based on adherence to traditions, duties, rules and maintenance of social order (Bennett & Delattre, 1978; Sommers, 1984; Wynne, 1986).

It turns out, then, that proponents of a character trait approach describe Western morality in an opposite way to that of social communication theorists and akin to the social communication characterization of other, presumably more traditional, cultures. Adding to this array of varying portrayals is the proposition that moral orientations within this society are divided by gender (Gilligan, 1982). Specifically, it is proposed that the morality of males is dominated by concerns with personal rights and justice, whereas the morality of females is dominated by concerns with care and interdependence within interpersonal relationships. The position on gender differences partly overlaps and is partly inconsistent with the social communication position. The proposed female orientation to interpersonal concerns and particularistic duties is somewhat akin to duty-based morality, but social communication theorists claim that it is a moral orientation characteristic of both genders in other societies and that both males and females in this society focus on rights and justice.

Elsewhere we have maintained that concerns with rights, freedoms, duties, and social order coexist in this and other cultures (Turiel, 1989a, 1989b). The extensive evidence on domain-specificity in morality and convention indicates that the judgments of individuals are heterogeneous in this regard. Our viewpoint on heterogeneity in judgments and contextual variations in the application of these judgments also leads us to expect that individuals maintain both justice and interpersonal concerns that vary systematically in accordance with relevant situational components. We recently conducted research (Smetana, Killen, & Turiel, in press) to ascertain whether, for both males and females, interpersonal concerns are separable from their moral judgments. We did not expect that justice or interpersonal concepts would necessarily be applied by males and females to the same situations. Rather, the expectations were that males and females would use each type of judgment and that their application might entail an interaction between gender and situation. Accordingly, it might even be that in certain situations females are more likely to be concerned with justice considerations than males.

The research examined children's judgments regarding the maintenance or fostering of interpersonal relations and moral issues concerning sharing, theft, fairness, and welfare. We constructed a series of hypothetical situations describing conflicts between considerations bearing on interpersonal relationships and moral considerations. Within each situation the circumstances were also varied through shifts in the type or extent of the interpersonal relationship (e.g., friend or sibling; closeness of the friendship) and in the salience of the moral issue.

Two studies were conducted, with each including third-, sixth-, and ninth-grade children; in each grade there were 20 children equally divided by gender. In each study subjects were presented with initial story situations and accompanying contextual variations. In the first study, the initial situations were designed to pose a moral consideration that was in conflict with an act that would maintain or promote a relationship with a friend (e.g., a boy is asked by a close friend not to share candy with another boy with whom the friend does not get along). In the second study the initial situations described conflicts between acts serving general moral ends (e.g., overall fairness) and acts that serve the specific needs of a sibling or close friend. Since space limitations prevent us from describing the procedures in detail, we have summarized in Table 12.1 the different situations and contextual variations for each study.

Three types of data were obtained from these studies. The main findings considered here are the evaluations of the protagonist's action in the initial situations and contextual variations. In addition, in making their evaluations subjects could take into account one or both of the considerations. Responses were, thus, coded for types of coordination of the moral and interpersonal components. Finally, probing of subjects' reasons or justifications for their evaluations were coded.

The findings on the evaluations made by males and females in each grade are presented in Tables 12.2 (Study 1) and 12.3 (Study 2). To interpret these results it is important to note that the conflicts in the situations and contextual variations were designed to provide what might constitute different commitments to interpersonal concerns by males and females. For instance, the interpersonal considerations in the initial situations of Study 1 were direct requests by friends to violate a moral consideration (equality in distribution and theft) for self-interested reasons. Our expectation was that both males and females would view the conflict in similar terms. By contrast, the initial situations in Study 2 described what might be perceived as interpersonal obligations: there were well-intentioned reasons for adhering to the interpersonal considerations. Story 1 of Study 2 was designed to pose an interpersonal tie particularly relevant to males (i.e., caring for a vulnerable younger sister) in conflict with a potentially unfair decision to a female made by a male. In story 2, females cooperated in order to be competitive in a contest, a traditional male activity. Story 3 posed the conflict in a more neutral way regarding gender (stealing to help a sibling in pain). Note also that within each story the contextual variations shifted the salience of either the interpersonal or moral considerations.

TABLE 12.1
Story Themes and Contextual Variations

Study 1

Story 1. *Sharing vs. friendship:* Bob brings candy to share with everyone. His close friend George does not want Bob to give candy to Tim. They do not get along and Tim has been picking on George.
   Interpersonal variations:
      a. Bob is asked by an acquaintance not to share with Tim.
      b. Bob is asked by his brother not to share.
   Moral variations:
      c. Bob, who is in charge of distributing lunches, does not give one to Tim.
      d. Bob inflicts physical harm on Tim.

Story 2. *Stealing vs. friendship:* Pat asks her close friend Diane to steal a set of pens accessible to Diane and much needed by Pat.
   Interpersonal variations:
      a. Diane is asked by an acquaintance to take pens.
      b. Diane is asked by her sister to take pens.
   Moral variations:
      c. Diane takes a pack of gum for her friend.
      d. Diane breaks a promise to engage in an activity with her friend.

Study II

Story 1. *Fairness vs. interpersonal relationship:* Sam, the leader of an afterschool club, considers letting his younger sister join the club to stop other children from teasing her. There is only space for one new member, and another girl is more deserving.
   Interpersonal variation:
      a. Sam considers letting a friend in to the club.
   Moral variation:
      b. The other girl would lose all her friends and be very unhappy if she were not in the club.

Story 2. *Fairness vs. friendship:* Amy is too sick to work on her science fair project and asks her best friend Sally to help her finish it. John, who is also competing in the science fair, tells her it would be unfair.
   Interpersonal variation:
      a. Sally is asked by her younger sister to help finish the work.
   Moral variation
      b. Sally is asked by a friend. The contest has an explicit rule prohibiting obtaining help.

Story 3: *Stealing vs. welfare of sibling:* Walking home with his brother Jimmy, Marvin trips and cuts his leg. Very worried about his brother and not having enough money to call their mother, Jimmy goes to a store, but the owner won't let him use his phone. Jimmy takes $10 lying on the register.
   Interpersonal variation:
      a. It is Jimmy's friend who is hurt.
   Moral variation:
      b. Jimmy lies to the store owner, telling him that the $10 belonged to him.

TABLE 12.2
Responses (%) in Study 1 Endorsing the Non-interpersonal Choice
(Sharing; not taking pens)

Story/Variation	Grade 3		Grade 6		Grade 9	
	Males	Females	Males	Females	Males	Females
1. Sharing Story						
Initial situation	100	88	63	88	86	75
Interpersonal variation-acquaintance	75	100	88	100	100	100
Interpersonal variation-sibling	88	75	63	100	43	75
Moral variation-greater need	100	88	88	100	86	100
Moral variation-harm	100	100	88	100	100	100
2. Stealing Story						
Initial situation	88	75	13	75	14	38
Interpersonal variation-acquaintance	100	100	75	100	71	88
Interpersonal variation-sibling	88	75	13	88	43	50
Moral variation-less need	100	100	63	88	71	63
Moral variation-trust violation	88	88	50	25	0	0

In general, the patterns of results in Tables 12.2 and 12.3 demonstrate variations in judgments that are more closely linked to differences in situations and contexts than the gender of the subjects. There are also some interesting age-related findings entailing an interaction with gender that are not readily interpretable and will require further investigation.

The least complicated finding was that the contextual variations produced expected shifts in judgments that were unrelated to the gender of the subject. For the most part, subjects supported noninterpersonal choices more often in Study 1 than in Study 2. This indicates that the well-intentioned reasons given in Study 2 influenced children's evaluations of the interpersonal choices. Furthermore, a change in the moral salience of the act produced changes in judgments. With increases in the moral salience of the acts, both males and females judged it wrong to favor the interpersonal considerations. Similarly, a change in the level of friendship (from a close friend to an acquaintance) produced shifts for both males and females in the same direction. These results show that males and females take both the moral and interpersonal considerations into account in their judgments, such that they are applied differently in different contexts.

TABLE 12.3
Responses (%) in Study 2 Endorsing the Noninterpersonal Choice
(Not admitting sister/not helping Amy/not taking money)

	Grade 3		Grade 6		Grade 9	
Story/Variation	Males	Females	Males	Females	Males	Females
1. Fairness vs. Interpersonal						
Initial situation	23	55	57	25	75	71
Interpersonal variation-friend	85	100	93	92	100	100
Moral variation-greater need	23	55	64	33	75	71
2. Fairness vs. Friendship						
Initial situation	15	18	36	8	17	36
Interpersonal variation-sibling	15	9	21	8	17	29
Moral variation-rule	92	91	79	75	92	86
3. Stealing vs. Welfare of Sibling						
Initial situation	62	73	50	33	58	64
Interpersonal variation-friend	77	73	29	42	50	64
Moral variation-lying	85	100	86	83	92	100

The comparisons among the different situations presented to subjects show an even more complicated pattern of application of the two types of judgments. In Story 1 of Study 1, there were no significant interactions of age and sex. In Story 2 of Study 1, there was a marginally significant interaction of the situation, age, and sex. In some situations (the Initial Situation and Sibling Variation) the interpersonal choices of grade 6 males were greater than those of grade 6 females. Additionally, in those situations the interpersonal choices of grade 3 males were less than those of grade 6 and grade 9 males. There were no differences, however, among females at each of the grades. In Study 2 we see a greater tendency of females at grade 6 to make interpersonal choices than the younger or older females. For males in Study 2 there was a decrease with age in the frequency of the interpersonal choices. Moreover, in Study 2, grade 9 males and females were similar to each other, with differences appearing among the stories (more ninth-graders made the interpersonal choice in Story 2 than in Story 1).

The results of this research are complex and raise a number of questions for additional studies. It is evident, however, that there are shifts in judgments based on situational variations and that those variations are more powerful than gender differences. Indeed, we failed to find any direct, dichotomous gender differences with regard to interpersonal concerns not only in evaluations of choices in the conflicts but also in the coordination of moral and interpersonal concerns and in the justifications for the evaluations. The analyses of coordinations showed that the children often attended to the moral and interpersonal components and attempted to coordinate them in arriving at an evaluative decision. The types of reasons or justifications invoked for these decisions included substantial use by all children of fairness and welfare concepts, as well as interpersonal considerations.

CONCLUSIONS

We have deliberately covered research evidence of a wide range to substantiate the proposition that explanations of individual–environment interactions should attend to differentiations in the judgments of persons and in situational contexts. Through examples of recent characterizations of the presumed ethos of this culture, we have shown that no consensus exists regarding its predominant social orientation. Instead, different researchers propose different and opposing characterizations of the cultural ethos. It seems that researchers stereotype persons and groups by imposing a consensus on the culture that does not exist among researchers. The imposition of such a consensus on groups brings with it the assumption of within-individual homogeneity that it is contradicted by the type of evidence we have reviewed. Perhaps the characterizations of the culture in homogeneous terms and the imposition of a consensus stems from what we perceive to be a current social scientific trend toward the reification of culture (for cross-cultural discussions of this issue, see Asch, 1952; Spiro, 1986; Turiel et al., 1987).

Our evidence indicated that the heterogeneity of individuals' social judgments stems from domain-specificity in systematic categories for understanding the social world. In turn, we have proposed an analogous notion of domain-specificity as a means for analyzing differentiated components of the social environment. In their development, children structure their environments and thereby contribute to the contextual variations evident in behavior and judgments.

REFERENCES

Asch, S. E. (1952). *Social psychology*. Englewood Cliffs, NJ: Prentice–Hall.
Asch, S. E. (1956). Studies of independence and conformity: A minority of one against a unanimous majority. *Psychological Monographs, 70*(9).
Bandura, A. (1977). *Social learning theory*. Englewood Cliffs, NJ: Prentice–Hall.
Bandura, A., & McDonald, F. J. (1963). The influence of social reinforcement and the behavior of

models in shaping children's moral judgments. *Journal of Abnormal and Social Psychology, 67,* 274–281.

Bellah, R. N., Madsen, R., Sullivan, W. M., Swidler, A., & Tipton, S. M. (1985). *Habits of the heart: Individualism and commitment in American life.* New York: Harper & Row.

Bennett, W. J., & Delattre, E. J. (1978). Moral education in the schools. *Public Interest, 50,* 81–98.

Brown, R., & Herrnstein, R. J. (1975). *Psychology.* Boston: Little, Brown.

Brownell, C. A. (1987). *Social context and the construction of social knowledge.* Paper presented at the biennial meeting of the Society for Research in Child Development, Baltimore.

Gelman, R., & Massey, C. M. (1987). The cultural unconscious as contributor to the supporting environments for cognitive development. Commentary in E. B. Saxe, S. R. Guberman, & M. Gearhart (Eds.), Social processes in early number development. *Monographs of the Society for Research in Child Development, 52*(2, Serial No. 216).

Gewirtz, J. L. (1972). Some contextual determinants of stimulus potency. In R. D. Parke (Ed.), *Recent trends in social learning theory* (pp. 7–33). New York: Academic Press.

Gilligan, C. (1982). *In a different voice: Psychological theory and women's development.* Cambridge, MA: Harvard University Press.

Haney, C., Banks, C., & Zimbardo, P. (1973). Interpersonal dynamics in a simulated prison. *International Journal of Criminology and Penology, 1,* 69–97.

Hogan, R. (1975). Theoretical egocentrism and the problem of compliance. *American Psychologist, 30,* 533–539.

Hollos, M. (1987). Learning in rural communities: Cognitive development in Norway and Hungary. In G. D. Spindler (Ed.), *Education and cultural process: Anthropological Approaches.* Prospect Heights, IL: Waveland Pres.

Kessen, W. (1979). The American child and other cultural inventions. *American Psychologist, 34,* 815–820.

Killen, M. (1987). *Contextual features of peer interaction.* Paper presented at the biennial meeting of the Society for Research in Child Development, Baltimore.

Latane, B., & Darley, J. M. (1970). *The unresponsive bystander: Why doesn't he help?* New York: Appleton.

Malinowski, B. (1926/1976). *Crime and custom in savage society.* Totowa, NJ: Littlefield, Adams.

Milgram, S. (1963). Behavioral study of obedience. *Journal of Abnormal and Social Psychology, 67,* 371–378.

Milgram, S. (1974). *Obedience to authority.* New York: Harper & Row.

Mills, C. W. (1956). *White collar: The American middle class.* New York: Oxford University Press.

Mischel, W. (1969). Continuity and change in personality. *American Psychologist, 24,* 1012–1018.

Mischel, W., & Mischel, H. N. (1976). A cognitive social-learning approach to morality and self-regulation. In T. Lickona (Ed.), *Moral development: Theory, research and social issues* (pp. 104–107). New York: Holt, Rinehart, & Winston.

Much, N. C., & Shweder, R. A. (1978). Speaking of rules: The analysis of culture in the breach. In W. Damon (Ed.), *New directions for child development: Vol. 2. Moral development* (pp. 19–39). San Francisco: Jossey–Bass.

Nisan, M. (1987). Moral norms and social conventions: A cross-cultural comparison. *Developmental Psychology, 23,* 719–725.

Nisbett, R. & Ross, L. (1980). *Human inference: Strategies and shortcomings of social judgment.* Englewood Cliffs, NJ: Prentice–Hall.

Nucci, L. P., & Nucci, M. S. (1982a). Children's social interactions in the context of moral and conventional transgressions. *Child Development, 53,* 403–412.

Nucci, L. P., & Nucci, M. S. (1982b). Children's responses to moral and social conventional transgressions in free-play settings. *Child Development, 53,* 1337–1342.

Nucci, L. P., & Turiel, E. (1978). Social interactions and the development of social concepts in preschool children. *Child Development, 49,* 400–407.

Piaget, J. (1932). *The moral judgment of the child.* London: Routledge & Kegan Paul.

Piaget, J. (1970). *Psychology and epistemology.* New York: Viking Press.

Riesman, D., Glazer, N., & Denney, R. (1953). *The lonely crowd: A study of the changing American character.* New York: Doubleday.

Sampson, E. E. (1977). Psychology and the American ideal. *Journal of Personality and Social Psychology, 35,* 767–782.

Sampson, E. E. (1978). Scientific paridigms and social values: Wanted—a scientific revolution. *Journal of Personality and Social Psychology, 36,* 1332–1343.

Saxe, G. B., Guberman, S. R., & Gearhart, M. (1987). Social processes in early number development. *Monographs of the Society for Research in Child Development, 52*(2, Serial No. 216).

Shweder, R. A. (1986). Divergent rationalities. In D. W. Fiske & R. A. Shweder (Eds.), *Metatheory in social science: Pluralisms and subjectivities* (pp. 163–196). Chicago: University of Chicago Press.

Shweder, R. A., Mahapatra, M., & Miller, J. G. (1987). Culture and moral development. In J. Kagan & S. Lamb (Eds.), *The emergence of morality in young children* (pp. 1–82). Chicago: University of Chicago Press.

Skinner, B. F. (1971). *Beyond freedom and dignity.* New York: Knopf.

Smetana, J. G. (1983). Social-cognitive development: Domain distinctions and coordinations. *Developmental Review, 3,* 131–147.

Smetana, J. G. (1984). Toddlers' social interactions regarding moral and conventional transgressions. *Child Development, 55,* 1767–1776.

Smetana, J. G. (1989). Toddlers' moral and conventional interactions. *Developmental Psychology, 4,* 499–509.

Smetana, J. G., Killen, M., & Turiel, E. (in press). Children's reasoning about interpersonal and moral conflicts, *Child Development.*

Sommers, C. H. (1984). Ethics without virtue: Moral education in America. *American Scholar, 53,* 381–389.

Spiro, M. (1986). Cultural relativism and the future of anthropology. *Cultural Anthropology, 1,* 259–286.

Turiel, E. (1983). *The development of social knowledge: Morality and convention.* Cambridge, England: Cambridge University Press.

Turiel, E. (1989a). The social construction of social construction. In W. Damon (Ed.), *Child development today and tomorrow.* San Francisco: Jossey–Bass.

Turiel, E. (1989b). Multifaceted social reasoning and educating for character, culture and development. In L. Nucci & A. Higgins (Eds.), *Moral development and character education: A dialogue.* Berkeley, CA: McCutchen.

Turiel, E., & Davidson, P. (1986). Heterogeneity, inconsistency, and asynchrony in the development of cognitive structures. In I. Levin (Ed.), *Stage and structure; Reopening the debate* (pp. 106–143). Norwood, NJ: Ablex.

Turiel, E., Killen, M., & Helwig, C. C. (1987). Morality: Its structure, functions and vagaries. In J. Kagan & S. Lamb (Eds.), *The emergence of moral concepts in young children* (pp. 155–244). Chicago: University of Chicago Press.

Turiel, E., Nucci, L. P., & Smetana, J. G. (1988). A cross-cultural comparison of what?: A critique of Nisan's (1987) study of morality and convention. *Developmental Psychology, 24,* 140–143.

Turiel, E., & Smetana, J. (1984). Social knowledge and action: The coordination of domains. In W. M. Kurtines & J. L. Gewirtz (Eds.), *Morality, moral behavior and moral development: Basic issues in theory and research* (pp. 261–282). New York: Wiley.

Vygotsky, L. S. (1962). *Thought and language.* Cambridge, MA:MIT Press.

Whyte, W. H. (1956). *The organization man.* New York: Simon & Schuster.

Wynne, E. A. (1986). The great tradition in education: Transmitting moral values. *Educational Leadership, 43,* 4–9.

Zimbardo, P. G. (1969). The human choice: Individuation, reason, and order versus deindividuation, impulse and chaos. In W. J. Arnold & D. Levine (Eds.), *Nebraska Symposium on Motivation* (Vol. 17, pp. 237–307). Lincoln: University of Nebraska Press.

13 Sex Differences in Moral Reasoning

Lawrence J. Walker

ABSTRACT

This chapter discusses the empirical evidence regarding the contentious issue of sex differences in moral reasoning and sex bias in theories of morality. Two claims regarding this issue have been raised: (a) that there are two sex-related orientations for moral decision-making, and (b) that Kohlberg's moral stage theory down-scores the moral reasoning of females. Evidence regarding the former claim indicates that sex differences in moral orientations are infrequent and that such differences can be best attributed to dilemma content. Evidence regarding the latter claim indicates that the overall pattern is one of nonsignificant sex differences in stage of moral reasoning development. Discussion focuses on the appropriate definition of mature moral reasoning.

Over the last decade, we have witnessed the resurrection of a controversial and difficult, if not intractable, issue—that of sex differences in moral development and sex bias in theories of morality.[1] The underlying theme, of course, is that of ideology in psychological theories. This issue seems to be more contentious than claims about sex differences in other areas, like cognitive or physical abilities,

---

[1]Some authors use the word *gender* instead of *sex* when discussing issues such as those dealt with in this chapter in an attempt to avoid the implication that the differences have a biological origin. However, the relative contributions of biological and social factors for sex-linked behaviors have not yet been clearly established. The research discussed in this chapter classified individuals on the basis of their biological sex and therefore the term *sex* will be used. I do not intend to imply biological causality for these differences (see Maccoby, 1980, p. 203).

since morality is so fundamental to our existence and so obviously value-laden. In large part, this issue of sex differences in moral reasoning has arisen from two claims made by Carol Gilligan (1982a) in her book, titled "In a Different Voice." Incidentally, although her work has been acclaimed by many, some commentators believe that "her conclusions can be taken to support traditional sex stereotypes" (Henley, 1985, p. 113), that such ideas "preserve the status quo and do not demand that either society or individuals change" (Hare-Mustin, 1987, p. 264), and that this "bandwagon" concept of a different voice "deters rather than advances the goals of feminist psychology" (Mednick, 1989, p. 1118).

It is important to differentiate the two claims that Gilligan makes (see Colby & Damon, 1983; Friedman, 1987). Her first claim is that there are two sex-related orientations for moral decision-making (rights/justice versus response/care). Her second claim (which is shared by several others) is that the currently dominant theory in moral psychology, that of Lawrence Kohlberg (1981, 1984), among many other influential theories of human development including those of Freud, Piaget, Erikson, Levinson, and McClelland, is insensitive to females' "different voice" on morality (that is, their response orientation) and denigrates their thought to lower stages, thereby caricaturing them as morally deficient and aberrant.

There is a certain elegance and breadth to Gilligan's writing, many of her arguments have intuitive appeal, and her vivid examples are a refreshing change from the tedious reporting of statistics that characterizes much of psychological writing. However, such notions should be subjected to empirical evaluation (Greeno & Maccoby, 1986). This chapter explores the evidence regarding both of these claims—through a review of the literature and the presentation of some findings of my research that specifically addressed these issues—beginning with moral orientations and then later, moral stages. It is hoped that the present confusion regarding sex differences in moral reasoning can be best addressed by a discussion of relevant empirical evidence.

MORAL ORIENTATIONS

Interest in this area was prompted by the popular reception of Gilligan's work (1977, 1982a, 1986b, 1986c, 1987; Gilligan, Ward, & Taylor, 1988; Gilligan & Wiggins, 1987; also see Langdale, 1986; Lyons, 1983; and Noddings, 1984) in which she proposed that the sexes typically differ in their basic life orientation, especially in conceptions of self and of morality. Her claim (1982b, 1987) that the sexes follow different developmental pathways is intended as a major challenge to the cognitive-developmental claim of the universality of stage sequences.

A moral orientation represents a conceptually distinctive framework or perspective for organizing and understanding the moral domain. Gilligan believes that males typically have a *justice/rights orientation* because of their individualistic and separate conception of self, their detached objectivity, their basing of identity on occupation, and their proclivity for abstract and impartial principles. Thus, she holds that males view morality as involving issues of conflicting rights. On the other hand (and she does describe the difference as if it were a dichotomy, representing fundamentally incompatible perspectives; Stocker, 1987), she believes that females typically have a *care/response orientation* because of their perception of the self as connected to and interdependent with others, their basing of identity on intimate relationships, their sensitivity not to endanger or hurt, their concern for the well being and care of self and others and for harmonious relationships in concrete situations. Thus, she holds that females view morality as involving issues of conflicting responsibilities. Note that Gilligan believes these orientations to be sex-related, but not sex-specific, and that the origins of these orientations are, at least in part, found in the young child's relational experiences of inequality/equality and attachment/detachment (Gilligan, 1986b, 1986c, 1987; Gilligan et al., 1988; Gilligan & Wiggins, 1987).

Several critics have provided theoretical analyses of Gilligan's views (e.g., Brabeck, 1983, 1987; Broughton, 1983; Boyd, 1983; Flanagan & Jackson, 1987; Hare-Mustin, 1987; Kittay & Meyers, 1987; Kohlberg, 1984; Mednick, 1989; Nails, 1983; Sichel, 1985) that will not be duplicated here. What is of concern here is the empirical validity of her claim. The evidence is currently quite limited, and many issues remain to be addressed. For example, Gilligan (1982a) provided only anecdotal data and her original study of moral orientations (1977) was limited to women and a single-context dilemma (viz., abortion). Ford and Lowery (1986), in a recent study, failed to find sex differences among undergraduate students who were asked to describe a moral conflict, read a paragraph outlining the response and rights orientations, and then rate the extent to which they had used these orientations in thinking about their conflict. Friedman, Robinson, and Friedman (1987) also failed to find sex differences among university students who rated the importance of rights and response considerations in resolving a series of moral dilemmas. Similarly, Forsyth, Nye, and Kelley (1988) found no sex differences in university students' endorsement of questionnaire items reflecting an ethic of care. Also to be noted is Archer and Waterman's (1988) review of research on four constructs deemed to reflect psychological individualism (vs. connectedness)—identity, self-actualization, internal locus of control, and principled moral judgment. They reported that the overall pattern was one of nonsignificant sex differences for all constructs.

However, Lyons (1983) interviewed 30 individuals (8–60+ years), asking them to discuss their own real-life moral dilemma. These interviews were analyzed for considerations of rights and response in three components of reasoning about the dilemma: its construction, resolution, and evaluation. Lyons reported support for Gilligan's claim of sex-related moral orientations: Response considerations were predominant for 75% of the females, whereas rights considerations were predominant for 79% of the males.

Gilligan and Attanucci (1988b) replicated this pattern with samples totaling 80 adolescents and adults (14–77 years). They found that a focus on response considerations was more likely in the moral dilemmas of females, whereas a focus on rights considerations was more likely for males. In both Lyons' (1983) and Gilligan and Attanucci's (1988b) studies, participants simply recounted one of their own moral problems. This suggests the possibility—and this is an important point—that their findings may be an artifact of the differing moral problems that the sexes encounter or choose to relate, rather than a basic difference in orientation in solving moral problems (Walker, 1986a).

As previously noted, Gilligan (1982a) describes the response orientation as entailing a concern for maintenance of personal relationships. Kohlberg (1984) similarly held that this orientation is "directed primarily to relations of special obligations to family, friends, and group members, relations which often include or presuppose general obligations of respect, fairness, and contract" (p. 349). In my research (Walker, 1989; Walker, de Vries, & Trevethan, 1987) presented shortly, I examined such suggestions by conducting a content analysis of the nature of the relationship in the real-life conflict—as either personal or impersonal. In this way it could be determined whether or not there are sex differences in the type of dilemma recalled, whether or not there is a relation between orientation and dilemma content, and whether or not there are sex differences in orientations within types of dilemmas.

If the sex difference in moral orientations is as pervasive and basic as Gilligan's theorizing implies, then it should also be evident in responses to standard moral dilemmas, not only idiosyncratic real-life dilemmas (Vasudev, 1988). Indeed, Gilligan in her 1982 book does provide anecdotes of females' supposedly distinctive reasoning in response to Kohlberg's dilemmas. Langdale (1986) analyzed moral orientations expressed in response to Kohlberg's Heinz dilemma and a hypothetical abortion dilemma and found that the sex difference in orientation was still evident. However, Langdale's analysis was only for the resolution component of her participants' reasoning and not for the construction and evaluation components. Johnston (1988) examined orientations in children's responses to two of Aesop's fables and found sex differences for one ("The Dog in the Manger"), but not the other ("The Porcupine and the Moles"). In another study (Donenberg & Hoffman, 1988), children were asked to respond to two hypothetical interpersonal dilemmas and to generate a real-life one. These researchers reported that girls produced a greater number of response considerations than did boys. However, that finding is not readily interpretable given that it may be an artifact of the finding that girls also gave more responses overall than did boys. Contrary evidence has been reported by Rothbart, Hanley, and Albert (1986) who found no sex differences in moral orientations in university students' responses to the Heinz dilemma and a hypothetical physical-intimacy dilemma. Similarly, Crown and Heatherington (1988) found no sex differences in moral orientations in university students' responses to a hypothetical competitive-athletics dilemma.

It should be noted though that Gilligan, Langdale, Lyons, and Murphy (1982) argued that the use of hypothetical dilemmas may obscure moral orientations because the moral problem has been preconstructed by the researcher, in contrast to real-life dilemmas in which subjects construct the problem as well as evaluate its resolution. For example, they argued that Kohlberg's dilemmas are typically constructed as conflicts of rights, with other issues ignored. In this regard, Langdale (1986) reported that the hypothetical Heinz and abortion dilemmas elicited more rights considerations than did real-life dilemmas (Lyons', 1983, data), and Rothbart et al. (1986) found that the Heinz dilemma elicited more rights reasoning than did real-life dilemmas; however, they also found that real-life dilemmas in turn elicited more rights reasoning than did the hypothetical physical-intimacy dilemma. This again suggests that dilemma content may strongly influence moral orientations. It would seem that an appropriate strategy would be to compare responses between real-life and hypothetical dilemmas, allowing participants to construct the problem in the hypothetical dilemmas and with questioning more open-ended, along the lines of questioning for the real-life dilemmas (as suggested by Gilligan et al., 1982).

Gilligan (1986a, p. 10) also claims that most people "focus on one orientation and minimally represent the other"—a claim that I interpret to mean that individuals will be consistent in the use of a single orientation. Langdale interprets Gilligan's claim similarly, arguing that a moral orientation represents a traditionally defined structured whole, which means that "most of an individual's moral reasoning will reflect a single underlying structure of thought both within and across situations" (Langdale, 1986, p. 31). Thus, it is important to determine whether individuals are consistent in their orientation across dilemmas or whether particular dilemmas elicit certain considerations, and furthermore, whether or not sex differences in orientations are pervasive.

Another issue concerning moral orientations is whether or not they entail a developmental pattern (Vasudev, 1988). Are adults more mature than children in terms of moral orientations? Is the sex-related pattern in moral orientations evidenced across the life-span? Lyons (1983) did report that moral orientations in real-life dilemmas were evident across the life-span but her sample was small (viz., 6 children, 11 adolescents, and 13 adults). Langdale (1986) reported a similar pattern for the Heinz dilemma with a larger sample ($N = 137$). My research (Walker, 1989; Walker et al., 1987) provides more extensive data regarding this issue of developmental trends in moral orientations for both real-life and hypothetical dilemmas, with a large sample representing a wide portion of the life-span (5–63 years) who were followed longitudinally over a 2-year interval. Thus, my research addressed the validity of the notion of sex-related moral orientations.

Procedure

The initial sample for my study[2] was composed of 80 family triads (mother, father, and child) for a total N of 240 individuals. The children were drawn from four age groups (Grades 1, 4, 7, and 10), with 10 boys and 10 girls in each group. Only seven individuals were unable to participate in the retest interview; and so the analyses reported here are based on the data of the 233 participants who were interviewed twice. The procedure and measures were the same at both interview times, which were separated by an interval of approximately 2 years.

Each family member was individually interviewed in a 45–90 minute session which was tape-recorded for later transcription and scoring. The interview had two parts: three hypothetical dilemmas (one of three alternate Kohlberg interview forms, randomly chosen) and the real-life dilemma. To allow participants to construct the conflict in each hypothetical dilemma, the standard issue was not initially made explicit; rather, after presenting the "facts" of each dilemma, the interviewer first asked a series of general questions that allowed participants to construct, resolve, and evaluate the solution for the conflict (i.e., "What is the problem? What are the considerations? What should be done and is it the right thing to do?"). These questions were then followed by the standard and other interviewer-determined probe questions. After responding to the hypothetical dilemmas, each participant was asked to discuss her or his conception of morality and to recall a recent real-life moral dilemma from his or her own experience. The interviewer probed regarding the participant's construction, resolution, and evaluation of this dilemma (following Lyons, 1982).

The scoring of moral orientations followed the procedures described in Lyons' (1982) manual, and was conducted blindly and by each dilemma separately (not by subject). Although the manual focuses on responses to real-life dilemmas, Lyons (1982, p. 168) stated that it could be applied to standard hypothetical dilemmas, and both Johnston (1988) and Langdale (1986) reported that they successfully did so. In scoring the hypothetical dilemmas, only responses to the initial non-orientation-specific questions were considered, not responses to the standard Kohlbergian probes since it is possible that a particular line of questioning might elicit reasoning representing one orientation or the other. Each consideration (i.e., scorable thought unit) presented by the participant was categorized as reflecting either the response or rights orientation, following guidelines in the manual. The relative number of considerations within each orientation determined the *modal orientation* for each dilemma ("rights," "response," or "split" if there was an equal number for each orientation). A more sensitive score, the *percent response score,* was also calculated as the percentage of all considerations that reflected the response orientation. (Gilligan

---

[2]For complete details regarding the participants, procedure, and results of this study, see Walker et al. (1987) and Walker (1989).

et al., 1982, and Lyons, 1982, 1983, described the derivation of such a score, but they failed to report any analyses. A percent rights score would be complementary to the percent response score and analyses would, therefore, be redundant.) Percent response scores were determined for both the hypothetical dilemmas and the real-life dilemma.

Interrater reliability for scoring rights and response considerations was determined by a second rater who independently scored 32 randomly selected interviews. For the hypothetical dilemmas, reliability was .77; and for the real-life dilemmas, .76. As a further check on the validity of the scoring, 16 randomly selected real-life dilemmas were independently scored by another rater who had been directly trained by Nona Lyons, the author of the scoring manual. In this case, reliability was .77.

Results

As noted earlier, Gilligan (1986a) holds that most people focus on one orientation and minimally represent the other; empirically, that means that a substantial proportion of the reasoning should reflect one orientation with relatively little reasoning reflecting the other orientation. Thus, it is important to determine whether or not most individuals are sufficiently consistent to warrant such a claim. To examine this basic issue, a score was calculated to represent the percentage of all considerations reflecting the *modal* moral orientation (rights or response) over the interview (three hypothetical and one real-life dilemma). What level of consistency should the concept imply? Since 50% represents the minimum possible (i.e., both orientations equal) and 100% represents perfect consistency (i.e., one orientation exclusively), I adopted an arbitrary criterion of 75% of greater—a criterion that has also been adopted by Gilligan and Attanucci (1988b). To examine this issue, the percentage of subjects who met the criterion of consistency over all dilemmas was determined. It was found that very few subjects were consistent in the use of a single orientation: 16.3% on the initial interview and 18.9% on the retest. Even when examining the single real-life dilemma, the extent of consistency was not great: Only about one-half of the participants met the criterion. Gilligan and Attanucci (1988b) also examined consistency in orientation usage with a single real-life dilemma and reported that only 66.3% met this criterion. An alternate approach in assessing this issue is to determine the percentage of subjects who evidenced the same modal moral orientation on the real-life dilemma for the two interviews. In my study, only 50.2% were found to be consistent over time; that is, half of the participants evidenced a different orientation in their reasoning on the retest than the initial interview. Pratt, Golding, Hunter, and Sampson (1988) addressed this issue of orientation consistency by asking each of the 40 adults in their sample to recall and discuss *two* real-life dilemmas. They found that only 60% of the subjects used the same modal orientation between the two dilemmas—a level not significantly different from chance. These data indicate that most individuals use both orientations to a significant degree, and thus analyses simply based on individuals' modal orientation should be interpreted with considerable caution, since it is not an accurate measure of their reasoning.

A more sensitive and appropriate measure of moral orientations would be the percent response score (recall that it was calculated as the percentage of all considerations that reflected the response orientation; a percent rights score would be complementary). In order to examine developmental trends, sex differences, and dilemma type differences in Gilligan's moral orientations, an ANOVA was conducted using response scores as the dependent variable, and with age group, sex, type of dilemma, and interview time as factors. This analysis yielded a complex pattern of findings: There was a significant effect of age (viz., increasing response scores with age), $F(4, 223) = 10.39$, $p < .001$; and a significant effect for type of dilemma with real-life dilemmas eliciting slightly more response reasoning than hypothetical dilemmas (46.3% vs. 42.8%), $F(1, 223) = 11.73$, $p < .001$. These two effects were qualified by an interaction between age and type of dilemma, $F(4, 223) = 7.37$, $p < .001$, which illustrated in Fig. 13.1. Subsequent analyses of this interaction determined that two groups of children (Grade 1/3 and 7/9) used more response reasoning on hypothetical dilemmas than the real-life one, whereas adults evidenced the opposite pattern. There were no significant differences for the other groups.

The pattern shown in this figure was qualified by two three-way interactions: Age × Type of dilemma × Time, $F(4, 233) = 3.20$, $p < .05$; and Age × Sex ×

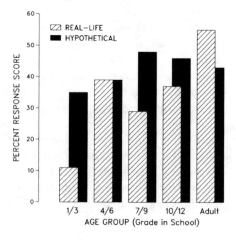

FIG. 13.1. Mean percent response scores across age groups for both dilemma types. From "A Longitudinal Study of Moral Reasoning" by L. J. Walker, 1989, *Child Development, 60*, p. 161. Copyright 1989 by the Society for Research in Child Development and reprinted with permission.

Type of dilemma, $F(4, 223) = 2.57$, $p < .05$. Beyond what has already been described, analyses of the Age $\times$ Type of dilemma $\times$ Time interaction indicated that Grade 7/9 children's greater use of response reasoning on the hypothetical dilemmas than the real-life one was significant only on the retest interview (51.7% vs. 19.8%) and not the initial interview (44.1% vs. 37.4%). Analyses of the Age $\times$ Sex $\times$ Type of dilemma interaction indicated that there were no sex differences on the hypothetical dilemmas, and none among children on the real-life dilemma; however, among adults on the real-life dilemma, women had higher response scores than men (59.6% vs. 50.2%). Incidentally, if modal moral orientations are examined (see Table 13.1), rather than response scores, then, among children there are no sex differences on either interview; whereas for adults, the sex-related pattern is evidenced on the initial interview but not on the retest, $\chi^2(2, N = 156) = 10.37$, $p < .01$, and 3.77, N.S., respectively.

In summary, this analysis of percent response scores indicated clear cross-sectional age trends, but no change in response reasoning over the 2-year interval. Sex differences were not found with standard dilemmas, nor among children with real-life dilemmas. The only sex difference evidenced was among adults with the real-life dilemmas. The pattern regarding the relation between type of dilemma and response reasoning was conflicting with two groups of children using more such reasoning with hypothetical dilemmas and with adults using more with real-life dilemmas.

TABLE 13.1.
Percentage of Subjects at each Modal Moral Orientation on the Real-Life Dilemma (both Children and Adults)

Group	Response	Rights	Split
		Moral Orientation	
	Initial interview		
Children			
boys	15.8	63.2	21.1
girls	25.6	53.8	20.5
Adults			
men	29.5	38.5	32.1
women	53.8	20.5	25.6
	Retest interview		
Children			
boys	7.9	73.7	18.4
girls	20.5	66.7	12.8
Adults			
men	51.3	38.5	10.3
women	53.8	26.9	19.2

I argued earlier that the sex-related pattern in moral orientations might be an artifact of dilemma content. The absence of sex differences with standard stimulus materials—the hypothetical dilemmas—is consistent with that view. It, thus, seems important to examine the content of the real-life dilemmas in order to determine if there is a relation between dilemma content and moral orientation, and if there are sex differences within types of dilemma content. To accomplish this, a content analysis of the real-life dilemmas was conducted in terms of the nature of the relationship that each moral conflict entailed (as either personal or impersonal). A "personal" moral conflict was interpreted as one involving a specific person or group of people with whom the subject has a significant relationship, defined generally as one of a continuing nature (e.g., a family member, friend, close neighbor, colleague, associate, partner). Examples of personal moral conflicts include whether or not to tell a friend that her husband was having an affair and whether or not to put one's father in a nursing home against his wishes. An "impersonal" moral conflict was interpreted as one involving a person or group of people whom the subject does not know well (a stranger or acquaintance) or is not specified or is generalized (e.g., students, clients), or as one involving institutions (e.g., police), or involving an issue primarily intrinsic to self. Examples of impersonal moral conflicts include whether or not to correct a clerk's error in failing to charge for an item and whether to absorb a business loss as an employer or cut employees' wages. (Interrater reliability was determined by another rater who independently classified all real-life dilemmas. There was 93.9% agreement.)

Then, a 2 (Sex) × 2 (Dilemma content: personal, impersonal) ANOVA was conducted for both the initial and retest interview, using the percent response score on the real-life dilemma as the dependent variable. The findings are summarized in Fig. 13.2. Both analyses indicated no main effect of sex and no interaction between sex and dilemma content. In other words, there are no sex differences in orientation use when dilemma content is held constant. However, a significant effect for dilemma content was found with higher response scores on the personal-relationship dilemmas than the impersonal-relationship ones for both the initial interview (52.3% vs. 40.0%) and the retest interview (56.9% vs. 33.7%), F's(1, 229) = 6.48 and 27.42, p's < .05 and .001, respectively. Since the only sex difference in moral orientations that has been revealed was for adults on the real-life dilemma (as discussed earlier), these Sex × Dilemma content ANOVAs were also conducted for this age group alone. Interestingly, there were no sex differences or interactions with sex for either interview. However, significant effects of dilemma content were found, mirroring the pattern just presented. Thus, the nature of the dilemma better predicts moral orientation than does individuals' sex. Note, although, that the type of dilemma does not perfectly predict moral orientation. Obviously, the same kind of dilemma can be interpreted within either a response or a rights framework (cf. Gilligan & Attanucci, 1988a).

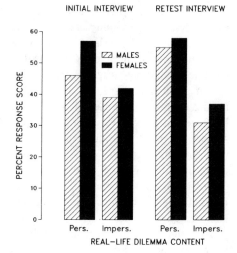

INITIAL INTERVIEW   RETEST INTERVIEW

FIG. 13.2. Mean percent response scores as a function of real-life dilemma content.

Pratt et al. (1988, Study 1) have reported similar findings to those of my study. In their research, three groups of adults (young-, middle-, and old-aged) recalled and discussed a real-life dilemma. The adults' moral orientation on this dilemma was determined and dilemma content was also classified (as relational vs. nonrelational—a typology similar to mine). Although there were sex differences in moral orientation, these differences disappeared when type of dilemma was controlled, again indicating that the content of a dilemma influences orientation. Actually, Pratt et al. reported that a sex difference in orientation was only found for one group of adults (viz., the middle-aged) and not the younger and older adults. They speculated that middle-aged adults are more likely to be active in the parenting role, a situation that is conducive to sex-role polarization. They tested this notion in a second study with a sample of adults of the same age: half of whom were parents and half, not. Only the parents evidenced a sex-related pattern in their orientations. This provides further evidence that the sex difference in moral orientation is of extremely limited generality.

Discussion

Gilligan (1982a) and others (e.g., Noddings, 1984) have proposed that there are two moral orientations: a rights orientation based on an individualistic conception of self and a justice conception of morality versus a response orientation based on an interdependent conception of self and a care conception of morality. One issue addressed by this study concerned intraindividual consistency in use of moral orientations. If each moral orientation represents a distinctive framework for understanding morality and is as basic to our functioning as has been proposed, then individuals should show a clear preference for one or the other which generalizes across moral problems, be they real-life or hypothetical. However, if most people use both orientations to a significant degree, then the validity of the notion as such is suspect, just as Kohlberg's moral stage concept would be invalid if most people used all stages in their reasoning. The findings indicated low levels of intraindividual consistency in both real-life and standard dilemmas. Apparently, most individuals use a considerable mix of both orientations—with no clear preference or focus. As such, the classification of individuals simply on the basis of modal moral orientation may be misleading and inaccurate, and the use of the term "orientation" inappropriate. Incidentally, this finding of low intraindividual consistency in orientation use has also recently been reported by Rothbart et al. (1986).

Although Gilligan argued against the use of hypothetical dilemmas because of their depersonalized nature, it is important to determine whether or not orientations are evidenced with standard stimulus materials. In this study, both orientations were scored in the hypothetical dilemmas, and, in general, responses to real-life and hypothetical dilemmas were similar, although two groups of children used response considerations less with real-life dilemmas than with hypothetical ones, and adults, more. Developmentally, there was a linear increase with age in response scores—a phenomenon not apparent in previous research with small samples. Younger children often conceptualized and resolved moral problems egocentrically, in terms of "effects to self" which, according to Gilligan, is characteristic of the rights orientation. Gilligan (1977) originally proposed developmental stages in the response orientation but, as yet, no scoring system has been developed to assess such stages and no supportive data have been presented.

Gilligan (1982a) proposed that these orientations are sex-related, but the data of this study indicated that sex differences were infrequent: only among adults and only on the real-life dilemma. The association between sex and orientation is not as general and basic as has been argued. Furthermore, a sex-related pattern in orientations was not found for standard dilemmas. In terms of modal moral orientations for the real-life dilemma, a significant relation between sex and orientation was found on the initial interview, but not on the retest, and then only for adults. When the content of these dilemmas was analyzed in terms of the nature of the relationship they entailed, it was found that personal-relationship dilemmas elicited a response orientation, whereas impersonal-relationship dilemmas elicited a rights orientation. However, within each type of dilemma content, sex differences in orientations were no longer evidenced. Thus, differences in moral orientations can be better attributed to the type of moral dilemma that subjects discuss than to their sex. But this is not to deny that the choice and construal of a dilemma may reflect one's orientation. However, the social experiences of males and females in everyday life do differ and may explain the nature of the moral dilemmas they relate. The sex differences in orientations that are sometimes evident may be due to the differing types of moral dilemmas that the sexes typically encounter.

Kohlberg's Moral Orientations

Gilligan's theorizing regarding moral orientations was actually predated by Kohlberg's (1976) proposal of a typology of four moral orientations (which are, of course, conceptually independent of his better known moral stages). These orientations are somewhat more closely related to the content, rather than the structure, of individuals' reasoning. It is possible to distinguish these orientations with the current scoring manual (Colby & Kohlberg, 1987). In scoring an interview, each moral judgment is classified, not only according to "stage," but also according to "element." Scores for the four orientations are derived from these scored elements. The *normative* orientation emphasizes maintenance of the normative order, with a focus on duties and rights defined by adherence to prescribed rules and roles. The *fairness* orientation emphasizes justice, with a focus on liberty, equity and equality, reciprocity and contract. The *utilitarianism* orientation emphasizes welfare and happiness consequences of moral actions for oneself or for others. The *perfectionism* orientation emphasizes attainment of dignity and autonomy, good conscience and motives, and harmony with self and others.

Kohlberg's typology of moral orientations seems to tap dimensions related to those described by Gilligan—there are many similar themes and distinctions. It is recognized, however, that Kohlberg's orientations are not a direct reflection of Gilligan's model and that her claims cannot be optimally explained *within* the framework of Kohlberg's theory (Smetana, 1984). Nevertheless, given Gilligan's claim of a pervasive sex difference and Kohlberg's description of moral orientations, it is reasonable to hypothesize that sex differences would be evident in his typology as well (although Gilligan has not made explicit predictions in this regard). Males would be expected to use the normative and fairness orientations because of their presumed focus on rights, duties, and justice; whereas females would be expected to use the utilitarianism and perfectionism orientations because of their focus on relationships, welfare, and caring.

There are four studies with data relevant to this issue. Pratt, Golding, and Hunter (1984) analyzed orientation usage with a sample of 60 adults (18–75 years). Overall, they found no sex differences on any of the orientations. However, among their high-stage subjects only ($n = 13$), men oriented more to fairness than did women, whereas women oriented more to perfectionism than did men. Similarly, I (Walker, 1986a) analyzed orientation usage with a sample of 62 adults (23–84 years) and found no sex differences on either the utilitarianism or perfectionism orientations. As predicted, men used the normative orientation more than did women (29.8% vs. 21.6%); but contrary to predictions, women used the fairness orientation more than men (19.9% vs. 12.9%). In another study, Pratt et al. (1988) found no sex differences in orientation usage in their sample of 72 adults (18–75 years).

These three studies reported equivocal data regarding sex differences in Kohlberg's moral orientations. They are limited in a couple of respects: first, they all involved samples of adults only; second, they all assessed orientation usage in response to hypothetical dilemmas. In a recent 2-year longitudinal study, I (Walker, 1989) examined Kohlberg's moral orientations with a sample of 233 children, adolescents, and adults who responded, not only to a set of hypothetical dilemmas, but who also discussed a real-life dilemma from their own experience. This design allowed for a more powerful test of the notion of sex differences in moral orientations. However, no sex differences were revealed. Interestingly, the two types of dilemmas (hypothetical vs. real-life) did elicit differing orientations. Hypothetical dilemmas elicited more of the normative and fairness (*rights*-like) orientations, whereas real-life dilemmas elicited more of the utilitarianism and perfectionism (*response*-like) orientations. Although this is Gilligan's prediction, it is supported only by the Kohlberg typology.

Thus, these studies indicate the almost complete absence of sex differences with Kohlberg's moral orientations. This raises the issue of the congruence between these alternate models of moral orientations. It could be expected that there would be a positive relation between response reasoning (as assessed by Gilligan's model) and the utilitarianism and perfectionism (response-like) orientations and that there would be a negative relation between response reasoning and the normative and fairness (rights-like) orientations. I (Walker, 1989) examined this issue with a correlational analysis. Although there was no consistent relation between response scores and either the fairness or utilitarianism orientations, the expected negative relation with the normative orientation (r's ranged between $-.07$ and $-.19$, depending on dilemma type and interview time) and the expected positive relation with the perfectionism orientation (r's ranged between .10 and .38) were found. Even these correlations are relatively weak, indicating that Gilligan's and Kohlberg's typologies of moral orientations are tapping somewhat different aspects of moral reasoning.

MORAL STAGES

Sex Bias in Kohlberg's Theory

Gilligan argues that Kohlberg's theory has not heard the "different voice" of females and is insensitive to their response orientation. Although the current controversy revolves around a contemporary theory of moral development, the issue is not new; historically, women have often been regarded as morally inferior to men—by common folk (e.g., witness the predominance of patriarchical societies), philosophers (see Lloyd's, 1983, review), and social scientists (e.g., Freud, 1927). The charge of sex bias might be warranted for two reasons. First, a theorist could advocate or popularize a poorly founded claim that the sexes are fundamentally different in moral orientation or in rate and endpoint of moral development. For example, Freud (1927) made the now notorious assertion that women lack moral maturity because of deficiencies in same-sex parental identification and consequent superego formation. Second, a theorist might offer no such opinion, but define and/or measure moral maturity in ways that inadvertently favor one sex or the other and thus create a false impression of real differences in moral maturity. The allegations of sex bias against Kohlberg's theory have been based primarily on the latter reason. Gilligan argues that Kohlberg's conception of morality is *androcentric* in that there is an emphasis (particularly at the higher stages) on what she describes as traditionally masculine values such as rights, rationality, individuality, abstraction, detachment, impersonality, and principles of justice.

A brief synopsis of Kohlberg's (1981, 1984) theory may be helpful at this point. Kohlberg argues that it is appropriate and useful to characterize moral reasoning in terms of a strict stage model. This model holds that moral reasoning stages represent holistic structures that are in an invariant, universal sequence and that constitute a hierarchy (Walker, 1988). In other words, individuals should be consistent in stage of reasoning across contents and contexts; their development should be irreversibly progressive, one stage at a time; and they should recognize the increased moral adequacy of successive stages of moral reasoning. Kohlberg has postulated six stages in the development of moral reasoning which are amply described elsewhere and need not be duplicated here. Kohlberg claimed empirical support for the first five stages but regarded Stage 6 primarily as a theoretical construct because of its absence in his longitudinal data (Colby, Kohlberg, Gibbs, & Lieberman, 1983).

Kohlberg (1976) claimed that the order of development through the stages is invariant, but predicted variability in rate and eventual end-point of development. There are two main determinants of rate of moral development: (a) attainment of prerequisite levels of cognitive and perspective-taking development (i.e., moral reasoning has a basis in cognition), and (b) exposure to appropriate sociomoral experiences (i.e., moral reasoning also has a basis in social interactions). Claims regarding the former determinant are derived from the cognitive-developmental assumption of structural parallelism which implies that isomorphic processes are involved in parallel stages in different domains of cognition. This claim has been supported by studies that indicate that attainment of a moral stage requires the prior or concomitant attainment of the parallel cognitive and perspective-taking stages (Walker, 1988).

Level of moral development is influenced not only by cognitive prerequisites

348 LAWRENCE J. WALKER

but also by exposure to sociomoral experiences (Kohlberg, 1973, 1976). Claims regarding this determinant are derived from the cognitive-developmental assumption that disequilibrium (or cognitive conflict) is the cognitive motivational mechanism that induces development (Walker, 1988). Thus, the experiences that promote moral development are often emotional, personal experiences involving responsibility and decision making—ones that entail cognitive conflict. The essential feature of these social experiences for moral development is the provision of role-taking opportunities in conflict situations. These experiences arise both through interpersonal relationships with family and friends and through real participation in the economic, political, and legal institutions of society through education, occupation, and citizenship activities. A number of studies have provided support for the notion that social experiences relate to moral development. For example, moderately strong relations have been found between moral development and level of education (Bielby & Papalia, 1975; Boldizar, Wilson, & Deemer, 1989; Buck, Walsh, & Rothman, 1981; Colby et al., 1983; Edwards, 1975; Pratt, Golding, & Hunter, 1983; Walker, 1986a) and between moral development and occupational status (Boldizar et al., 1989; Buck et al., 1981; Edwards, 1975; Walker, 1986a). Other social experiences that have been found to relate positively to moral development include: political and social activity (Fontana & Noel, 1973; Haan, Smith, & Block, 1968; Keasey, 1971), living independently rather than with parents or in residences (Edwards, 1975; Haan et al., 1968), joint household decision-making (Walker, 1986a), and family and peer discussions (Berkowitz, Gibbs, & Broughton, 1980; Buck et al., 1981; Haan, 1985; Holstein, 1972; Parikh, 1980; Powers, 1983, 1988).

Kohlberg's theory, of course, does not predict that any particular experiences are necessary for attainment of a given stage. Those experiences that will affect moral development are ones that induce rethinking of current modes of moral reasoning. Thus, the number of years someone sits in a classroom is not a direct index of the amount of relevant experience (there is no educational threshold for each stage). What is of concern is whether or not life experience, including but not only educational experience, encourages reflection on, and discussion of, social and moral issues; that is, its quality, not quantity. Similarly, whether or not someone is employed is not of much concern. What is of concern is the extent to which the occupation permits responsibility, communication, and decision making. Individuals who are in low-level occupations (which are where many women in the labor force are employed) tend to be denied the opportunity for significant moral decision-making on the job. In fact, running a household may provide more opportunity for such experiences than many occupations, including some in which men predominate.

Baumrind (1986) regards the relation between moral development and sociomoral experiences (especially education) as a "serious challenge" to the theory. In contradistinction, I interpret the relation as evidence for the theory's construct validity. Educational level has been found to correlate with most developmental variables. Of what value is education if it has no impact on moral thought, and what would be the validity of a theory concerned with the development of moral reasoning that did not evidence such a relation (Rest & Thoma, 1985)?

If there is sex bias in Kohlberg's approach, how could it have arisen? A trite response is that, because Kohlberg is a man, he has taken a masculine point of view in theorizing about moral development. An equally trite rejoinder would be to point out his numerous female colleagues, including the senior author of recent editions of the scoring manual (Colby & Kohlberg, 1987). A second, and much more serious, possible source of bias is that the stages have been constructed from the longitudinal data provided by an exclusively male sample (Colby et al., 1983). This lack of representativeness would be a real threat to the generalizability of the model if the stages are not universal (as claimed by cognitive-developmental theory) and could easily be a source of sex bias; but to date, no data have been presented to show that females do not follow Kohlberg's sequence of stages. In fact, several studies of the sequentiality of the stages demonstrate that males and females do develop through the stages in the same order (Erickson, 1980; Snarey, Reimer, & Kohlberg, 1985; Walker, 1982, 1989). Nonetheless, it is impossible to determine whether the same stages and sequence would have been derived if females had been studied originally. A third potential source of bias is the predominance of male protagonists in the moral dilemmas used as stimulus materials in eliciting reasoning. Females may have difficulty relating to these male protagonists and thus exhibit artifactually lower levels of moral reasoning. The effect of protagonists' sex on moral reasoning has been examined in a number of studies. Bussey and Maughan (1982) found more advanced reasoning with same-sex protagonists (for male subjects only). Freeman and Giebink (1979) also found more advanced reasoning with same-sex protagonists (for female subjects only). On the other hand, Orchowsky and Jenkins (1979) found more advanced reasoning with opposite-sex protagonists, and Donenberg and Hoffman (1988), Garwood, Levine, and Ewing (1980), Greene and Vulcano (1987), and Turiel (1976) all found no evidence of differential responding when protagonist sex was varied. Thus, the data are equivocal regarding this potential source of bias.

To summarize, it is possible that sex bias exists in Kohlberg's theory, in particular because of his reliance on a male sample to construct and validate the stages, but this remains to be determined; and it is important to note that a sex difference in moral development is not a theoretical claim of his model. To address this issue a review of the literature was undertaken to examine the consistency of sex differences in moral reasoning. If females' moral reasoning is poorly captured by Kohlberg's model, as has been alleged, then they should evidence lower levels of moral reasoning than do males.

Before presenting the review, there is a cautionary point to note. Some critics (e.g., Baumrind, 1986; Gilligan, 1982a) hold that findings of difference are indicative of bias, but differences only indicate bias if they do not accurately reflect reality. For example, males have been found to be heavier than females on average and Caucasians to be taller than Orientals, but that hardly implies that our systems of weight and height measurement are biased. Demonstrating that a theory is biased requires more than findings of difference between groups. A sex difference may simply be a reflection of a male-dominated society that restricts females' opportunities for growth, not an indication of a biased theory. Assuming that the sexes do not differ, the minimal (but certainly not sufficient) basis for an interpretive claim of sex bias against a theory would be consistent evidence indicating greater moral maturity for males than for females.

Review of Sex Differences in Moral Reasoning Development

This review of the literature covered all studies using Kohlberg's measure in which sex differences in the development of moral reasoning were examined. It included the studies from my 1984 *Child Development* review article plus studies published since that article went to press and others that have recently come to my attention. Criteria for the review were as follows: (a) A study was excluded if only one sex was assessed or if age and sex were confounded (e.g., a comparison of mothers and their sons). (b) Studies were also excluded if there was no analysis of sex differences (e.g., Alker & Poppen, 1973, and Fishkin, Keniston, & MacKinnon, 1973, claimed sex differences but failed to provide either descriptive or inferential analyses in substantiation) or if analyses were questionable (e.g., Lockwood, 1975, used incorrect error terms in his ANOVA). (c) Studies in which the design involved selecting subjects according to stage were excluded. (d) Also omitted from the review were studies that presented data that had been reported in another study and thus redundant (e.g., D. Candee, personal communication, November 1, 1982 (also see Candee & Kohlberg, 1987), provided rescored data[3] previously reported by Haan, 1975, and Haan et al., 1968; Speicher-Dubin, 1982, presented rescored data that had been reported, in part, by Haan, Langer, & Kohlberg, 1976, Haan, Weiss, & Johnson, 1982, and Kuhn, Langer, Kohlberg, & Haan, 1977; and Snarey et al., 1985, presented rescored data previously reported, in part, by Bar-Yam, Kohlberg, & Naame, 1980). (e) Finally, studies using some objective, recognition-type measure of moral reasoning, such as the Defining Issues Test (DIT), instead of Kohlberg's measure, were not included. These studies were excluded because: they are not

---

[3]Although Candee reanalyzed only a subsample ($N = 321$) of Haan et al.'s total sample ($N = 510$), this review reports only the finding based on Candee's data because: (a) he rescored the data according to the current scoring system, (b) his data include mixed stage subjects that had been excluded by Haan et al., and (c) the secondary analysis of his data yields a more highly significant finding than that of Haan et al.'s data (thus providing a more liberal test of sex differences).

appropriate for children and early adolescents, they do not stage-type (instead yield continuous indices like the "P" or "D" scores), they rely on stage definitions that differ somewhat from Kohlberg's (cf. Kohlberg, 1981; Rest, 1979), and Thoma (1986) has already provided a comprehensive review and meta-analysis of DIT research which revealed that, overall, females scored significantly *higher* than males, although the magnitude of this difference was small.

The review covered all studies in which Kohlberg's measure was used to examine sex differences in moral reasoning. A number of researchers who did not analyze sex differences did, however, present enough data (e.g., the number of males and females at each moral stage) to allow me to do a secondary analysis. For my 1984 review, secondary analyses were typically conducted via the Kolmogorov-Smirnov test. Baumrind (1986) argued that this test was inappropriate because it is too conservative. In my rejoinder (Walker, 1986b), however, I noted that, although the Kolmogorov-Smirnov test is less powerful than the Mann-Whitney test (favored by Baumrind) for detecting differences in central tendency especially with large sample sizes and many ties (Lehmann, 1975), it is more powerful in detecting differences with small samples and differences other than central tendency (e.g., dispersion, skewness). The Kolmogorov-Smirnov test was chosen because it is a test of *all* possible alternatives to the null hypothesis that the distribution of two groups is identical. Thus, Siegel (1956, p. 157) concluded that "of all tests for any kind of difference, the Kolmogorov-Smirnov test is the most powerful." Nevertheless, in order to provide the most liberal test of sex differences in moral reasoning development, secondary analyses were conducted via both the Mann-Whitney and Kolmogorov-Smirnov tests; however, the conclusions regarding the significance of a finding were congruent in all cases.

The present review included 80 studies with a total of 152 samples, and involved a total of 10,637 subjects. The pattern revealed by the review is quite apparent: of the 152 samples, a nonsignificant difference was reported for the vast majority (130, or 85.5%). Females had higher scores in 9 samples (5.9%), whereas males had higher scores in 13 samples (8.6%). The few differences favoring females tended to occur in homogeneous samples of school and university students (Arbuthnot, 1983; Biaggio, 1976; Blatt & Kohlberg, 1975; Krebs & Gillmore, 1982; Lei & Cheng, 1984; Noam, Powers, Hauser, & Jacobson, 1985; Saltzstein, Diamond, & Belenky, 1972; Turiel, 1976). Baumrind (1986) dismissed these findings of differences by alluding to girls' "accelerated general development," but she did not cite evidence of this general sex difference. Her belief seems contrary to the available data regarding the consistency and magnitude of sex differences in general (Maccoby & Jacklin, 1974).

The few differences favoring males tended to occur either in homogeneous samples of students (Bussey & Maughan, 1982; Candee, 1982; Gielen, 1986; Haan, 1986; Speicher-Dubin, 1982) or in heterogeneous samples of adults (Baumrind, 1986; Holstein, 1976; Parikh, 1980; Powers, 1983; Speicher-Dubin, 1982). These samples are described as heterogeneous since the sexes differed in levels of education and occupation—a situation, of course, that reflects contemporary society. Since education and occupation are sociomoral experiences that may explain variability in moral development, it could be expected, in those studies involving the confounding of sex with education and/or occupation, that sex differences in moral reasoning would be attenuated, if not eliminated, when levels of these experiences were controlled. As predicted, whenever researchers (Baumrind, 1986; Powers, 1983; Speicher-Dubin, 1982) controlled in some manner for these sociomoral experiences, sex differences in moral reasoning disappeared. Speicher-Dubin compared the moral reasoning development of men and women within the same SES level (reflecting both occupation and education) and found no differences. Both Baumrind and Powers statistically controlled for education and/or occupation and found that sex differences disappeared in their samples. Baumrind also conducted an analysis of sex differences within education level but, unfortunately, it entailed a confounding of sex and education at both high and low education levels (the only levels where there were differences); and so her conclusion that there are sex differences in moral reasoning within educational levels is not warranted (Walker, 1986b). My presentation of these analyses of sex differences in moral reasoning within level of education and occupation should not be construed as an attempt to "explain away" these findings (cf. Gilligan & Attanucci, 1988a), but rather as an illustration of the point that, when differences occurred, they are generally explicable in terms of the theory's predictions regarding variability in moral development.

Some critics (e.g., Baumrind, 1986) argue that only the data of adults are relevant to the question of sex differences in moral reasoning development and that a review which includes the data of children, adolescents, and youth is biased against the finding of differences. Baumrind's argument is based on the notion that bias in Kohlberg's theory arises from sex differences at the highest level of moral reasoning. However, she did not explain how there is bias at that level but not at lower ones. If the theory and/or measures are biased (as Baumrind claimed elsewhere in her Discussion), then sex differences could occur at any level. Other critics do argue that Kohlberg's theory is pervasively biased against the thinking of females of all ages (e.g., Gilligan, 1982a, chap. 2, argued that his approach is insensitive to the moral reasoning of girls). In any event, adults do reason at almost all stages. There are no convincing reasons to focus exclusively on the data of adults.

Thus, the overall pattern yielded by the review is one of nonsignificant sex differences. This is not to deny that there are a few studies with particular samples that did yield significant differences; however, such a small number would be expected by chance.

Meta-analysis

Although it is clear that the conclusion to draw from this review is that the moral reasoning of males and females is more similar than different, such a vote-counting method of integrating findings has limitations—limitations that are

largely overcome by meta-analytic techniques. The traditional review is susceptible to biases in interpretation (e.g., in discounting findings) and furthermore,
simply determines whether findings were significant or not, making no assessment of the size of the effect. If the effect is moderate, the findings may tend to
be nonsignificant, but cumulatively favor a given direction. Meta-analysis is a
more powerful and objective method than summary impression, allowing reviewers to include information beyond a simple box-score and to combine statistically the results of a series of studies. (See Rosenthal, 1984, for a comprehensive discussion of meta-analytic procedures.)

One of the most powerful, yet simple and routinely applicable methods is the
Stouffer method. It is based on the Z score (i.e., the standard normal deviate)
associated with the one-tailed p value of the relevant test statistic and is calculated by summing these Z scores and dividing by the square root of the number of
samples. A meta-analysis indicates the probability level for the overall pattern of
findings. I conducted such a meta-analysis with the studies included in the
review, testing the hypothesis that males are more advanced in moral reasoning
than are females. (For those studies involving secondary analyses, the Z score
used was the larger of those yielded by the Mann-Whitney and Kolmogorov-
Smirnov tests. Also note that some researchers failed to report the statistics on
which they made inferences of no difference or reported statistics without indicating direction and so, following convention, an exact finding of no difference
was assumed, i.e., $p = .50$.) The meta-analysis indicated that, although the
pattern was in the predicted direction; it was not significant, $Z = +1.08$, one-
tailed $p = .14$.

This finding probably overestimates the extent of sex differences in moral
reasoning given the "file-drawer problem" which increases Type I error (Rosenthal, 1979). Many studies did not report sex differences (presumably because
they found none), although subjects of both sexes participated (i.e., a reporting
bias). Also, there may exist many studies that did examine sex differences but
remain unknown because they found nonsignificant differences and the process
of publication is biased toward selecting studies with significant findings (i.e., a
publication bias). Both of these biases lead one to suspect that the review overestimates sex differences. Also, note that a meta-analysis entails a one-tailed test
and is extremely powerful in detecting differences, especially with a large
number of samples such as is the present case. Meta-analyses sometimes lead to
rejection of the null hypothesis with minuscule and trivial effects (Light &
Pillemer, 1984). For example, Thoma's (1986) meta-analysis of DIT research
indicated a significant difference favoring females, but the magnitude of this
effect was minuscule (accounting for less than one-half of 1% of the variance).

In order to place the finding of the review and meta-analysis in some context
and to determine its practical importance, I also calculated the mean effect size.
One of the most suitable measures of effect size is Cohen's d, the standardized
mean difference. According to Cohen (1977), an effect size of .8 is considered
large, .5 is moderate, and .2 is small. The effect size was found to be extremely

small, $d = +.046$, which means that sex explains only one-twentieth of 1% of the variance in moral reasoning development, $r^2 = .0005$. Cohen also suggested expressing the relationship in terms of the area of both populations combined that is not overlapped, which also was found to be extremely small, $U_1 = 3.5\%$.

One explanation offered for the occasional finding of sex differences among older studies is that earlier versions of Kohlberg's scoring system were inadequate, in particular confusing content and structure. There have been significant revisions in both stage descriptions and scoring procedures (Colby & Kohlberg, 1987). Colby (1978), for example, claimed that revisions should eliminate any tendency to underestimate females' moral reasoning because of particular content. To examine this suggestion, I conducted a meta-analytic comparison of the findings (Rosenthal, 1984) yielded by studies that used earlier versus current scoring systems. A small number of recent studies failed to report which version of the scoring system was used. My attempts to obtain this information from authors were unsuccessful in two cases, so those two studies were excluded from the analysis. (This is not a problem, of course, with earlier studies published before the Standard Issue Scoring System was available.) Of the remaining studies, 44 used an early version and 34 used the current one. The meta-analysis tested the hypothesis that sex differences favoring males are more likely with earlier scoring systems. The meta-analytic comparison indicated that, contrary to the prediction, differences favoring males tend to be more likely with the current scoring system, $Z = -1.58$; however, this finding did not quite reach significance, $p = .06$. Rosenthal (1984, p. 89) argued that, when the bulk of the findings has been incorrectly predicted, a two-tailed test is more appropriate, in which case, $p = .11$.

To summarize, then, given the minuscule effect size and the nonsignificant meta-analysis, one is forced to conclude that no nontrivial relation exists—the evidence is that the sexes are more alike than different—the distributions are really overlapping. "We are not two species; we are two sexes" (Luria, 1986, p. 318). The data cannot support the rejection of the null hypothesis. There is no empirical support for the claim that Kohlberg's theory down-scores the moral thinking of females. One cannot help but wonder why the myth that males are more advanced in moral reasoning persists in the face of so little evidence.

Moral Stages and Moral Orientations

A final issue concerns the relation between moral stage and moral orientation. Gilligan holds that Kohlberg's approach tends to undervalue the response orientation, categorizing such reasoning at lower stages. Langdale's (1986) data supported this claim since she found that individuals with a response orientation scored significantly lower in moral reasoning development than did those with a rights orientation (however, her data were restricted to the Heinz dilemma only). Recall that in my study (Walker, 1989; Walker et al., 1987), the 233 participants

responded to Kohlberg's standard dilemmas and discussed a personally generated real-life dilemma, which were scored not only for moral orientation but also
for moral stage. It, thus, provides more comprehensive data regarding the empirical relation between moral stage and orientation.

If Gilligan's arguments are correct, then individuals with a response orientation should be lower in moral development than those with a rights orientation.
To investigate this issue, ANOVAs were conducted examining the relation between orientation (response, rights, split) and moral development for both dilemma types and interview times. The dependent variable for these analyses was the
weighted average score (WAS) which is a composite score based on the percent
usage of reasoning over all stages and with a range from 100 (pure Stage 1) to
500 (pure Stage 5). The ANOVAs for the hypothetical dilemmas yielded no
effects, providing no support for Gilligan's claim. However, the ANOVAs for
the real-life dilemmas revealed significant effects for orientation, $F(2, 230) =$
10.47 and 15.33, p's < .001, for the initial and retest interviews, respectively.
Figure 13.3 displays the relevant data. On the initial interview, individuals with
either a response or split orientation evidenced a *higher* level of moral development than did those with a rights orientation; whereas, on the retest interview,
individuals with a response orientation were again higher than those with a rights
orientation (but those with a split orientation did not differ significantly from
either other group). Pratt et al. (1988) similarly reported a positive correlation
between level of moral development and response reasoning for women (but not
men) in their sample. Thus, these findings fail to support the notion that
Kohlberg's theory and scoring system are biased against the "female" response
orientation and, in fact, indicate the opposite. There is no evidence to support

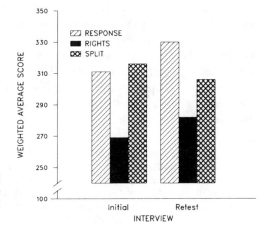

FIG. 13.3. Mean weighted
average scores on the real-life
dilemma as a function of modal
moral orientation.

Gilligan's (1986b, p. 45) claim that "the primary use of the care orientation thus creates a liability within Kohlberg's framework." Indeed, one of the intriguing findings of my study was that individuals at a higher level of moral development tended to be split in their orientations—to evidence substantial amounts of both response and rights reasoning. This suggests that Kohlberg's conceptualization of mature moral thinking does entail a coordination or integration of these two orientations. Lyons' (1982) scoring system for these orientations, however, is a disjunctive one wherein considerations are scored as reflecting *either* a rights or a response perspective and cannot be scored as coordinated.[4] There is no reason to assume that the rights and response orientations are mutually exclusive. Certainly the data of this study indicate that Kohlberg's theory is not simply reflected by the rights orientation.

CONCLUSIONS

In conclusion, then, what can be said about the issue of sex differences in moral reasoning and sex bias in theories of morality? Obviously, there is, as yet, only limited support for Gilligan's claim of different moral orientations for females and males, and no support for the claim that Kohlberg's theory down-scores the moral thinking of females or those with a response orientation. All of this does not deny the contribution that Gilligan and others have made to our understanding of moral development with the emphasis on care, response, interdependence, and commitment. But this emphasis raises many, as yet unanswered, questions. For example, to what does Gilligan attribute this sex difference in orientations—to nature or to nurture? Gilligan and Wiggins (1987) did argue that the origins of these orientations were, in part, found in socialization factors like the child's experiences of inequality and detachment, but did not address the question of whether there are also biological origins. Also, what is Gilligan's definition of mature moral development and how might it be attained (Auerbach, Blum, Smith, & Williams, 1985)? Gilligan seems to have provided three incompatible responses. First, she argues most frequently that the response orientation is superior to the rights orientation (implying that females are more moral than males). Second, she sometimes argues that the two orientations are equally valid and acceptable for the respective sexes. Third, she suggests that each orientation is deficient without the other and that maturity is a synthesis of rights and response (see Gilligan, 1982a, p. 174). However, her description of the origins

---

[4]Recently, Gilligan and her colleagues (Brown, 1987; also see Ward, 1988) have introduced a revised scoring system that differs in some important respects from Lyons' earlier system. First, it represents a more interpretive, hermeneutic approach and thus provides for only global scoring (and not in terms of "considerations" as in Lyons' system). Second, it allows for a coding of a mixed orientation. Third, it emphasizes the alignment of self with orientation. It remains to be determined whether this revised scoring system will yield a different pattern of findings.

of these orientations in the dimensions of detachment/attachment and inequality/equality certainly implies their psychological incompatibility (Flanagan & Jackson, 1987; cf. Gilligan, 1986c). Furthermore, the morality of response and care does not seem to be complete in itself (Held, 1987). For example, it does not include the notions of impartiality and universalizability (Flanagan & Adler, 1983; Hill, 1987); it has no mechanism by which to resolve conflicts of responsibility or to handle corrupt kinds of care (Flanagan & Jackson, 1987); and it does not go beyond interpersonal relationships to include responsibility for others with whom one does not interact personally.

Yet, the allegations against Kohlberg's theory have had considerable appeal. Kohlberg's (1981) philosophical defense of his model of moral reasoning development may impart the view expressed by Gilligan and others that he considers thinking at the higher stages to be abstract, inflexible, detached, disinterested, individualistic, impersonal, indifferent to the concrete realities of interpersonal relationships, and overly concerned with issues of justice. This view, I believe, is based on a limited or mis-understanding of the theory, especially principled moral reasoning; first, because it fails to recognize the self-limiting scope of Kohlberg's approach to moral development. His is a *cognitive* theory that deals with the adequacy of justifications for solutions to moral conflicts. It does not speak directly to the issues of moral emotions and behaviors, although Kohlberg (1984) has admitted the necessity and desirability of enlarging the moral domain beyond "cognition." Although morality certainly is more than a matter of "cold cognition," it is, however, customarily understood to refer to voluntary actions governed by some internal mechanism, so it would seem that a focus on moral cognition is, at the very least, a legitimate and appropriate starting point for a theory and research enterprise.

Second, this criticism fails to recognize the contextual basis of principled moral judgment in action (vs. in abstract descriptions). Kohlberg (1982, 1984) argued that there is no conflict between using moral principles and being contextually relative in moral judgment. Principled moral reasoning is contextually relative since it can be sensitive to aspects of a given situation in ways that rule-bound reasoning cannot (see Friedman, 1987, for a helpful discussion of this point). Further, through the process of ideal reciprocal role-taking, principled reasoning avoids the biasing impact of vested interests by evaluating the moral legitimacy of the claims of *real* people in *real* situations—something that Gilligan seems unwilling to adopt. Boyd's (1979) interpretation of principled moral reasoning in terms of its accompanying "psychological postures" demonstrated the concrete aspects underlying such reasoning. Other psychological postures inherent in mature moral reasoning are open-mindedness and principledness—that is, principle-seeking, not rigid rule-applying. It should be remembered that principled moral thinking is not the exclusive domain of philosophers, but is also used by activists such as Gandhi, Martin Luther King, and Mother Teresa of Calcutta (Kohlberg, 1981).

Also central to the conception of Stage 6 moral reasoning is the principle of "respect for persons" as ends, not means (as argued by Boyd, 1983; Kohlberg, Boyd, & Levine, 1986), a principle that has not been sufficiently emphasized in previous interpretations. Respect for persons not only entails the adjudicating of conflicting interests and rights, but also implies a willingness to dialogue with others in seeking agreement, an attitude of identification and empathic connection with others (i.e., active sympathy), an obligation to promote good and prevent harm—that is, both a principle of justice and a principle of care. (See Kohlberg, 1984, pp. 486–490, for an example of a high-stage woman who articulates a respect-for-persons principle that integrates justice and care concerns.) It should now be apparent that a morality of justice and rights and a morality of care and response are not in opposition, although Gilligan (1987) continues to argue "against the implication that these two perspectives are readily integrated or fused" (p. 30). Not only are they compatible but they are interdependent. Moral problems do not force a choice between justice and caring.

ACKNOWLEDGMENT

A portion of the research presented in this chapter was supported by grants from the Social Sciences and Humanities Research Council of Canada and was reported in a series of articles published in *Child Development* (1984, 1986, 1987, 1989). I gratefully acknowledge the research collaboration of Brian de Vries and Shelley D. Trevethan, the work of numerous research assistants, and the helpful comments of many colleagues and reviewers.

REFERENCES

Alker, H. A., & Poppen, P. J. (1973). Personality and ideology in university students. *Journal of Personality, 41,* 653–671.

Arbuthnot, J. (1983). Attributions of responsibility by simulated jurors: Stage of moral reasoning and guilt by association. *Psychological Reports, 52,* 287–298.

Archer, S. L., & Waterman, A. S. (1988). Psychological individualism: Gender differences or gender neutrality. *Human Development, 31,* 65–81.

Auerbach, J., Blum, L., Smith, V., & Williams, C. (1985). Commentary on Gilligan's "In a different voice". *Feminist Studies, 11,* 149–161.

Bar-Yam, M., Kohlberg, L., & Naame, A. (1980). Moral reasoning of students in different cultural, social, and educational settings. *American Journal of Education, 88,* 345–362.

Baumrind, D. (1986). Sex differences in moral reasoning: Response to Walker's (1984) conclusion that there are none. *Child Development, 57,* 511–521.

Berkowitz, M. W., Gibbs, J. C., & Broughton, J. M. (1980). The relation of moral judgment stage disparity to developmental effects of peer dialogues. *Merrill-Palmer Quarterly, 26,* 341–357.

Biaggio, A. M. B. (1976). A developmental study of moral judgment of Brazilian children and adolescents. *Interamerican Journal of Psychology, 10,* 71–78.

Bielby, D. D., & Papalia, D. E. (1975). Moral development and perceptual role-taking ego-centrism: Their development and interrelationship across the life-span. *International Journal of Aging and Human Development, 6,* 293–308.

Blatt, M. M., & Kohlberg, L. (1975). The effects of classroom moral discussion upon children's level of moral judgment. *Journal of Moral Education, 4,* 129–161.

Boldizar, J. P., Wilson, K. L., & Deemer, D. K. (1989). Gender, life experiences, and moral judgment development: A process-oriented approach. *Journal of Personality and Social Psychology, 57,* 229–238.

Boyd, D. R. (1979). An interpretation of principled morality. *Journal of Moral Education, 8,* 110–123.

Boyd, D. R. (1983). Careful justice or just caring: A response to Gilligan. *Proceedings of the Philosophy of Education Society, 38,* 63–69.

Brabeck, M. (1983). Moral judgment: Theory and research on differences between males and females. *Developmental Review, 3,* 274–291.

Brabeck, M. (1987). Gender and morality: A response to Philibert and Sayers. *New Ideas in Psychology, 5,* 209–214.

Broughton, J. M. (1983). Women's rationality and men's virtues: A critique of gender dualism in Gilligan's theory of moral development. *Social Research, 50,* 597–642.

Brown, L. M. (Ed.). (1987). *A guide to reading narratives of moral conflict and choice for self and moral voice.* Unpublished manuscript, Harvard University Graduate School of Education GEHD Study Center, Cambridge, MA.

Buck, L. Z., Walsh, W. F., & Rothman, G. (1981). Relationship between parental moral judgment and socialization. *Youth and Society, 13,* 91–116.

Bussey, K., & Maughan, B. (1982). Gender differences in moral reasoning. *Journal of Personality and Social Psychology, 42,* 701–706.

Candee, D., & Kohlberg, L. (1987). Moral judgment and moral action: A reanalysis of Haan, Smith, and Block's (1968) Free Speech Movement data. *Journal of Personality and Social Psychology, 52,* 554–564.

Cohen, J. (1977). *Statistical power analysis for the behavioral sciences* (rev. ed). New York: Academic.

Colby, A. (1978). Evolution of a moral-developmental theory. In W. Damon (Ed.), *New directions for child development: Moral development* (No. 2, pp. 89–104). San Francisco: Jossey-Bass.

Colby, A., & Damon, W. (1983). Listening to a different voice: A review of Gilligan's *In a different voice. Merrill-Palmer Quarterly, 29,* 473–481.

Colby, A., & Kohlberg, L. (1987). *The measurement of moral judgment* (Vols. 1–2). New York: Cambridge University Press.

Colby, A., Kohlberg, L., Gibbs, J., & Lieberman, M. (1983). A longitudinal study of moral judgment. *Monographs of the Society for Research in Child Development, 48*(1–2, Serial No. 200).

Crown, J., & Heatherington, L. (1988, August). *Gender and athletics: Judgment and moral reasoning about competitive encounters.* Paper presented at the meeting of the American Psychological Association, Atlanta.

Donenberg, G. R., & Hoffman, L. W. (1988). Gender differences in moral development. *Sex Roles, 18,* 701–717.

Edwards, C. P. (1975). Societal complexity and moral development: A Kenyan study. *Ethos, 3,* 505–527.

Erickson, V. L. (1980). The case study method in the evaluation of developmental programs. In L. Kuhmerker, M. Mentkowski, & V. L. Erickson (Eds.), *Evaluating moral development* (pp. 151–176). Schenectady, NY: Character Research Press.

Fishkin, J., Keniston, K., & MacKinnon, C. (1973). Moral reasoning and political ideology. *Journal of Personality and Social Psychology, 27,* 109–119.

Flanagan, O. J., Jr., & Adler, J. E. (1983). Impartiality and particularity. *Social Research, 50*, 576–596.

Flanagan, O. J., Jr., & Jackson, K. (1987). Justice, care, and gender: The Kohlberg-Gilligan debate revisited. *Ethics, 97*, 622–637.

Fontana, A. F., & Noel, B. (1973). Moral reasoning in the university. *Journal of Personality and Social Psychology, 27*, 419–429.

Ford, M. R., & Lowery, C. R. (1986). Gender differences in moral reasoning: A comparison of the use of justice and care orientations. *Journal of Personality and Social Psychology, 50*, 777–783.

Forsyth, D. R., Nye, J. L., & Kelley, K. (1988). Idealism, relativism, and the ethic of caring. *Journal of Psychology, 122*, 243–248.

Freeman, S. J. M., & Giebink, J. W. (1979). Moral judgment as a function of age, sex, and stimulus. *Journal of Psychology, 102*, 43–47.

Freud, S. (1927). Some psychological consequences of the anatomical distinction between the sexes. *International Journal of Psycho-analysis, 8*, 133–142.

Friedman, M. (1987). Care and context in moral reasoning. In E. F. Kittay & D. T. Meyers (Eds.), *Women and moral theory* (pp. 190–204). Totowa, NJ: Rowman & Littlefield.

Friedman, W. J., Robinson, A. B., & Friedman, B. L. (1987). Sex differences in moral judgments? A test of Gilligan's theory. *Psychology of Women Quarterly, 11*, 37–46.

Garwood, S. G., Levine, D. W., & Ewing, L. (1980). Effect of protagonist's sex on assessing gender differences in moral reasoning. *Developmental Psychology, 16*, 677–678.

Gielen, U. P. (1986). Moral reasoning in radical and non-radical German students. *Behavior Science Research, 20*, 71–109.

Gilligan, C. (1977). In a different voice: Women's conception of the self and of morality. *Harvard Educational Review, 47*, 481–517.

Gilligan, C. (1982a). *In a different voice: Psychological theory and women's development*. Cambridge, MA: Harvard University Press.

Gilligan, C. (1982b). New maps of development: New visions of maturity. *American Journal of Orthopsychiatry, 52*, 199–212.

Gilligan, C. (1986a, Spring). [Letter to D. Baumrind]. *Newsletter of the APA Division on Developmental Psychology*, pp. 10–13.

Gilligan, C. (1986b). Remapping development: The power of divergent data. In L. Cirillo & S. Wapner (Eds.), *Value presuppositions in theories of human development* (pp. 37–53). Hillsdale, NJ: Lawrence Erlbaum Associates.

Gilligan, C. (1986c). Remapping the moral domain: New images of the self in relationship. In T. C. Heller, M. Sosna, & D. E. Wellbery (Eds.), *Reconstructing individualism: Autonomy, individuality, and the self in Western thought* (pp. 237–252). Stanford, CA: Stanford University Press.

Gilligan, C. (1987). Moral orientation and moral development. In E. F. Kittay & D. T. Meyers (Eds.), *Women and moral theory* (pp. 19–33). Totowa, NJ: Rowman & Littlefield.

Gilligan, C., & Attanucci, J. (1988a). Much ado about . . . knowing? noting? nothing? A reply to Vasudev concerning sex differences and moral development. *Merrill-Palmer Quarterly, 34*, 451–456.

Gilligan, C., & Attanucci, J. (1988b). Two moral orientations: Gender differences and similarities. *Merrill-Palmer Quarterly, 34*, 223–237.

Gilligan, C., Langdale, S., Lyons, N., & Murphy, J. M. (1982). *The contribution of women's thought to developmental theory: The elimination of sex bias in moral development research and education*. Unpublished manuscript, Harvard University, Cambridge, MA.

Gilligan, C., Ward, J. V., & Taylor, J. M. (Eds.). (1988). *Mapping the moral domain: A contribution of women's thinking to psychological theory and education*. Cambridge, MA: Harvard University Graduate School of Education.

Gilligan, C., & Wiggins, G. (1987). The origins of morality in early childhood relationships. In J.

Kagan & S. Lamb (Eds.), *The emergence of morality in young children* (pp. 277–305). Chicago: University of Chicago Press.

Greene, S. D., & Vulcano, B. A. (1987, June). *The association of sex, sex-role, and sex of protagonist with level of moral judgment.* Paper presented at the meeting of the Canadian Psychological Association, Vancouver. (abstract published in *Canadian Psychology, 28*(2a), Abstract No. 229).

Greeno, C. G., & Maccoby, E. E. (1986). How different is the "Different Voice"? *Signs: Journal of Women in Culture and Society, 11,* 310–316.

Haan, N. (1975). Hypothetical and actual moral reasoning in a situation of civil disobedience. *Journal of Personality and Social Psychology, 32,* 255–270.

Haan, N. (1985). Processes of moral development: Cognitive or social disequilibrium? *Developmental Psychology, 21,* 996–1006.

Haan, N. (1986). Systematic variability in the quality of moral action, as defined by two formulations. *Journal of Personality and Social Psychology, 50,* 1271–1284.

Haan, N., Langer, J., & Kohlberg, L. (1976). Family patterns of moral reasoning. *Child Development, 47,* 1204–1206.

Haan, N., Smith, M. B., & Block, J. (1968). Moral reasoning of young adults: Political-social behavior, family background, and personality correlates. *Journal of Personality and Social Psychology, 10,* 183–201.

Haan, N., Weiss, R., & Johnson, V. (1982). The role of logic in moral reasoning and development. *Developmental Psychology, 18,* 245–256.

Hare-Mustin, R. T. (1987). The gender dichotomy and developmental theory: A response to Sayers. *New Ideas in Psychology, 5,* 261–267.

Held, V. (1987). Feminism and moral theory. In E. F. Kittay & D. T. Meyers (Eds.), *Women and moral theory* (pp. 111–128). Totowa, NJ: Rowman & Littlefield.

Henley, N. M. (1985). Psychology and gender. *Signs: Journal of Women in Culture and Society, 11,* 101–119.

Hill, T. E., Jr. (1987). The importance of autonomy. In E. F. Kittay & D. T. Meyers (Eds.), *Women and moral theory* (pp. 129–138). Totowa, NJ: Rowman & Littlefield.

Holstein, C. B. (1976). Irreversible, stepwise sequence in the development of moral judgment: A longitudinal study of males and females. *Child Development, 47,* 51–61.

Johnston, D. K. (1988). Adolescents' solutions to dilemmas in fables: Two moral orientations— two problem solving strategies. In C. Gilligan, J. V. Ward, & J. M. Taylor (Eds.), *Mapping the moral domain: A contribution of women's thinking to psychological theory and education* (pp. 49–71). Cambridge, MA: Harvard University Graduate School of Education.

Keasey, C. B. (1971). Social participation as a factor in the moral development of preadolescents. *Developmental Psychology, 5,* 216–220.

Kittay, E. F., & Meyers, D. T. (Eds.). (1987). *Women and moral theory.* Totowa, NJ: Rowman & Littlefield.

Kohlberg, L. (1973). Continuities in childhood and adult moral development revisited. In P. B. Baltes & K. W. Schaie (Eds.), *Life-span developmental psychology: Personality and socialization* (pp. 179–204). New York: Academic.

Kohlberg, L. (1976). Moral stages and moralization: The cognitive-developmental approach. In T. Lickona (Ed.), *Moral development and behavior: Theory, research, and social issues* (pp. 31–53). New York: Holt, Rinehart and Winston.

Kohlberg, L. (1981). *Essays on moral development: Vol. 1. The philosophy of moral development.* San Francisco: Harper & Row.

Kohlberg, L. (1982). A reply to Owen Flanagan and some comments on the Puka-Goodpaster exchange. *Ethics, 92,* 513–528.

Kohlberg, L. (1984). *Essays on moral development: Vol. 2. The psychology of moral development.* San Francisco: Harper & Row.

Kohlberg, L., Boyd, D., & Levine, C. (1986). Die wiederkehr von Stufe 6: Der moralische stand-punkt der hochsten entwicklungsstufe [The return of Stage 6: The moral standpoint of the highest developmental stage]. In W. Edelstein & G. Nunner-Winkler (Eds.), *Zur bestimmung der moral: Eine diskussion zwischen philosophen und sozialwissenschaftlern* [On the determination of mor-als: A discussion between philosophers and social scientists]. Frankfurt: Suhrkamp.

Krebs, D., & Gillmore, J. (1982). The relationship among the first stages of cognitive develop-ment, role-taking abilities, and moral development. *Child Development, 53,* 877–886.

Kuhn, D., Langer, J., Kohlberg, L., & Haan, N. S. (1977). The development of formal operations in logical and moral judgment. *Genetic Psychology Monographs, 95,* 97–188.

Langdale, C. J. (1986). A re-vision of structural-developmental theory. In G. L. Sapp (Ed.), *Handbook of moral development: Models, processes, techniques, and research* (pp. 15–54). Birmingham, AL: Religious Education Press.

Lehmann, E. L. (1975). *Nonparametrics: Statistical methods based on ranks.* San Francisco: Hold-en-Day.

Lei, T., & Cheng, S. (1984). *A little but special light on the universality of moral judgment development.* Unpublished manuscript, National Taiwan University, Taipei.

Light, R. J., & Pillemer, D. B. (1984). *Summing up: The science of reviewing research.* Cambridge, MA: Harvard University Press.

Lloyd, G. (1983). Reason, gender, and morality in the history of philosophy. *Social Research, 50,* 490–513.

Lockwood, A. L. (1975). Stage of moral development and students' reasoning on public policy issues. *Journal of Moral Education, 5,* 51–61.

Luria, Z. (1986). A methodological critique. *Signs: Journal of Women in Culture and Society, 11,* 316–321.

Lyons, N. P. (1982). *Conceptions of self and morality and modes of moral choice: Identifying justice and care in judgments of actual moral dilemmas.* Unpublished doctoral dissertation, Harvard University, Cambridge, MA.

Lyons, N. P. (1983). Two perspectives: On self, relationships, and morality. *Harvard Educational Review, 53,* 125–145.

Maccoby, E. E. (1980). *Social development: Psychological growth and the parent-child rela-tionship.* New York: Harcourt Brace Jovanovich.

Maccoby, E. E., & Jacklin, C. N. (1974). *The psychology of sex differences.* Stanford, CA: Stanford University Press.

Mednick, M. T. (1989). On the politics of psychological constructs: Stop the bandwagon, I want to get off. *American Psychologist, 44,* 1118–1123.

Nails, D. (1983). Social-scientific sexism: Gilligan's mismeasure of man. *Social Research, 50,* 643–664.

Noam, G., Powers, S., Hauser, S., & Jacobson, A. (1985). *Structural-developmental psychology and psychopathology: Ego development and moral development in psychiatric patients and high school students.* Unpublished manuscript, Radcliffe College, Cambridge, MA.

Noddings, N. (1984). *Caring: A feminine approach to ethics and moral education.* Berkeley, CA: University of California Press.

Orchowsky, S. J., & Jenkins, L. R. (1979). Sex biases in the measurement of moral judgment. *Psychological Reports, 44,* 1040.

Parikh, B. (1980). Development of moral judgment and its relation to family environmental factors in Indian and American families. *Child Development, 51,* 1030–1039.

Powers, S. I. (1983). Family interaction and parental moral development as a context for adolescent moral development: A study of patient and non-patient adolescents. *Dissertation Abstracts Inter-national, 43,* 3753B. (University Microfilms No. 83-08,501).

Powers, S. I. (1988). Moral judgement development within the family. *Journal of Moral Educa-tion, 17,* 209–219.

Pratt, M. W., Golding, G., & Hunter, W. J. (1983). Aging as ripening: Character and consistency of moral judgment in young, mature, and older adults. *Human Development, 26,* 277–288.

Pratt, M. W., Golding, G., & Hunter, W. J. (1984). Does morality have a gender? Sex, sex role, and moral judgment relationships across the adult lifespan. *Merrill-Palmer Quarterly, 30,* 321–340.

Pratt, M. W., Golding, G., Hunter, W. J., & Sampson, R. (1988). Sex differences in adult moral orientations. *Journal of Personality, 56,* 373–391.

Rest, J. R. (1979). *Development in judging moral issues.* Minneapolis: University of Minnesota Press.

Rest, J. R., & Thoma, S. J. (1985). Relation of moral judgment development to formal education. *Developmental Psychology, 21,* 709–714.

Rosenthal, R. (1979). The "file-drawer problem" and tolerance for null results. *Psychological Bulletin, 86,* 638–641.

Rosenthal, R. (1984). *Meta-analytic procedures for social research.* Beverly Hills, CA: Sage.

Rothbart, M. K., Hanley, D., & Albert, M. (1986). Gender differences in moral reasoning. *Sex Roles, 15,* 645–653.

Saltzstein, H. D., Diamond, R. M., & Belenky, M. (1972). Moral judgment level and conformity behavior. *Developmental Psychology, 7,* 327–336.

Sichel, B. A. (1985). Women's moral development in search of philosophical assumptions. *Journal of Moral Education, 14,* 149–161.

Siegel, S. (1956). *Nonparametric statistics for the behavioral sciences.* New York: McGraw-Hill.

Smetana, J. G. (1984). Morality and gender: A commentary on Pratt, Golding, and Hunter. *Merrill-Palmer Quarterly, 30,* 341–348.

Snarey, J. R., Reimer, J., & Kohlberg, L. (1985). Development of social-moral reasoning among kibbutz adolescents: A longitudinal cross-cultural study. *Developmental Psychology, 21,* 3–17.

Speicher-Dubin, B. (1982). Relationships between parent moral judgment, child moral judgment and family interaction: A correlational study. *Dissertation Abstracts International, 43,* 1600B. (University Microfilms No. 82-83,231).

Stocker, M. (1987). Duty and friendship: Toward a synthesis of Gilligan's contrastive moral concepts. In E. F. Kittay & D. T. Meyers (Eds.), *Women and moral theory* (pp. 56–68). Totowa, NJ: Rowman & Littlefield.

Thoma, S. J. (1986). Estimating gender differences in the comprehension and preference of moral issues. *Developmental Review, 6,* 165–180.

Turiel, E. (1976). A comparative analysis of moral knowledge and moral judgment in males and females. *Journal of Personality, 44,* 195–208.

Vasudev, J. (1988). Sex differences in morality and moral orientation: A discussion of the Gilligan and Attanucci study. *Merrill-Palmer Quarterly, 34,* 239–244.

Walker, L. J. (1982). The sequentiality of Kohlberg's stages of moral development. *Child Development, 53,* 1330–1336.

Walker, L. J. (1984). Sex differences in the development of moral reasoning: A critical review. *Child Development, 55,* 677–691.

Walker, L. J. (1986a). Experiential and cognitive sources of moral development in adulthood. *Human Development, 29,* 113–124.

Walker, L. J. (1986b). Sex differences in the develoment of moral reasoning: A rejoinder to Baumrind. *Child Development, 57,* 522–526.

Walker, L. J. (1988). The development of moral reasoning. *Annals of Child Development, 5,* 33–78.

Walker, L. J. (1989). A longitudinal study of moral reasoning. *Child Development, 60,* 157–166.

Walker, L. J., de Vries, B., & Trevethan, S. D. (1987). Moral stages and moral orientations in real-life and hypothetical dilemmas. *Child Development, 58,* 842–858.

364   LAWRENCE J. WALKER

Ward, J. V. (1988). Urban adolescents' conceptions of violence. In C. Gilligan, J. V. Ward, & J. M. Taylor (Eds.), *Mapping the moral domain: A contribution of women's thinking to psychological theory and education* (pp. 175–200). Cambridge, MA: Harvard University Graduate School of Education.

Author Index

A

Abelson, R. P., 18, 20, 69, 84, 87
Abrahami, A., 284, 303
Abramovitch, R., 121, 134
Achtenhagen, F., 213, 226
Adalbjaarmardottir, S., 92, 111
Addison, W., 121, 134
Adler, J. E., 357, 360
Ahn, R., 76, 85
Ajzen, I., 12, 17, 20, 22
Albert, M., 336, 337, 344, 363
Alker, H. A., 350, 358
Allen, A., 162, 167
Allport, G. W., 63, 84
Althof, W., 195, 226
Altman, I., 249, 253, 256, 261, 262, 277
Altman, M., 284, 303
Amatruda, C. S., 173, 174, 188
Ames, L. B., 173, 188
Anderson, J. R., 267, 275
Anderson, L. M., 243, 244
Anderson, N. H., 264, 276
Apel, K. -O., 201, 226
Arbuthnot, J., 351, 358
Archer, S. L., 335, 358
Argyris, D.,27, 33, 44, 45
Arnold, M. B., 15, 20
Aronfreed, J., 68, 84, 113, 187
Asch, S. E., 311, 313, 314, 317, 329
Asher, S. R., 121, 122, 135
Astin, A. W., 231, 244

Atkinson, J. W., 15, 22
Attanucci, J., 27, 28, 44, 45, 336, 339, 342, 352, 360
Auerbach, J., 356, 358
Austin, J. L., 249, 255, 275

B

Backman, C., 163, 167
Bakeman, R., 123, 134
Bakhtin, M., 27, 29, 44
Ballachey, E. L., 14, 22
Bandura, A., 17, 20, 316, 329, 330
Banks, C., 311, 330
Banks, W. C., 140, 169
Bar-Tal, D., 1, 2, 9, 14, 16, 17, 20, 21, 172, 187
Bar-Tal, Y., 2, 17, 19, 21
Bar-Yam, M., 284, 303, 350, 358
Bardige, B., 27, 44, 45
Barnett, M. A., 73, 79, 84, 86
Baron, R. A., 15, 20
Bassett, P., 296, 299, 303
Batson, C. D., 64, 65, 66, 70, 73, 74, 79, 81, 83, 84, 88
Baudonniere, P. M., 123, 138
Baumrind, D., 141, 137, 348, 349, 351, 352, 358
Beardslee, W., 92, 113
Bearison, D. J., 120, 125, 135
Bebeau, M. J., 200, 226
Beeghly, M., 176, 187
Beeghly-Smith, M., 176, 187

365

Subject Index